Sources and Debates in Modern British History

'This is a collection of documents of immense richness from a wide variety of sources: parliamentary debates, official reports, cartoons, novels, high intellects, among others. They stretch from the 18th century to the present, from Adam Smith to Mrs Thatcher. Dealing with state and society, workers and women, culture and empire, each short document is succinctly introduced. Every chapter concludes with invaluable bibliographies reflecting the most important current historiographical debates. Through a close study of these extremely well-selected documents, students will be able to come to a thorough knowledge and understanding of the compelling story of Britain since 1714, its rise to being the most powerful country in the world, and its subsequent decline.'

Peter Stansky, *Stanford University*

'*Sources and Debates in Modern British History* is an excellent way to introduce undergraduates to primary sources. The editorial material shows students how these historical figures were in conversation with each other, while the questions for discussion encourage students to analyze the documents individually and in groups. I highly recommend this book for undergraduates.'

Carol Engelhardt Herringer, *Wright State University*

'Ellis Wasson's *Sources and Debates in Modern British History* is an unusually well chosen and wide angling collection of major primary sources, which will prove of great value to undergraduates and graduate students alike who are studying modern British history. This collection makes available valuable primary source material about the great events and trends which shaped modern Britain. It is also notable for the wide range and even handedness of the material selected, a tribute to Dr. Wasson's editorial skills.'

Bill Rubinstein, *Aberyswyth University*

Sources and Debates in Modern British History

1714 to the present

A John Wiley & Sons, Ltd., Publication

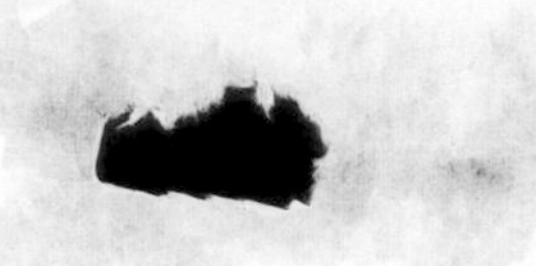

This edition first published 2012

Blackwell Publishing was acquired by John Wiley & Sons in February 2007. Blackwell's publishing program has been merged with Wiley's global Scientific, Technical, and Medical business to form Wiley-Blackwell.

Registered Office
John Wiley & Sons Ltd, The Atrium, Southern Gate, Chichester, West Sussex, PO19 8SQ, UK

Editorial Offices
350 Main Street, Malden, MA 02148-5020, USA
9600 Garsington Road, Oxford, OX4 2DQ, UK
The Atrium, Southern Gate, Chichester, West Sussex, PO19 8SQ, UK

For details of our global editorial offices, for customer services, and for information about how to apply for permission to reuse the copyright material in this book please see our website at www.wiley.com/wiley-blackwell.

Library of Congress Cataloging-in-Publication Data

Sources and debates in modern British history : 1714 to the present / edited by Ellis Wasson. – 1st ed.
p. cm.
Includes bibliographical references and index.
ISBN 978-1-4443-3371-8 (cloth) – ISBN 978-1-4443-3372-5 (pbk.)
1. Great Britain–History–18th century–Sources. 2. Great Britain–History–19th century–Sources. 3. Great Britain–History–20th century–Sources. I. Wasson, Ellis Archer, 1947–
DA470.S73 2012
941.08–dc23

2011033839

A catalogue record for this book is available from the British Library.

This book is published in the following electronic formats: ePDFs ISBN: 9781444399004; ePub ISBN: 9781444399011; Mobi ISBN: 9781444399028

Set in 10.5/13pt Minion by Thomson Digital, India
Printed in Singapore by Ho Printing Singapore Pte Ltd

1 2012

Dedicated to

David, Margaret, and Carson

Contents

List of Documents

Part I: The Eighteenth Century

List of Figures

Preface

How to Analyze Historical Documents

Written records are the primary means through which we learn about the past. If you want to study human society before writing was discovered, turn to archeology. Of course, understanding even recent events can be enhanced by studying material culture and physical remains. Industrial archeology is a thriving activity, and art history tells us much about the past. With the arrival of technology capable of recording the human voice, oral evidence became important. Images on film also have taken their place in the historian's arena. This volume includes a number of cartoons and other illustrations that enhance our understanding of the themes discussed, but such items cannot be the main focus of a historian. History flows from what people said about themselves and their society. The remains of this evidence we call "documents," the foundation of our discipline.

What is so fascinating about documents is their variety and incompleteness. On the one hand, a plethora of material exists in the form of letters, diaries, memoirs, government records, business accounts, newspapers, and e-mails. On the other hand, what survives and what does not is often governed by chance. The observations of the literate, of course, are much more likely to come down to us than the feelings and opinions of those who could not read or write. However, court records, military recruitment data, and slave ship account books, for example, can be pieced together in ways that reveal a good deal about people who were incapable of offering direct evidence themselves.

The Biases Inherent in Historical Evidence

Students need to be alert to certain structural biases that exist in the surviving evidence. Britain's elite is particularly well documented because no conquering armies or revolutionary incendiaries devastated cities, libraries, record repositories, and country houses, as happened in most other European countries over the last three centuries.[1] The aristocracy in Britain is one of the few in the world in the twenty-first century to retain titles of rank officially recognized by the government, and hundreds of patrician families continue to live in ancestral houses acquired in some cases five or six hundred years ago. Today family records once kept in musty "muniment rooms" have often made their way to county record offices or through auction rooms to American university libraries. An amazing amount has survived.

Of course, even among the elite chance had a good deal to do with what exists today. Houses burned down, roofs leaked, trunks were mislaid, irresponsible heirs threw out what ought to have been kept, and people with too much free time on their hands or conscious of keeping the family reputation clean doctored and destroyed precious materials. During a research expedition, I came across the diary of the sixth duke of Devonshire where passages had been inked out by some later hand to conceal information he or she considered threatening or embarrassing, while Queen Victoria's diary was, after her death, edited and copied by one of her daughters who then destroyed the original. After World War II some politicians (or their descendants) who had been "Appeasers" or even Nazi sympathizers "weeded" their correspondence to remove embarrassing letters. For years our understanding of the "enclosure movement" that transformed English agriculture was skewed by the fact that the last stage was carried out by parliamentary legislation, leaving an easily traced written record. Only later did historians begin to understand that most of the process had taken place *earlier* through mutual agreements that were much harder to track down. Even fraud can take place. We know of at least one US Supreme Court justice who manufactured letters written years after the events described in them in ways that cast himself in a flattering light.[2] For many years accusations were made that the British Government had composed a fake diary revealing Sir Roger Casement (see document 9.18) as a homosexual. This document was used to discredit his reputation and to clear the way for a sentence of death for treason to be carried out. The length and complexity of the diary has convinced most scholars that it was in fact genuine, though used inappropriately. More recently, a diary purportedly written by Adolf Hitler, at first accepted by a leading expert as genuine, was later shown to be a forgery. Oral history can be unreliable. When recollections made decades after an event are compared with contemporary written records, discontinuities and errors almost always appear. Over time the human mind unconsciously reshapes and reorders the past.

1 The Irish suffered tragic losses when their national record collection containing documents of immense value and antiquity was set on fire during the civil war in 1922 and many aristocratic country houses were burned to the ground by the IRA (Irish Republican Army). Some destruction of British records took place during World War II as a result of German air attacks, but most important documents were stored in places of safety between 1939 and 1945.

2 Justice Frank Murphy.

Be alert to the fact that rich people's records are more likely to survive than those created by poor people, and winners (in war, business, and politics, etc.) are more likely to leave an ample paper trail than losers. The most powerful single selector, however, is chance. That poses the question whether the records we do have are representative and give a balanced portrait of the time from which they came – or does random selection mislead, misrepresent, leave gaping holes, and overemphasize aspects of the past? The answer to this question is never easy to find, and, ironically, is made more difficult by the ever-increasing amount of material that does survive. When the telephone arrived, much that had once been communicated by letter, both by politicians writing to each other from offices in buildings on the opposite side of the same street and by family members sharing intimate thoughts, was lost. Technology, however, did not staunch the onslaught of material spewing out of printing presses operated by steam engines, distributed by railways and motorized vehicles, whizzing along telegraph wires, and accumulating in mountains to fulfill the needs of a fully literate and increasingly prosperous society. A biographer of an eighteenth-century prime minister could – sometimes in a few years, in other cases over much of a lifetime – be reasonably confident that she could read every existing word spoken by or written by, to, or about her subject. Biographers of Margaret Thatcher or Tony Blair have no hope of even making more than a modest dent in the billions of words that fall into those categories about their subjects, to say nothing about e-mails and audio and video tapes of radio and television shows, and so on. This has not stopped historians from going about their appointed tasks, but the prospect for recent historians is daunting. On the other hand, the modern biographer may, through careful selection, make a pretty complete collection of what it is vital to know, while the writer about the eighteenth century will always have lingering doubts about what did not survive.

What Are the Questions to Ask?

All of the above is a warning to be wary, but not a discouragement to go ahead. The chase after documents can provide all the thrill of a big game hunt or solving a crime. Many a researcher has found the collection of evidence more enjoyable than the writing up of the finds. Famous anticipated "big books" have never appeared in print. Assuming that knowing about the past is important, which historians are more than ready to argue is true, accumulating and analyzing the raw materials from which it is written are crucial tasks. Because, as I have suggested above, the understanding of historical evidence is complex and challenging, students in history classes ought to learn how to do it. Aside from the books listed in a history syllabus, which are inherently valuable, and the arts of verbal and written expression that the study of history cultivates, the most important single skill one can come away with from a course of study is the ability to analyze evidence, both in terms of individual documents and in linking and comparing them. These skills are almost universally applicable in life and are used by lawyers, physicians, entrepreneurs, policewomen, journalists, and almost everybody when they are buying a used car or selecting a spouse.

What should you be looking for as you survey these documents? First, ask who wrote the document. Often this is fairly obvious: a man or a woman, an aristocrat or a manual laborer, a Protestant or a Catholic, a Scot or an Irishman. How does the person's education, social rank, class, gender, nationality, religion, trade, business, office, or whatever affect what they say? Sometimes the authorship is obscure. One should nevertheless speculate.

Testimony before a government committee can be tricky to analyze. Will a worker feel free to make a public criticism of his employer, who might be sitting in the room at the time? Who is the audience being addressed by the document? Knowing whether something is intended for public or private consumption is of vital importance. Diaries offer a whole range of problems. Why is the person writing one? Someone of modest background may well feel the document is not likely to survive or will be read only within a family circle. A monarch or prime minister knows his or her document will survive and contribute to shaping their reputation, unless they give orders for its destruction at their death.

Memoirs, of course, must be handled with kid gloves. Almost every author of an autobiography has an axe to grind. Why else write it? Of course, some authors may just want to make money, which encourages exaggerations and sensationalizing. Most authors want to promote their own reputations, strike back at enemies, and encourage particular views. Few memoirs contain a record of the mistakes and errors of judgment the author made during his or her career.

Speeches are sometimes made to enlighten, guide, and inform, but more often to exculpate mistakes, gain followers, crush opponents, and enhance reputations. Letters written between government officials or close friends may contain unvarnished opinions, but letters written to newspapers are often full of misinformation. In all cases, however frank and open a source may appear, the document can only reflect the point of view of an individual, who has limited access to information and a unique set of personal experiences and prejudices of which they may be entirely unaware. All of us look at the world through a set of glasses, actually more like binoculars, that are clouded and peculiar. Analyzing historical documents is one of the ways that we can become more self-aware about our own misinformed, selfish, self-satisfied, and ignorant points of view, although history also offers the hope that courage, education, and kindness can help us be better informed, more generous, and less rigid about our ideas and opinions.

Success in analyzing evidence relies heavily on context. The date of a document is critical. Something written before an event is very different than one written with hindsight. Eyewitness accounts may be preferred to second-hand accounts, although many problems exist with evidence presented by actual participants or bystanders. The latter may be a bit more objective than the former; however, the active player may understand more about what is going on behind the scenes while the outside observer sees only the surface. Over the years the police have often found eyewitness testimony unreliable. People may see only part of the event; their adrenalin may be unleashed by fear, which drastically reduces their ability to make cool judgments. If you have ever witnessed an event, whether it be a crime or a public protest, and then read accounts of it in newspapers written by journalists who are supposedly trained to be accurate, you will almost always be amazed by the differences between your own memories of what happened and the description provided in the press.

The really difficult thing to remember when analyzing documents is that the past is a foreign country. The problem is not just one of identifying and understanding unique points of view. The shape and nature of the whole of society is constantly changing. People in the past looked at the world from personal perspectives standing on a platform which we cannot now clamber aboard. Think of the changes in fashion in clothes over time. Correcting for our "modern" views (which will someday seem quaint, vulgar, or impenetrable to our descendants) is a huge challenge. On issues ranging from the morality of slavery to capital punishment attitudes change profoundly. For example, present-day concerns with clerical celibacy in the Roman Catholic Church and the emergence of gay liberation have led some people to speculate that the great nineteenth-century writer and prelate, John, Cardinal Newman (see document 6.10), was a homosexual. That he may have felt attracted to other men is possible, though no significant evidence has come to light about that. What is anachronistic about making Newman into a "gay" figure is that Victorian male Catholic clerics simply did not think of themselves in that way. Sexual activity, whatever its nature, contravened the vow of celibacy, and the whole record of Newman's life suggests that he took his devotion to the teachings of the Church very seriously. More to the point, "gayness" did not exist as an identity in his period. No one, let alone an authentically saintly clergyman, would have defined themselves in terms of sexual orientation. The present discussion of his sexuality is all about our contemporary concerns and not about Victorian reality.[3]

It is also well to remember that just because jet airplanes and computers were absent in the nineteenth century does not mean that people living then were any less intelligent than we are now. If we could converse with them, they might well ask how it is with all our fancy technology we invented a means to eliminate human life from the planet, or within the lifetimes of many people now living a great modern state deliberately murdered millions of innocent people in gas chambers.

Above all, be critical. Take each document and treat it as if it were a delicate and intricate machine whose mechanism is concealed. By examining the exterior minutely much information about the interior can be obtained. Shaking, rattling, and rolling also helps. Much of what we can say about historical evidence is speculative, and we gain a firmer foothold only by drawing together and comparing pieces of evidence, using sources as building blocks that interlock with each other to form a foundation. Often some blocks are missing altogether, and holes in the foundation appear. But foundations can stand with holes in them, if the surrounding material is robust and fitted in the right positions. Good luck!

3 See Anthony Kenny, "Cardinal of Conscience," *TLS*, July 30, 2010, 3.

This Book

The problem with textbooks is that they oversimplify because they have to be short enough to be read in a limited amount of time. The advantage of documents is that they can, in a brief space, offer an authentic slice of the past. Unfortunately, limitations on length have forced me to reduce those slices to extracts; only fragments of long and complex documents can be included here. Nevertheless, they allow the reader to make direct contact with the minds and voices of people who lived hundreds of years ago. Space also imposes severe restrictions on the number of documents that can be included. Of the millions of possibilities only a few hundred could be selected. To suggest this volume is a balanced and representative account of the issues and evidence that has survived over three centuries of British and Irish history is ridiculous. I hope I have touched on most of the topics of the very greatest importance, but even that aspiration can only be partially achieved. What is presented here has an element of the randomness of the evidence that has survived overall.

I have tried to include extracts from "cardinal" documents, works of seminal importance. Adam Smith, Charles Darwin, and Winston Churchill are examples of figures whose words shaped the history of Britain and the world. On the other hand, other documents are not necessarily ones every historian would include in a source collection but which illustrate a theme central to the period being covered. Here selection has been more personal but I hope not whimsical or irrational. Some documents were chosen for the gripping nature of the narrative that brings history "alive." I have looked for documents that offer opportunities for alternative interpretations. Sometimes I have juxtaposed sources to illustrate opposing contemporary views. I have included some poetry, art, and fiction, usually to illustrate a historical theme rather than to try to provide examples of the best literature or painting of the time. To do the latter would require doubling or more the length of this book.

In a number of instances I have indicated links with or suggested comparisons between documents within chapters and sometimes across centuries. I have tried to provide enough background for each document to make this book useable in a variety of courses and contexts. Its usefulness can be enhanced by pairing it with my textbook, *A History of Modern Britain: 1714 to the Present.* Material in the textbook provides additional background on the authors of many of the documents and a context for answering some of the questions I pose in the introductory paragraphs.

At the end of each chapter you will find lists of topics about which historians have disagreed and sources that illustrate various views on the subject. Sometimes these are celebrated disputes now largely resolved. Others are ongoing discussions even as I write. History is a never-ending conversation. I have also listed a number of counterfactual questions to consider. Historians have always analyzed the possibilities of alternative outcomes. Today "virtual history" (also called "counterfactual history") has become fashionable. [4] It addresses the question "What if?" Examining how things might have turned out in different circumstances can enhance our understanding of the past. It is one of the ways to avoid the trap of regarding history as predetermined or inevitable.

Note: I have modernized and Americanized punctuation and spelling in most cases. When necessary, I have explained confusing language or references in the introductory paragraph or in brackets in the text.

4 E.g., Niall Ferguson, ed., *Virtual History: Alternatives and Counterfactuals* (London, 1997).

Abbreviations

£	pound (unit of British currency)
AHR	*American Historical Review*
AS	*Ageing and Society*
BH	*Business History*
BHR	*Business History Review*
BJECS	*British Journal of Eighteenth-Century Studies*
BJS	*British Journal of Sociology*
CC	*Continuity and Change*
CJH	*Canadian Journal of History*
CSSH	*Comparative Studies of Society and History*
EcHR	*Economic History Review*
EEH	*Explorations in Economic History*
FR	*Feminist Review*
HJ	*Historical Journal*
HT	*History Today*
HW	*History Workshop*
IJURR	*International Journal of Urban and Regional Research*
IRSH	*International Review of Social History*
JBS	*Journal of British Studies*
JEH	*Journal of Economic History*
JHD	*Journal of Historical Demography*
JIH	*Journal of Interdisciplinary History*
JMH	*Journal of Modern History*
JSH	*Journal of Social History*
MP	Member of Parliament
P&P	*Past & Present*
PH	*Parliamentary History*
PS	*Population Studies*

SH	*Social History*
SR	*Social Research*
TCBH	*Twentieth-Century British History*
TLS	*Times Literary Supplement*
TRHS	*Transactions of the Royal Historical Society*

Part I

The Eighteenth Century

CHAPTER ONE

State and Empire

Britain became a great power with a large empire overseas in the eighteenth century. Episodes such as the Civil War (1642–49), the Cromwellian Commonwealth (1649–60), and the Glorious Revolution (1688–89) had focused attention and resources at home. As the eighteenth century progressed, Britons remained divided about constitutional matters yet the political system emerged as a strong and flexible instrument. It also provided a stable platform for commercial growth and overseas expansion. It helped Britain weather challenges from Louis XIV and Louis XV, Jacobites and Irish rebels, English radicals and American patriots, and the existential threat of invasion by French revolutionaries and Napoleon Bonaparte.

The secrets of British stability and growth in the eighteenth century lay partly in the nature of the intellectual environment and economic developments, which are discussed in Chapters 2 and 3. What factors discussed in the documents of this chapter contributed to British prosperity and strength? Why were concerns about understanding the ground rules of the political system so salient?

As you read the documents in this chapter, consider the following questions:

- What were the perceived strengths and weaknesses of the British political system?
- How did the British constitution function and what did the authors of these documents perceive the role of the various elements in it to be?
- What was the relationship between Britain and its colonies in the eighteenth century?

Sources and Debates in Modern British History: 1714 to the Present, First Edition. Edited by Ellis Wasson.

Published 2012 by Blackwell Publishing Ltd.

The Constitution

1.1 Viscount Bolingbroke, The Idea of the Patriot King *(written 1738, pub. 1749)*[1]

Henry St John, Viscount Bolingbroke (1678–1751), served in government under Queen Anne. His opposition to the Hanoverian succession led to a period of exile in France. He returned in 1723 and worked against Sir Robert Walpole and the Whigs. He had a strong influence on the royal tutor and later prime minister, the earl of Bute, and on the latter's pupil and master, King George III, a monarch who came to believe he was pursuing the national interest above the bickering of self-interested political factions.

What was the British constitution like in 1738? What does Bolingbroke see as the foundations of government? Did he believe in "divine right" monarchy in the manner of Louis XIV of France? To what degree would Bolingbroke and Burke (see documents 1.5 and 1.10) agree or disagree about government?

Now we are subject, by the constitution of human nature, and therefore by the will of the Author of this and every other nature, to two laws. . . . By the first . . . I mean the universal law of reason; and by the second the particular law, or constitution of laws, by which every distinct community has chosen to be governed.

The obligation of submission to both, is discoverable by so clear and so simple a use of our intellectual faculties, that it may be said properly enough to be *revealed to us by God*; and though *both* these laws cannot be said properly to be given him, yet our obligation to submit to the *civil* law is a principal paragraph in the *natural* law, which he has most manifestly given us. In truth we can no more doubt of the obligations of both these laws, than of the existence of the lawgiver. As supreme Lord over all his works, his *general* providence regards immediately the *great commonwealth* of mankind; but then, as supreme Lord likewise, his authority gives a sanction to the *particular bodies* of law which are made under it. . . . It follows, therefore, that he who breaks the *laws of his country* resists the *ordinance of God*, that is, the law of his nature. . . .

. . . The *just authority* of *kings*, and the *due obedience* of *subjects*, may be deduced with the utmost certainty. And surely it is far better for kings themselves to have their authority thus founded on principles incontestable, and on fair deductions from them, than on the chimeras of madmen, or, what has been more common, the sophisms of knaves. A *human right*, that cannot be controverted, is preferable surely to a *pretended divine right*, which every man must believe implicitly, as few will do, or not believe at all.

[1] Viscount Bolingbroke, *The Works of the Late Right Honourable Henry St John, Lord Viscount Bolingbroke*, 8 vols (London, 1809), IV, 237–41, 263.

But the principles we have laid down do not stop here. A divine right in kings is to be deduced evidently from them. A divine right to govern *well*, and conformably to the constitution at the head of which they are placed. A divine right to govern *ill*, is an absurdity: to assert it is blasphemy. A people may choose, or hereditary succession may raise, a *bad* prince to the throne; but a *good* king alone can derive his right to govern from *God*. The reason is plain: good government alone can be in the divine intention. . . . [Nor can it] be said without absurd impiety, that he confers a right to oppose his intention.

The office of kings is then of *right divine*, and their persons are to be reputed *sacred*. As *men*, they have no such *right*, no such sacredness belonging to them: as *kings* they have both, unless they forfeit them. Reverence for government obliges to reverence governors, who, for the sake of it, are raised above the level of other men: by reverence for governors, independently of government, any further than reverence would be due to their virtues if they were private men, is preposterous, and repugnant to common sense. The spring from which this legal reverence, for so I may call it, arises, is *national*, not *personal*.

All this is as true of *hereditary*, as it is of *elective* monarchs; though the scribblers for tyranny, under the name of monarchy, would have us believe that there is something more august, and more scared in one than the other. They are sacred *alike*, and this attribute is to be ascribed, or not ascribed to them, as they answer, or do not answer, the *ends* of their institution. . . .

To conclude . . . I think a *limited monarchy* the best of governments, so I think a *hereditary monarchy* the best of monarchies. I said a *limited monarchy*; for an unlimited monarchy, wherein arbitrary will, which is in truth no rule, is however the sole rule, or stands instead of all rule of government, must be allowed so great an absurdity, both in reason informed and uninformed by experience, that it seems a government fitter for savages than for civilized people. . . .

In fine, the constitution will be reverenced by him as the *law of God* and of *man*; the *force* of which binds the king as much as the meanest subject, and the *reason* of which binds him *much more*.

1.2 Third duke of Atholl to J. Mackenzie (Dec. 10, 1770)[2]

During the eighteenth century Britain exercised less restraint over the press than any other European country. Nonetheless the House of Commons repeatedly tried to block reports of debates made by journalists sitting in the gallery and imprisoned a number of printers. The struggle culminated in the 1771 "Printers' Case" in which the courts ruled that the press had the right to print reports of the proceedings in the lower house. After a long struggle, the House of Lords similarly succumbed. Rockingham Whigs and the followers of

2 Michael W. McCahill, *The House of Lords in the Age of George III (1760–1811)* (Oxford, 2009), 172.

William Pitt the Elder tried to block motions to suppress journalists. In 1770 the Lords ordered "strangers" to leave the chamber during a debate on the Falkland Islands crisis with Spain. The duke of Atholl (1729–74) described the scene on December 10, 1770. The ban, however, lasted only until 1775, after which further attempts to suppress public reports on debates failed.

Why were published debates useful? Why was the government unable to keep the proceedings of Parliament secret? How serious were the political divisions among the landed elite? In what ways did the British constitution encourage the growth of the public sphere? Why might many aristocrats be reluctant to open debates to the press?

The minority have all this session of Parliament endeavored to represent the Weakness of Britain in every Part of the globe. By sea and land, and in her forts and garrisons. This the duke of Manchester was doing today in a very strong manner so as might invite an Enemy to attack us, he was stopped by Lord Gower who said the House was so full of Strangers that if such discourse went on the House must be cleared, as everything that was said would be taken down in shorthand and published to the world. Whereupon it was moved to clear the House, which by a standing order takes place of Every other motion, and none can speak till it be done; However, Lord Chatham [Pitt the Elder] stood up and attempted to speak but the House would not hear him, and drowned his voice with the Cry clear the House, clear the House. Which he took so much amiss that he immediately walked out and 16 other Peers who have voted in the minority this session followed him. This affair I doubt not will be a fine topic for newspapers and opposition writers. There are faults on all sides and every days experience convinces me that planting trees is more agreeable and more honest business than either supporting or opposing ministers.

1.3 *Horace Walpole,* Memoirs of the Reign of King George the Third *(written between 1766 and 1784)*[3]

Horace Walpole (1717–97), the son of the first prime minister, Sir Robert Walpole, was an attentive observer of the political system in the mid-eighteenth century. Here he summarizes the Whig interpretation of the British constitution. Because it was not set down in a single document and many elements were based on tradition and custom, disagreements often cropped up when one party competed with another for advantage within the political system. Many of these disputes had to do with procedure, but broad

[3] Horace Walpole, *Memoirs of the Reign of King George the Third*, ed. Sir Denis Le Marchant (Philadelphia, 1845), I, 191–2.

philosophical differences also existed. One should be careful, however, about attributing conflict to the "unwritten" nature of the constitution. In fact much of it was written down in statutes. One can identify serious disagreements about the American constitution in the opinions of the Supreme Court and in contests between the executive and legislative branches, even though it is a single document.

How does Walpole's version of the constitution differ from Bolingbroke's (document 1.1)? How did the British constitution, as described by Walpole, differ from the American one? Why is personal liberty dependent on freedom of speech and the press?

The legislature consists of the three branches of King, Lords, and Commons. Together they form our invaluable Constitution, and each is a check on the other two. But it must be remembered at the same time, that while any two are checking, the third is naturally aiming at extending and aggrandizing its power. The House of Commons has not seldom made this attempt like the rest. The Lords, as a permanent and as a proud body, more constantly aim at it: the Crown always. Of liberty, a chief and material engine is the liberty of the Press; a privilege for ever sought to be stifled and annihilated by the Crown. . . . Liberty of speech and liberty of writing are the two instruments by which Englishmen call on one another to defend their countrymen.

1.4 *George Grenville,* Diary *(Mar. 23, 1764)*[4]

George Grenville (1712–70) recorded a discussion with King George III (1738–1820) about the still evolving office of prime minister. Sir Robert Walpole had emerged in the 1720s as the key intermediary between the Cabinet Council and King George II, but the minister denied that he was any more than first among equals. Gradually, the term "first minister" (later variants included "premier") entered common usage, and the life of a government came to stand or fall on his decisions. At this time the Secretaries of the Northern and Southern Departments (of which Lord Egremont, referred to below, was one) divided responsibilities for both domestic and foreign affairs between them, and some exercised power nearly comparable to the prime minister's. George III's decision, which he repeated frequently throughout his reign, though not always, allowed premiers increasingly to consolidate ministerial control in their own hands.

What were the advantages to the king of making one man solely responsible for the conduct of an administration? What were the disadvantages?

4 W.J. Smith, ed., *The Grenville Papers* (London, 1852–3), II, 500.

[His Majesty said] ... now, all the world confessed it as well as himself, that it was necessary to lodge the power of the government in one man alone, and that Mr. Grenville was the person in whom he wished to see it; that when Lord Egremont [died 1763] was alive, it was necessary from particular circumstances to make that power more equal in the three Ministers; that he meant it should be in him; that to him he gave, and would give his confidence; that it would be necessary for Mr. Grenville to keep certain managements with the two Secretaries of State and the Duke of Bedford, but that must be at his own discretion, for that it was his desire and purpose that all recommendations and appointments come through Mr. Grenville.

1.5 *Edmund Burke,* Reflections on the Revolution in France *(1790)*[5]

Edmund Burke (1729–97) was appalled by the French Revolution (1789–99) even though he had made a spirited defense of the American colonists in the 1770s and supported Whiggish opposition to English oppression in Ireland. Even before the Revolution moved into its more radical phase, Burke denounced it in a clarion call for upholding tradition and gradual reform of existing institutions in the face of the predations of abstract theory. His polemic against revolution has become a cardinal document in the discussion of modern democracy.

On what did Burke base the legitimacy of the British political system? Why did he think the constitution must be anchored in the past? Could such a system adjust easily to change? What would Burke be likely to say about the recently ratified constitution of the United States? Is it surprising that Burke should defend the right of large landowners to a predominant role in government when he had risen as an aide to Whig aristocrats and had himself established a landed estate which he intended to pass on to his heir, and hoped to gain membership in the House of Lords?

You will observe, that from Magna Charta [1215] to the Declaration of Right [1689], it has been the uniform policy of our constitution to claim and assert our liberties, and an *entailed inheritance* derived to us from our forefathers, and to be transmitted to our posterity; as an estate specially belonging to the people of this kingdom without any reference whatever to any more general or prior right. By this means our constitution preserves a unity in so great a diversity of its parts. We have an inheritable crown; an inheritable peerage; and a house of commons and a people inheriting privileges, franchises, and liberties, from a long line of ancestors.

5 Edmund Burke, *The Works of the Right Honourable Edmund Burke*, 3 vols (London, 1782), III, 58–9, 80–1, 89–93.

This policy appears to me to be the result of profound reflection; or rather the happy effect of following nature, which is wisdom without reflection, and above it. A spirit of innovation is generally the result of a selfish temper and confined views. People will not look forward to posterity, who never look backward to their ancestors. Besides, the people of England well know, that the idea of inheritance furnishes a sure principle of conservation, and a sure principle of transmission; without at all excluding a principle of improvement. . . . Whatever advantages are obtained by a state proceeding on these maxims, are locked fast as in a sort of family settlement. . . .

Nothing is a due and adequate representation of a state that does not represent its ability, as well as its property. But as ability is a vigorous and active principle, and as property is sluggish, inert and timid, it never can be safe from the invasions of ability, unless it be, out of all proportion, predominant in the representation. It must be represented to in great masses of accumulation, or it is not rightly protected. The characteristic essence of property, formed out of the combined principles of its acquisition and conservation, is to be *unequal*. The great masses therefore which excite envy, and tempt rapacity, must be put out of the possibility of danger. Then they form a natural rampart about the lesser properties in all their gradations. . . .

The power of perpetuating our property in our families is one of the most valuable and interesting circumstances belonging to it, and that which tends the most to the perpetuation of society itself. It makes our weakness subservient to our virtue; it grafts benevolence even upon avarice. The possession of family wealth, and of the distinction which attends hereditary possession . . . are the natural securities for this transmission. [The House of Lords and the House of Commons are filled with landowners.] Let those large proprietors be what they will, and they have their chance of being among the best, they are, at the very worst, the ballast in the vessel of the commonwealth. . . .

[Admirers of the French Revolution in England] despise experience as the wisdom of unlettered men; and as for the rest, they have wrought under-ground a mine that will blow up at one grand explosion all examples of antiquity, all precedents, charters, and acts of parliament. They have "the rights of men." Against these there can be no prescription; against these no agreement is binding. . . . Against these their rights of men let no government look for security in the length of its continuance, or in the justice and lenity of its administration.

. . . Government is not made in virtue of natural rights, which may and do exist in total independence of it; and exist in much greater clearness, and in a much greater degree of abstract perfection: but their abstract perfection is their practical defect. Government is a contrivance of human wisdom to provide for human *wants*. Men have a right that these wants should be provided for by this wisdom. Among these wants is . . . the want, out of civil society, of a sufficient restraint upon their passions. Society requires not only that the passions of individuals should be subjected, but that . . . the inclinations of men should be frequently thwarted, their will controlled, and their passions brought into subjection . . . Liberties and restraints vary with times and circumstances, . . . they cannot be settled upon any abstract rule; and nothing is so foolish as to discuss them upon that principle. . . . The science of constructing a commonwealth, or renovating it, or reforming it, is, like every other experimental science, not to be taught *à priori.* Nor is it a short experience that can instruct us in that practical science; because the real effects of moral causes are not always immediate; but that with which in the first instance is prejudicial may be excellent in its remoter operation; and its excellence may arise even from the ill effects it produces in the beginning. The reverse also happens; and very plausible schemes, with very pleasing commencements, have often shameful and lamentable conclusions. . . . It is with infinite caution that any man ought to venture upon pulling down an edifice which has answered in any tolerable degree for ages the common purposes of society, or of building it up again, without having models and patterns of approved utility before his eyes.

1.6 *Charles James Fox, speech in the House of Commons (May 11, 1791)*[6]

One of the ironies of British politics in the years immediately before and after the French Revolution is that the principal party leaders – William Pitt the Younger, Charles James Fox, Henry Addington, and the earl of Liverpool – came from recently risen families, often of quite humble origins only a generation or two previously. Yet no men could be found who more vigorously defended the aristocratic order. It is also ironic that the more progressive party, the Whigs, who were initially in sympathy with the early achievements of the French Revolution, was led, aside from Fox (1749–1806), by magnate families often of old lineage and massive estates, while the Tory leaders included many more "new" men. Fox's grandfather had been a servant, but his father earned a fortune and a peerage in politics. He stood on the left of the parliamentary political spectrum but, as the following passage suggests, was sympathetic to aristocratic rule.

Why might Fox sing the praises of the aristocracy? When he spoke of democracy, what did he mean by the term? The House of Commons was filled with members of the landowning gentry and the sons of peers, so how could it be seen as democratic? Does the fact that this speech was delivered two years after the French Revolution commenced have any significance? What might Fox think of the monarchy? Was Fox correct in thinking that hereditary dynasties of politicians emerge in democracies?

. . . He laid it down as a principle never to be departed from, that every part of the British dominions ought to possess a government, in the constitution of which

[6] *The Parliamentary History of England*, ed. William Cobbett (London, 1817), XXIX, 409–10.

monarchy, aristocracy and democracy were mutually blended and united; nor could any government be a fit one for British subjects to live under, which did not contain its due weight of aristocracy, because that, he considered to be the proper poise of the constitution, the balance that equalized and meliorated the powers of the two other extreme branches, and gave stability and firmness to the whole. It became necessary to look what were the principles on which aristocracy was founded, and he believed it would be admitted to him, that they were two-fold, namely, rank and property, or both united. In this country the House of Lords formed the aristocracy, and that consisted of hereditary titles, in noble families of ancient origin, or possessed by peers newly created on account of their extended landed property. He said that prejudice for ancient families, and that sort of pride which belonged to nobility, was right to be encouraged in a country like this; otherwise one great incentive to virtue would be abolished and the national dignity as well as its domestic interest would be diminished and weakened. There was also such a thing to be remembered, which gave additional honor to our House of Lords, as long established respect for the persons and families of those who, in consequence either of their own superior talents and eminent services, or of one or both in their ancestors, constituted the peerage. This he observed, was by no means peculiar to pure aristocracies such as Venice and Genoa, nor even to despotic or to mixed governments. It was to be found in democracies, and was there considered as an essential part of the Constitution; affection to those whose families had best served the public being always entertained with the warmest sincerity and gratitude. Thus in the ancient republics of Athens and Rome, they all knew the respect paid to those who had distinguished themselves by their services for the commonwealth.

Threats to the Political and Social Order

1.7 John Wilkes, speech in the House of Commons (Mar. 21, 1776)[7]

The radical businessman John Wilkes (1727–97) attacked the ministry of the earl of Bute, which earned him the enmity of King George III. Later he opposed government policy regarding the Thirteen Colonies during the War of Independence. At one point he fled into exile for fear of prosecution for printing obscene material in his journal, *The North Briton*. He was repeatedly elected to Parliament and then denied his seat. He became widely popular across the country. Eventually he established a conservative, respectable career that culminated in being elected Lord Mayor of London. Figure 1.1 shows John Wilkes as drawn by William Hogarth.

[7] *The Parliamentary Register*, III, Mar. 21, 1776, 440.

What is Wilkes's case for enacting parliamentary reform? Does he advocate universal suffrage? Did his social class have anything to do with his opinions? To what degree may this be a personal crusade to rectify what he felt was ill treatment by the king and Parliament and to what degree were his views ideologically driven?

Figure 1.1 "John Wilkes" by William Hogarth (1769).

How has Hogarth portrayed Wilkes? How might people of different social classes have reacted to this engraving?

The disfranchising of the mean, venal, and dependent boroughs would be laying the axe to the root of corruption and [executive] influence, as well as aristocratical tyranny. . . . Burgage tenures [votes tied to the control of property that could be easily manipulated by a landowner], and private property in a share of the legislature [property owners being able to select MPs], are monstrous absurdities in a free state, as well as an insult to common sense. I wish, Sir, an English parliament to speak the free, unbiased sense of the body of the English people, and of every man among us, of each individual, who may justly be supposed to be comprehended in a fair majority. The meanest mechanic, the poorest peasant and day-laborer, has important rights respecting his personal liberty, that of his wife and children, his property, however inconsiderable, his wages, his earnings, the very price and value of each day's hard labor, which are in many trades and manufactures regulated by the power of Parliament. Every law relative to marriage, to the protection of a wife, sister, or daughter, against violence and brutal lust, to every contract or agreement with a rapacious or unjust master, interest the manufacturer, the cottager, the servant, as well the rich subjects of the state. Some share therefore in the power of making those laws, which deeply interest them, and to which they are expected to pay obedience, should be reserved even to this inferior, but most useful, set of men in the community. We ought always to remember this important truth, acknowledged by every free state, that all government is instituted for the good of the mass of the people to be governed.

1.8 Thomas Paine, Common Sense *(1776)*[8]

The radical Thomas Paine (1737–1809) was the son of a rural stay- (corset) maker and was himself a failed businessman, later an excise officer, and then a school teacher. In the pamphlet *Common Sense*, he analyzed what in his eyes were the defects of the British constitution. Initially, his work had a greater impact in North America, where he had fled his troubles at home, than it did in Britain.

Was Paine's assessment of the power of the monarchy and the aristocracy accurate? In speaking to an audience remote from London, why might he focus on the role of George III? What aspects of the British legal system and constitution does he neglect to mention because they might undermine his argument? Was patriotism the only reason George III became more popular as he grew older?

[8] Thomas Paine, *The Political Works of Thomas Paine* (Springfield, 1826), 143, 145.

I know it is difficult to get over local or long-standing prejudices, yet if we will suffer ourselves to examine the component parts of the English constitution, we shall find them to be base remains of two ancient tyrannies. . . .

First – The remains of monarchical tyranny in the person of the king.

Secondly – The remains of aristocratical tyranny in the persons of the peers. . . .

By being hereditary, [they] are independent of the people; wherefore in a *constitutional sense* they contribute nothing towards the freedom of the state.

To say that the constitution of England is a union of [the king, Lords, and Commons] reciprocally *checking* each other, is farcical; either the words have no meaning, or they are flat contradictions.

To say that the Commons is a check on the king, presupposes two things:

First – That the king is not to be trusted without being looked after, or in other words, that a thirst for absolute power is the natural disease of monarchy.

Secondly – That the Commons, by being appointed for that purpose, are either wiser or more worthy of confidence than the crown.

But as the same constitution which gives the Commons a power to check the king by withholding [financial allocations], gives afterwards the king a power to check the Commons, by empowering him to reject their other bills; it again supposes that the king is wiser than those whom it has already supposed to be wiser than him. A mere absurdity!

There is something exceedingly ridiculous in the composition of monarchy; it first excludes a man from the means of information, yet empowers him to act in cases where the highest judgment is required. The state of a king shuts him from the world, yet the business of a king requires him to know it thoroughly; wherefore the different parts, by unnaturally opposing and destroying each other, prove the whole character to be absurd and useless. . . .

That this crown is the overbearing part in the English constitution, needs not to be mentioned, and that it derives its whole consequence merely from being the giver of places and pensions, is self-evident, wherefore, though we have been wise enough to shut and lock a door against absolute monarchy, we at the same time have been foolish enough to put the crown in possession of the key.

The prejudice of Englishmen in favor of their own government by king, Lords and Commons, arises as much or more from national pride than reason.

1.9 *Thomas Paine,* The Rights of Man *(1791)*[9]

Tom Paine (see document 1.8) attacked Burke's (document 1.5) assertion of the legitimacy of the constitutional settlement made after the Glorious Revolution of 1688. Paine had traveled to the Thirteen Colonies in the 1770s and helped arouse the populace against monarchical rule. He went

[9] Thomas Paine, *The Political Works of Thomas Paine* (Springfield, 1826), 7–8.

to Paris after the outbreak of revolution in France, and was a strong supporter of radicalism there.

Why and on what grounds did Paine criticize the existing system in general and Burke in particular? How effective is his criticism? Was it true that Parliament could pass unchangeable enactments binding on all future Parliaments?

The English parliament of 1688 did a certain thing, which for themselves and their constituents, they had a right to do, and which it appeared right should be done: but, in addition to this right, which they professed by delegation, *they set up another right by assumption*, that of binding and controlling posterity to the end of time. The case, therefore, divides itself into two parts; the right which they possessed by delegation, and the right which they set up by assumption. The first is admitted; but with respect to the second, I reply:

There never did, there never will, and there never can exist a parliament of any description of men, or any generation of men, in any country, possessed of the right or the power of binding and controlling posterity to the "*end of time*," or of commanding forever how the world shall be governed, or who shall govern it: And therefore all such clauses, acts or declarations, by which the makers of them attempt to do what they have neither the right nor the power to do, nor the power to execute, are in themselves null and void. Every age and generation must be free to act for itself, *in all cases*, as the ages and generations which preceded it. The vanity and presumption of governing beyond the grave, is the most ridiculous and insolent of all tyrannies. Man has no property in man: neither has any generation a property in the generations which are to follow. . . . It is the living, and not the dead, that are to be accommodated.

1.10 Edmund Burke, Reflections on the Revolution in France *(1790)*[10]

Burke's attack on the French Revolution has been discussed above (document 1.5). What disturbed Burke so much about the French Revolution? Was his willingness to ignore the defective characters of the French royal family mere sentiment or did it have importance in his argument? Could xenophobia have led him to exaggerate the depravity of the French? Would you say his argument that the tyranny overthrown in France was considerably more benign than the one by which it was replaced valid? What might lead revolutions to produce tyrannies worse than those they overthrew?

[10] Edmund Burke, *The Works of the Right Honourable Edmund Burke*, 3 vols (London, 1792), III, 61–2, 110–14, 125.

> . . . Your constitution [in France], it is true, whilst you were out of possession [Burke is referring here to failure of the Estates General to meet between 1614 and 1789], suffered waste and dilapidation; but you possessed in some parts the walls, and in all the foundations of a noble and venerable castle. You might have repaired those walls; you might have built on those foundations. . . . You had the elements of a constitution very nearly as good as could be wished.
>
> . . . But you chose to act as if you had never been molded into civil society, and had everything to begin anew. You began ill, because you began by despising every thing that belonged to you.

Burke denounced the attacks on the royal family and their forced removal from Versailles to Paris. How do you account for the survival of the British monarchy in this period?

> Little did I dream that I should have lived to see such disasters fallen upon [the queen] in a nation of gallant men, in a nation of men of honor and of cavaliers. I thought ten thousand swords must have leaped from their scabbards to avenge even a look that threatened her with insult. But the age of chivalry is gone. That of sophisters, economists, and calculators, has succeeded; and the glory of Europe is extinguished forever. Never, never more, shall we behold that generous loyalty to rank and sex, that proud submission, that dignified obedience, that subordination of the heart, which kept alive, even in servitude itself, the spirit of an exalted freedom. The unbought grace of life, the cheap defense of nations, the nurse of manly sentiment and heroic enterprise is gone! It is gone, that sensibility of principle, that chastity of honor, which felt a stain like a wound, which inspired courage whilst it mitigated ferocity, which ennobled whatever it touched, and under which vice itself lost half its evil, by losing all its grossness. . . .
>
> All pleasing illusions, which made power gentle, and obedience liberal, which harmonized the different shades of life, and which, by a bland assimilation, incorporated into politics the sentiments which beautify and soften private society, are to be dissolved by this new conquering empire of light and reason. All the decent drapery of life is to be rudely torn off. All the superadded ideas, furnished from the wardrobe of a moral imagination, which the heart owns, and the understanding ratifies, as necessary to cover the defects of our naked shivering nature, and to raise it to dignity in our estimation, are to be exploded as a ridiculous, absurd, and antiquated fashion.
>
> . . . When the old feudal and chivalrous spirit of *Fealty*, which, by freeing kings from fear, freed both kings and subjects from the precautions of tyranny, shall be extinct in the minds of men, plots and assassinations will be anticipated by preventive murder and preventive confiscation, and that long roll of grim and bloody maxims, which form the political code of all power, not standing on its honor, and the honor of those who are to obey it. Kings will be tyrants from policy when subjects are rebels from principle.

When ancient opinions and rules of life are taken away, the loss cannot possibly be estimated. From that moment we have no compass to govern us; nor can we know distinctly to what port we steer. . . .

Nothing more certain, than that our manners, our civilization, and all the good things which are connected with manners and with civilization, have, in this European world of ours depended for ages upon two principles: and were indeed the result of both combined; I mean the spirit of a gentleman, and the spirit of religion. The nobility and clergy, the one by profession, the other by patronage, kept learning in existence, even in the midst of arms and confusions, and whilst governments were rather in their causes, than formed. Learning paid back what it received to nobility and to priesthood: and paid it with usury by enlarging their ideas, and by furnishing their minds. Happy if they had all continued to know their insoluble union, and their proper place! Happy if learning, not debauched by ambition, had been satisfied to continue, the instructor, and not aspired to be master! Along with its natural protectors and guardians, learning will be cast into the mire, and trodden down under the hoofs of a swinish multitude. . . .

Your literary men [the French *philosophes*], and your politicians . . . essentially differ in these points. They have no respect for the wisdom of others; but they pay it off by very full measure of confidence in their own. With them it is sufficient motive to destroy an old scheme of things, because it is an old one. As to the new, they are in no sort of fear with regard to the duration of the building run up in haste; because duration is no object to those who think little or nothing has been done before their time, and who place all their hopes in discovery . . .

1.11 Thomas Paine, The Rights of Man *(1791)*[11]

Tom Paine challenged Burke's attack on the French "Declaration of the Rights of Man." He was serving as a deputy in the French legislature when he was caught up in the Terror. He escaped execution only by chance. This experience somewhat tempered his enthusiasm for revolution. On what grounds did Paine challenge Burke's arguments? How persuasive is his reasoning? What was Paine likely to put on his list of Rights of Man?

Mr. Burke with his usual outrage, abused the *Declaration of the Rights of Man*, published by the National Assembly of France [1789], as the basis on which the constitution of France is built. This he calls "paltry and blurred sheets of paper about the rights of man." Does Mr. Burke mean to deny that man has any rights? If he does, then he must mean that there are no such things as rights anywhere, and that he has none himself; for who is there in the world but man? But if Mr. Burke

[11] Thomas Paine, *The Rights of Man* (Putnam's, New York, 1894), 303, 309 and (Ecker, New York, 1894), 190.

means to admit that man has rights, the question then will be: What are those rights, and how man came by them originally? . . .

It has been thought a considerable advance towards establishing the principles of Freedom to say that Government is a compact between those who govern and those who are governed; but this cannot be true, because it is putting the effect before the cause; for as man must have existed before governments existed, there necessarily was a time when governments did not exist, and consequently there could originally exist no governors to form such a compact with.

The fact therefore must be that the *individuals themselves*, each in his own personal and sovereign right, *entered into a compact with each other* to produce government: and this is the only mode in which governments have a right to arise, and the only principle on which they have a right to exist. . . . Governments must have arisen either *out* of the people or *over* the people. Mr. Burke has made no distinction. He investigates nothing to its source, and therefore he confounds everything. . . .

[Challenging Burke's emphasis on following tradition, Paine wrote] Government by precedent, without any regard to the principle of the precedent, is one of the vilest systems that can be set up. In numerous instances the precedent ought to operate as a warning, and not as an example, and requires to be shunned instead of imitated; but instead of this, precedents are taken in the lump, and put at once for Constitution and law.

Either the doctrine of precedents is policy to keep man in a state of ignorance, or it is a practical confession that wisdom degenerates in governments as governments increase in age, and can only hobble along by the stilts and crutches of precedents. How is it that the same persons who would proudly be thought wiser than their predecessors appear at the same time only as the ghosts of departed wisdom? How strangely is antiquity treated! . . .

If the doctrine of precedents is to be followed, the expenses of government need not continue the same. Why pay men extravagantly who have but little to do? If everything that can happen is already in precedent, legislation is at an end, and precedent, like a dictionary, determines every case. Either, therefore, government has arrived at its dotage, and requires to be renovated, or all the occasions for exercising its wisdom have already occurred.

The Sinews of Empire

1.12 *Daniel Defoe,* A Tour through the Whole Island of Great Britain *(1724–26)*[12]

Daniel Defoe (1660–1731), the author of the first great English novel, *Robinson Crusoe* (1719), described the dockyards of the Royal Navy near Rochester on

[12] Daniel DeFoe, *A Tour through the Whole Island of Great Britain* (London, 1724), 20–4.

the River Medway east of London, close to the mouth of the Thames. The Royal Navy ensured the security of the island nation and protected its commerce and overseas empire. It was also the largest manufacturing organization in Britain, and its great battleships were the most complex machines as yet devised by man.

Why was it important for Britain to invest heavily in naval power? What did a very large and highly skilled ocean-going force allow Britain to do? What sort of economy would allow a country to assemble and maintain such a force? Was naval success an indicator that the British system of government was more efficient than its competitors in raising tax revenue and encouraging industrial development? Perhaps the success of the navy was more due to the skills of its officers and the organization established by officials?

This being the chief arsenal of the Royal Navy of Great Britain. The buildings here are indeed like the ships themselves, surprisingly large, and in their several kinds beautiful. The warehouses, or rather streets of ware-houses, and storehouses for laying up the naval treasure are the largest in dimension, and the most in number, that are any where to be seen in the world. The ropewalks for making cables, and the forges for anchors and other ironwork, bear a proportion to the rest as also the wetdock for keeping masts, and yards of the greatest size, where they lie sunk in water to preserve them, the boatyard, the anchor yard; all like the whole, monstrously great and extensive, and are not easily described.

We come next to the stores themselves, for which all this provision is made; and first, to begin with the ships that are laid up there. The sails, the rigging, the ammunition, guns, great and small shot, small arms, swords, cutlasses, half pikes, with all the other furniture belonging to the ships that ride at their moorings in the river Medway. These take up one part of the place, where the furniture of every ship lies in particular warehouses by themselves, and may be take out on the most hasty occasion without confusion, fire excepted. . . .

The particular government of these yards, as they are called is very remarkable, the commissioners, clerks, accountants, etc. within doors, the store-keepers, yard-keepers, dock-keepers, watchmen, and all other officers without doors, with the subordination of all officers one to another respectively, as their degree and offices require, is admirable. . . .

The expedition that has been sometimes used here in fitting out men of war, is very great, and as the workmen relate it, 'tis indeed incredible . . . The *Royal Sovereign*, a first rate of 106 guns, was riding at her moorings, entirely unrigged, and nothing but her three masts standing, as is usual when a ship is laid up, and that she was completely rigged, all her masts up, her yards put to, her sails bent, anchors and cables on board, and the ship sailed . . . in three days. . . . a thousand or fifteen hundred men to be employed in it and more if they were wanted . . . The dexterity of the English sailors in those things is not to be matched by the world.

1.13 Sir William Keith, A Short Discourse on the Present State of the Colonies in America with Respect to the Interest of Great Britain *(1740)*[13]

Sir William Keith (1669–1749) was governor of Pennsylvania from 1712 to 1726. He advocated a mercantilist policy which viewed colonies as existing solely for the benefit of the mother country. The latter extracted as much as it could of the natural resources and sent back manufactured goods in a closed system that excluded the colonies from trading with other markets.

How would Adam Smith (see document 2.10) have viewed Keith's arguments? How did Sir William's political arguments accord with British traditions of liberty and parliamentary representation? What might be the reaction of the residents of the Thirteen Colonies to this discourse? What did they gain by remaining British colonists?

Every act of a dependent provincial government therefore ought to terminate in the advantage of the mother state unto whom it owes it's being, and by whom it is protected in all its valuable privileges . . .

It has ever been the maxim of all polite nations, to regulate their Government to the best advantage of their trading interest: wherefore it may be helpful to take a short view of the principle benefits arising to *Great Britain* from the trade of the colonies.

1. The colonies take off and consume above one sixth Part of the woollen manufactures exported from *Britain*, which is the chief staple of *England*, and main support of the landed interest.
2. They take off and consume more than double that Value in Linen and callicoes, which is either the product of *Britain* and *Ireland*, or partly the profitable returns made for that product carried to foreign countries.
3. The luxury of the colonies, which increases daily, consumes great quantities of *English* manufactured silk, haberdashery, household furniture, and trinkets of all sorts; also a very considerable value of East India goods.
4. A great revenue is raised to the crown of *Britain* by Returns made in the Produce of the plantations, especially in tobacco, which at the same time helps England to bring nearer to a Balance their unprofitable trade with *France*.
5. Those colonies promote the interest and trade of *Britain*, by a vast increase of shipping and seamen, which enables them to carry great quantities of fish to *Spain*, *Portugal*, *Leghorn*, etc., furs, logwood, and rice to *Holland*, whereby they help *Great Britain* considerably in the Balance of trade with those countries.
6. If reasonably encouraged, the colonies are now in a Condition to furnish Britain with as much of the following commodities as it can demand, *viz.* masts for

[13] William L. Saunders, ed., *The Colonial Records of North Carolina, State of North Carolina* (Raleigh, 1886), II, 626–9.

the Navy, and all sorts of timber, hemp, flax, pitch, tar, oil, rosin, copper ore, with pig and bar iron, by means whereof the balance of trade to *Russia* and the *Baltic* may be very much reduced in favor of *Great Britain*.

7. The profits arising to all those colonies by trade is returned in bullion or other useful effects to *Great Britain*, where the superfluous cash, and other riches acquired in *America* must center, which is not one of the least securities that *Britain* has to keep the colonies always in due subjection.
8. The colonies upon the main are the granary of *America*, and a necessary support to the sugar plantations of the West Indies, which could not subsist without them.

By this short view of trade in general we may plainly understand, that those colonies can be very beneficially employed both for *Great Britain* and themselves, without interfering with any of the staple manufactures in *England*. . . .

From what has been said of the nature of colonies, and the restriction that ought to be laid on their trade, it is plain that none of the *English* plantations in *America* can with any reason or good sense pretend to claim an absolute legislative Power within themselves . . . They cannot be possessed of any rightful capacity to contradict, or evade the true intent and force of any act of Parliament, wherewith the wisdom of *Great Britain* may think fit to affect them from time to time . . .

North America

1.14 William Pitt [the Elder], speech in the House of Commons (Jan. 14, 1766)[14]

William Pitt the Elder, first earl of Chatham (1708–78), was credited with greatly expanding the empire by war in the 1750s and early 1760s. Here he seems to strike a somewhat different note in the aftermath of the hugely unpopular Stamp Act of 1765 imposed on the Thirteen Colonies. A number of leading British politicians, including Burke and Fox, also urged conciliation and respect toward the colonies.

What might account for Pitt's position? Did Pitt's view reflect the majority of opinion in the British political class? Why might Parliament and the king think they could impose their will on the American colonies? Had Pitt been prime minister in 1776, would the American Revolution have happened?

The gentleman tells us America is obstinate; America is almost in open rebellion. I rejoice that America has resisted. Three millions of people so dead to all the feelings of liberty as voluntarily to submit to be slaves, would have been fit instruments to make slaves of the rest. . . . Even under former arbitrary reigns,

[14] *The Parliamentary History of England*, ed. William Cobbett (London, 1813), XVI, 104–5 and 107–8.

parliaments were ashamed of taxing a people without their consent, and allowed them representatives. . . .

I am no courtier of America. I stand up for this kingdom. I maintain that the parliament has the right to bind, to restrain America. Our legislative power over the colonies is sovereign and supreme. When it ceases to be sovereign and supreme, I would advise every gentleman to sell his lands, if he can, and embark for that country. When two countries are connected together, like England and her colonies, without being incorporated, the one must necessarily govern; the greater must rule the less; but so rule it as not to contradict the fundamental principles that are common to both. . . .

The Americans have not acted in all things with prudence and temper. They have been wronged. They have been driven to madness by injustice. Will you punish them for the madness you have occasioned? Rather let prudence and temper come first from this side. I will undertake for America that she will follow the example. . . .

Upon the whole, I will beg leave to tell the House what is really my opinion. It is, that the Stamp Act be repealed absolutely, totally, and immediately. That the reason for the repeal be assigned, because it was founded on an erroneous principle. At the same time let the sovereign authority of this country over the colonies be asserted in as strong terms as can be devised, and be made to extend to every point of legislation whatsoever; that we may bind their trade, confine their manufactures, and exercise every power whatsoever except that of taking their money out of their pockets without consent.

1.15 Horace Walpole to the countess of Upper Ossory (Oct. 15, 1776)[15]

Opinions among the political elite about the rebellion of the Thirteen Colonies were sharply divided. In the following passage Horace Walpole (see document 1.3) expressed grave concern about the impact of the war on Britain. To many Britons the loss of the colonies was seen as the beginning of the end of British greatness. How could that be? Did he think Britain would succeed in holding onto the colonies? How did he see the colonies in relation to Britain's other foreign interests?

About the American news, I say what I always have thought and said, that whatever way this war ends, it will be fatal to this country. The liberty of America made it flourish to the prodigious height it did. If governed by an army, instead of inviting settlers and trade, it will be deserted and be a burthen to us, as Peru and Mexico, with all their mines, have been to Spain. The war has already drained us of men; if the army could be brought back, how many, between climate, and others chances, will return? Our ships are entering their third winter in those seas,

[15] *The Letters of Horace Walpole, Earl of Orford*, ed. Peter Cunningham, 9 vols (London, 1857), VI, 385–6.

and we have flung away in those three years what should have lessened our debt, and prepared against a war with France. The plea for the last peace was our inability of proceeding with the war. Are we in the condition we were in 1763? How soon we shall have a French war, I know not; it is much talked of already at Paris; but come when it will, then will be the moment of judging of this war with the Colonies. I believe France will then recover Canada, with interest; and for the East Indies, which our fleets, supported by our trade, obtained, I have always looked on them as a vision, which made us drunk with riches, which will be a burthen to maintain, and which will vanish like a scene in the Arabian tales. I have not less gloomy ideas of your Ireland, where I conclude the first storm will burst.

1.16 *John Adams, letter to John Jay (June 2, 1785)*[16]

John Adams (1735–1826), a founding father and second President of the United States, was appointed the first minister (ambassador) to Great Britain and presented his credentials to King George III on June 2, 1785 at St James's Palace. How did Adams, who a few years earlier could have been hanged for treason had the revolutionaries lost, respond to the meeting with his former sovereign? Were his declarations sincere? What were the king's emotions likely to have been?

The Marquis of Carmarthen returned, and desired me to go with him to his majesty! I went with his lordship through the levee room into the king's [office]; the door was shut, and I was left with his majesty and the secretary of state alone. I made the three reverences; one at the door, another about half way, and a third before his presence, according to the usage established at this and all the northern courts of Europe, and then addressed myself to his majesty in the following words:

"Sir – The United States of America have appointed me their minister plenipotentiary to your majesty, and have directed me to deliver to your majesty this letter which contains the evidence of it. It is in obedience to their express commands, that I have the honor to assure your Majesty of the unanimous disposition and desire to cultivate the most friendly and liberal intercourse between your Majesty's subjects and their citizens, and of their best wishes for your majesty's health and happiness, and for that of your royal family.

The appointment of a minister from the United States to your majesty's court will form an epoch in the history of England and of America. I think myself more fortunate than all my fellow-citizens, in having the distinguished honor to be the first to stand in your Majesty's royal presence in a diplomatic character; and I shall esteem myself the happiest of men, if I can be instrumental in recommending my country more and more to your Majesty's royal benevolence, and of restoring

16 *Public and Private Life of George the Third* (London, 1821), 429.

an entire esteem, confidence, and affection, or, in better words, the old good nature and the old good humor between people, who, though separated by an ocean, and under different governments, have the same language, a similar religion, and kindred blood. I beg your majesty's permission to add, that, although I have some time before been intrusted by my country, it was never in my whole life in a manner so agreeable to myself."

The king listened to every word I said, with dignity, but with an apparent emotion.

India

1.17 "Narrative of J.Z. Holwell," The Annual Register *(1758)*[17]

The British headquarters in India at Calcutta fell to the Newab (ruler) of Bengal in 1756. This is an eyewitness account written by one of the prisoners of the horrific first night the British spent in captivity in what came to be known as "the Black Hole of Calcutta."

What does the treatment of the prisoners tell us about Indian attitudes toward the British? What does the incident suggest about the ability of Europeans to sustain imperial control in distant places? Did the conduct of the prisoners accord with the image of European superiority asserted by Edward Gibbon in document 3.4? Is an eyewitness account likely to be completely or even marginally reliable? What circumstances might make this account more or less accurate?

Figure to yourself, my friend, if possible, the situation of a hundred and forty-six wretches, exhausted by continual fatigue and action, crammed together in a cube of eighteen feet, in a close sultry night, in Bengal, shut up to the eastward and southward (the only quarters from whence air could reach us) by dead walls, and by a wall and a door to the north, open only to the westward by two windows, the strongly barred with iron, from which we could receive scarce any the least circulation of fresh air. . . .

We had been but a few minutes confined before every one fell into a perspiration so profuse, you can form no idea of it. This brought on a ragging [*sic*] thirst, which increased in proportion as the body was drained of its moisture. . . .

Until the water came, I had myself not suffered much from thirst, which instantly grew excessive. We had no means of conveying it into the prison, but by hats forced through the bars; and thus myself and Messieurs Coles and Scott (notwithstanding the pains they suffered from their wounds) supplied them as fast as possible. . . . Though we brought full hats within the bars, there ensued such

17 *The Annual Register . . . for 1758* (London, 1791), 279–81 and 283–5.

violent struggles, and frequent contests to get at it, that before it reached the lips of any one, there would be scarcely a small tea cup full left in them. . . .

By half an hour past eleven, the much greater number of those living were in an outrageous delirium, and the others quite ungovernable; few retaining any calmness, but the ranks next the windows. They all now found, that water, instead of relieving, rather heightened their uneasiness; and, *Air*, *air*, was the general cry. Every insult that could be devised against the guard, all the opprobrious names and abuse . . . were repeated to provoke the guard to fire upon us, every man that could, rushing tumultuously towards the windows, with eager hopes of meeting the first shot. . . . They whose strength and spirits were quite exhausted, laid themselves down and expired quietly upon their fellows: others who had yet some strength and vigour left, made a last effort for the windows, and several succeeded by leaping and scrambling over the backs and heads of those in the first ranks; and got hold of the bars, from which there was no removing them. Many to the right and left sunk with the violent pressure, and were soon suffocated; and the stench arising from the dead bodies [grew] intolerable . . .

[After release was ordered:] As the door opened inwards, and as the dead were piled up against it, and covered all the rest of the floor, it was impossible to open it by any efforts from without; it was therefore necessary that the dead should be removed by the few that were within, who were become so feeble, that the task, though it was the condition of life, was not performed without the utmost difficulty, and it was 20 minutes after the order came, before the door could be opened.

About a quarter after six in the morning, the poor remains of 146 souls, being no more than three and twenty, came out of the Blackhole alive, but in a condition which made it very doubtful whether they would see the morning of the next day . . . . The bodies were dragged out of the hole by the soldiers, and thrown promiscuously into the ditch of an unfinished ravelin, which was afterwards filled with earth.

1.18 Edmund Burke, speech in the House of Commons (Dec. 1, 1783)[18]

Edmund Burke (see documents 1.5 and 1.10), as a senior advisor to the Whig elite, placed great emphasis on individual liberty and supported the calls for granting representation to the Thirteen Colonies in North America. He devoted enormous time and energy to rooting out corruption in the British administration in India. He refers here in particular to the "nabobs," self-made men who returned to England often with vast fortunes after a career with the East India Company. He believed that colonies were held by the mother country as a trustee, which was a philosophy ultimately dangerous to the continuance of empire.

[18] *The Works of the Right Hon. Edmund Burke*, ed. Henry Rogers (London, 1841), I, 282–3.

> Why might Burke's Irish nationality have made him alert to colonial misrule? Did he object to the idea of empire in the first place? How do you square his conservatism in the face of the French Revolution with his sympathy for those who suffered from tyrannical rule in India and America?

Our conquest [of India], after twenty years, is as crude as it was the first day. The natives scarcely know what it is to see the grey head of an Englishman. Young men (boys almost) govern there, without society, and without sympathy with the natives. They have no more social habits with the people, than if they still resided in England; nor, indeed, any species of intercourse but that which is necessary to making a sudden fortune, with a view to a remote settlement. Animated with all the avarice of age, and all the impetuosity of youth, they roll in one after another; wave after wave; and there is nothing before the eyes of the natives but an endless, hopeless prospect of new flights of birds of prey and passage, with appetites continually renewing for a food that is continually wasting. Every rupee of profit made by an Englishman is lost for ever to India. With us are no retributory superstitions, by which a foundation of charity compensates, through ages, to the poor, for the rapine and injustice of the day. With us no pride erects stately monuments which repair the mischiefs which pride had produced, and which adorn a country out of its own spoils. . . .

. . . English youth in India drink the intoxicating draught of authority and dominion before their heads are able to bear it, and as they are full grown in fortunes long before they are ripe in principle, neither nature nor reason have any opportunity to exert themselves for remedy of the excesses of their premature power. The consequences of their conduct, which in good mind, (and many of there are probably such) might produce penitence or amendment, are unable to pursue the rapidity of their flight. Their prey is lodged in England; and the cries of India are given to seas and winds, to be blown about, in every breaking up of the monsoon, over a remote and unhearing ocean. In India all the vices operate by which sudden fortune is acquired; in England are often displayed by the same persons, the virtues which dispense hereditary wealth. Arrived in England, the destroyers of the nobility and gentry of a whole kingdom will find the best company in this nation, at a board of elegance and hospitality. Here the manufacturers and husbandman will bless the just and punctual hand that in India has torn the cloth from the loom, or wrested the scanty portion of rice and salt from the peasant of Bengal, or wrung from him the very opium in which he forgot his oppressions and his oppressor. They marry into your families; they enter into your senate; they ease your estates with loans . . . Our Indian government is in its best state of grievance. It is necessary that the corrective should be uncommonly vigorous; and the work of men, sanguine, warm, and even impassioned in the cause. But it is an arduous thing to plead against abuses of a power which originates from your own country, and affects those whom we are used to consider as strangers.

HISTORIANS' DEBATES

What forces shaped the development of the law and punishment system and its reform during the eighteenth century?

Richard R. Follett, *Evangelicalism, Penal Theory, and the Politics of Criminal Law Reform in England, 1808–1830* (New York, 2001); V.A.C. Gatrell, *The Hanging Tree: Execution and the English People 1770–1868* (Oxford, 1994); Douglas Hay, *et al.*, *Albion's Fatal Tree: Crime and Society in Eighteenth-Century England* (New York, 1975); Michael Ignatieff, *A Just Measure of Pain: The Penitentiary in the Industrial Revolution, 1750–1850* (New York, 1978); Peter Linebaugh, *The London Hanged: Crime and Civil Society in the Eighteenth Century* (London, 1991); Leon Radzinowicz, *A History of English Criminal Law and Its Administration from 1750*, vol. I: *The Movement for Reform 1750–1833* (New York, 1948); E.P. Thompson, *Whigs and Hunters: The Origin of the Black Act* (London, 1975).

How serious a threat were the Jacobites? What motivated support for the Rising of 1745?

L. Colley, *Britons: Forging the Nation, 1707–1837* (New Haven, 1992); Eveline Cruikshanks, *Political Untouchables: The Tories and the '45* (London, 1979); David Daiches, *Charles Edward Stuart: The Life and Times of Bonnie Prince Charlie* (London, 1973); Bruce Lenman, *The Jacobite Cause* (Glasgow, 1986); Bruce Lenman, *The Jacobite Risings in Britain, 1689–1746* (London, 1980); F.J. McLynn, *France and the Jacobite Risings of 1745* (Edinburgh, 1981); Frank McLynn, *The Jacobites* (London, 1985); Paul Kleber Monod, *Jacobitism and the English People, 1688–1788* (Cambridge, 1989); Daniel Szechi, *Jacobitism and Tory Politics 1710–1714* (Edinburgh, 1984); A.J. Youngson, *The Prince and the Pretender: A Study in the Writing of History* (London, 1985).

Sir Lewis Namier famously argued that politics during much of the eighteenth century was about squabbles over patronage and jockeying among various aristocratic factions, not motivated by political principle or ideology. Subsequent historians have questioned his interpretation. How much of a role did principle and ideology play in party politics?

Lewis Namier, *England in the Age of the American Revolution*, 2nd ed. (London, 1961); Lewis Namier, *The Structure of Politics at the Accession of George III*, 2nd ed. (New York, 1957); John Brewer, *Party Ideology and Popular Politics at the Accession of George III* (London, 1976); Ian R. Christie, "Party Politics in the Age of Lord North's Administration," *PH* 6 (1987), 47–68; J.C.D. Clark, *The Dynamics of Change: The Crisis of the 1750s and the English Party Systems* (Cambridge, 1982); Linda Colley, *In Defiance of Oligarchy: The Tory Party 1714–1760* (Cambridge, 1982); Linda Colley, *Lewis Namier* (London, 1989); H.T. Dickinson, *Liberty and Property: Political Ideology in Eighteenth-Century Britain* (London, 1977); B.W. Hill, *The Growth of Parliamentary Parties 1689–1742* (London, 1976); B.W. Hill, *British Parliamentary Parties 1742–1832* (London, 1985); Geoffrey Holmes, ed., *Britain after the Glorious Revolution 1689–1714* (London, 1969); Frank O'Gorman, *The Emergence of the British Two-Party System 1760–1832*, (London, 1982); James J. Sack, *From Jacobite to Conservative: Reaction and Orthodoxy in Britain, c. 1760–1832* (Cambridge, 1993); Peter D.G. Thomas, "Party Politics in Eighteenth-Century Britain: Some Myths and a Touch of Reality," *BJECS* 10 (1987), 201–10.

Particular focus has been aimed at the question of to what degree the eighteenth-century Whigs formed a coherent and principled party.

Herbert Butterfield, *Sincerity and Insincerity in Charles James Fox: The Raleigh Lecture in History, British Academy, 1971* (London, 1972); John W. Derry, *The Regency Crisis and the Whigs, 1788–1789* (Cambridge, 1963); W.M. Elofson, *The Rockingham Connection and the Second Founding of the Whig Party, 1768–1773* (Montreal, 1996); J.P. Kenyon, *Revolution Principles: The*

Politics of Party, 1689–1720 (Cambridge, 1977); Austin Mitchell, *The Whigs in Opposition 1815–1830* (Oxford, 1967); L.G. Mitchell, *Charles James Fox* (Oxford, 1992); Frank O'Gorman, *The Rise of Party in England: The Rockingham Whigs, 1760–1782* (London, 1975); Frank O'Gorman, *The Whig Party and the French Revolution* (London, 1967); James J. Sack, *The Grenvillites, 1801–1829: Party Politics and Factionalism in the Age of Pitt and Liverpool* (Urbana, 1979); E.A. Smith, *Whig Principles and Party Politics: Earl Fitzwilliam and the Whig Party 1748–1833* (Manchester, 1975).

What sort of king was George III? A tyrant, an incompetent, a noble man?

Jeremy Black, *America's Last King* (New Haven, 2006); John Brooke, *King George III* (London, 1972); John Bullion, "The Prince's Mentor: A New Perspective on the Friendship between George III and Lord Bute during the 1750s," *Albion* 21 (1989), 34–55; Herbert Butterfield, *George III and the Historians*, rev. ed. (New York, 1959); Herbert Butterfield, *George III, Lord North, and the People, 1779–1780* (London, 1949); I.R. Christie, "George III and the Historians Thirty Years On," *History* 71 (1986), 205–21; Linda Colley, *Britons: Forging the Nation, 1707–1837* (New Haven, 1992); B.W. Hill, "Executive Monarchy and the Challenge of Parties 1689–1832: Two Concepts of Government and Two Historiographical Interpretations," *HJ* 13 (1970), 379–401; Marilyn Morris, *The British Monarchy and the French Revolution* (New Haven, 1998); Lewis Namier, "King George III: A Study of Personality," in *Personalities and Powers* (London, 1955), and "The King and His Ministers," in *Crossroads of Power* (London, 1962); Richard Pares, *King George III and the Politicians* (Oxford, 1954); E.A. Reitan, *George III: Tyrant or Constitutional Monarch?* (Boston, 1964).

COUNTERFACTUALS TO CONSIDER

What if the Jacobite risings in 1715 or 1745 had succeeded? What if Britain had won the American War of Independence? What if Napoleon had successfully invaded Britain? What if there had been a revolution in Britain in 1790?

CHAPTER TWO

Economy and Society

Sometime in the eighteenth century Britain became the crucible for the first industrialized economy. Full development of the factory system, however, did not take place until the middle years of the nineteenth century. Historians still debate the timing and causes of this process. Moreover, no clear sense of class, in its purely economic sense, existed in a society that still thought in terms of ranks and orders. An important change was the development of a robust social group variously described as the middling classes or bourgeoisie. The middling orders helped foster a consumer revolution, which in part was spurred by their desire to emulate the style of life and manners – honor and politeness – of the aristocracy and gentry. The respect for the elite sustained social stability while the proportion of society enjoying prosperity expanded. Perceptions of gender and family were more diverse than is sometimes realized.

Mercantilism had been the dominant system in economic thought, but gradually during the eighteenth century a series of thinkers began to challenge the underlying assumptions of state-controlled expansion. Indeed a new school of thought, known as "classical economics," addressed a wide range of issues. Surely it was no accident that the avatars of modern capitalism emerged as Britain gathered momentum for a spectacular economic expansion?

As you read the documents in this chapter, consider the following questions:

- How did people perceive each other in terms of social rank and relationships?
- What was the place and importance of trade and commerce in British society?

Sources and Debates in Modern British History: 1714 to the Present, First Edition. Edited by Ellis Wasson.

Published 2012 by Blackwell Publishing Ltd.

- What were the forces economists believed produced and endangered wealth and what could the government do to create prosperity?

Honor and Manners

2.1 *Daniel Defoe,* The Complete English Tradesman *(1726)*[1]

Daniel Defoe (see document 1.12) wrote extensively about commerce and business. He was keenly aware of the transformation and interrelationship between finance and government. The synergy between commerce and war was accelerating rapidly during the eighteenth century. Defoe also understood the interlocking nature of the landed and business elites: both were entrepreneurial and willing to work with each other to the extent that the boundaries between them were blurred in a way almost unique in Europe. By "tradesman" he does not mean artisans or others who worked with their hands but the equivalent of a modern "businessman."

Why might the landed elite accept the situation that Defoe describes? What was distinctive about English society that led it on a different path than that taken by France, Germany, or Austria? Why might businessmen and their families emulate and embrace the values of "polite" society? How would one define a "gentleman" in England?

As so many of our noble and wealthy families, as we have shown, are raised by and derived from trade, so it is true, and indeed it cannot well be otherwise, that many of the younger branches of our gentry, and even of the nobility itself, have descended again into the spring from whence flowed, and have become tradesmen: and thence it is that, as I said above, our tradesmen in England are not, as it generally is in other countries, always of the meanest of our people. Nor is trade itself in England, as is in other countries, the meanest thing the men can turn their hand to; but, on the contrary, trade is the readiest way for men to raise their fortunes and families; and therefore it is a field for men of figure and of good families to enter upon. . . .

As to the wealth of the nation, that undoubtedly lies chiefly among the trading part of the people; and though there are a great many families raised within few years, in the late war, by great employments and by great actions abroad, to the honor of the English gentry, yet how many more families among the tradesmen have been raised to immense estates, even during the same time, by the attending circumstances of the war; such as the clothing, the paying, the victualling and furnishing, etc., both army and navy. And by whom have the prodigious taxes been paid, the loans supplied, and money advanced upon all occasions? . . .

[1] Daniel Defoe, *The Complete English Tradesman* (London, 1841), I, 242–3.

[A landed] estate [is] a pond, but trade's a spring: the first, if it keeps full, and the water wholesome, by the ordinary supplies and drains from the neighboring grounds, it is well, and it is all that is expected; but the other is an inexhausted current, which not only fills the pond, but is continually running over, and fills all the lower ponds and places about it. . . .

Trade is so far here from being inconsistent with [being] a gentleman, that, in short, trade in England makes gentlemen, and has peopled this nation with gentlemen; for after a generation or two, the tradesman's children, or at least their grandchildren, come to be as good gentlemen, statesmen, parliament men, privy counselors, judges, bishops, and noblemen, as those of the highest birth and the most ancient families.

2.2 Lord Hastings to the ninth earl of Huntingdon (Mar. 15, 1743)[2]

The Horace referred to here was Sir Robert Walpole's brother, Horatio, a diplomat later created first Baron Walpole of Wolterton (1678–1757, in 1742 still a member of the House of Commons). Dueling continued to be an important element in aristocratic life during the eighteenth century. Increasingly Enlightenment values, religion and other factors led to its demise in Britain during the first half of the nineteenth century, although it survived much longer on the Continent.

What might the balance be between ideas about honor and masculine identity in the survival of the duel? Was the fact that Walpole and Chetwynd were wearing swords merely a sign of gentlemanly status or a practical necessity? To what degree was this a "political" duel as opposed to a "social" one about status?

I was told every particular of the battle between Mr. William Chetwynd and Mr. Horace Walpole, by the Speaker [of the House of Commons], Mr. Onslow. The quarrel begun behind the Speaker's chair, who was gone into his private chamber. Mr. Horace Walpole talked about some affairs during his brother's ministration, on which Mr. Chetwynd bid him not rub up old sores. "Why," says Horace, "you would have had my brother and I hanged" – on which they went out and came to . . . Pipe's Ground. But one of the clerks followed these two bravo's, Chetwynd being fifty-nine, Horace Walpole sixty-four (one hundred and twenty-three betwixt them), and the Speaker says Horace Walpole has a sort of crutch. He found them a-fighting in prodigious passions and Chetwynd wounded. He took up their sticks which they had laid before them in great ceremony, and struck their swords. But it did not signify, for they passed at one another with

2 *Report on the Manuscripts of the Late Reginald Rawdon Hastings, volume III* (London, 1934), 38. For another account, see also W.S. Lewis, Warren Hunting Smith, and George L. Lam, eds., *Horace Walpole's Correspondence with Sir Horace Mann*, vol. II: *1742–1745* (New Haven, 1954), 191–2.

Figure 2.1 "The Prodigal Son" by Thomas Rowlandson (1785). Library of Congress.

The man lying on the sofa looking rather the worse for wear is the Prince of Wales (later King George IV). On the right, looking even worse, is the Whig leader Charles James Fox (see document 1.6). The scene is set in a bordello. Both men were drunkards and gamblers. Their conduct contrasts rather sharply from that advocated by Lord Chesterfield (document 2.3), which suggests that Sydney Smith (document 5.12) might have been right about alcohol consumption among the upper classes. "Politeness" and manners were unevenly spread across society even within the same social ranks. The cartoon also illustrates an important aspect of eighteenth-century British society: journalists were largely at liberty to criticize members of the royal family and senior political leaders. Public discourse was genuinely free. What made the elite accept being subjected to fierce satire? Who might form the market for which Rowlandson intended this engraving?

great fury again, especially Mr. Chetwynd who, enraged at being wounded, bent his sword against a button of Horace. The Speaker immediately put Horace under arrest, and sent to take care of Mr. Chetwynd, and went to see himself. He says his sword is bent very much and that the force it was pushed with, if it had not been for the button, would have carried it through Horace's body. Chetwynd is wounded on the hip. Horace Walpole says he thought it was a great and hard thing to fight a duel, because young fellows used to make such ado about it, but he says there is nothing at all in it now, he finds.

2.3 *Fourth earl of Chesterfield to his son (Oct. 19, 1748)*[3]

The letters of the earl of Chesterfield (1694–1773) to his illegitimate son contain many passages that reflect the values and manners of the eighteenth-century landed elite (but see Figure 2.1 for a contrast in conduct). Chesterfield

[3] *Letters Written by the Earl of Chesterfield to His Son* (Philadelphia, 1876), 195–8.

owned a large estate, descended from an old family, held high office, and was a cultured man. What attitudes and values does this letter suggest he holds? Why should a rich and powerful man value politeness and manners? Why does he encourage insincerity? What is his attitude toward people who do not understand his version of good manners? Who are those people?

Having, in my last, pointed out what sort of company you should keep, I will now give you some rules for your own conduct in it; rules which my own experience and observation enable me to lay down and communicate to you with some degree of confidence. . . . I shall say nothing with regard to your bodily carriage and address, but leave them to the care of your dancing-master, and to your own attention to the best models; remember however, that they are of consequence. . . .

Talk often, but never long: in that case, if you do please, at least you are sure not to tire your hearers. . . .

Tell stories very seldom, and absolutely never but where they are very apt, and very short. Omit every circumstance that is not material, and beware of digressions. To have frequent recourse to narrative betrays great want of imagination.

Never hold anybody by the button, or the hand, in order to be heard out; for, if people are not willing to hear you, you had much better hold your tongue than them. . . .

Take, rather than give, the time of the company you are in. If you have parts, you will show them, more or less, upon every subject; and, if you have not, you had better talk sillily upon a subject of other people's than of your own choosing.

Avoid as much as you can, in mixed companies, argumentative polemical conversations; which, though they should not, yet certainly do, indispose, for a time, the contending parties towards each other; and, if the controversy grows warm and noisy, endeavor to put an end to it by some genteel levity or joke. . . .

Above all things, and upon all occasions, avoid speaking of yourself, if it be possible. Such is the natural pride and vanity of our hearts, that it perpetually breaks out, even in people of the best parts, in all the various modes and figures of egotism. . . .

Neither retail nor receive scandal, willingly; defamation of others may, for the present, gratify the malignity of the pride of our hearts, cool reflection will draw very disadvantageous conclusions from such a disposition; and in the case of scandal, as in that of robbery, the receiver is always thought as bad as the thief. . . .

I need not (I believe) advise you to adapt your conversation to the people you are conversing with; for I suppose you would not, without this caution, have talked upon the same subject and in the same manner to a Minister of state, a bishop, a philosopher, a captain, and a woman. A man of the world must, like the chameleon, be able to take every different hue, which is by no means a criminal or abject, but a necessary complaisance, for it relates only to manners, and not to morals. . . .

Loud laughter is the mirth of the mob, who are only pleased with silly things; for true wit or good sense never excited a laugh since the creation of the world. A man of parts and fashion is therefore only seen to smile, but never heard to laugh.

2.4 *Thomas Paine,* The Rights of Man *(1791)*[4]

Tom Paine (documents 1.8, 1.9, and 1.11) despised the aristocracy and the landed interest. One of the means by which the elite sustained their wealth and power was through the practice of primogeniture, leaving the bulk of their estate to the eldest son (or, if they had only daughters, to a more distant male relative) at the expense of younger sons and daughters. The latter were given educations and dowries or "portions," usually in cash, to meet the expenses of starting a career in the army, law, or business. The practice prevented large blocks of land from being diminished by subdivision over the generations. Primogeniture made the English aristocracy one of the richest and most powerful in Europe, whereas on the Continent aristocratic estates were often rapidly reduced in size through multiple inheritance.

What were Paine's arguments against primogeniture? How would parents feel about disinheriting their younger children? What forces made them overcome their love for their younger progeny? Why were protests made by younger siblings against the favoritism shown to older brothers very rare? Could the pressure to restore prosperity be a spur to achievement among younger sons and also reinforce the system? Why does Paine fail to mention that argument? Did this practice make aristocrats unfit legislators?

The nature and character of aristocracy shows itself to us in this law. It is a law against every law of nature, and Nature herself calls for its destruction. Establish family justice and aristocracy falls. By the aristocratical law of primogenitureship, in a family of six children five are exposed. Aristocracy has never more than one child. The rest are begotten to be devoured. They are thrown to the cannibal for prey, and the natural parent prepares the unnatural repast.

As everything which is out of nature in man affects, more or less, the interest of society, so does this. All the children which the aristocracy disowns (which are all except the eldest) are, in general, cast like orphans on a parish, to be provided for by the public, but at a greater charge. Unnecessary offices and places in governments and courts are created at the expense of the public to maintain them.

With what kind of parental reflections can the father or mother contemplate their younger offspring? By Nature they are children, and by marriage they are heirs; but by aristocracy they are bastards and orphans. They are the flesh and blood of

[4] Thomas Paine, *The Political Works of Thomas Paine* (Springfield, 1826), 57–9.

their parents in one line, and nothing akin to them in the other. To restore, therefore, parents – relations to each other, and man to society – and to exterminate the monster aristocracy, root and branch – the French Constitution [of the Revolution] destroyed the law of *primogentitureship*. . . .

Aristocracy is kept up by family tyranny and injustice. . . . There is an unnatural unfitness in an aristocracy to be legislators for a nation. Their ideas of *distributive justice* are corrupted at the very source. They begin life by trampling on all their younger brothers and sisters, and relations of every kind, and are taught and educated to do so. With what ideas of justice or honor can that man enter a house of legislation, who absorbs in his own person the inheritance of a whole family of children or doles out to them some pitiful portion with the insolence of a gift?

The Struggle for Life and Wealth

2.5 *Daniel Defoe,* A Tour through the Whole Island of Great Britain *(1724–26)*[5]

Daniel Defoe (see documents 1.12 and 2.1) was a man of business but also a journalist. He was likely to exaggerate, but he was a shrewd observer. The "City" was the financial and commercial heart of Britain and the "Court" the center of government. By this time London was the largest city in the world.

What did Defoe think was most striking about London? Why was it so prosperous? Make a list of the most important institutions he mentions. Are they what you would expect a commentator to notice in a great royal capital city? Why was London unique?

London, as a city only, and as its walls and liberties line it out, might, indeed, be viewed in a small compass; but when I speak of London, now in the modern acceptation, . . . how much father it may spread, who knows? New squares, and new streets rising up every day to such a prodigy of buildings, that nothing in the world does, or ever did, equal it, except old Rome in Trajan's time . . .

It is the disaster of London, as to the beauty of its figure, that it is thus stretched out in buildings, and as the convenience of the people directs, whether for trade, or otherwise; and this has spread the face of it in a most straggling, confused manner, out of all shape, uncompact, and unequal; neither long nor broad, round or square . . .

The extent or circumference of the continued buildings of the cities of London and Westminster and borough of Southwark, all which, in the common acceptation, is called London, amounts to thirty-six miles . . .

5 Daniel Defoe, *Curious and Diverting Journies through the Whole Island of Great Britain* (London, 1734), not numbered.

The Royal Exchange, the greatest and finest of the kind in the world. . . . Though this Exchange cost the citizens an immense sum of money . . . yet it was so appropriated to the grand affairs of business, that the rent or income of it for many years, full answered the interest of the money laid out in building it. . . .

The churches in London are rather convenient than fine, not adorned with pomp and pageantry as in Popish countries; but, like the true Protestant plainness, they have made very little of ornament either within them or without. . . . But the beauty of all the churches in the city, and of all the Protestant churches in the world, is the cathedral of St. Paul's. . . .

The City is the centre of its commerce and wealth. The Court of its gallantry and splendor. . . . Between the Court and City, there is a constant communication of business to that degree, that nothing in the world can come up to it. . . .

The equality, however, being thus preserved, and a perfect good understanding between the Court and City having so long flourished, this union contributes greatly to the flourishing circumstances of both, and the public credit is greatly raised by it. . . . No sum is so great, but the Bank [of England] has been able to raise. . . .

By this great article of public credit, all the king's business is done with cheerfulness, provisions are now bought to victual the fleets without difficulty, and at reasonable rates. The several yards where the ships are built and fitted out, are currently paid: the magazines of military and naval stores kept full: in a word, by this very article of public credit, of which Parliament is the foundation (and the City, are the architectures or builders) all those great things are now done with ease . . .

The Bank is kept in Grocer's Hall, a very convenient place, and, considering its situation, so near the Exchange, a very spacious, commodious place. . . . In the next street is the Excise Office. In this one office is managed an immense weight of business, and they have in pay, as I am told, near four thousand officers. . . .

The Post Office . . . is grown very considerable. This office maintains now, packet boats to Spain and Portugal, which never was done before: so the merchants' letters for Cadiz or Lisbon, which were before two and twenty days in going over France and Spain to Lisbon, oftentimes arrive there now, in nine or ten days from Falmouth. . . . The penny post [in London is now] come also into so exquisite a management, that nothing can be more exact, and 'tis with the utmost safety and dispatch, that letters are delivered at the remotest corners of the town, almost as soon as they could be sent by a messenger, and that from four, five, six to eight times a day, according to the distance of the place makes it practicable. . . .

The city of London, and parts adjacent as also all the south of England, is supplied with coals, called therefore seal-coal, from Newcastle upon Tyne, and from the coast of Durham, and Northumberland. This trade is so considerable, that it is esteemed the great nursery of our best seamen. The quantity of coals, which it is supposed are [annually] burnt and consumed in and about this city, is supposed to be about five hundred thousand chalder, every chalder containing thirty-six bushels, and generally weighing about thirty hundred weight. ... A fleet of five hundred to seven hundred sail of ships, comes up the river at a time, yet they never want a market. ...

There are in London, notwithstanding we are a nation of liberty, more public and private prisons, and houses of confinement, than any city in Europe, perhaps as many as in all the capital cities of Europe put together.

2.6 *Arthur Young,* A Tour in Ireland *(1780)*[6]

The Englishman Arthur Young (1741–1820) was an expert on farming and published numerous books about his tours around the British Isles and on the Continent examining agricultural life and practices. His visit to Ireland in 1776 prompted him to comment on the diet of the poor in Ireland and England. At the time the extraordinary nutritional value of potatoes had not yet been scientifically examined.

What were the principal differences between the diets of the English and Irish poor? The plentiful potatoes available to the Irish poor described by Young were not always available. Terrible famines periodically visited Ireland in the eighteenth century and even more catastrophically in the 1840s. Why might Young fail to mention the precarious nature of Irish existence, so reliant on a single crop, when compared to the life of the English poor, who never encountered sustained mass starvation in the eighteenth or nineteenth centuries? Do you detect evidence of racism in Young's account of Ireland? What was Young's view of the Irish landowning elite?

The food of the common Irish, potatoes and milk, have been produced more than once as an instance of the extreme poverty of the country, but this I believe is an opinion embraced with more alacrity than reflection. I have heard it stigmatized as being unhealthy, and sufficiently nourishing for the support of hard labor, but this opinion is very amazing in a country, many of whose poor people are as athletic in their form, as robust, and as capable of enduring labor as any upon earth. The idleness seen among many when working for those who oppress them is a very contrast to the vigor and activity with which the same people work when themselves alone reap the benefit of their labor. To what country must we have recourse for a stronger instance than lime carried by little miserable mountaineers thirty miles on horses backs to the foot of their hils, and up the

6 Arthur Young, *A Tour in Ireland*, 2nd ed. (London, 1780), 116–19.

steeps on their own. When I see the people of the country in spite of political oppression with well formed vigorous bodies, and their cottages swarming with children; when I see their men athletic, and their women beautiful, I know not how to believe them subsisting on an unwholesome food.

At the same time, however, that both reason and observation convince me of the justice of these remarks, I will candidly allow that I have seen an excess in the laziness of great numbers, even when working for themselves, and such as apparent weakness in their exertions when encouraged to work, that I have had my doubts of the heartiness of their food. But here arise fresh difficulties, were their food ever so nourishing I can easily conceive an habitual inactivity of exertion would give them an air of debility compared with a more industrious people. . . . Granting their food to be the cause, it decides very little against potatoes, unless they were tried with good nourishing beer instead of their vile potations of whisky. When they are encouraged, or animate themselves to work hard, it is all by whisky, which though it has a notable effect in giving a perpetual motion to their tongues, can have but little of that invigorating substance which is found in strong beer or porter, probably it has an effect as pernicious, as the other is beneficial. One circumstance I should mention, which seems to confirm this, I have known the Irish reapers [who emigrated to England to find jobs] work as laboriously as any of our own men, and living upon potatoes which they procured from London, but drinking nothing but ale. If their bodies are weak, I attribute it to whisky, not potatoes; but it is still a question with me whether their miserable working arises from any such weakness, or from an habitual laziness. A friend of mine refused Irishmen work in Surrey [England], saying his bailiff could do nothing but settle their quarrels.

But of this food there is one circumstance which must ever recommend it, they have a belly full, and that let me add is more than the superfluities of an Englishman leaves to his family: let any person examine minutely into the receipt and expenditure of an English cottage, and he will find that tea, sugar, and strong liquors, can come only from pinched bellies. I will not assert that potatoes are a better food than bread and cheese; but I have no doubt of a bellyful of the one being much better than half a bellyful of the other; still less have I that the milk of the Irishman is incomparably better than the small beer, gin, or tea of the Englishman; and this even for the father, how much better must it be for the poor infants; milk to them is nourishment, is health, is life.

If any one doubts the comparative plenty, which attends the board of a poor native of England and Ireland, let him attend to their meals: the sparingness with which our laborer eats his bread and cheese is well known; mark the Irishman's potato bowl placed on the floor, the whole family upon heir hams around it, devouring a quantity almost incredible, the beggar seating himself to it with a hearty welcome, the pig taking his share as readily as the wife, the cocks, hens, turkeys, geese, the cur, the cat, and perhaps the cow – and all partaking of the same dish. No man can often have been a witness of it without being convinced of the plenty, and I will add the cheerfulness, that attends it.

2.7 *Richard Guest,* A Compendious History of the Cotton-Manufacture *(1823)*[7]

Richard Guest was among the earliest historians of the Industrial Revolution. Not only did he give a detailed account of the rise of the cotton industry, but also he wrote about the social impact of economic change that unfolded during the second half of the eighteenth and the early years of the nineteenth centuries.

What kind of evidence did Guest produce to illustrate and support his assertions? Do his many positive and negative judgments suggest fairness, nostalgia, or perhaps an inability to understand the changes taking place?

The progress of the Cotton Manufacture introduced great changes in the manners and habits of the people. The operative workmen being thrown together in great numbers, had their faculties sharpened and improved by constant communication. Conversation wandered over a variety of topics not before essayed; the questions of Peace and War, which interested them importantly, inasmuch as they might produce a rise or fall of wages, became highly interesting, and this brought them into the vast field of politics and discussions on the character of their Government, and the men who composed it. They took greater interest in the defeats and victories of their country's arms, and from being only a few degrees above their cattle in the scale of intellect, they became Political Citizens. . . .

The facility with which the weavers changed their masters, the constant effort to find out and obtain the largest remuneration for their labor, the excitement to ingenuity which the higher wages for fine manufactures and skilful workmanship produced, and a conviction that they depended mainly on their own exertions, produced in them that invaluable feeling, a spirit of freedom and independence, and that guarantee for good conduct and improvement of manners, a consciousness of the value of character and of their own weight and importance.

The practical truth of these remarks must be obvious to every one who has served on the jury at Lancaster, and compared the bright, penetrating, shrewd and intelligent jurors from the south of the county [the industrial heartland], with the stupidity and utter ignorance of those from its northern parts [still primarily agricultural]; and to every one who witnessed the fervor and enthusiasm with which the people in the manufacturing districts flew to arms, in 1803, to defend their firesides against a foreign invader [during a threatened French invasion attempt]. What crowding to drills; what ardor and alacrity to learn the use of arms there then was, and how much stronger and more rapid the feeling of independence,

[7] Richard Guest, *A Compendious History of the Cotton-Manufacture* (Manchester, 1823), 37–9.

both national and individual, is found to be among a highly-civilized dense manufacturing population, than among a scattered half-informed peasantry.

The amusements of the people have changed with their character. The athletic exercises of quoits, wrestling, football, prison-bars, and shooting with the long-bow are become obsolete and almost forgotten; and it is to be regretted that the present pursuits of pleasures of the laboring class are of a more effeminate cast. They are now pigeon-fanciers, canary-breeders and tulip-growers. The field sports, too, have assumed a less hardy and enterprising character. Instead of the squire with his merry harriers and a score or two of ruddy, broad-chested yeomen, scouring the fields on foot heedless of thorn and briar, and scorning to turn aside for copse or ditch, we now see half a dozen fustian masters and shopkeepers with three or four greyhounds and as many beagles, attacking the poor hare with such a superiority, both as respects scent and fleetness, as to give her no chance of escape, and pouncing upon their game like poachers, rather than pursuing it with the fairness and hardiness of hunters.

The Poor Law

2.8 Samuel Whitbread and William Pitt (the Younger), speeches in the House of Commons (Feb. 12, 1796)[8]

The Poor Laws intended to support those unable to work were enacted in the reign of Queen Elizabeth I. Over the years they had also come to be used to support those who could not find work or were paid too little to survive on their wages alone. Samuel Whitbread (1758–1815), an immensely wealthy brewer, great landowner, and brother-in-law of the Whig prime minister, the second Earl Grey, stood on the radical end of his party. He had a special interest in progressive reforms, and in 1796 introduced a bill to allow magistrates to set minimum wages for laborers. The prime minister, William Pitt the Younger (1759–1806), responded in the negative and the bill was rejected.

The first census was not taken until 1800. Many believed, contrary to the actual situation, that the number of people was shrinking. How might the lack of accurate information about population growth affect the debate on the Poor Law? As a businessman, Whitbread might have been expected to resist government interference in the economy. What might have motivated him to advocate giving powers to local officials to set wage rates? What economic theorists influenced the thinking of William Pitt? How might events during the year of the debate have affected the economic and social thinking of politicians?

[8] *The Parliamentary History of England*, ed. William Cobbett (London, 1818), XXXI, 703–11.

Mr. Whitbread ... He appealed to the sense of the House whether the situation of the laboring poor in this country was such as any feeling or liberal mind would wish? He did not mean that the wages of the laborer were inadequate for his subsistence and comfort in times of temporary scarcity and unusual hardship; but even at the period preceding such distress, the evil had prevailed. In most parts of the country, the laborer had long been struggling with increasing misery, till the pressure had become almost too grievous to be endured, while the patience of the sufferers under their accumulated distresses had been conspicuous and exemplary. And did not such distress, supported with so much fortitude, merit relief from the legislature? Were it necessary to refer to any authority, he could quote the writings of Dr. Price, in which he showed that in the course of two centuries, the price of labor had not increased more than three or at most four-fold; whereas the price of meat had increased in the proportion of six or seven; and that of clothing, no less than fourteen or fifteen-fold in the same period. The poor-rates [taxes collected to pay for helping the indigent], too, had increased since the beginning of this century from £600,000, at which they were then estimated, to upwards of three millions. Nor was this prodigious increase in the poor-rates to be ascribed to the advance of population; for it was doubtful whether any such increase had taken place. At the present period the contrary seemed to be the case. By the pressure of the times, marriage was discouraged; and among the laborious classes of the community, the birth of a child, instead of being hailed as a blessing, was considered a curse. For this serious evil a remedy was required, and to this was the bill directed. It was his wish to rescue the laboring poor from a state of slavish dependence; to enable the [agricultural laborer], who dedicated his days to incessant toil, to feed, to clothe and to lodge his family with some degree of comfort; to exempt the youth of this country from the necessity of entering the army or navy, and from flocking to great towns for subsistence; and to put it in the power of him who ploughed and sowed and threshed the corn, to taste the fruits of his industry, by giving him a right to a part of the produce of his labor. ...

Mr. Pitt ... The present situation of the laboring poor in this country was certainly not such as could be wished, upon any principle, either of humanity or policy. That class had of late been exposed to hardships which they all concurred in lamenting, and were equally actuated by a desire to remove. ... The statement of Dr. Price was erroneous, as he compared he earnings of the laborer at the period when the comparison is instituted, with the price of provisions, and the earnings of the laborer at the present day, with the price of the same articles, without adverting to the change of circumstances, and to the difference of provisions. Corn [wheat], which was then almost the only food of the laborer was now supplied by cheaper substitutions ... Trade, industry and barter would always find their own level, and be impeded by regulations which violated their natural operation and deranged their proper effect ... The evil, in his opinion, originated in a great measure, in the abuses which had crept into the Poor Laws of this country, and the complicated mode of executing them ... The Laws of Settlement [which required recipients of poor relief to return to their native parish to receive it] prevented workmen from going to that market where he could dispose of his industry to the greatest advantage, and the capitalist, from employing the person who was qualified to procure him the best returns for his advances. These laws had at once increased the burdens of the poor, and taken from the collective resources of the state to supply wants which their operation had occasioned, and to alleviate a poverty which they tended to perpetuate. Such were the institutions which misguided benevolence had introduced . . . He conceived, that to promote the free circulation of labor, to remove the obstacles by which industry is prohibited from availing itself of its resources, would go far to remedy the evils, and diminish the necessity of applying for relief to the poor-rates . . . He should wish, therefore, that an opportunity were given for restoring the original purity of the poor laws, and of removing those corruptions by which they had been obscured . . . Let us, said he, make relief in cases where there are a number of children, a matter of right and an honor, instead of a ground for opprobrium and contempt. This will make a large family a blessing and not a curse; and this will draw a proper line of distinction between those who are able to provide for themselves by their labor, and those who, after having enriched their country with a number of children, have a claim upon its assistance for their support. . . . Such a plan would convert the relief granted to the poor into an encouragement to industry, instead of being, as it is by the present Poor Laws, a premium to idleness, and a school for sloth.

2.9 Thomas Robert Malthus, An Essay on the Principle of Population *(1807)*[9]

The Reverend Thomas Robert Malthus (1766–1834, pronounced "Malt-huss," see document 2.11) was an Anglican clergyman and professor of history and political economy at a college operated by the East India Company. He was pessimistic about helping the poor. He argued that population would always expand to the limits of the food available to feed it, and subsidizing the income of the poor ultimately created more suffering than if harsh conditions existed to discourage the excessive births of children.

How does Malthus's view of population growth compare to that of Whitbread and Pitt (document 2.8)? How would Malthus account for the fact that the Poor Laws had been in operation for over two centuries without causing famine and catastrophe? Compare Malthus's views about the treatment of the poor with those of Herbert Spencer (documents 6.14 and 6.15).

[9] T.R. Malthus, *An Essay on the Principle of Population*, 4th ed. (London, 1807), II, 96–7.

The poor laws of England tend to depress the general condition of the poor in these two ways. Their first obvious tendency is to increase population without increasing the food for its support. A poor man may marry with little or no prospect of being able to support a family without parish assistance. They may be said therefore in some measure to create the poor which they maintain; and as the provisions of the country must, in consequence of the increased population, be distributed to every man in smaller proportions, it is evident that the labor of those who are not supported by parish assistance, will purchase a smaller quantity of provisions than before, and consequently, more of them must be driven to apply for assistance.

Secondly the quantity of provisions consumed in workhouses, upon a part of the society that cannot in general be considered as the most valuable part, diminishes the shares, that would otherwise belong to more industrious, and more worthy members, and thus, in the same manner, forces more to become dependent. If the poor in the workhouses were to live better than they now do, this new distribution of the money of the society would tend more conspicuously to depress the condition of those out of the workhouses, by occasioning a rise in the price of provisions.

Fortunately for England, a spirit of independence still remains among the peasantry. The poor laws are strongly calculated to eradicate this spirit. They have succeeded in part; but had they succeeded as completely as might have been expected, their pernicious tendency would not have been so long concealed.

Hard as it may appear in individual instances, dependent poverty ought to be held disgraceful. Such a stimulus seems to be absolutely necessary to promote the happiness of the great mass of mankind; and every general attempt to weaken this stimulus, however benevolent its apparent intention, will always defeat its own purpose. If men be induced to marry from the mere prospect of parish provision, they are not only unjustly tempted to bring unhappiness and dependence upon themselves and children, but they are tempted, without knowing it, to injure all in the same class with themselves.

Economic Theory

2.10 Adam Smith, An Inquiry into the Nature and Causes of the Wealth of Nations *(1776)*[10]

Adam Smith (1723–90) was a Scottish political economist who taught logic and moral philosophy at the University of Glasgow. He was one of the most important figures in the "Scottish Enlightenment," an intellectual movement

[10] Adam Smith, *An Inquiry into the Nature and Causes of the Wealth of Nations* (London, 1809), 2–3, 5, and 6 and (Edinburgh, 1843), 3, 23–6, 184–6, 201, and 286. The order of some of the paragraphs has been modified.

of importance and remarkable distinction, particularly in light of Scotland's small size compared with France or England. Smith's most important book, *The Wealth of Nations*, though in part founded on the earlier work of other economists, challenged existing economic theory and gained him international renown. He provided an intellectual foundation for "classical" economic theory, nineteenth-century liberalism, and modern market capitalism.

What characteristics of Smith's work placed him in the company of the leading thinkers of the Enlightenment? Why were his ideas widely embraced by British politicians, merchants, manufacturers, and landed aristocrats? Why would he be an enthusiastic advocate of the application of machinery to the industrial process? What was his reasoning for advocating free trade and rejecting mercantilism? We have found that unrestrained greed and individualism can produce ecological catastrophe and that children born into poverty have virtually no chance of escaping the fate of their parents. How would Smith respond to these points?

Division of Labor

The greatest improvement in the productive powers of Labor, and the greater skill, dexterity, and judgment with which it is anywhere directed, or applied, seem to have been the effects of its division.

This great increase of the quantity of work, which, in consequence of the division of labor, the same number of people are capable of performing, is owing to three different circumstances: first, to the increase of dexterity in every particular workman; secondly, to the saving of the time which is commonly lost in passing from one species of work to another; and lastly to the invention of a great number of machines which facilitate and abridge labor, and enable one man to do the work of many.

To take an example, therefore, from a very trifling manufacture; but one in which the division of labor has been very often taken notice of, the trade of the pin-maker; a workman not educated to this business ... could scarce, perhaps, with his utmost industry, make one pin in a day, and certainly could not make twenty. But in the way in which this business is now carried on ... it is divided into a number of branches ... One man draws out the wire, another straightens it, a third cuts it, a fourth points it, a fifth grinds it at the top for receiving the head: to make a head requires two or three distinct operations; to put it on is a peculiar business; to whiten the pins is another; it is even a trade by itself to put them into the paper; and the important business of making a pin is, in this manner, divided into about eighteen distinct operations ... I have seen a small manufactory of this kind where ten men only were employed ... They could, when they exerted themselves, make ... upwards of forty-eight thousand pins in a day. ... But if they had all wrought separately and independently, and without any of them having been educated to this peculiar business, they certainly could not each of them have made twenty, perhaps not one pin in a day . . .

The Operation of the Market Governed by Supply and Demand

There is in every society or neighborhood an ordinary or average rate of wages and profit in every different employment of labor and stock. This rate is naturally regulated, as I shall show hereafter, partly by the general circumstances of society, their riches or poverty, their advancing, stationary, or declining condition; and partly by the particular nature of each employment.

There is likewise in every society or neighborhood an ordinary or average rate of rent, which is regulated too, as I shall show hereafter, partly by the general circumstances of the society or neighborhood in which the land is situated, and partly by the natural or improved fertility of the land.

These ordinary or average rates may be called the natural rates of wages, profit, and rent, at the time and place in which they commonly prevail.

When the price of any commodity is neither more nor less than what is sufficient to pay the rent of the land, the wages of the labor, and the profits of the stock employed in raising, preparing, and bringing to market, according to their natural rates, the commodity is then sold for what may be called its natural price. . . .

The actual price at which any commodity is commonly sold is called its market price. It may either be above, or below, or exactly the same as its natural price.

The market price of every particular commodity is regulated by the proportion between the quantity which is naturally brought to market and the demand of those willing to pay the natural price of the commodity, or the whole value of the rent, labor, and profit which must be paid in order to bring it thither. . . .

When the quantity of any commodity which is brought to market falls short of the effectual demand . . . some . . . will be willing to give more. A competition will immediately begin among them, and the market price will rise more or less above the natural price, according either to the greatness of the deficiency, or the wealth and wanton luxury of the competitors, happen to animate more or less the eagerness of the competition. . . .

It is the interest of all those who employ their land, labor, or stock in bringing any commodity to market, that the quantity never should exceed the effectual demand; and it is in the interest of all other people that it never should fall short of that demand. . . .

A monopoly granted either to an individual or to a trading company has the same effect as a secret in trade or manufactures. The monopolists, by keeping the market constantly understocked, by never fully supplying the effectual demand, sell their commodities much above their natural price . . .

. . . The exclusive privileges of corporations, statutes of apprenticeship, and all those laws which restrain in particular employments the competition to a smaller number than might otherwise go into them, have the same tendency, though to a lesser degree. They are sort of enlarged monopolies . . . and in whole classes of employments, keep up the market price of particular commodities above the natural price . . .

Free Trade

. . . Nations have been taught that their interest consisted in beggaring all their neighbors. Each nation has been made to look with an invidious eye upon the prosperity of all the nations with which it trades, and to consider their gain as its own loss. Commerce, which ought naturally to be, among nations as among individuals, a bond of union and friendship, has become the most fertile source of discord and animosity. The capricious ambition of kings and ministers has not . . . been more fatal to the repose of Europe than the impertinent jealousy of merchants and manufacturers. . . .

That it was the spirit of monopoly which originally both invented and propagated this doctrine, cannot be doubted; and they who first taught it were by no means such fools as they who believed it. In every country it always is and must be the interest of the great body of the people to buy whatever they want of those who sell it cheapest. The proposition is so very manifest that it seems ridiculous to take any pains to prove it; nor could it ever have been called in question had not the interested sophistry of merchants and manufacturers confounded the common sense of mankind. . . . It is the interest of the merchants and manufacturers of every country to secure to themselves the monopoly of the home market. Hence in Great Britain, and in most other European countries, the extraordinary duties upon almost all goods imported by alien merchants. . . .

The wealth of a neighboring nation, however, though dangerous in war and politics, is certainly advantageous in trade. In a state of hostility it may enable our enemies to maintain fleets and armies superior to ours; but in a state of peace and commerce it must likewise enable them to exchange with us to a greater value, and to afford a better market, either for the immediate produce of our industry, or for whatever is purchased with that produce. . . .

To give the monopoly of the home market to the produce of domestic industry, in any particular art or manufacture, is in some measure to direct people in what manner they ought to employ their capitals, and must, in almost all cases, be either a useless or a hurtful regulation. If the produce of domestic can be brought there as cheap as that of foreign industry, the regulation is evidently useless. If it cannot, it must generally be hurtful. . . .

If a foreign country can supply us with a commodity cheaper than we ourselves can make it, better buy it of them with some part of the produce of our own industry, employed in a way in which we have some advantage. The general industry of the country, being always in proportion to the capital which employs it, will not thereby be diminished. . . .

Laissez Faire

All systems, either of preference or restraint, therefore, being thus completely taken away, the obvious and simple system of natural liberty establishes itself of its own accord. Every man, so long as he does not violate the laws of justice, is left perfectly free to pursue his own interest his own way, and to bring both his industry and capital into competition with those of any other man, or order of men. The sovereign is completely discharged from a duty, in the attempting to perform which he must always be exposed to innumerable delusions, and for the proper performance of which no human wisdom or knowledge could ever be sufficient; the duty of superintending the industry of private people, and of directing it toward the employments most suitable to the interest of society. According to the system of natural liberty, the sovereign has only three duties to attend to; three duties of great importance, indeed, but plain and intelligible to common understandings; first, the duty of protecting society from the violence and invasion of other independent societies; secondly, the duty of protecting, as far as possible, every member of the society from the injustice or oppression of every other member of it, or the duty of establishing an exact administration of justice; and thirdly, the duty of erecting and maintaining certain public works and certain public institutions, which it can never be for the interest of any individual, or small number of individuals, to erect and maintain; because the profit could never repay the expense to any individual or small number of individuals, though it may frequently do much more than repay it to a great society. . . .

As every individual, therefore, endeavors as much as he can both to employ his capital in the support of domestic industry . . . and by directing that industry in such a manner as its produce may be of the greatest value, he intends only his own gain, and he is in this, as in many other cases, led by an invisible hand to promote an end which was no part of his intention. . . . By pursuing his own interest he frequently promotes that of the society more effectually than when he really intends to promote it. I have never known much good done by those who affected to trade for the public good.

2.11 *Thomas Robert Malthus,* An Essay on the Principle of Population *(1798)*[11]

The demographer T.R. Malthus (see document 2.9) was pessimistic about the natural restraints on population growth, which helped to gain "classical" economics the sobriquet the "dismal science." Malthus challenged the more positive view of the natural world espoused by Enlightenment thinkers. In particular he derided William Godwin's (1756–1836) notions of helping

[11] Thomas Robert Malthus, *Parallel Chapters from the First and Second Editions of An Essay on the Principle of Population 1798: 1803* (New York, 1895) 5, 4, 6–8 and the 7th ed. (London, 1872), 6–8.

to improve social and economic conditions of the poor. Such efforts would produce a "Malthusian" crisis by encouraging excessive population growth, bringing misery to all. In later editions of his work he was willing to allow that moral restraint, by delaying or avoiding marriage, could help alleviate his grim litany of war, poverty, famine, disease, and infanticide as the primary brake on population growth. The *Essay* influenced the thinking of David Ricardo (see document 5.18) and later Charles Darwin (see documents 6.12 and 6.13).

How might Malthus's clerical background have influenced his views? Why might many manufacturers have enthusiastically embraced Malthusian principles? In what way can you say that the ideas of Adam Smith (document 2.10) and Malthus are alike? Is it likely that Malthus's work helped or hindered Britain's economic growth in the nineteenth century? Did Malthus's predictions turn out to be correct in the nineteenth and twentieth centuries? In the twenty-first?

I have read some of the speculations on the perfectibility of man and of society with great pleasure. I have been warmed and delighted with the enchanting picture which they hold forth. I ardently wish for such happy improvements. But I see great and, to my understanding, unconquerable difficulties in the way to them. These difficulties it is my present purpose to state; declaring, at the same time, that so far from exulting in them, as a cause of triumphing over the friends of innovation, nothing would give me greater pleasure than to see them completely removed. . . .

I think I may fairly make two postulata.

First, that food is necessary to the existence of man.

Secondly, that the passion between the sexes is necessary and will remain nearly in its present state.

These two laws, ever since we have had any knowledge of mankind, appear to have been fixed laws of our nature; and as we have not hitherto seen any alteration in them, we have no right to conclude that they will ever cease to be what they are now, without an immediate act of power in that Being who first arranged the system of the universe; and for the advantage of His creatures, still executes, according to fixed laws, all its various operations. . . .

Assuming, then, my postulata as granted, I say that the power of population is indefinitely greater than the power in the earth to produce subsistence for man.

Population, when unchecked, increases in a geometrical ratio. Subsistence only increases in an arithmetical ratio. A slight acquaintance with numbers will show the immensity of the first power in comparison of the second.

By that law of our nature which makes food necessary to the life of man, the effects of these two unequal powers must be kept equal.

This implies a strong and constantly operating check on population from the difficulty of subsistence. This difficulty must fall somewhere; and must necessarily be severely felt by a large portion of mankind.

Through the animal and vegetable kingdoms, nature has scattered the seeds of life abroad with the most profuse and liberal hand. She has been comparatively sparing in the room, and the nourishment necessary to rear them. The germs of existence contained in this spot of earth, with ample food, and ample room to expand in, would fill millions of worlds in the course of a few thousand years. Necessity, that imperious all pervading law of nature, restrains them within the prescribed bounds. The race of plants, and the race of man cannot, by any efforts of reason, escape from it. Among plants and animals its effects are waste of seed, sickness, and premature death. Among mankind, misery and vice. The former, misery, is an absolutely necessary consequence of it. Vice is a highly probable consequence, and we therefore see it abundantly prevail; but it ought not, perhaps, to be called an absolutely necessary consequence. The ordeal of virtue is to resist all temptation to evil.

This natural inequality of the two powers of population and of the production in the earth, and that great law of our nature which must constantly keep their efforts equal, form the great difficulty that to me appears insurmountable in the way to perfectibility of society. . . .

Consequently, if the premises are just, the argument is conclusive against the perfectibility of the mass of mankind. . . .

The ultimate check to population appears to be a want of food, arising necessarily from the different ratios according to which population and food increase. But this ultimate check is never the immediate check, except in cases of actual famine.

The immediate check may be stated to consist in all those customs, and all those diseases, which seem to be generated by a scarcity of the means of subsistence; and all those causes, independent of this scarcity, which tend prematurely to weaken and destroy the human frame.

These checks to population, which are constantly operating with more or less force in every society, and keep down the number to the level of the means of subsistence, may be classed under two general heads – the preventive and the positive checks.

The preventive check, as far as it is voluntary, is peculiar to man, and arises from that distinctive superiority in his reasoning faculties which enables him to calculate distant consequences. Man cannot look around him and see the distress which frequently presses upon those who have large families; he cannot contemplate his present possessions or earnings which he now nearly consumes himself, and calculate the amount of each share, when with a little addition they must be divided, perhaps, among seven or eight, without feeling a doubt whether, if he follow the bent of his inclinations, he may be able to support the offspring which he will probably bring into the world. . . .

These considerations are calculated to prevent, and certainly do prevent, a great number of persons in all civilized nations from pursuing the dictate of nature in an early attachment to one woman. . . .

The positive checks to population are extremely various, and include every cause, whether arising from vice or misery, which in any degree contributes to shorten the natural duration of human life. Under this head, therefore, may be enumerated all unwholesome occupations, severe labor and exposure to the seasons, extreme poverty, bad nursing of children, great towns, excesses of all kinds, the whole train of common diseases and epidemics, wars, plague, and famine.

2.12 *Jeremy Bentham,* A Manual of Political Economy *(1789)*[12]

Jeremy Bentham (1748–1832) was the father of "Utilitarianism" and associated with the ideas of laissez-faire enunciated by Adam Smith and other classical economists. Bentham offered many proposals for political and social reform covering everything from prisons to the secret ballot. His thinking continued to influence political debates deep into the nineteenth century (see J.S. Mill, document 6.9). His preserved body, fully clothed, may be seen in a box at University College London, to which he donated it.

To what degree were Malthus and Bentham in agreement or disagreement? What kind of a moral system underpinned Utilitarianism? To what degree were Bentham's ideas implemented in British society and government during the nineteenth century? What flaws do you see in his argument?

According to the principle of utility in every branch of legislation, the object and end in view should be the production of the maximum of happiness in a given time in the community in question.

In the instance of this branch of the art [of political economy], the object or end in view should be the production of that maximum of happiness, in so far as this more general end is promoted by the production of the maximum of wealth and maximum of population.

The practical questions, therefore, are . . . how far the end in view is best promoted by individuals acting for themselves? And in what cases these ends may be best promoted by the hands of government? . . .

With the view of causing an increase to take place in the mass of national wealth, or with a view to increase of the means of subsistence or enjoyment, without some special reason, the general rule is that nothing ought to be done or attempted by government. The motto or watchword of government on these occasions ought to be – *Be quiet.*

For this quietism there are two main reasons: 1. Generally speaking, any interference for this purpose on the part of the government is *needless.* The wealth of the whole community is composed of the wealth of the several individuals belonging to it taken together. But to increase his particular portion is, generally speaking, among the constant objects of each individual's exertions and care.

12 J. Bowring, ed., *The Works of Jeremy Bentham,* 11 vols (Edinburgh, 1843), III, 33–5.

Generally speaking, there is no one who knows what is for your interest so well as yourself – no one who is disposed with so much ardor and constancy to pursue it.

. . . With few exceptions, and those not very considerable ones, the attainment of the maximum of enjoyment will be most effectually secured by leaving each individual to pursue his own maximum of enjoyment, in proportion as he is in possession of the means.

. . . The request which agriculture, manufactures and commerce present to governments, is modest and reasonable as that which Diogenes made to Alexander: "*Stand out of my sunshine.*" We have no need of favor – we require only a secure and open path.

HISTORIANS' DEBATES

What were the principal causes of industrialization? Was it primarily driven by an intellectual/ideological stimulus, by technological innovations, or by other political, social, demographic, or economic factors?

David C. Allen, *The British Industrial Revolution in Global Perspective* (Cambridge, 2009); N.F.R. Crafts, *British Economic Growth during the Industrial Revolution* (Oxford, 1985); N.F.R. Crafts and C.K. Harley, "Output Growth and the Industrial Revolution. A Restatement of the Crafts–Harley View," *EcHR* 45 (1992), 703–30; Phyllis Deane and W.A. Cole, *British Economic Growth, 1688–1959: Trends and Structure*, 2nd ed. (Brookfield, VT, 1993); Jan de Vries, *The Industrious Revolution* (Cambridge, 2008); David S. Landes, *The Unbound Prometheus: Technological Change and Industrial Development in Western Europe from 1750 to the Present* (Cambridge, 1969); P. Mathias, *The First Industrial Nation: An Economic History of Britain, 1700–1914*, 2nd ed. (London, 1983); Joel Mokyr, *The Enlightened Economy: An Economic History of Britain 1700–1850* (New Haven, 2009); J.U. Nef, *The Rise of the British Coal Industry*, 2 vols (London, 1932); Sidney Pollard, *Peaceful Conquest: The Industrialization of Europe, 1760–1970* (Oxford, 1982); W.W. Rostow, *The Stages of Economic Growth: A Non-Communist Manifesto*, 2nd ed. (Cambridge, 1971); Charles Sabel and Jonathan Zeitlin, "Historical Alternatives to Mass Production: Politics, Markets, and Technology in Nineteenth-Century Industrialization," *P&P* 108 (1985), 133–76.

Was there a consumer revolution in eighteenth-century Britain? And what was its character?

Jan de Vries, *The Industrious Revolution* (Cambridge, 2008); Elizabeth Kowaleski-Wallace, *Consuming Subjects: Women, Shopping, and Business in the Eighteenth Century* (New York, 1997); Beverly Lemire, *Dress, Culture, and Commerce: The English Clothing Trade before the Factory, 1660–1800* (London, 1997); Neil McKendrick, John Brewer, and J.H. Plumb, *The Birth of a Consumer Society: The Commercialization of Eighteenth-Century England* (London, 1982); Carole Shammas, *The Pre-industrial Consumer in England and America* (Oxford, 1990); Amanda Vickery, "Women and the World of Goods," in *Consumption and the World of Goods*, ed. John Brewer and Roy Porter (London, 1993); Amanda Vickery, *Behind Closed Doors: At Home in Georgian England* (New Haven, 2009); Lorna Weatherill, *Consumer Behavior and Material Culture in Britain 1660–1760* (London, 1988).

Was the English landed elite open or closed to social mobility and where did new entrants come from? Lawrence Stone argued that the central paradigm of the modern development of Britain rested on that question. His own answer was that it was largely closed. His critics disagree.

Lawrence Stone and J.F. Stone, *An Open Elite? England, 1540–1880* (Oxford, 1984); D. Cannadine, "No Entrance," *New York Review of Books* (Dec. 20, 1984), 85; H. Perkin, "An Open Elite," *JBS* 24 (1985), 496–501; D. and E. Spring, "The English Landed Elite, 1540–1880," *Albion* 17 (1985), 149–80 and 393–6; D. and E. Spring, "Social Mobility and the English Landed Elite," *CJH* 21 (1986), 333–51; Ellis Wasson, *Born to Rule: British Political Elites* (Stroud, 2000); Ellis Wasson, *The Role of Ruling Class Adaptability in the British Transition from Ancien Regime to Modern State* (Lewiston, NY, 2010).

What was the balance between increased fertility and decreased mortality in the rise of population after 1750?

M. Anderson, "Historical Demography after *The Population History of England*," *JHD* 4 (1984–85); D.V. Glass and D.E.C. Eversley, eds., *Population in History: Essays in Historical Demography* (London, 1965); J.A. Goldstone, "The Demographic Revolution in England: A Re-examination," *PS* 49 (1986); T. McKeown, *The Modern Rise of Population* (London, 1976); R.B. Outhwaite, "The Age at Marriage in England from the Late Seventeenth to the Nineteenth Century," *TRHS* 23 (1973), 55–70; P.E. Razzell, "Population Change in Eighteenth-Century England: A Reinterpretation," *EcHR* 18 (1965), 312–32; E.A. Wrigley, *Continuity, Chance and Change: The Character of the Industrial Revolution in England* (Cambridge, 1988); E.A. Wrigley and R.S. Schofield, *The Population History of England, 1541–1871: A Reconstruction* (London, 1981).

Historians argue about the decline of a patriarchal family and the rise of "affective individualism."

Elisabeth Badinter, *The Myth of Motherhood* (London, 1981); Melvin Konner, *Childhood* (London, 1992); Lloyd de Mause, ed., *The History of Childhood* (London, 1974); Robert Hinde, in *Childhood Social Development*, ed. Harry McGurk (London, 1992); Linda Polock, *Forgotten Children: Parent–Child Relationships from 1500 to 1900* (Cambridge, 1983); Edward Shorter, *The Making of the Modern Family* (London, 1977); Lawrence Stone, *The Family, Sex and Marriage, 1500–1800* (London, 1977); Randolph Trumbach, *The Rise of the Egalitarian Family* (New York, 1978); Nicholas Tucker, "Boon or Burden?," *HT* (Sept. 1993), 28–35.

COUNTERFACTUALS TO CONSIDER

What if Britain had not industrialized? Would the population have continued to expand as it did in Ireland and ultimately have led to a Malthusian catastrophe? Or might Britain have declined into minor status similar to the Dutch United Provinces, which it resembled in many ways? What if the English Enlightenment had been as radical as the one in France? What if there had been no Poor Law?

CHAPTER THREE

Culture and Identity

The Enlightenment was not the dominant culture in Europe in the eighteenth century. The Church and traditional customs and practices reinforced orthodoxy and conservatism among the high and the low. Nonetheless the ideas of rationalism, humanity, and reform were spreading and began to arouse opposition to slavery and even to the suppression of women. Scotland made a strong contribution to the cause with Adam Smith (document 2.10) and David Hume (documents 3.1 and 3.2) in the lead, but the movement differed from the one in France in being less overtly challenging to the established structure of society and government. The English Enlightenment was also less controversial, more traditional, and, with some exceptions, more conservative in nature. Thus one of the destabilizing forces that led to revolution in Paris in 1789 did not emerge in London. The Enlightenment evoked powerful counter-movements, most notably Romanticism. Evangelicalism in religion could also be a conservative force, although it contributed to the anti-slavery campaign and later to political reform. The Atlantic archipelago was moving toward a more unified sense of "Britishness," although this was never true among most Catholic Irish people. Important differences remained between England and Scotland as well.

To what degree could Britain still be called an "*ancien régime*" state comparable to France where regional separatism, a powerful church, censorship, and entrenched forces of ignorance reigned? How self-aware were British people becoming about their beliefs, assumptions, prejudices, and place in the world?

Sources and Debates in Modern British History: 1714 to the Present, First Edition. Edited by Ellis Wasson.

Published 2012 by Blackwell Publishing Ltd.

As you read the documents in this chapter, consider the following questions:

- What were some of the significant intellectual and cultural changes taking place in the eighteenth century and what were their consequences?
- What were some of the leading characteristics and institutions of the *ancien régime* in Britain?
- In what ways did people of different nationalities, religions, and genders see the world differently?

The Scottish Enlightenment

3.1 *David Hume,* An Enquiry Concerning Human Understanding *(1772)*[1]

Adam Smith (see document 2.10) was the brightest star of the Scottish Enlightenment, but many other impressive writers and thinkers emerged out of a society that placed great value on education and had affinities with European culture and learning. David Hume (1711–76), a leading philosopher of the Scottish Enlightenment, was critical of superstition, but also he doubted that reason was omnipotent, particularly in the realm of morality. He was the most skeptical among all the *philosophes* of the Scottish Enlightenment about religion. His decision to write a history of England (1754–62) rather than Scotland is suggestive about where the interests and loyalties of the Scottish elite lay.

What was his method in doubting the validity of miracles? What had he to say about the value of religion in guiding one to virtue? How would Smith and Malthus (documents 2.10 and 2.11) have responded to Hume's thought? Compare this document with document 3.5.

there is no god, therefore no miracles

I flatter myself that I have discovered an argument . . . , which, if just, will, with the wise and learned, be an everlasting check to all kinds of superstitious delusion, and consequently will be useful as long as the world endures; for so long, I presume, will the accounts of miracles and prodigies be found in all history, sacred and profane. . . .

A wise man proportions his belief to the evidence. . . .

A miracle is a violation of the laws of nature; and as a firm and unalterable experience has established these laws, the proof against a miracle, from the very nature of the fact, is as entire as any argument from experience can possibly be imagined. Why is it more than probable, that all men must die; that lead cannot, of itself, remain suspended in the air; that fire consumes wood, and

[1] David Hume, *An Enquiry Concerning Human Understanding*, ed. L.A. Selby-Bigge (Oxford, 1894), 110–16.

is extinguished by water; unless it be, that these events are found agreeable to the laws of nature, and there is required a violation of these laws, or in other words, a miracle to prevent them? Nothing is esteemed a miracle, if it ever happens in the common course of nature. It is no miracle that a man, seemingly in good health, should die on a sudden; because such a kind of death, though more unusual than any other, has yet been frequently observed to happen. But it is a miracle that a dead man should come to life; because that has never been observed in any age or country. There must, therefore, be uniform experience against every miraculous event, otherwise the event would not merit that appellation. And as an uniform experience amounts to a proof, there is here a direct and full *proof*, from the nature of the fact, against the existence of any miracle . . .

The plain consequence is (and it is a general maxim worthy of our attention), "That no testimony is sufficient to establish a miracle, unless the testimony be of such a kind, that its falsehood would be more miraculous, than the fact, which it endeavours to establish . . ." When anyone tells me, that he saw a dead man restored to life, I immediately consider with myself, whether it be more probable, that this person should either deceive or be deceived, or that the fact, which he relates, should really have happened. I weigh the one miracle against the other; and according to the superiority, which I discover, I pronounce my decision, and always reject the greater miracle. If the falsehood of his testimony would be more miraculous, than the event which he relates; then, and not till then, can he pretend to command my belief or opinion.

In the foregoing reasoning we have supposed, that the testimony, upon which a miracle is founded, may possibly amount to an entire proof, and that the falsehood of that testimony would be a real prodigy: But it is easy to shew, that we have been a great deal too liberal in our concession, and that there never was a miraculous event established on so full an evidence.

3.2 *David Hume,* An Enquiry Concerning the Principles of Morals *(1751)*[2]

Hume's ideas about reason and morality were highly influential. He argued that reason alone could not induce ethical actions. They must be motivated by emotion and passion.

What characteristics of this argument can be said to make Hume "enlightened"? To what in Hume's work would conservatives and traditionalists have objected? How would French *philosophes* have responded to Hume?

2 *The Philosophical Works of David Hume* (Boston, 1843), IV, 230–5.

There has been a controversy started of late, much better worth examination, concerning the general foundation of MORALS; whether they be derived from REASON or from SENTIMENT; whether we attain the knowledge of them by a chain of argument and induction, or by an immediate feeling and finer internal sense; whether, like all sound judgment of truth and falsehood, they should be the same to every rational intelligent being; or whether, like the perception of beauty and deformity, they be founded entirely on the particular fabric and constitution of the human species. . . .

The end of all moral speculations is to teach us our duty; and, by proper representations of the deformity of vice and beauty of virtue, begat correspondent habits, and engage us to avoid the one, and embrace the other. But is this ever to be expected from inferences and conclusions of the understanding, which of themselves have no hold of the affections, or set in motion the active powers of men? They discover truths: But where the truths which they discover are indifferent, and beget no desire or aversion, they can have no influence on conduct and behavior. What is honorable, what is fair, what is becoming, what is noble, what is generous, takes possession of the heart, and animates us to embrace and maintain it. What is intelligible, what is evident, what is probable, what is true, procures only the cool assent of the understanding; and gratifying a speculative curiosity, puts an end to our researches.

Extinguish all warm feeling and prepossessions in favor of virtue, and all disgust or aversion to vice; render men totally indifferent towards these distinctions; and morality is no longer a practical study, nor has any tendency to regulate our lives and actions.

These arguments on each side (and many more might be produced) are so plausible, that I am apt to suspect they may, the one as well as the other, be solid and satisfactory, and that *reason* and *sentiment* concur in almost all moral determinations and conclusions. The final sentence, it is probable, which pronounces characters and actions amiable, or odious, praiseworthy or blameable; that which stamps on them the mark of honor or infamy, approbation or censure; that which renders morality an active principle, and constitutes virtue our happiness, and vice our misery. . . .

The other scientific method, where a general abstract principle is first established, and is afterwards branched out into a variety of inferences and conclusions, may be more perfect in itself, but suits less the imperfection of human nature, and is a common source of illusion and mistake, in this as well as other subjects. Men are now cured of their passion for hypotheses and systems in natural philosophy, and will hearken to no arguments but those which are derived from experience. It is full time they should attempt a like reformation in all moral disquisitions; and reject every system of ethics, however subtle or ingenious, which is not founded on fact and observation.

The English Enlightenment

3.3 Letter by Lady Mary Wortley Montagu (Apr. 1, 1717)[3]

Lady Mary Wortley Montagu (1689–1762) suffered a bout of smallpox that permanently disfigured her face. Her brother died from the frequently fatal disease. Her sojourn in Constantinople (now Istanbul) while her husband served as the British ambassador to the Ottoman Empire allowed her to observe the Turkish method of dealing with the scourge. Lady Mary helped establish inoculation in Britain, both by having her children subjected to it and by becoming an effective public advocate. In 1796 Edward Jenner introduced a safer preventative system of vaccination. Through this chain of developments the disease was eventually eradicated.

In what ways did Lady Mary's observations reflect the influence of the Enlightenment? Why did medical advancements such as smallpox inoculation, to which the Princess of Wales (1719–72) also contributed, and, during the nineteenth century, Queen Victoria's enthusiasm for the use of anesthetics and improvements in nursing introduced by Florence Nightingale offer such a fertile field for women to play a role in the public sphere?

The smallpox, so fatal and so general amongst us, is here [in Turkey] entirely harmless, by the invention of ingrafting, which is the term they give it. There is an old set of women, who make it their business to perform the operation, every autumn, in the month of September, when the great heat is abated. People send to one another to know if any of their family has a mind to have the small-pox; they make parties for this purpose, and when they are met (commonly fifteen or sixteen together), the old women comes with a nut-shell full of the matter of the best sort of small pox, and asks what vein you please to have opened. She immediately rips open that you offer to her, with a large needle (which gives you no more pain that a common scratch), and puts into the vein as much matter as can lie upon the head of her needle, and after that, binds up the little wound with a hollow bit of shell . . . The children or young patients play together all the rest of the day, and are in perfect health to the eighth. Then the fever begins to seize them, and they keep their beds two days, very seldom three. They have very rarely above twenty or thirty [pox marks] in their faces, which never mark; and in eight days time they are as well as before the illness. . . . There is no example of any one that has died in it, and you may believe I am well satisfied of the safety of this experiment, since I intend to try it on my dear little son.

[3] George Paston, *Lady Mary Wortley Montagu and Her Times* (London, 1907), 264.

I am patriot enough to take pains to bring this useful invention into fashion in England, and I should not fail to write to some of our doctors very particularly about it, if I knew any one of them that I thought had virtue enough to destroy such a considerable branch of their revenue, for the good of mankind.

3.4 *Edward Gibbon,* The Decline and Fall of the Roman Empire *(1776–88)*[4]

Edward Gibbon (1737–94) is best remembered as the author of one of the first modern works of historical scholarship, *The Decline and Fall of the Roman Empire.* He brought a secular and analytical view to a subject previously studied largely through uncritical and often religious perspectives. Gibbon understood how both to research individual events and to step back to reflect on the big picture. His vision charted the way for future historical scholarship.

What are the strengths and weaknesses of Gibbon's faith in the power of reason? How might Enlightenment ideas have affected English attitudes toward empire? In what ways did the Enlightenment change the way history was written?

[Future conflicts between European states] cannot essentially injure our general state of happiness, the system of arts, and laws, and manners, which so advantageously distinguish, above the rest of mankind, the Europeans and their colonies. The savage nations of the globe are the common enemies of civilized society; and we may inquire, with anxious curiosity, whether Europe is still threatened with a repetition of those calamities, which formerly oppressed the arms and institutions of Rome. ...

The military art has been changed [in Europe] by the invention of gunpowder; which enables man to command the two most powerful agents of nature, air and fire. Mathematics, chemistry, mechanics, architecture, have been applied to the service of war; and the adverse parties oppose to each other the most elaborate modes of attack and of defense. ... Cannon and fortifications now form an impregnable barrier against the Tartar horse; and Europe is secure from any future irruption of Barbarians. ...

Should these speculations be found doubtful or fallacious, there still remains a more humble source of comfort and hope. The discoveries of ancient and modern navigators, and the domestic history, or tradition, of more enlightened nations, represent the *human savage*, naked both in mind and body, and destitute of laws, of arts, of ideas, and almost language. From this abject condition, perhaps the primitive and universal state of man,

[4] Edward Gibbon, *The History of the Decline and Fall of the Roman Empire*, 2nd ed. (London, 1846), III, 441–5.

he has gradually arisen to command the animals, to fertilize the earth, to traverse the ocean, and to measure the heavens. His progress in the improvement and exercise of his mental and corporal faculties had been irregular and various; infinitely slow in the beginning, and increasing by degrees with redoubled velocity: ages of laborious ascent have been followed by a moment of rapid downfall; and the several climates of the globe have felt the vicissitudes of light and darkness. Yet the experience of four thousand years should enlarge our hopes, and diminish our apprehensions: we cannot determine to what height the human species may aspire in their advances towards perfection; but it may be safely presumed, that no people, unless the face of nature is changed, will relapse into their original barbarism.

3.5 *James Boswell,* Life of Samuel Johnson *(event 1773, pub. 1791)*[5]

Dr Samuel Johnson (1709–84), the author of one of the first dictionaries of the English language, embraced the Enlightenment idea of organizing and recording knowledge. Unlike many of the French and Scottish *philosophes*, however, he was conservative and religious. In England many writers and thinkers of the Enlightenment era were sympathetic to orthodoxy and supporters of the established political system. The clergyman Malthus (see documents 2.9 and 2.11) is a notable example of this phenomenon. Here Johnson comments (in 1773) on Hume's ideas about miracles (see document 3.1).

Compare Johnson's analysis of the belief in miracles to Hume's provided above. How do they differ? What consequences might the differences between men such as Johnson and Voltaire have had on their respective countries during the later years of the eighteenth century?

Why, sir, the great difficulty of proving miracles should make us very cautious in believing them. But let us consider, although God has made Nature to operate by certain fixed laws, yet it is not unreasonable to think that he may suspend those laws in order to establish a system highly advantageous to mankind. Now the Christian religion is a most beneficial system, as it gives us light and certainty where we were before in darkness and doubt. The miracles which prove it are attested by men who had no interest in deceiving us; but who, on the contrary, were told that they should suffer persecution, and did actually lay down their lives in confirmation of the truth of the facts which they asserted. Indeed, for some centuries the heathens did not pretend to deny the miracles; but said they were performed by the aid of evil spirits. This is a circumstance of great weight. Then, sir, when we

5 James Boswell, *Life of Samuel Johnson*, ed. John Wilson Croker (Albany, 1889), I, 355.

take the proofs derived from prophecies which have been so exactly fulfilled, we have most satisfactory evidence. Supposing a miracle possible, as to which, in my opinion, there can be no doubt, we have as strong evidence for the miracles in support of Christianity as the nature of the thing admits.

3.6 *James Boswell,* Life of Samuel Johnson *(event 1767, pub. 1791)*[6]

King George III took an interest in the arts and literature. He conferred a substantial pension on Dr Johnson (see document 3.5) to honor the latter's work in producing his celebrated dictionary. The king collected a large library at Buckingham House (later Buckingham Palace), which his son, King George IV, donated to the nation. It is still preserved in a spectacular central space in the present national library. The account of this exchange between the king and the scholar is taken from Boswell's biography of Johnson based on Johnson's recollections of the event. Johnson occasionally visited the king's library, which was open to literary men. When the librarian informed George III of these visits, the king requested that he be informed of Johnson's next appearance, which took place in February 1767.

How would you assess the king's intelligence and character based on this passage? How can we judge the accuracy of this account? What does it convey about the English Enlightenment and the British monarchy in the eighteenth century? Why was English society less fertile ground than the *ancien régime* in France for vitriolic criticism of the existing order, at least by the literate classes?

[The librarian] stepped forward hastily to Dr. Johnson, who was still in a profound study, and whispered him, "Sir, here is the King." Johnson started up, and stood still. His Majesty approached him, and at once was courteously easy. . . .

His Majesty inquired if he was then writing anything. He answered he was not, for he had pretty well told the world what he knew, and must now read to acquire more knowledge. The King then said, "I do not think you borrow much from anybody." Johnson said he thought he had already done his part as a writer. "I should have thought so, too," said the King, "if you had not written so well." Johnson observed to me upon this, that "No man could have paid a handsomer compliment, and it was fit for a King to pay. It was decisive." . . .

His Majesty having observed to him that he supposed he must have read a great deal; Johnson answered that he thought more than read; that he had

[6] James Boswell, *Life of Samuel Johnson,* ed. John Wilson Croker (Albany, 1889), I, 424–7.

read a great deal in the early part of his life, but having fallen into ill health, he had not been able to read much, compared with others; for instance, he said he had not read much, compared with Dr. Warburton [Bishop of Gloucester]. Upon which the King said that he heard Dr. Warburton was a man of such general knowledge that you could scarce talk with him on any subject on which he was not qualified to speak; and that his learning resembled Garrick's [great Shakespearean actor] acting, in its universality. His Majesty then talked of the controversy between Warburton and Lowth [Bishop of Oxford, a master of sarcasm], which he seemed to have read, and asked Johnson what he thought of it. Johnson answered, "Warburton has most general, most scholastic learning; Lowth is the more correct scholar. I do not know which of them calls names best." "Why, truly," said the King, "when once it comes to calling names, argument is pretty well at an end."

His Majesty then asked him what he thought of Lord Lyttelton's [medieval] history, which was then just published. Johnson said he thought his style pretty good, but he had blamed Henry the Second rather too much. "Why," said the King, "they seldom do these things by halves." – "No, sir," answered Johnson, "not to kings." . . .

The King then asked him what he thought of Dr. Hill [botanist and quack]. Johnson answered that he was an ingenious man, but had no veracity; and immediately mentioned, as an instance of it, an assertion of that writer that he had seen objects magnified to a much greater degree by using three or four microscopes at a time than by using one. "Now," added Johnson, "everyone acquainted with microscopes knows that the more of them he looks through, the less the object will appear." – "Why," replied the King, "this is not only telling an untruth, but telling it clumsily; for, if that be the case, everyone who can look through a microscope will be able to detect him."

3.7 Fourteenth earl of Morton, "Hints offered to the consideration of Captain Cooke" (n.d. 1768?)[7]

The eighteenth century was an age of exploration. Although commercial motives were at the forefront of European expansion across the globe, the spirit of the Enlightenment was also strong. The earl of Morton, President of the Royal Society (the principal scientific organization in Britain), which sponsored Captain James Cook's first expedition to the Pacific in 1768–71, set out some guidelines on how to treat native inhabitants of territories being explored.

[7] J.C. Beaglehole, ed., *The Journals of Captain James Cook on His Voyages of Discovery, vol. I: The Voyage of the Endeavour, 1768–1771* (Cambridge, 1955), 514–15.

What does this document tell us about eighteenth-century European attitudes toward less "civilized" cultures? Was this approach likely to be typical of English opinion at the time? Among army and naval officers? Government officials? How do you account for Morton's instructions?

To exercise the utmost patience and forbearance with respect to the Natives of the several Lands where the Ship may touch.

To check the petulance of the Sailors, and restrain the wanton use of Fire Arms.

To have it still in view that sheding the blood of those people is a crime of the highest nature: They are human creatures, the work of the same omnipotent Author, equally under his care with the most polished European; perhaps being less offensive, more entitled to his favor.

They are the natural, and in the strictest sense of the word, the legal possessors of the several Regions they inhabit.

No European Nation has the right to occupy any part of their country, or settle among them without their voluntary consent.

Conquest over such people can give no just title; because they could never be the Aggressors.

They may naturally and justly attempt to repell intruders, whom they may apprehend are come to disturb them in the quiet possession of their country, whether that apprehension be well or ill founded.

Therefore should they in a hostile manner oppose a landing, and kill some men in the attempt, even this would hardly justify firing among them, 'till every other gentle method had been tried.

There are many ways to convince them of the Superiority of Europeans, without slaying any of those poor people. . . .

Upon the whole, there can be no doubt that the most savage and brutal Nations are more easily gained by mild, than by rough treatment.

Education

3.8 *Edward Gibbon,* Memoirs *(written 1752–53, prepared for pub. c.1794)*[8]

Edward Gibbon (see document 3.4) came from a comfortable gentry background. He was educated at Westminster School, and, as was not uncommon among the landed elite, sent to Oxford University at the age of 15. Oxford was a medieval institution that had from time to time produced great scholars and

[8] Edward Gibbon, *Memoirs*, ed. William D. Howells (Cambridge, MA, 1882), 79, 82–3.

divines. Cambridge and Oxford were the only universities in England during the eighteenth century. Students were largely engaged in studying to become clergymen or, if they were patricians, gaining some polish in what amounted to a "finishing" school. Faculty members were required to be celibate clergymen. The English universities suffered in comparison to the more vigorous and rigorous Scottish institutions of higher learning, of which there were four, even though Scotland was a much smaller country. However, the picture was not quite as dark as Gibbon painted it.

Gibbon's unedifying view of the faculty was made possible by his social rank. Can educational achievement be high in an institution where money outweighs merit? Yet, isn't that the case in elite American universities today? Why might Scotland have had a stronger tradition of educational meritocracy? Why might the power of the Church of England at Oxford and Cambridge have stifled intellectual rigor? Why might the Oxford faculty have been so enthusiastic for Tory politics?

To the University of Oxford *I* acknowledge no obligation; and she will as cheerfully renounce me for a son, as I am willing to disclaim her for a mother. I spent fourteen months at Magdalen College [the university was a confederation of colleges]; they proved the fourteen months the most idle and unprofitable of my whole life: the reader will pronounce between the school and the scholar; but I cannot affect to believe that Nature had disqualified me for all literary pursuits. The specious and ready excuse of my tender age, imperfect preparation, and hasty departure, may doubtless be alleged; nor do I wish to defraud such excuses of their proper weight. Yet in my sixteenth year I was not devoid of capacity or application; even my childish reading had displayed an early though blind propensity for books; and the shallow flood might have been taught to flow in a deep channel and a clear stream. In the discipline of a well-constituted academy, under the guidance of skilful and vigilant professors, I should gradually have risen from translations to originals, from the Latin to the Greek classics, from dead languages to living science: my hours would have been occupied by useful and agreeable studies, the wanderings of fancy would have been restrained, and I should have escaped the temptations of idleness, which finally precipitated my departure from Oxford. . . .

Our colleges are supposed to be schools of science as well as of education; nor is it unreasonable to expect that a body of literary men, devoted to a life of celibacy, exempt from the care of their own subsistence, and amply provided with books, should devote their leisure to the prosecution of study, and that some effects of their studies should be manifested to the world. The shelves of their library groan under the weight of [many volumes written by medieval scholars]. . . . If I inquire into the manufactures of the [modern] monks of Magdalen, if I extend the inquiry to the other colleges of Oxford and Cambridge, a silent blush, or a

Oxford = blush

scornful frown, will be the only reply. The [faculty members] of my time were decent easy men, who supinely enjoyed the [income from the endowment]; their days were filled by a series of uniform employments, – the chapel and the hall, the coffee-house and the common room, till they retired, weary and well satisfied, to a long slumber. From the toil of reading, or thinking, or writing, they had absolved their conscience; and the first shoots of learning and ingenuity withered on the ground, without yielding any fruits to the owners or the public. As a gentleman commoner [those from families of gentle birth and good income like Gibbon], I was admitted to the society of the [faculty members], and fondly expected some questions of literature would be amusing and instructive topics of their discourse. Their conversation stagnated in a round of college business, Tory politics, personal anecdotes, and private scandal . . .

3.9 *Hannah More to the Bishop of Bath and Wells (1801)*[9]

Sunday schools made a huge contribution to the education of the working classes during the nineteenth century. At the peak in the mid-nineteenth century perhaps as many as four out of five children attended Sunday school some of the time. The movement began within the Church of England under aristocratic patronage, although Nonconformists had long been advocates of educating children both in the Bible and in secular subjects. It is uncertain how much religious teaching was absorbed, but illiteracy largely disappeared during the course of the century. One of the important sources of energy within the Anglican Church during this period were Evangelicals. Hannah More (1745–1833), a notable member of the Clapham Sect, which included famous anti-slavery advocates such as William Wilberforce, strongly supported Sunday schools.

Why were anti-slavery activities and education two causes considered appropriate for women to enter civic life in an active way similar to men? What was it about the Evangelical movement that impelled activism? Was Hannah More interested more in religious education or literacy? Why was she afraid of "enthusiasm" and Jacobinism? How did she see education helping in preventing these two "evils"?

When I settled in this country [Somerset] thirteen years ago, I found the poor in many of the villages in a deplorable state of ignorance and vice. There were, I think, no Sunday-schools in the whole district, except one in my own parish, which had been established by our respectable rector, and another in the adjoining parish . . . This drew me to the more neglected villages, which being distant, made it very laborious. Not one school here

9 William Roberts, *Memoirs of the Life and Correspondence of Mrs. Hannah More* (New York, 1834), II, 72–5.

did I ever attempt to establish without the hearty concurrence of the clergyman of the parish. My plan of instruction is extremely simple and limited. They learn, on week days, such coarse works as may fit them for servants. I allow no writing for the poor. My object is not to make fanatics but to train up the lower classes in habits of industry and piety. I knew no way of teaching morals but by teaching principles; nor of inculcating Christian principles without imparting a good knowledge of Scripture. I own I have labored this point diligently. My sisters and I always teach them ourselves every Sunday, except during our absence in the winter. By being out about thirteen hours, we have generally contrived to visit two schools the same day, and to carry them to their respective churches. When we had more schools, we commonly visited them on a Sunday. The only books we use in teaching are two little tracts, called "Questions for the Mendip Schools" ... [and] "The Church Catechism" (these are framed, and half a dozen hung up in the room.) The Catechism, broken into short questions, Spelling-books, Psalter, [the Book of] Common Prayer, Testament, Bible. The little ones repeat "Watt's Hymns." The Collect is learned every Sunday. They generally learn the Sermon on the Mount, with many other chapters and psalms. Finding that what the children learned at school they commonly lost at home by the profaneness and ignorance of their parents, it occurred to me in some of the larger parishes to invite the latter to come at six on Sunday evening, for an hour, to the school, together with the elder scholars. A plain printed sermon and a printed prayer is read to them, and a psalm is sung. I am not bribed by my taste, for unluckily, I do not delight in music, but observing that singing is a help to devotion in others, I thought it right to allow the practice.

For many years I have given away, annually, nearly 200 Bibles, Common Prayer- Books, and Testaments. To teach the poor to read without providing them with *safe* books, has always appeared to me an improper measure, and this consideration induced me to enter upon the laborious undertaking of the Cheap Repository Tracts. ...

I need not inform your lordship why the illiterate, when they become religious, are more liable to enthusiasm than the better informed. They have a coarse way of expressing their religious sentiments, which often appears to be enthusiasm, when it is only vulgarity or quaintness. But I am persuaded your lordship will allow that this does not furnish a reason why the poor should be left destitute of religious instruction. That the knowledge of the Bible should lay men more open to the delusions of fanaticism on the one hand, or of Jacobinism on the other, appears so unlikely, that I should have thought the probability lay all on the other side.

I do not vindicate enthusiasm; I dread it. But can the possibility that a few should become enthusiasts be justly pleaded as an argument for giving them all up to actual vice and barbarism?

The Romantic Movement

3.10 William Wordsworth, "Lines Composed a Few Miles Above Tintern Abbey" (1798)

Romanticism was in part a reaction to the Enlightenment. Although the movement spread widely through architecture, music, and painting, a number of poets, notably William Blake (see documents 3.11 and 3.20), Samuel Taylor Coleridge (1772–1834), Percy Bysshe Shelley (1792–1822), and Lord Byron (1788–1824), are particularly closely associated with the movement that lasted well into the nineteenth century. No poet surpassed William Wordsworth (1770–1850) in the force of his devotion to individual creativity and expressiveness in the face of what Romantics saw as the soulless rationalism of the *philosophes.* His meditation on the medieval ruins of Tintern Abbey drew together religious, historical, emotional, and imaginative themes dear to the movement. His exaltation of the Welsh landscape becomes a challenge to the notion of nature operating merely as a giant machine. What was the relationship between reason and nature explored by Wordsworth? Why did he choose an abandoned medieval religious building to meditate upon? What would Hume (documents 3.1 and 3.2) and Wordsworth have had to say to each other?

I have learned
To look on nature not as in the hour
Of thoughtless youth; but hearing oftentimes
This still, sad music of humanity,
Nor harsh nor grating, though of ample power
To chasten and subdue. And I have felt
A presence that disturbs me with the joy
Of elevated thoughts; a sense sublime
Of something far more deeply interfused,
Whose dwelling is the light of setting suns,
And the round ocean and the living air,
And the blue sky, and in the mind of man:
A motion and a spirit, that impels
All thinking things, all objects of all thought,
And rolls through all things. Therefore am I still
A lover of the meadows and the woods,
And mountains; and of all that we behold
From this green earth; of all the mighty world
Of eye and ear, – both what they half create,
And what perceive; well pleased to recognize

In nature and the language of the sense
  The anchor of my purest thoughts, the nurse,
The guide, the guardian of my heart, and soul
  Of all my moral being.

3.11 William Blake, "The Tiger" (1794)

The poet and artist William Blake (1757–1827) famously combined Romantic hostility to industrialization with a simple love of country. A number of the leading Romantics, though not all, became political conservatives in the face of the French Revolution. Blake remained radical and intensely religious. Many of his qualities were encompassed in the poem below. Why might Blake have chosen a tiger to symbolize nature?

Tiger! Tiger! burning bright
  In the forests of the night,
What immortal hand or eye
  Could frame thy fearful symmetry?

In what distant deeps or skies
  Burnt the fire of thine eyes?
On what wings dare he aspire?
  What the hand dare seize the fire?

And what shoulder, and what art,
  Could twist the sinews of thy heart?
And when thy heart began to beat,
  What dread hand? and what dread feet?

What the hammer? what the chain?
  In what furnace was thy brain?
What the anvil? what dread grasp?
  Dare its deadly terrors clasp?

When the stars threw down their spears,
  And watered heaven with their tears,
Did he smile his work to see?
  Did he who made the Lamb make thee?

Tiger! Tiger! burning bright
  In the forests of the night,
What immortal hand or eye
  Dare frame thy fearful symmetry?

Women

3.12 Jonathan Swift, "The Furniture of a Woman's Mind" (1727)[10]

Jonathan Swift (1667–1745) was an Anglo-Irish writer and clergyman who became Dean of St Patrick's Cathedral in Dublin. He is perhaps best known as the author of *Gulliver's Travels* (1726) and *A Modest Proposal* (1729). Swift's poem below reflects the assumptions of many eighteenth-century men that women were unreasonable, duplicitous, frivolous, and inconsistent.

Swift was a celebrated satirist. Do you detect any irony here? Swift's social circle included a number of intelligent and well-informed women. How could he have reconciled the views expressed in this poem with his personal experience?

A set of phrases learn'd by rote;
  A passion for a scarlet coat;
When at a play to laugh, or cry,
  Yet cannot tell the reason why;
Never to hold her tongue a minute,
  While all she prates has nothing in it;
Whole hours can with a coxcomb sit,
  And take his nonsense all for writ;
Her learning mounts to read a song,
  But half the words pronouncing wrong;
Has every repartee in store
  She spoke ten thousand times before;
. . .

  If chance a mouse creeps in her sight,
Can finely counterfeit a fright;
  So sweetly screams, if it comes near her,
She ravishes all hearts to hear her.
  Can dexterously her husband tease,
By taking fits whene'er she please;
  By frequent practice learns the trick
At proper seasons to be sick;
  Thinks nothing gives one airs so pretty,
At once creating love and pity;
  . . .

[10] Jonathan Swift, *Works* (London, 1801), VII, 371–2.

3.13 *James Boswell,* Life of Samuel Johnson *(event 1778, pub. 1791)*[11]

This account of a conversation between Dr Johnson (see documents 3.5 and 3.6) and Mrs Mary Morris Knowles (1733–1807) in 1778 illustrates an eighteenth-century male attitude toward women. Mrs Knowles was a Quaker intellectual and literary figure. Would this be a typical topic for conversation in the eighteenth century? Was Mrs Knowles likely to have been a typical representative of female opinion? What might her Quaker background have contributed to her opinions? Would his strong belief in the doctrines of the Church of England have influenced Johnson on this subject? Did either the Enlightenment or Romanticism have much to say about the equality of women?

Mrs. Knowles affected to complain that men had much more liberty allowed them than women. JOHNSON: "Why, madam, women have all the liberty they should wish to have. We have all the labor and the danger, and the women all the advantage. We go to sea, we build houses, we do everything, in short, to pay court to the women." MRS. KNOWLES. "The Doctor reasons very wittily, but not convincingly. Now, take the instance of building; the mason's wife, if she is ever in liquor, is ruined; the mason may get himself drunk as often as he pleases, with little loss of character; nay, may let his wife and children starve." JOHNSON. "Madam, you must consider, if the mason does get himself drunk, and let his wife and children starve, the parish will oblige him to find security for their maintenance. We have different modes of restraining evil. Stocks for the men, a ducking-stool for women, and a pound for beasts. If we require more perfection from women than from ourselves, it is doing them honor. And women have not the same temptations that we have; they may always live in virtuous company; men must live in the world indiscriminately . . ." MRS. KNOWLES. "Still, Doctor, I cannot help thinking it a hardship that more indulgence is allowed to men than to women. It gives a superiority to men, to which I do not see how they are entitled." JOHNSON. "It is plain, madam, one or the other must have the superiority. As Shakespeare says, 'If two men ride on a horse, one must ride behind.'" . . . MRS. KNOWLES. "Well, I hope that in another world the sexes will be equal." BOSWELL. "That is being too ambitious, madam. We might as well desire to be equal with the angels. We shall all, I hope, be happy in a future state, but we must not expect to be all happy in the same degree. A worthy carman [laborer] will get to heaven as well as Sir Isaac Newton. Yet, though equally good, they will not have the same degrees of happiness." JOHNSON. "Probably not."

11 James Boswell, *Life of Samuel Johnson*, ed. John Wilson Croker (Albany, 1889), II, 167–8.

3.14 *Mary Wollstonecraft,* A Vindication of the Rights of Women *(1791)*[12]

Mary Wollstonecraft (1759–97) wrote the first important book on the rights of women based on the reasoning of Enlightenment ideas. She was inspired by the achievements of the French Revolution and urged the male leadership to go further than it turned out they were willing to go on the issue of female equality.

Why might her appeal have fallen on deaf ears? Why did women's rights make no significant advances in Britain as the Enlightenment and the French Revolution unfolded? How does her work compare with the other writers of the English Enlightenment? What arguments did she use to support equal rights?

When men contend for their freedom, and to be allowed to judge for themselves respecting their own happiness, it [seems to them] not inconsistent and unjust to subjugate women . . . Who made man the exclusive judge, if women partake with him the gift of reason?

In this style, argue tyrants of every denomination, from the weak king to the weak father of a family; they are eager to crush reason; yet always assert that they usurp its throne only to be useful. Do you not act a similar part, when you *force* all women, by denying them civil and political rights, to remain immured in their families groping in the dark? For surely, sir, you will not assert that a duty can be binding which is not founded on reason? If, indeed, this be their destination, arguments may be drawn from reason; and thus augustly supported, the more understanding women acquire, the more they will be attached to their duty – comprehending it – for unless they comprehend it, unless their morals be fixed on the same immutable principle as those of man, no authority can make them discharge it in a virtuous manner. They may be convenient slaves, but slavery will have its constant effect, degrading the master and the abject dependent.

But, if women are to be excluded, without having a voice, from a participation of the natural rights of mankind, prove first, to ward off the charge of injustice and inconsistency, that they want reason – else this flaw in your NEW CONSTITUTION will ever show that man must, in some shape, act like a tyrant; and tyranny, in whatever part of society it rears its brazen front, will ever undermine morality. . . .

Women cannot, by force, be confined to domestic concerns; for they will, however ignorant, intermeddle with more weighty affairs, neglecting private duties

[12] Mary Wollstonecraft, *A Vindication of the Rights of Women* (London, 1891), ix–x.

only to disturb, by cunning tricks, the orderly plans of reason which rise above their comprehension.

Besides, whilst they are only made to acquire personal accomplishments, men will seek for pleasure in variety, and faithless husbands will make faithless wives; such ignorant beings, indeed, will be very excusable when, not taught to respect public good, nor allowed any civil rights, they attempt to do themselves justice by retaliation. . . .

Let there be, then no coercion *established* in society, and the common law of gravity prevailing, the sexes will fall into their proper places. And, now that more equitable laws are forming your citizens, marriage may become more sacred; your young men may choose wives from motives of affection, and your maidens allow love to root out vanity.

Slavery

3.15 John Newton, letter to his wife (Jan. 26, 1753)[13]

John Newton (1725–1807) was for many years involved in the slave trade between Africa and the Caribbean and served as captain of a slave ship. Later he changed his views and became a clergyman preaching against the trade. His authorship of the hymn "Amazing Grace" (1779, written while he was still a slave trader) made his name immortal. British ships brought more slaves to the Americas than those of all other countries combined.

At what stage of his career was he likely to have written this letter? What was his justification for Europeans enslaving Africans? Are there contradictions between his religion and his commercial activities? Many slavers and slave owners pointed to the acceptance of slavery in the Bible. What might have changed Newton's mind about the morality of the slave trade?

The three greatest blessings of which human nature is capable, are, undoubtedly religion, liberty, and love. In each of these how highly has God distinguished me! But here are whole nations around me [in Africa], whose languages are entirely different from each other, yet I believe they all agree in this, that they have no words among them expressive of these engaging ideas: from whence I infer, that the ideas themselves have no place in their minds. And as there is no medium between light and darkness, these poor creatures [Africans] are not only strangers to the advantages I enjoy, but are plunged in all the contrary evils. Instead of the present blessings, and bright future prospects of Christianity, they are deceived and harassed by necromancy, magic, and all the train of superstitions that fear, combined with ignorance, can produce

13 *The Works of John Newton*, 4 vols (New Haven, 1824), 71–3.

in the human mind. The only liberty of which they have any notion, is an exemption from being sold; and even from this very few are perfectly secure that it shall not some time or other, be their lot: for it often happens, that a man who sells another on board ship, is himself bought and sold in the same manner, and perhaps in the same vessel, before the week is ended. As for love, there may be some softer souls among them that I have met with; but for the most part, when I have tried to explain this delightful word, I have seldom been in the least understood; and when I have spoken of its effects I have never been believed. . . . Their passions are strong; but few, indeed, have any notion of what I mean by tenderness.

3.16 Lord Mansfield, Judgment in the Somersett Case (June 22, 1772)[14]

The Scottish aristocrat Lord Mansfield (1705–93, son of the fourth Viscount Stormont), as Chief Justice of the King's Bench, heard the case of a slave brought to England from the West Indies who refused to return there with his master. The case was ultimately settled on a technicality, but the implications were huge, as Mansfield recognized in the last line of his judgment. His decision, followed by other judges in subsequent cases, gradually took the effect of ending the state of slavery in England and Wales, though not the empire.

Might the fact that a black half-African girl, daughter of Mansfield's nephew and a slave, was living as a ward in the chief justice's house and being raised alongside his daughter have an effect on his decision in the Somersett case? Was his Scottish background of any significance? Mansfield argued that English common law did not recognize the state of slavery. What is common law? What does Mansfield's decision and its reception by other judges in subsequent cases tell us about the English judicial system in the eighteenth century?

I shall recite the return to the writ of Habeas Corpus, as the ground of our determination . . . The captain of the ship on board of which the negro was taken, makes his return to the writ in terms signifying that there have been, and still are, slaves to a great number in Africa; and that the trade in them is authorized by the laws and opinions of Virginia and Jamaica; "that they are goods and chattels; and, as such, saleable and sold. That James Somersett" is a negro of Africa, and long before the return of the king's writ was brought to be sold, and was sold to Charles Steuart, esq. then in Jamaica, and has not been manumitted since; that Mr. Steuart, having occasion to transact business, came over hither, with an intention to return; and brought

14 *A Complete Collection of State Trials*, ed. T.B. Howell (London, 1816), XX, 80–2.

Somersett to attend and abide with him, and to carry him back as soon as the business should be transacted. That such intention has been, and still continues; and that the negro did remain till the time of his departure in the service of his master Mr. Steuart, and quitted it without his consent. . . .

The state of slavery is of such a nature, that it is incapable of being introduced on any reasons moral or political, but only by positive law, which preserves its force long after the reasons, occasion, and time itself from whence it was created, is erased from memory. It is so odious, that nothing can be suffered to support it, but positive law. Whatever inconveniences, therefore, may follow from the decision, I cannot say this case is allowed or approved by the law of England; and therefore the black must be discharged.

3.17 *James Boswell,* Life of Samuel Johnson *(event 1777, pub. 1791)*[15]

Dr Johnson (documents 3.5, 3.6, and 3.13) spoke to his friend and biographer, the Scottish lawyer and landowner James Boswell, about slavery in 1777. Johnson, not having any children of his own, left his estate to his black servant Francis Barber, a former slave.

How might Johnson's political conservatism and religious devotion have affected his views on slavery? Most Tories supported the institution of slavery and the rights of slave owners. Yet on this issue, Johnson stood with the *philosophes* of the Enlightenment (Figure 3.1). Why did Boswell append such a vigorous defense of slavery? What might have made him more sympathetic to the institution than Johnson?

He had always been very zealous against slavery in every form, in which I with all deference thought that he discovered "a zeal without knowledge." Upon one occasion, when in company with some very grave men at Oxford, his toast was, "Here's to the next insurrection of the negroes in the West Indies." His violent prejudice against our West Indian and American settlers appeared whenever there was an opportunity. Toward the conclusion of his "Taxation No Tyranny," he says, "How is it that we hear the loudest *yelps* for liberty among the drivers of negroes?" . . .

[Johnson wrote], "it is impossible not to conceive that men in their original state were equal; and very difficult to imagine how one would be subjected to another but for violent compulsion. An individual may indeed forfeit his liberty by a crime, but he cannot by that crime forfeit the liberty of his children. What is true of a criminal seems likewise of a captive. A man may accept life from a conquering enemy on condition of perpetual servitude; but it is very doubtful whether he can entail that servitude on his descendants,

15 James Boswell, *Life of Samuel Johnson*, ed. John Wilson Croker (Albany, 1889), VII, 20–4.

for no man can stipulate without commission for another. The condition which he accepts, his son or grandson perhaps would have rejected. … [A slave] suing for his freedom is certainly subject to no law but that of violence, to his present master; who pretends no claim to his obedience but that he bought him from a merchant of slaves, whose right to sell him never was examined. … Whoever is [so] exposed to sale is condemned to slavery without appeal, by whatever fraud or violence he might have been originally brought into the merchant's power. … The laws of Jamaica afford a negro no redress. His color is considered as a sufficient testimony against him. It is to be lamented that moral right should ever give way to political convenience." …

Figure 3.1 "Am I not a man and a brother?" Anti-slavery medallion, by Josiah Wedgwood (1730–95) c.1787. © The Trustees of the British Museum. PY 1887.0307.1.683/digital image no. 00198711001.

Slavery abolitionism was one of the first modern mass reform movements. Men and women, members of the middle class and the aristocracy, placed increasing pressure on the government to act. The slave trade was abolished in 1807 and slavery in the empire in 1833. How is the slave portrayed in this medallion? Who could afford to purchase such an object, which was produced by one of the highest quality manufacturers in the world at that time? What were the religious and secular ideas that motivated the abolitionist movement?

[Boswell rejects his friend's argument.] I will resolutely say that his unfavorable notion of [slavery] was owing to prejudice, and imperfect or false information. The wild and dangerous attempt which has for some time been persisted in to obtain an act of our Legislature to abolish so very important and necessary a branch of commercial interest, must have been crushed at once, had not the insignificance of the zealots who vainly took the lead in it made the vast body of planters, merchants, and others, whose immense properties are involved in the trade, reasonably enough suppose that there could be no danger . . . To abolish a *status*, which in all ages God has sanctioned and man has continued would not only be *robbery* to an innumerable class of our fellow-subjects, but it would be extreme cruelty to the African savages, a portion of whom it saves from massacre, or intolerable bondage in their own country, and introduces into a much happier state of life; especially now when their passage to the West Indies and their treatment there is humanely regulated. To abolish that trade would be to "shut the gates of mercy on mankind."

3.18 Olaudah Equiano, The Interesting Narrative of the Life of Olaudah Equiano Written by Himself *(1789)*[16]

Olaudah Equiano (c.1745–97) was an African perhaps born in what is now Nigeria or perhaps in South Carolina to slave parents. If the latter, his account of slaving on the African coast and the "Middle Passage" could still have been based on eyewitness accounts picked up from other slaves. In his memoir, which sold very well, he describes being seized by slave traders and shipped to Barbados in the Caribbean. He was later freed and lived in England where he was active in the abolition of slavery movement.

Very few Africans were able to leave any kind of account of their experiences of the "Middle Passage," but can the historian place trust in the accuracy of this one? What use is a document like this to historians? Compare this document to John Newton's description of African slaves (document 3.15).

The first object which saluted my eyes when I arrived on the coast was the sea, and a slave ship, which was then riding at anchor and waiting for its cargo. These filled me with astonishment, which was soon converted into terror . . . When I was carried on board, I was immediately handled and tossed up to see if I were sound by some of the crew, and I was now persuaded that I had gotten into a world of bad spirits and that they were going to kill me. . . . Indeed, such were the horrors of my views and fears at the moment that, if ten thousand worlds had been my own, I would have freely parted with

16 *The Interesting Narrative of the Life of Olaudah Equiano*, 9th ed. (London, 1794), 46–52.

them all to have exchanged my condition with that of the meanest slave in my own country. When I looked round the ship too and saw a large furnace or copper boiling and a multitude of black people of every description chained together, every one of their countenances expressing dejection and sorrow, I no longer doubted of my fate. . . . We were . . . to be eaten by those white men with horrible looks, red faces, and loose hair. . . .

I was soon put down under the decks, and there I received such a salutation in my nostrils as I had never experienced in my life: so that with the loathsomeness of the stench and crying together, I became so sick and low that I was not able to eat, nor had I the least desire to taste anything. I now wished for my last friend, Death, to relieve me; but soon, to my grief, two of the white men offered me eatables, and on my refusing to eat, one of them held me fast by the hands and laid me across I think a windlass, and tied my feet while the other flogged me severely. I had never experienced anything of this kind before, and although, not being used to the water, I naturally feared that element the first time I saw it, yet nevertheless could I have got over the nettings I would have jumped over the side, but I could not . . .

The stench of the hold while we were on the coast was so intolerably loathsome that it was dangerous to remain there for any time, and some of us had been permitted to stay on the deck for fresh air; but now that the whole ship's cargo were confined together it became absolutely pestilential. The closeness of the place and the heat of the climate, added to the number in the ship, which was so crowded that each has scarcely room to turn himself around, almost suffocated us . . . and brought on a sickness among the slaves, of which many died . . . This wretched situation was again aggravated by the galling of the chains, now become insupportable . . . The shrieks of the women and the groans of the dying rendered the whole a scene of horror almost inconceivable.

National Identities

3.19 Logbook, HMS Neptune, *Battle of Trafalgar (Oct. 21, 1805)*[17]

The battle of Trafalgar was the most important British naval victory of the nineteenth century. It made Napoleon's plan to invade the home island impossible, and it guaranteed British naval supremacy around the globe for a century. As his ships went into battle off the southwestern coast of Spain against a combined French and Spanish fleet, Admiral Lord Nelson

17 William Stanhope Lovell [Babcock], *Personal Narrative of Events, from 1799 to 1815*, 2nd ed. (London, 1879), 46–7.

(1758–1805) famously signaled: "England expects every man will do his duty." Yet the patriotic symbols, music, and emotions engulfing the ships and sailors appears to have been "British" not "English." Was this merely a matter of the two words, England and Britain, having become interchangeable or was the description below nearer the truth than the admiral's message? Many of the sailors in the fleet were Irish, Scots, and Welsh. How likely were they to feel "British"? To what degree do you think the flags, music, and cheers were orchestrated by the high command to manipulate the men, or were the sentiments expressed likely to have been authentic?

. . . In our fleet, union jacks [the British flag] and ensigns were made fast to the fore and fore-topmast-stays, as well as to the mizzen-rigging, besides one at the peak, in order that we might not mistake each other in the smoke, and to show the enemy our determination to conquer. . . . The bands playing "God Save the King," "Rule Britannia," and "Britons Strike Home"; the crews stationed on the forecastles of the different ships, cheering the ship ahead of them when the enemy began to fire, sent those feelings to our hearts that ensured victory.

3.20 William Blake, "And Did Those Feet in Ancient Time" (1804)

William Blake (see document 3.11), a revolutionary and mystic, influenced the rise of the Romantic movement. The following poem was set to music in 1916 by Sir Hubert Parry. The stirring result, entitled "Jerusalem," became in the second half of the twentieth century an unofficial "English" national anthem. The reference in the first verse is to the legend of a young Jesus traveling to England with his uncle, Joseph of Arimathea, which suggested that England had a special place in the divine plan of a Christian universe. The "dark Satanic Mills" in verse two is often taken as a reference to industrialization. However, it may be a religious allusion.

Why might eighteenth-century Englishmen see themselves as having a special claim on divine favor? Does the poem suggest that it was England, not Britain, that was so lucky, or was Blake simply using the term, as it often was, to refer to the whole island?

And did those feet in ancient time.
  Walk upon England's mountains green:
And was the holy Lamb of God,
  On England's pleasant pastures seen!

And did the Countenance Divine,
  Shine forth upon our clouded hills?
And was Jerusalem builded here,
  Among these dark Satanic Mills?

Bring me my Bow of burning gold;
  Bring me my Arrows of desire:
Bring me my Spear: O clouds unfold!
  Bring me my Chariot of fire!

I will not cease from Mental Fight,
  Nor shall my Sword sleep in my hand:
Till we have built Jerusalem,
  In England's green & pleasant Land.

3.21 Robert Burns, "Scots Wha Hae" (1793)

Robert Burns (1759–96) is the national poet of Scotland. He wrote the following patriotic song in 1793. It is a supposed speech by Robert the Bruce, King of Scots before the Battle of Bannockburn with the English in 1314. Burns had radical sympathies and may have intended the song to lend support to the cause of reform or even revolution in a dangerous moment for the English after the French declaration of war in 1793. The original verse was "Scots" dialect in which Burns composed his poetry. The version here has been modified into modern English. The first line in the original reads "Scots, wha hae wi' Wallace bled" while the last reads in Scots, "Let him on wi me." Wallace was a celebrated enemy of the English.

Burns initially issued the poem anonymously. Why? What does he imply about the existing state of relations between England and Scotland after nearly a century of union? Why might the Scots turn the lyrics into the national song for much of the next two centuries?

Scots, who have with Wallace bled,
  Scots, whom Bruce has often led,
Welcome to your gory bed
  Or to victory.

Who will be a traitor knave?
  Who will fill a coward's grave?
Who so base as be a slave? –
  Let him turn, and flee.

Who for Scotland's King and Law
  Freedom's sword will strongly draw,

Freeman stand or freeman fall,
  Let him follow me.

By oppression's woes and pains,
  By your sons in servile chains,
We will drain our dearest veins
  But they shall be free.

Lay the proud usurpers low,
  Tyrants fall in every foe,
Liberty is in every blow,
  Let us do or die!

3.22 *Edmund Burke, "A Letter to Sir Hercules Langrishe" (1792)*[18]

Edmund Burke (documents 1.5 and 1.10) was born in Ireland of a Protestant father and Catholic mother. He judged the support given by the British government to the Protestant Ascendancy in Ireland ill judged and unnatural. Burke believed the social structures of the two countries differed due to the exclusion of Catholics from Parliament or ownership of large landed estates while at the same time many poor Protestants were privileged politically. In his view what effect did this difference have on Irish society? Why would a strong supporter of aristocratic rule be unhappy with the system in Ireland?

We know that the Government of Ireland (the same as the British) is not in its constitution *wholly* Aristocratical; and, as it is not such in its form, so neither is it in its spirit. If it had been inveterately aristocratical, exclusions might be more patiently submitted to. The lot of one plebian would be the lot of all; and a habitual reverence and admiration of certain families might make the people content to see government wholly in hands to whom it naturally seemed to belong. But our constitution has a *plebian member*, which forms an essentially integral part of it. A plebian oligarchy is a monster in itself: and no people, not absolutely domestic or predial slaves will long endure it.... I hold it to be absolutely impossible for two million plebeians, composing certainly a very clear and decided majority in that class, to become so far in love with six or seven hundred thousand of their fellow citizens (to all outward appearances plebeians like themselves, and many of them tradesmen, servants, and otherwise inferior to some of them) as to see with satisfaction, or even patience, an exclusive power vested in them....

[18] *The Works of the Right Hon. Edmund Burke*, ed. Henry Rogers (London, 1891), I, 545–6.

HISTORIANS' DEBATES

J.G.A. Pocock launched a debate on the degree to which it was possible to write "English" history, excluding Wales, Scotland, and Ireland, and about the importance of writing transnational "British" history.

J.G.A. Pocock, "British History: A Plea for a New Subject", *JMH* 47 (1975), 601–28. Glenn Burgess, ed., *The New British History* (London, 1999); Tony Claydon, "Problems with the British Problem," *PH* 16 (1997), 221–7; S.J. Connolly, ed., *Kingdoms United? Great Britain and Ireland since 1500* (Dublin, 1999); Steven G. Ellis and Sarah Barber, eds., *Conquest and Union: Fashioning a British State 1485–1725* (Harlow, 1995); Alexander Grant and Keith J. Stringer, eds., *Uniting the Kingdom? The Making of British History* (London, 1995).

To this problem has been added, at least for the colonial period in the Americas, the idea of writing "Atlantic" history: David Armitage, ed., *Greater Britain, 1516–1775* (Burlington, VT, 2004); Nicholas Canny, ed., *The Oxford History of the British Empire*, vol. 1: *The Origins* (Oxford, 1998): Peter Marshall, ed., *The Oxford History of the British Empire*, vol. 2: *The Eighteenth Century* (Oxford, 1998).

Debates over slavery in the British Empire cover many topics including the linking of slave emancipation to the decline of the planter class in the West Indies and whether the profits from the slave trade contributed to the capital formation necessary for industrialization.

Roger Anstey, *The Atlantic Slave Trade and British Abolition, 1760–1810* (London, 1975); H. Beckles, "Economic Interpretations of Caribbean History," in *General History of the Caribbean*, vol. 6: *Methodology and Historiography*, ed. B.W. Higman (London, 1999); Thomas Bender, ed., *The Antislavery Debate: Capitalism and Abolitionism as a Problem in Historical Interpretation* (Berkeley, 1992); Michael Carton, *Sinews of Empire: A Short History of British Slavery* (New York, 1974); H. Cateau and S.H.H. Carrington, eds., *"Capitalism and Slavery", Fifty Years Later: Eric Eustace Williams – A Reassessment of the Man and His Work* (New York, 2000); David Biron Davis, *The Problem of Slavery in the Age of Revolution, 1770–1823* (Oxford, 1999); Seymour Drescher, *Capitalism and Antislavery: British Mobilization in Comparative Perspective* (London, 1986); David Eltis, *Economic Growth and the Ending of the Transatlantic Slave Trade* (New York, 1987); John J. McCusker, "Growth, Stagnation, or Decline? The Economy of the British West Indies, 1763–1790," in *The Economy of Early America: The Revolutionary Period, 1763–1789*, ed. Ronald Hoffman, John J. McCusker, and Russell R. Menard (Charlottesville, 1988); Sidney W. Mintz, *Sweetness and Power: The Place of Sugar in Modern History* (New York, 1985); Kenneth Morgan, *Slavery, Atlantic Trade and the British Economy, 1660–1800* (Cambridge, 2000); J.R. Oldfield, *Popular Politics and British Anti-Slavery: The Mobilisation of Public Opinion against the Slave Trade, 1787–1807* (Manchester, 1995); Lowell J. Ragatz, *The Fall of the Planter Class in the British Caribbean, 1763–1833* (New York, 1928); David Richardson, "The Slave Trade, Sugar, and British Economic Growth, 1748–1776," *JIH* 17 (1987), 139ff.; David Beck Ryden, *West Indian Slavery and British Abolition, 1783–1807* (Cambridge, 2010); Barbara L. Solow and Stanley L. Engerman, eds., *British Capitalism and Caribbean Slavery: The Legacy of Eric Williams* (Cambridge, 1987); J.R. Ward, *British West Indian Slavery, 1750–1834: The Process of Amelioration* (Oxford, 1988); J.R. Ward, "The Profitability of Sugar Planting in the British West Indies, 1650–1834," *EcHR* 31 (1978), 197–213; Eric Williams, *Capitalism and Slavery* (Chapel Hill, 1944).

Was Methodism a conservative or more a progressive or even radical force?

Henry Abelove, *The Evangelist of Desire: John Wesley and the Methodists* (Stanford, 1990); Alan D. Gilbert, "Religion and Political Instability in Early Industrial England," in *The Industrial Revolution and British Society*, ed. Patrick K. O'Brien and Roland Quinalt (Cambridge, 1993); Elie Halévy, *England in 1815* (London, 1949); David Hempton, *Methodism and Politics in British Society, 1750–1850* (London, 1984); Bernard Semmel, *The Methodist Revolution* (New York, 1973); E.P. Thompson, *The Making of the English Working Class* (London, 1963).

Was the Old Poor Law a harsh means of repression or more of a positive and/or humane institution?

Mark Blaug, "The Myth of the Old Poor Law and the Making of the New," *JEH* 23 (1963), 151–84; Joanna Innes, "The 'Mixed Economy of Welfare' in Early Modern England: Assessments of the Opinions from Hale to Malthus (c.1683–1803)," in *Charity, Self-Interest, and Welfare in the English Past*, ed. Martin Daunton (New York, 1996); Steve King, "Reconstructing Lives: The Poor, the Poor Law, and Welfare in Calverley, 1650–1820," *SH* 22 (1997), 318–38; Norma Landau, "The Laws of Settlement and the Surveillance of Immigration in Eighteenth-Century Kent," *CC* 3 (1988), 391–420; Lynn Hollen Lees, *The Solidarities of Strangers: The English Poor Laws and the People, 1700–1948* (Cambridge, 1998); Dorothy Marshall, *The English Poor Law in the Eighteenth Century* (London, 1926); Mark Neuman, *The Speenhamland County: Poverty and the Poor Laws in Berkshire, 1782–1834* (New York, 1982); K.D.M. Snell, *Annals of the Labouring Poor: Social Change and Agrarian England 1660–1900* (Cambridge, 1985); Peter M. Solar, "Poor Relief and English Economic Development before the Industrial Revolution," *EcHR* 48 (1995), 1–22; E.P. Thompson, *Customs in Common* (London, 1991); Sidney Webb and Beatrice Webb, *English Poor Law History*, vol. 1: *The Old Poor Law* (London, 1927).

COUNTERFACTUALS TO CONSIDER

What if the 1798 Irish rebellion had succeeded? Could Ireland then have become a staging ground for a French invasion of Britain? What if Britain had treated the non-Western peoples encountered on voyages of discovery and trading missions as the earl of Morton (document 3.7) recommended? What if the British colonies had never accepted slavery?

Part II

The Nineteenth Century

CHAPTER FOUR

State and Empire

The continued expansion of the middle classes, discontent among workers, and the example of the French Revolution made the British ruling class alert to demands for reform of the political system. These were not the only forces at work in impelling change forward. The Whig ideology played a role. Not all aristocrats, however, favored concession. The peaceful extension of the franchise was not inevitable, but it did take place in 1832. Though the electorate was only modestly extended, the precedent for further change was established, a consequence lamented by conservatives and embraced by working people. As the electorate expanded both Liberals and Tories sought to win more votes and changed their approach to government.

The example of the American Revolution was not lost on the political elite. Attempts were made to reconstruct the governance of the remaining colonies and, whether by accident or design, more and more territory was added to the burgeoning empire. Britain's vulnerability to competition in holding on to both its empire and its place as the world's leading economy became evident late in the century and drew it into a vast and tragic conflict in 1914. (For further discussion of imperialism and war, see Chapter 6.)

As you read the documents in this chapter, consider the following questions:

- Why was reform of Parliament rather than the overthrow of the monarchy and aristocracy the goal adopted by all but some fringe elements of the British (but not Irish) population in the nineteenth century?
- What was distinctive about the principal political parties in the nineteenth century and how did they change over time?
- What were the strengths and weaknesses of the British Empire in the nineteenth century?

Sources and Debates in Modern British History: 1714 to the Present, First Edition. Edited by Ellis Wasson.

Published 2012 by Blackwell Publishing Ltd.

Radicalism and Protest

4.1 *William Cobbett,* Cobbett's Political Register *(Nov. 2, 1816)*[1]

William Cobbett (1763–1835) edited the radical *Political Register.* In the troubled years immediately after Waterloo his paper was widely read among the workers in the North, although many radical journalists distrusted his pro-Tory past and faith in parliamentary reform. In this address to workingmen in 1816 Cobbett makes a passionate plea for reform but not revolution.

What were Cobbett's main points of criticism of the existing regime? What did he think was the remedy? Would this have been an effective solution? How radical were his proposals in the context of late eighteenth- and early nineteenth-century Europe? Would most of the people he was addressing be able to purchase and read his publication? Who would read his paper?

As it is the labor of those who toil which makes a country abound in resources, so it is the same class of men, who must, by their arms, secure its safety and uphold its fame. Titles and immense sums of money have been bestowed upon numerous Naval and Military commanders. Without calling the justice of these in question, we must assert that the victories were obtained by *you* [members of the working classes] and your fathers and brothers and sons in co-operation with those Commanders, who, with *your* aid have done great and wonderful things . . .

With this correct idea of your own worth in your minds, with what indignation must you hear yourselves called the Populace, the Rabble, the Mob, the Swinish Multitude [see document 1.10]; and with what greater indignation, if possible, must you hear the projects of those cool and cruel and insolent men, who, now that you have been, without any fault of yours, brought into a state of misery, propose to narrow the limits of parish relief, to prevent you from marrying in the days of your youth, or to thrust you out to seek your bread in foreign lands, never more to behold your parents and friends? . . .

. . . As to the cause of your present miseries, it is the enormous amount of the taxes, which the government compels us to pay for the support of its army, its placemen, its pensioners, etc. and for the payment of the interest of its debt . . .

The remedy is what we have now to look to, and that remedy consists wholly and solely of such a reform in the Commons' or People's House of Parliament, as shall give to every payer of direct taxes a vote at elections, and as shall cause the Members to be elected annually.

[1] George Saintsbury, ed., *Political Pamphlets* (New York, 1892), 184–5 and 208–9.

4.2 William Hazlitt, "What Is the People?" (Mar. 7, 1818)[2]

William Hazlitt (1778–1830) was a scourge of the ruling class and "Old Corruption," the use of government positions for personal profit and the employment of tax revenue to support relatives with sinecures and pensions and win friends through patronage. This passage was written in 1818 at the height of the social and economic unrest after the end of the Napoleonic Wars. Who were the "State paupers"? Why did he criticize government officials? What was his remedy likely to be?

Legitimate Governments (flatter them as we will) are not another Heathen mythology. They are neither so cheap nor so splendid as the Delphian edition of Ovid's Metamorphoses. They are indeed "Gods to punish," but in other respects "men of our infirmity." They do not feed on ambrosia or drink nectar; but live on the common fruits of the earth, of which they get the largest share, and the best. The wine they drink is made of grapes: the blood they shed is that of their subjects: the laws they make are not against themselves: the taxes they vote, they afterwards devour. They have the same wants that we have: and, having the option, very naturally help themselves first, out of the common stock, without thinking that others are to come after them . . . Our State-paupers have their hands in every man's dish, and fare sumptuously every day. They live in palaces, and loll in coaches. In spite of Mr. Malthus, their studs of horses consume the produce of our fields, their dog-kennels are glutted with food that would maintain the children of the poor. They cost us so much a year in dress and furniture, so much in stars and garters [honorific orders of knighthood], blue ribbons, and grand crosses, – so much in dinners, breakfasts, and suppers, and so much in suppers, breakfasts, and dinners. These heroes of the Income-tax, Worthies of the Civil List, Saints of the Court calendar . . . have their naturals and non-naturals, like the rest of the world, but at a dearer rate . . . You will find it easier to keep them a week than a month; and at the end of that time, waking from the sweet dream of Legitimacy, you may say with Caliban, "Why, what a fool was I to take this drunken monster for a God."

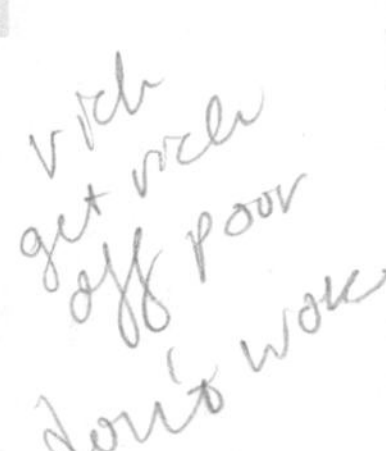

4.3 Samuel Bamford's description of the "Peterloo Massacre" (Aug. 16, 1819)[3]

The movement for parliamentary reform had begun to gather momentum in the later eighteenth century, but accelerated in the wake of the disruption and

[2] *The Collected Works of William Hazlitt*, ed. A.R. Waller and Arnold Glover, 12 vols (London, 1902), III, 287.

[3] Henry Dunckley, *Bamford's Passages in the Life of a Radical and Early Days* (London, 1893), II, 141–2, 149–53, 155–6.

suffering in the years immediately after the defeat of Napoleon (post 1815). Support was drawn from all ranks in society. Aristocratic Whigs such as the second Earl Grey, middle-class bankers like Thomas Attwood, artisans such as the tailor Francis Place, and many inarticulate laborers had different visions of what the political order ought to look like, but all eyes focused on the composition of the electorate and of the House of Commons. Radical protests erupted across the country and made even hardened Tories uneasy as they reflected on the events in France in the 1790s. Peaceful demonstrations such as that held at St Peter's Field in Manchester in 1819 made conscious references to aspects of the French Revolution that were chilling to the privileged elite. The following eyewitness account by Samuel Bamford (1788–1872), a handloom weaver and radical, describes the "Peterloo" Massacre of 1819 when 80,000 unarmed protestors were attacked by mounted cavalry, leaving 15 dead and hundreds wounded.

There is evidence that the London government urged moderation in dealing with protests while the Manchester magistrates wanted to crush the protest with force. Why might the two groups differ in their approach? How reliable do you think Bamford's account of the "Peterloo Massacre" is? Why were handloom weavers likely to be radicalized? Why might a large protest take place at Manchester? Why was the radical focus on Parliament and not on overthrow of the monarchy and aristocracy?

First were selected twelve of the most comely and decent-looking youths, who were placed in two rows of six each, with each a branch of laurel held presented in his hand, as a token of amity and peace; then followed the men of several districts in fives; then the band of music, an excellent one; then the colors: a blue one of silk, with inscriptions in golden letters, "Unity and Strength," "Liberty and Fraternity;" a green one of silk, with golden letters, "Parliaments Annual," "Suffrage Universal;" and betwixt them, on a staff, a handsome cap of crimson velvet with a tuft of laurel, and the cap tastefully braided, with the word "Libertas" in front. . . .

At the sound of the bugle not less than three thousand men formed a hollow square, with probably as many people around them, and, an impressive silence having been obtained, I reminded them that they were going to attend the most important meeting that had ever been held for Parliamentary Reform, and I hoped their conduct would be marked by a steadiness and seriousness befitting the occasion, and such as would cast shame upon their enemies, who had always represented the reformers as a mob-like rabble . . . Not to offer any insult or provocation by word or deed; nor to notice any persons who might do the same to them, but to keep such persons as quiet as possible; for if they began to retaliate, the least disturbance might serve as a pretext for dispersing the meeting. If the peace officers should come to arrest myself or any other person, they were not to offer any resistance . . .

I may say with truth that we presented a most respectable assemblage of laboring men . . .

We learned that other parties were on the field before us . . . [one group] had been led by Doctor Healy, walking before a pitch-black flag, with staring white letters, forming the words, "Equal Representation or Death," "Love" – two hands joined and a heart . . .

[I] saw a party of cavalry in blue and white uniform come trotting, sword in hand round the corner of a garden wall, and to the front row of new houses, where they reined up in a line. . . .

"Oh," some one made reply, "they are only come to be ready if there should be any disturbance in the meeting." . . .

On the cavalry drawing up they were received with a shout of goodwill, as I understood it. They shouted again, waving their sabers over their heads; and then, slackening rein, and striking spur into their steeds, they dashed forward and began cutting the people . . .

On the breaking of the crowd the [soldiers] wheeled, and, dashing whenever there was an opening, they followed, pressing and wounding. Many females appeared as the crowd opened; and striplings or mere youths were also found. Their cries were piteous and heart-rending, and would, one might have supposed, have disarmed any human resentment: but here their appeals were in vain. Women, white-vested maids, and tender youth, were indiscriminately sabred or trampled; and we have reason for believing that few were the instances in which forbearance was vouchsafed which they so earnestly implored.

4.4 *John Wade,* The Extraordinary Black Book *(1831)*[4]

John Wade (1788–1875) was a radical writer who researched corruption and published the famous *Extraordinary Black Book* in 1831. The Church of England was neck deep in "Old Corruption" with a multitude of ranks and jobs that produced some very high salaries. Bishops lived in palaces and sat in the House of Lords and exercised political as well as ecclesiastical patronage.

Why might a radical be out of sympathy with the Church of England? How likely was it that the clergy would take party political positions and oppose reform? The Church encouraged charity and supervised its disbursement. Why might Wade believe that clergymen resisted state assistance for the poor? Who was the intended audience for this book?

The clergy, from superior education, from their wealth and sacred profession, possess greater influence than any other order of men, and all the influence they possess is as subservient to government as the army or navy, or any other branch of

[4] John Wade, *The Extraordinary Black Book*, new ed. (London, 1831), 23.

public service. Upon every public occasion the consequence of this influence is apparent. There is no question, however unpopular, which may not obtain countenance by the support of the clergy: being everywhere, and having much to lose, and a great deal to expect, they are always active and zealous in devotion to the interests of those on whom their promotion depends. Hence their anxiety to attract notice at county, corporate, and sessional meetings. Whenever a loyal address is to be obtained, a popular petition opposed, or hard measure carried against the poor, it is almost certain that some reverend rector, very reverend dean, or venerable archdeacon, will make himself conspicuous.... [Among the higher clergy] hostility to reform, subservience to ministers, and alacrity in supporting them on all occasions, is sure to be rewarded.

Constitutional Reform 1829–32

4.5 Sir Robert Peel, 2nd Baronet, speech in the House of Commons (Mar. 5, 1829)[5]

Sir Robert Peel (1788–1850), the Tory leader in the House of Commons, made an about-face in 1829 and accepted the necessity of passing Catholic Emancipation. The legislation removed the laws preventing Roman Catholics from holding public office (except the Crown).

Was this a pragmatic or principled decision? What made Peel reverse himself? Why was this an important constitutional reform? Why had Tories favored retaining Catholic disabilities and Whigs opposed them? In what part of the kingdom was this law most burdensome and reform most radical? What does it say about the British political system in the 1820s, 1830s, and 1840s that the leaders of the traditional conservative political order, the duke of Wellington and Peel, abandoned crucial tenets of their party creed relating to Catholics and free trade and agreed not to reverse the legislation on parliamentary reform?

Sir, I approach this subject, almost overpowered by the magnitude of the interests it involves, and by the difficulties with which it is surrounded. I am not unconscious of the degree to which those difficulties are increased by the peculiar situation of him on whom the lot has been cast to propose this measure, and to enforce the expediency of its adoption.... I believe that the time has come when less danger is to be apprehended to the general interests of the empire and to the spiritual and temporal welfare of the Protestant Establishment, in attempting to adjust the Catholic Question, than in allowing it to remain any longer in its present state...

5 *The Speeches of the Late Right Honourable Sir Robert Peel, Bart.*, 4 vols (London, 1853), I, 698–9.

I do not think it was an unnatural or unreasonable struggle. I resign it, in consequence of the conviction that it can be no longer advantageously maintained; from believing that there are not adequate materials or sufficient instruments for its effectual and permanent continuance. I yield, therefore, to a moral necessity which I cannot control, unwilling to push resistance to a point which might endanger the Establishments that I wish to defend.

4.6 *Lord John Russell, speech in the House of Commons (Mar. 1, 1831)*[6]

A combination of public pressure from both the middle and working classes, anger among ultra-Tories over Catholic Emancipation, ardent advocacy by a group of young Whig grandees, the death of King George IV, missteps by the prime minister the duke of Wellington, and skilful political maneuvering on the part of the Whig leader Lord Grey led to the appointment of a Whig ministry in 1830. Its goal was to enact a reform of Parliament by incorporating middle-class voters into the electorate, eliminate archaic constituencies that had so few voters on the rolls that landowners could select MPs without any opposition, and grant seats to large industrial and commercial districts that did not enjoy representation.

Lord John Russell (1792–1878), a younger son of one of the richest and most important Whig aristocrats in Britain, the duke of Bedford, was given the task of introducing the First Reform Bill in the House of Commons to an excited reception on the part of his own party and groans of disapproval and even horror from Tories on the opposite benches.

What are the principal arguments Russell deploys in advocating the need for reform? What was his understanding of the role of class in politics? How might his own background have affected his view of reform and government? Did he base his ideas on principle or pragmatism? What did he hope to achieve? What sort of people do you think he wanted to see represented in Parliament?

. . . The House of Commons underwent various changes, till the principle on which it was founded was lost sight of, I will not now detain the House by explaining. There can be no doubt, however, that [during the Middle Ages] the House of Commons did represent the people of England. No man of common sense pretends that this assembly now represents the commonalty or people of England. If it be a question of right, therefore, right is in favor of reform.

Let us now look at the question as one of reason. Allow me to imagine, for a moment, a stranger from some distant country, who should arrive in England to examine our institutions . . . He would have been told that the proudest boast of this celebrated country was its political freedom. If, in addition to this, he had

6 *Selections from Speeches of Earl Russell 1817 to 1841*, 2 vols (London, 1870), I, 304–7 and 331–5.

heard that once in six years this country, so wise, so renowned, so free, chose its representatives to sit in the great council where all the ministerial affairs were discussed and determined, he would be not a little curious to see the process by which so important and solemn an operation was effected. What then would be his surprise if he were taken by this guide, whom he had asked to conduct him to one of the places of election, to a green mound and told that this green mound sent two members to parliament, or to be taken to a stone wall with three niches in it and told that these three niches sent two members to parliament . . . But his surprise would increase to astonishment if he were carried into the north of England, where he would see large flourishing towns, full of trade and activity, containing vast magazines of wealth and manufactures, and were told that these places had no representatives in the assembly which was said to represent the people. . . . After seeing all this, would he not wonder that a nation which had made such progress in every kind of knowledge, and which valued itself for its freedom, should permit so absurd and defective a system or representation any longer to prevail? But whenever arguments of this kind have been urged it has been replied . . . "We agree that the house of commons is not, in fact, sent here by the people; we agree that, in point of reason, the system by which it is sent is full of anomaly and absurdity; but government is a matter of experience, and so long as people are satisfied with the actual working of the House of Commons, it would be unwise to embark in theoretical change." Of this argument, I confess, I always felt the weight, and so long as the people did not answer the appeals of the friends of reform, it was indeed an argument not to be resisted. But what is the case at the moment? The whole people call loudly for reform . . .

I arrive at the last objection which may be made to the plan we propose. I shall be told, in the first place, that we overturn the institutions of our ancestors. I maintain that, in departing from the letter, we preserve the spirit of those institutions. . . . I believe that no reform that can be introduced will have the effect of preventing wealth, probity, learning, and wit from having their proper influence upon elections. . . .

It may be said, too that one great injurious effect of the measures I propose will be to destroy the power and privilege of the aristocracy. This I deny . . . Whenever the aristocracy reside, receiving large incomes, performing important duties, relieving the poor by charity, and evincing private worth and public virtue, it is not in human nature that they should not possess a great influence upon public opinion and have an equal weight in electing persons to serve their country in parliament. Though such persons may not [any longer] have the direct nomination of members . . . I contend that they will have as much influence as they ought to have. But if by aristocracy those persons are meant who do not live among the people, who know nothing of the people, and who care nothing for them – who seek honors without merit, places without duty, and pensions without service – for such an aristocracy I have no sympathy . . .

To establish the constitution on a firm basis, you must show that you are determined not to be the representatives of a small class or of a particular interest, but to form a body who, representing the people, springing from the people, and sympathizing with the people, can fairly call on the people to support the future burdens of the country.

4.7 *Thomas Babington Macaulay, speech in the House of Commons (Mar. 2, 1831)*[7]

The famous historian of middle-class origins, Thomas Babington Macaulay (1800–59), was, as a young man, an active Whig politician. His speeches during the parliamentary reform debates in 1831 and 1832 became among the best known orations of the nineteenth century.

Why was he opposed to universal suffrage? What did he hope the bill would achieve? To what degree did his speech reflect liberal principles? What was his attitude toward class and politics? What did he mean by "the spirit of the age"? Is he making a Burkean (documents 1.5 and 1.10) argument?

[The] principle is plain, rational and consistent. It is this, to admit the middle class to a large and direct share in the representation, without any violent shock to the institutions of the country. . . . I say, sir, that there are countries in which the condition of the laboring-classes is such that they may safely be entrusted with the right of electing members of the legislature. If the laborers of England were in that state in which I, from my soul, wish to see them, if employment were always plentiful, wages always high, food always cheap, if a large family were considered not as an encumbrance but as a blessing, the principle objections to universal suffrage would, I think, be removed . . . But, unhappily, the laboring classes in England . . . are occasionally in a state of great distress. We know what effect distress produces, even on people more intelligent than the great body of the laboring-classes can possibly be. We know that it makes even wise men irritable, unreasonable and credulous; eager for immediate relief, heedless of remote consequences . . . that it blinds their judgment, that it enflames their passions, that it makes them prone to believe those who flatter them and to distrust those who would serve them. . . . I hold it to be clearly expedient that, in a country like this, the right of suffrage should depend on a pecuniary qualification.

. . . I support this bill because it will improve our institutions, but I support it also because it tends to preserve them. That we may exclude those whom it is necessary to exclude, we must admit those whom it may be safe to admit.

. . . Turn where we may, within, around, the voice of great events in proclaiming to us, "Reform, that you may preserve." Now therefore, while everything at home and abroad forebodes ruin to those who persist in a hopeless struggle against the spirit of the age, now, while the crash of the proudest throne of the Continent

7 Thomas Babington Macaulay, *Speeches of Lord Macaulay Corrected by Himself* (London, 1877), 2–3, 9.

[Charles X of France was deposed in 1830] is still resounding in our ears; . . . now while the heart of England is still sound; now, while the old feelings and old associations retain a power and a charm which may too soon pass away; . . . take counsel . . . Pronounce in a manner worthy of the expectation with which this great debate has been anticipated, and of the long remembrance which it will leave behind. Renew the youth of the State. Save property divided against itself. Save the multitude, endangered by their own ungovernable passions. Save the aristocracy, endangered by its own unpopular power. Save the greatest, and fairest, and most highly civilized community that ever existed, from calamities which may in a few days sweep away all the rich heritage of so many ages of wisdom and glory.

4.8 Sir Robert Peel, 2nd Baronet, speeches in the House of Commons (1831)[8]

The Tory leader, Sir Robert Peel (see document 4.5), worked tirelessly and fiercely to block passage of the Reform Bill. Why was he so fearful of a bill that the Whigs claimed would preserve aristocratic power and extend the franchise only to the middle classes (of which Peel's father, a textile manufacturer, had been a member)? On what grounds could he argue that the monarchy and aristocracy were a better guarantee for liberty than democracy? Why might he have been flexible about Catholic Emancipation but rigid on electoral reform? Is he making a Burkean argument (documents 1.5 and 1.10)?

July 6, 1831

It is triumphantly asked, will you not trust the people of England? Do you charge them with disaffection to the monarchy and to the constitution under which they live? I answer, that without imputing disaffection to the people, or a deliberate intention on their part to undermine the monarchy, or to destroy the peerage, my belief is, that neither the monarchy nor the peerage can resist with effect the decrees of a House of Commons that is immediately obedient to every popular impulse, and that professes to speak the popular will . . .

I have been uniformly opposed to reform up on principle, because I was unwilling to open a door which I saw no prospect of being able to close . . .

September 21, 1831

This bill does not violate the forms of the constitution – I admit it, but I assert, that while it respects those forms, it destroys the balance of opposing, but not hostile powers: it is a sudden and violent transfer of an authority, which has hitherto been shared by all orders in the state in just proportions, exclusively to one. In short, all its tendencies are, to substitute, for a mixed form of government, a pure

[8] *The Speeches of the Late Right Honourable Sir Robert Peel, Bart.*, 4 vols (London, 1853), II, 328, 332, 391–4, 433.

unmitigated democracy . . . to yield without resistance, and against our reason, to the prevailing – perhaps the temporary – current of popular feeling.

December 17, 1831

On this ground I take my stand, not opposed to a well-considered reform of any of our institutions which need reform, but opposed to this reform in our constitution, because it tends to root up the feelings of respect, the feelings of habitual reverence and attachment, which are the only sure foundations of government. I will oppose to the last the undue encroachments of that democratic spirit to which we are advised to yield without resistance. We may make it supreme – we may establish a republic full of energy – splendid in talent – but in my conscience I believe fatal to our liberty, our security and our peace.

4.9 Sir Robert Peel, 2nd Baronet, "Tamworth Manifesto" (Dec. 18, 1834)[9]

After the passage of the Reform Act which he so vigorously opposed, the leader of the Tory Party, Sir Robert Peel (documents 4.5 and 4.8), issued an electoral platform in which he accepted that what the Whigs had enacted was irreversible. Why might he have decided to give up his opposition? What was he likely to oppose in the future? Why might the manifesto be seen as a fundamental document of modern Conservatism?

With respect to the Reform Bill itself, I will repeat now the declaration which I made when I entered the House of Commons as a Member of the Reformed Parliament, that I consider the Reform Bill a final and irrevocable settlement of a great Constitutional question – a settlement which no friend to the peace and welfare of the country would attempt to disturb, either by direct or by insidious means. . . .

If by adopting the spirit of the Reform Bill, it be meant that we are to live in a perpetual vortex of agitation; that public men can only support themselves in public estimation by adopting every popular impression of the day, – by promising the instant redress of anything which anybody may call an abuse, – by abandoning altogether that great aid of government – more powerful than either law or reason – the respect for ancient rights, and the deference to prescriptive authority; if this be the spirit of the Reform Bill, I will not undertake to adopt it. But if the spirit of the Reform Bill implies merely a careful review of institutions, civil and ecclesiastical, undertaken in a friendly temper, combining, with the firm maintenance of established rights, the correction of proved abuses and the redress of real grievances, – in that case, I can for myself and colleagues undertake to act in such a spirit and with such intentions.

9 Sir Robert Peel, *Memoirs*, ed. Lord Stanhope and E. Cardwell, 2 vols (London, 1856–7), II, 61–6.

4.10 *Benjamin Disraeli,* Sybil or the Two Nations *(1845)*[10]

Benjamin Disraeli (1804–81), later Conservative prime minister (1868, 1874–80) was a young novelist in 1845. His political vision was as much governed by his sense of how people acted, the influence of duty and honor, for example, as it was by notions of legislation. One of his greatest insights was the idea that cross-class parties could be effective and that an alliance of workers and the landed elite might be possible. He was to instigate a further extension of the franchise in 1867 that added a substantial number of workingmen to the electorate.

In this passage from one of his novels, what was his assessment of the impact of reform? Was this what Lord Grey's government intended? How would Tories have felt about his arguments? Could the anti-Semitism against which he sometimes had to struggle have made him more alert than many Conservatives to the need for changes in society?

Are we then to conclude, that the only effect of the Reform Act has been to create in this country another of those class interests which we now so loudly accuse as the obstacles to general amelioration? Not exactly that. The indirect influence of the Reform Act has been not inconsiderable, and may eventually lead to vast consequences. It set men a-thinking; it enlarged the horizon of political experience; it led the public mind to ponder somewhat on the circumstance of our national history; to pry into the beginnings of some social anomalies, which they found, were not so ancient as they had been led to believe, and which had their origin in causes very different from what they had been educated to credit; and insensibly it created and prepared a popular intelligence to which one can appeal, no longer hopelessly, in an attempt to dispel the mysteries with which for nearly three centuries it has been the labour of party writers to involve a national history, and without the dispersion of which no political position can be understood and no social evil remedied.

4.11 *Thomas Escott,* England: Its People, Polity and Pursuits *(1885)*[11]

In 1885 the journalist Thomas Escott (1844–1924) looked back at the impact of the Reform Act of 1832 on English society. Does he mean that the Reform Act did not remove the aristocracy from power? Does his explanation of sustained aristocratic authority seem persuasive? Was he discounting the

[10] Benjamin Disraeli, *Sybil or the Two Nations* (London, 1907), 36.
[11] T.H.S. Escott, *England: Its People, Polity and Pursuits*, rev. ed. (London, 1885), 330–1.

impact of the explosive growth of commercial and manufacturing wealth during the nineteenth century?

The era of enlargement of English society dates from the Reform Bill of 1832, and if it has brought with it some contradictions, anomalies, and inconveniences, it has also been instrumental in the accomplishment of great and undoubted good. It has substituted, in a very large degree, the prestige of achievement for the prestige of position. . . . Before the eventful year of 1832, there existed a society in England very like the old exclusive society of Vienna [the Habsburg court]. The chief and indeed almost only road to it lay through politics, and politics were for the most part a rigidly aristocratic profession. Occasionally men of the people made their way out of the crowd, and became personages in and out of the House of Commons; but most of the places under Government were in the hands of the great families, as also were the close boroughs, and the tendency was to fill each from among the young men of birth and fashion. The Reform Bill admitted an entirely new element into political life, and threw open the whole of the political area. A host of applicants for Parliamentary position at once came forward, and as a consequence the social citadel was carried by persons who had nothing to do with the purely aristocratic section which had hitherto been paramount. The patrician occupants of the captured stronghold, if they were somewhat taken aback by the blow which had been dealt them, accepted the situation and decided upon their future tactics with equal wisdom and promptitude. If the new-comers were to be successfully competed with, they saw that they must compete with them on the new ground, and must assert their power as the scions of no *fainéant* [indolent] aristocracy. The impulse given to the whole mass of the patriciate was immense, and the sum of the new-born or newly-displayed energies as surprising as it was satisfactory. The man of pleasure ceased to be the type to which it was expected, as a matter of course, that all those born in the purple should conform.

Further Parliamentary Reform

4.12 *The People's Petition of 1838*[12]

English workers and radical politicians disappointed by the results of the First Reform Act pressed for a more complete reform of Parliament. One of the leaders of what became the "Chartist" movement, James "Bronterre" O'Brien (1805–64), wrote of the Reform Act the year after it was passed: "We

12 R.G. Gammage, *History of the Chartist Movement 1833–1854* (London, 1894), 88–90.

foresaw that its effect would be to detach from the working classes a large portion of the middle ranks, who were *then* more inclined to act with the people than with the aristocracy that excluded them."[13] Petitions signed by massive numbers of people were presented to the House of Commons in 1839, 1842, and 1848, each time rejected by Parliament. The Chartist movement (which made a conscious reference to the famous Magna Carta of 1215) eschewed violence, although some of its leaders eventually began to appeal for physical force.

What did the Chartists believe was the problem with England? Why did they want MPs to be paid? Were they demanding *universal* suffrage? Many MPs saw the Charter as a revolutionary document. Was it? Why did Parliament reject the petition? What led workers and radicals to choose a peaceful, constitutional approach to reform, while in much of the rest of Europe repeated violent episodes of rebellion and revolution punctuated the nineteenth century?

To the Honorable the [House of] Commons of Great Britain and Ireland, in Parliament assembled, the petitioners of the undersigned, their suffering countrymen humbly sheweth: For three-and-twenty years we have enjoyed a profound peace. Yet, with all these elements of national prosperity, and with every disposition and capacity to take advantage of them, we find ourselves overwhelmed with public and private suffering. We are bowed down under a load of taxes; which, notwithstanding, fall greatly short of the wants of our rulers; our traders are trembling on the verge of bankruptcy; our workmen are starving; capital brings no profit, and labour no remuneration; the home of the artificer is desolate, and the warehouse of the pawnbroker is full; the workhouse is crowded, and the manufactory is deserted. We have looked on every side, we have searched diligently in order to find out the causes of a distress so sore and so long continued. We can discover none in nature or in Providence. Heaven has dealt graciously by the people; but the foolishness of our rulers has made the goodness of God of none effect. The energies of a mighty kingdom have been wasted in building up the power of selfish and ignorant men, and its resources squandered for their aggrandizement. The good of a party has been advanced to the sacrifice of the good of the nation; the few have governed for the interest of the few, while the interest of the many has been neglected, or insolently and tyrannously trampled upon. It was the fond expectation of the people that a remedy for the greater part, if not the whole, of their grievances, would be found in the Reform Act of 1832. . . .

They regarded that Act as a wise means to a worthy end; as the machinery of an improved legislation, when the will of the masses would be at length potential. They have been bitterly and basely deceived. The fruit which looked so fair to the eye has turned to dust and ashes when gathered. The Reform Act has effected a

[13] E.P. Thompson, *The Making of the English Working Class* (New York, 1963), 821.

transfer of power from one domineering faction to another, and left the people as helpless as before. Our slavery has been exchanged for an apprenticeship to liberty, which has aggravated the painful feeling of our social degradation, by adding to it the sickening of still deferred hope. We come before your Honorable House to tell you, with all humility, that this state of things must not be permitted to continue; that it cannot long continue without very seriously endangering the stability of the throne and the peace of the kingdom; and that if by God's help and all lawful and constitutional appliances, an end can be put to it, we are fully resolved that it shall speedily come to an end.

We tell your honorable House that the capital of the master must be no longer be deprived of its due reward; that the laws which make food dear, and those which by making money scarce, make labor cheap, must be abolished; that taxation must be made to fall on property, not on industry; that the good of the many, as it is the only legitimate end, so must it be the sole study of Government. . . .

Required as we are, universally, to support and obey the laws, nature and reason entitle us to demand, that in the making of the laws, the universal voice shall be implicitly listened to. . . .We demand Universal suffrage. . . .We demand the ballot. . . .We demand Annual Parliaments. . . .We demand . . . that to every [MP] shall be assigned, out of the public taxes, a fair and adequate remuneration for the time which he is called upon to devote to the public service. . . . Universal suffrage will, and it alone can, bring true and lasting peace to the nation; we firmly believe that it will also bring prosperity. May it therefore please your Honorable House . . . to have a law passed granting to every male of lawful age, sane mind, and unconvicted of crime, the right of voting for members of Parliament; and directing all future elections of members of Parliament to be in the way of secret ballot . . .

4.13 William Gladstone, speech in the House of Commons (Apr. 27, 1866)[14]

In 1866 the Liberal Party proposed a second reform bill that was intended to expand the franchise to include a substantial number of workingmen. The Tories actually passed an act in 1867 to fix other parts of the electoral system that they felt gave the Liberals an advantage, but in the process it brought more manual laborers into the electorate than either side had initially expected (to the discomfort of many Conservatives). The following extracts from an 1866 speech in favor of reform by William Gladstone (1809–98), onetime follower of Peel and later Liberal prime minister, reveals the evolving nature of Liberal thought about democracy.

[14] *Parliamentary Debates*, CLXXXIII, Apr. 27, 1866, c. 143–51.

Was Gladstone simply repeating Macaulay's (document 4.7) argument that reform was necessary to preserve? Why didn't he advocate universal suffrage? What were his views about class and politics? What did he see as the qualifications for being admitted to the electorate?

When I heard it stated by a gentleman of ability that to touch the questions of enfranchising any portion of the working class was domestic revolution, I thought it time to remind him that the performance of the duties of citizenship does give some presumption of the capacity for civil rights, and that the burden of proof, that exclusion from such rights is warrantable or wise or (as it may be) necessary, lies upon those who exclude. . . . I heard [someone] describing these working men at from £7 to £10 [annual value of property], not once only it must be now be said, as an invading army, and as something more, as an invading ambush, as a band of enemies, which was to bring ruin and conflagration as the purpose of its mission, into a city all fore-doomed. . . .

[Another member] has said that we have given no reason for our Bill; and he likewise said that we know nothing of those 204,000 persons, who it is proposed to enfranchise in boroughs. . . . Now, Sir, we too know something of those men, but what we know is very different from the supposed knowledge of [the MP who spoke]. [He] asked, "Do you think the franchise is good in itself, or do you wish to improve the institutions of the country?" Sir, I find here no dilemma. My answer is, we want to do both. The extension of the franchise within safe and proper limits is good. It will array more persons in support of the institutions of the country, and that is another good. . . . I think that the influence of the separate classes is too strong, and that the influence of the public interest properly so called, as distinguished from the interest of sets, groups, and classes is too weak. . . . I believe that the composition of the House [of Commons] might be easily improved; and that the increased representation of the working classes would supply us more largely with that description of Members whom we want, who would look not to the interests of classes, but to the public interest.

. . . I am justified, then, in stating that the working classes are not adequately represented in this House. They are not, it is admitted represented in any proportion to their numbers. . . . I may boldly proceed to say they are not represented in proportion to their intelligence, their virtue, or their loyalty.

. . . Sir, let us for a moment consider the enormous and silent changes which have been going forward among the laboring population. . . . Let us try and raise our views above the fears, the suspicions, the jealousies, the reproaches, and the recriminations of this place and this occasion. . . . Is there or is there not, I ask, a steady movement of the laboring classes, and is or is not that movement a movement onwards and upwards? . . .

You cannot fight against the future. Time is on our side. The great social forces which move onwards in their might and majesty, and which the tumult of our debates does not for a moment impede or disturb – those great social forces are against [the Conservative Party]; they are marshaled on our side...

4.14 *Sir Henry Campbell-Bannerman, speech in the House of Commons (June 24, 1907)*[15]

The House of Lords came to be seen as increasingly anachronistic in the post–Third Reform Act (1884–85) democracy that was emerging in Britain. A crisis was reached in 1910 that led to the removal of its veto on legislation repeatedly passed by the Commons. The third marquess of Salisbury and other Conservatives fought a rearguard action to preserve the power of the aristocracy by arguing that the Lords could force governments to use a general election as a public referendum on controversial legislation. In this speech, Sir Henry Campbell-Bannerman (1836–1908), the leader of the Liberal Party, challenged that doctrine.

Why didn't the Chartists and, later, the Victorian Liberal Party call for the abolition of the House of Lords much earlier? With the abolition of the Lords' veto in 1911 was full democracy achieved? Why was the hereditary House of Lords retained, if it could no longer overturn legislation popular with the voters? Why was a hereditary element allowed to remain in the British Parliament throughout the twentieth century?

What meaning does the supremacy of the House of Commons convey to the minds of the House of Lords? In the first place, it is a matter of common knowledge that its working varies according to circumstances. When [the Conservative Party] are in power... there is never a suggestion that the checks and balances of the Constitution are to be brought into play; here is never a hint that this House is anything but a clear and faithful mirror of the settled opinions and desires of the country, or that the arm of the executive falls short of being the instrument of the national will...

... Witness the transition that takes place the moment a Liberal House of Commons comes into being. A complete change comes over this constitutional doctrine of the supremacy of this Chamber... Now they challenge it; and it becomes a deferred supremacy – a supremacy which is to arrive, it may be, at the next election, or the election after that, or may be never at all... I have never been able to discover by what process the House of Lords professes to ascertain whether or not our decisions correspond with the sentiments of the electors; but what I do know is that this House has to... carry on its existence in a state of suspense, knowing that our measures are liable to be amended, altered, rejected and delayed.

15 *Parliamentary Debates*, CLXXVI, June 24, 1907, c. 912–15, 925–6.

It is a singular thing, when you come to reflect upon it, that the representative system should only hold good when one Party is in office, and should break down to such an extent that the non-elective House must be called in to express the mind of the country whenever the country lapses into Liberalism. [The House of Commons it seems is] to be pulled up by the House of Lords as soon as its ventures inroads upon the pet prejudices and interests of that which used to be the ruling class in this kingdom.

... Let the country have the fullest use in all matters of the experience, wisdom, and patriotic industry of the House of Lords in revising and amending and securing full consideration for legislative measures; but, and these words sum up our whole policy, the Commons shall prevail.

4.15 Sidney Low, The Governance of England *(1904)*[16]

All constitutions, whether they appear in a single document or as a collection of statutes and conventions, adapt over time. Few, if any, have lasted longer, however, than the British one in terms of unchanged outward appearance. At the same time, repeated reforms and shifting conventions have altered the substance beyond recognition. Journalist and academic Sidney Low (1857–1932) captured the ever-changing nature of the British polity in his introduction to a book on government.

How do you account for the adaptability of the British constitution? Has the retention of outward forms helped or hindered the development of democratic institutions? Can an evolutionary approach to reform keep pace with modernity?

There is one reason why the English method of government is so hard to describe. Any account of it must be like the picture of a living person. If you want to see exactly how the original appears, you do not refer to a photograph taken twenty or thirty years ago. The features may be the same, but their expression, their proportion, and their whole character have changed. In the interval between one examination of our public polity and another, the formal part may not have greatly altered, but the conventional, the organic, the working portion has been modified in all sorts of ways. The structural elements, it is true, exhibit a wonderful superficial permanence. The Crown, the two Houses of Parliament, the Council of Ministers, the Electorate, the Judicature, and the mutual relations of these various powers and authorities, are the material of all the historians and jurists. There is the same machine, or at least a machine which is painted to look the same....

[16] Sidney Low, *The Governance of England* (New York, 1904), 5–6.

Other constitutions have been built; that of England has been allowed to grow, and so the organism has gradually adapted itself to its environment. Its development has been biological rather than mechanical.

Party Ideologies

4.16 Walter Bagehot on Disraeli (1859)[17]

The journalist and expert on the British political system, Walter Bagehot (1826–77), commented in 1859 on the Tory leader in the Commons and eventual prime minister, Benjamin Disraeli (see document 4.10). How do you account for the fact that a Jewish "outsider" could become leader of the aristocratic Tory Party, a favorite of Queen Victoria, owner of a landed estate, and earl of Beaconsfield (created 1876)? Was he a man without principles, a pure opportunist? Why did Bagehot's list of causes he embraced not contain "Whig" or "Liberal"? Was it possible for someone to be a Tory-Radical? What would such a person advocate?

Beginning without rank, without connection, without wealth, – with every difficulty in his path which the prejudices of race could conjure up, – without entering into the convictions or understanding the political traditions either of the party he was to defend or of the party he was to assail, – wholly destitute of the kind of practical sagacity which most easily inspires Englishmen with confidence, – with an ill-regulated literary ambition and a false melodramatic taste that were well calculated to increase tenfold the existing prejudices against him, it is difficult to conceive a greater marvel than the brilliant success which Mr. Disraeli has achieved, singlehanded, in a sphere of life usually thought singularly exclusive to unassisted adventurers.

The success of this great party-leader is, we believe, traceable to two principal gifts – a very sensitive and impressionable, but extremely unoriginal imagination, and a dexterity seldom equaled in working up all the impressions he receives into materials for personal attacks. . . . He has never had a political faith, – he probably does not know what it means. . . .

He has adopted the opinions of parties as he would adopt a national costume. "Tory," "Radical," "Tory-Radical," "Free-Trader," "Protectionist," "Conservative," "Reformer," no creed has come amiss to him, and amidst them all he has maintained the same clear eye for the personal qualities of those around him, and the same determined will to use them for individual or party ends.

Disrali supports self not county

[17] Walter Bagehot, *The Economist* XVII (July 2, 1859), 725–26.

4.17 Benjamin Disraeli, "Crystal Palace" speech (June 24, 1872)[18]

Disraeli (see documents 4.10 and 4.16) summed up his political philosophy in this 1872 speech. He was an advocate of social reforms that would win working-class votes and outbid the Liberals who were still wedded to laissez-faire attitudes toward the government and economy. Was Disraeli correct to emphasize that English social and political conditions led to the working class preferring home-grown political ideologies? Did his Burkean (documents 1.5 and 1.10) notion that a landed aristocracy was still vital to defend liberty valid in the Victorian era? What would he designate as England's unique qualities? Was his criticism of the Liberal Party accurate?

. . . The tone and tendency of Liberalism cannot be long concealed. It is to attack the institutions of the country under the name of Reform, and to make war on the manners and customs of the people of this country under the pretext of Progress. During the forty years that have elapsed since the commencement of this new system – although the superficial have seen upon its surface only the contentions of political parties – the real state of affairs has been this: the attempt of one party to establish in this country cosmopolitan [that is from the Continent] ideas, and the efforts of another – unconscious efforts, sometimes, but always continued – to recur to and resume those national principles to which they attribute the greatness and glory of the country. . . .

Now, I have always been of opinion that the Tory party has three great objects. The first is to maintain the institutions of the country – not from any sentiment of political superstition, but because we believe that they embody the principles upon which a community like England can alone safely rest. The principles of liberty, of order, of law, and of religion ought not to be entrusted to individual opinion or to the caprice and passion of the multitudes, but should be embodied in a form of permanence and power. We associate with the Monarchy the ideas which it represents – the majesty of the law, the administration of justice, the fountain of mercy and of honor. We know that in the Estates of the Realm [the peerage, clergy, and MPs] and the privileges they enjoy, is the best security for public liberty and good government. We believe that a national profession of faith can only be maintained by an Established Church, and that no society is safe unless there is a public recognition of the Providential government of the world, and of the future responsibility of man. Well, it is a curious circumstance that during all these same forty years of triumphant Liberalism, every one of these institutions has been attacked and assailed – I say, continuously attacked and assailed. . . .

The assault of Liberalism on the House of Lords has been mainly occasioned by the prejudice of Liberalism against the land laws of this country. But in my opinion,

[18] *Selected Speeches of the Late Right Honourable the Earl of Beaconsfield*, ed. T.E. Kebbel, 2 vols (London, 1882), II, 524–8.

and in the opinion of wiser men than myself, and of men in other countries besides this, the liberty of England depends much upon the landed tenure of England – upon the fact that there is a class which can alike defy despots and mobs, around which the people may always rally, and which must be patriotic from its intimate connection with the soil. . . .

When I say "Conservative," I use the word in the purest and loftiest sense. I mean that the people of England, and especially the working classes of England, are proud of belonging to a great country, and wish to maintain its greatness – that they are proud of belonging to an Imperial country, and are resolved to maintain, if they can, their empire – that they believe, on the whole, that the greatness and the empire of England are to be attributed to the ancient institutions of the land. . . .

I say with confidence that the great body of the working class of England utterly repudiate [radicalism]. They have no sympathy with [it]. They are English to the core. They repudiate cosmopolitan principles. They adhere to national principles.

4.18 Lord Randolph Churchill, "Elijah's Mantel," The Fortnightly Review *(1883)*[19]

The Tory opportunist Lord Randolph Churchill (1849–95), son of the seventh duke of Marlborough and father of Winston Churchill, attempted to steal the march on the Liberals with what he claimed to be Disraeli's greatest legacy, social reforms under the flag of "Tory Democracy." Does his language suggest that his party was motivated by *noblesse oblige* or a belief in the rights of the people? Or was this just a way to buy votes? Why might radicals criticize "Tory Democracy"?

[Disraeli developed] a scheme of social progress and reform, of dimensions so large and wide-spreading that many volumes would not suffice to explain its details. By it is shadowed forth, and in it is embraced, a social revolution which, passing by and diverting attention from wild longings for organic change, commences with the little piddling Boards of Health which occupy and delight the Local Government Department, comprises Lord Salisbury's plans for the amelioration of the dwellings of the poor, carries with it Lord Carnarvon's ideal of compulsory national insurance, includes Sir Wilfrid Lawson's temperance propaganda, preserves and reclaims commons and open spaces favored by Mr. Bryce, constructs people's parks, collects and opens to the masses museums, libraries, art-galleries, does not disdain the public washhouses of Mr. Jesse Collings. Public and private thrift must animate the whole, for it is from public thrift that the funds for these largesses can be drawn, and it is by private thrift alone that their results can be utilized and appreciated. The expression "Tory

[19] Lord Randolph Churchill, "Elijah's Mantle," *The Fortnightly Review*, n.s., XXXIII (1883), 621.

Democracy" has excited the wonder of some, the alarm of others, and great and bitter ridicule from the Radical party.

4.19 *William Gladstone, speech at Blackheath, Greenwich (Oct. 28, 1871)*[20]

Mid-nineteenth-century Liberals believed in rational progress through economic growth unhindered by government intervention, although men such as prime minister William Gladstone (see document 4.13) gradually began to see the need for more activist legislation. In this speech he listed the accomplishments that were central to his vision of Liberalism in the 1860s and 1870s.

How did this agenda differ from the Whig reforms of the 1830s or the Liberal reforms such as the enactment of old age pensions (see document 4.20) paid by the government of the first decade of the twentieth century? How does his account of Liberalism accord with Disraeli's (document 4.17) and Churchill's (document 4.18) assertions? Why did Gladstone, unlike Disraeli, neglect to mention the empire?

. . . Within these eighteen years, [the working class] has been invested largely with the Parliamentary franchise, and [the working man] now sees himself at the point where he may reasonably hope that before he is six or eight months older he will be protected in the free exercise of that franchise by means of the [secret] Ballot. The Parliament has passed an Act which aims at securing for all his children, under all circumstances, a good primary education, and which provides that, if unhappily he be unable himself to meet the cost, it shall be defrayed for him by the State and by his wealthier neighbors. While this provision has been made for primary education endeavors have been made through reforming the Universities, and the Abolition of [religious] Tests, and through an extensive dealing with the public and grammar schools of the country, to establish the whole of our schools in a hierarchy of classes . . . so that, wherever there is in the boy a capacity to rise he may with facility, pass on from point to point and may find open to him the road to distinction. But education would not be of great use to the people unless the materials of study were accessible. Therefore at no small cost of political effort the material of paper has been set free of duty, and every restriction in stamp [charges] or otherwise upon the Press has been removed, and the consequence has been the creation of a Press which for the lowness of its price, for the general excellence – aye, for the general wisdom and moderation with which it is written, and for the vast extent of its circulation, I might almost venture to call it not only an honor to the nation, but the wonder of the world. And in order that the public

[20] *The Times*, Oct. 30, 1871, 3.

service might indeed be a public service – in order that we might not have among the civil offices of the State that which we had complained of in the Army – namely, that the service was not the property of the nation, but of the officers – we have now been enabled to remove from the entry into the Civil Service the barriers of nomination, patronage, jobbing, favoritism in whatever form; and every man belonging to the people of England, if he so please to fit his children for the purpose of competing for places in the public service, may do it entirely irrespective of the question of what is his condition in life or the amount of means with which he may now happen to be or not to be blessed.... Though there may remain much to be done – I am the last to deny it, I am the first to admit it; but there is reason [for the working class] to look with patience and indulgence upon a system under which such results have been accomplished; some reason for that loyalty to the Throne, and that attachment to the law which are the happy characteristics of the people of this country....

[Government and the legislature can only do so much.] It is the individual mind, the individual conscience; it is the individual character, on which mainly human happiness or human misery depends. The social problems, which confront us are many and formidable. Let the Government labor to its utmost, let the Legislature spend days and nights in your service; but, after the very best has been achieved, the question whether the English father is to be the father of a happy family and the center of a united home is a question which must depend mainly upon himself.

4.20 Henry Herbert Asquith, speech in the House of Commons (July 9, 1908)[21]

Herbert Asquith (1852–1928), who became Liberal prime minister in 1908, introduced legislation to establish old age pensions funded in part by general taxation, a powerful step in the direction of collectivism even if the actual benefits to old persons was still very modest. What would Gladstone have said about this legislation (document 4.19)? Would Adam Smith (document 2.10) have approved? How would Asquith have explained the difference between Liberalism and socialism?

Who are these old men and women? ... They are the veterans of industry, people of almost endless toil, who have fought for and won the industrial and commercial supremacy of Great Britain. Is their lot and end to be the Bastille of the everlasting pauperism? We claim these pensions as right.... [The laborer] has a right to some consideration from the State. Here in a country rich

[21] *Parliamentary Debates*, CXCII, July 9, 1908, c. 197.

beyond description there are people poverty-stricken beyond description. There can be no earthly excuse for the condition of things which exists in this country today. If it be necessary to have a strong Army and Navy to protect the wealth of the nation, do not let us forget that it is the veterans of industry who have created that wealth; and let us accept this as an installment to bring decency and comfort to our aged men and women.

4.21 The Fabian Society, Manifesto *(1884)*[22]

The Fabian Society, established in 1883, was named after a Roman general who won a war against the Carthaginians by attrition rather than direct confrontation. Fabians embraced socialist ideas achieved through democratic means. Though its leaders were mainly middle-class intellectuals rather than politicians, the Fabian commentary on British society had considerable influence and flowed directly into the formation of policy by the Labour Party in subsequent decades. The following summary of the Society's ideas was written by the playwright George Bernard Shaw in 1884.

Why might prosperous members of the middle class become socialists? Why did they believe socialism could be achieved without violent revolution? How would they have answered Adam Smith (document 2.10) regarding the role of the state? Which of these reforms was later enacted and which never put into place? How did they differ from the Liberal Party of Gladstone and Asquith (documents 4.19 and 4.20)?

The Fabians are associated for spreading the following opinions held by them and discussing their practical consequences.

That under the existing circumstances wealth cannot be enjoyed without dishonor or foregone without misery.

That it is the duty of each member of the State to provide for his or her wants by his or her own Labor.

That a life interest in the Land and Capital of the nation is the birthright of every individual born within its confines and that access to this birthright should not depend upon the will of any private person other than the person seeking it.

That the most striking result of our present system of farming out the national Land and Capital to private persons has been the division of Society into hostile classes, with large appetites and no dinners at one extreme and large dinners and no appetites at the other.

That the practice of entrusting the Land of the nation to private persons in the hope that they will make the best of it has been discredited by the consistency with

[22] [G.B. Shaw], *A Manifesto, Fabian Tract No. 2* (London, 1884), 1–2.

which they have made the worst of it; and that Nationalization of the Land in some form is a public duty.

That the pretensions of Capitalism to encourage Invention and to distribute its benefits in the fairest way attainable, have been discredited by the experience of the nineteenth century.

That, under the existing system of leaving the National Industry to organize itself Competition has the effect of rendering adulteration, dishonest dealing and inhumanity compulsory.

That since Competition amongst producers admittedly secures to the public the most satisfactory products, the State should compete with all its might in every department of production.

That such restraints upon Free Competition as the penalties for infringing the Postal monopoly, and the withdrawal of workhouse and prison labor from the markets, should be abolished.

That no branch of Industry should be carried on at a profit by the central administration.

That the Public Revenue should be levied by a direct Tax; and that the central administration should have no legal power to hold back for the replenishment of the Public Treasury any portion of the proceeds of Industries administered by them.

That the State should compete with private individuals – especially with parents – in providing happy homes for children, so that every child may have a refuge from the tyranny or neglect of its natural custodians.

That Men no longer need special political privileges to protect them against Women and that the sexes should henceforth enjoy equal political rights.

That no individual should enjoy any Privilege in consideration for services rendered to the State by his or her parents or other relations.

That the State should secure a liberal education and an equal share in the National Industry to each of its units.

That the established Government has no more right to call itself the State than the smoke of London has to call itself the weather.

That we had rather face a Civil War than such another century of suffering as the present one has been.

The Empire

4.22 *First earl of Durham,* Report on the Affairs of British North America *(1839)*[23]

Sometimes also called the "white dominions," Canada, Australia, New Zealand, and in some senses South Africa formed a group of colonies

[23] *Report on the Affairs of British North America*, Parliamentary Papers (1839), No. 3, 27–31, 100–1.

in which settlers from Britain either subordinated or wiped out the native populations. The loss of the Thirteen Colonies in North America suggested that Britain should take a different tack in managing its remaining "settler" colonies. The earl of Durham (1792–1840), an advanced Whig, was sent out by Lord Melbourne's government (1834–41) to propose reforms in the governance of Canada. His report, largely written by aides, became a model for the future role of all the colonies of settlement.

Why were the British successful in retaining strong links with Canada, Australia, and New Zealand until after World War II, while they failed to do so with the Thirteen Colonies in the 1770s and 1780s? To what degree was this a "Whig" as opposed to a "British" document? Why was it not adopted as a template for the governance of India? Was it fear of losing more colonies or commitment to democratic principles that persuaded Britain to accord the colonies of settlement self-government?

It may be fairly said, that the natural state of government in [the colonies composing British North America] is that of collision between the executive and the representative body. In all of them the administration of public affairs is habitually confided to those who do not co-operate harmoniously with the popular branch of the legislature; and the Government is constantly proposing measures which the majority of the Assembly reject, and refusing its assent to bills which that body has passed.

A state of things, so different from the working of any successful experiment of representative government, appears to indicate a deviation from sound constitutional principles or practice . . .

It was not until some years after the commencement of the present century that the population of Lower Canada began to understand the representative system which had been extended to them, and that the Assembly evinced any inclination to make use of its powers. Immediately, however, upon its so doing, it found how limited those powers were, and entered upon a struggle to obtain the authority which analogy pointed out as inherent in a representative assembly. Its freedom of speech immediately brought into collision with the Governor; and the practical working of the Assembly commenced by its principle [*sic*] leaders being thrown into prison . . .

The wisdom of adopting the true principle of representative government and facilitating the management of public affairs, by entrusting it to the persons who have the confidence of the representative body, has never been recognized in the government of the North American Colonies . . .

It is difficult to understand how any English statesman could have imagined that representative and irresponsible government could be successfully combined. . . .

The preceding pages have sufficiently pointed out the nature of those evils, to the extensive operation of which, I attribute the various practical grievances and the present unsatisfactory condition of the North American Colonies. It is not by weakening, but strengthening the influence of the people on its Government; by confining within much narrower bounds than those hitherto allotted to it, and not by extending the interference of the imperial authorities in the details of colonial affairs, that I believe that harmony is to be restored, where dissension has so long prevailed . . . It needs no change in the principles of government, no invention of a new constitutional theory, to supply the remedy which would, in my opinion, completely remove the existing political disorders. It needs but to follow out consistently the principles of the British constitution, and introduce into the Government of these great Colonies those wise provisions, by which alone the working of the representative system can in any country be rendered harmonious and efficient . . . I would not impair a single prerogative of the Crown. . . . But the Crown must, on the other hand, submit to the necessary consequences of representative institutions.

4.23 Rudyard Kipling, "Our Lady of the Snows" (1897)[24]

The dominions of Australia and Canada remained deeply attached to the mother country of Britain well into the twentieth century (see document 4.22). Even today the British queen is their head of state. The poet Rudyard Kipling (1865–1936) was moved to write the following poem when he heard that Canada spontaneously and voluntarily granted preferential tariffs to imports from Great Britain.

What is the tone of this poem? Do you detect any of the ambivalence about empire that appeared in some of Kipling's other work? Was Kipling's conception of empire based more on economic or political grounds?

A Nation spoke to a Nation,
  A Queen sent word to a Throne
"Daughter am I in my mother's house,
  But mistress in my own.
The gates are mine to open,
  As the gates are mine to close,
And I set my house in order,"
  Said our Lady of the Snows.
. . .
"My speech is clean and single,
  I talk of common things –

[24] *Official Report of the Debates of the House of Commons of the Dominion of Canada*, XLIV, April 28, 1897, c. 1428.

Words of the wharf and the market-place
  And the ware the merchant brings:
Favour to those I favour,
  But a stumbling block to foes.
Many there be that hate us,"
  Said our Lady of the Snows.

"I called my chiefs to council
  In the din of a troubled year;
For the sake of a sign ye would not see,
  And a word ye would not hear.
This is our message and answer;
  This is the path we chose:
For we be also a people,"
  Said our Lady of the Snows.

"Carry the word to my sisters –
  To the Queens of the East and the South.
I have proven faith in the Heritage
  By more than the word of the mouth.
They that are wise may follow
  Ere the world's war-trumpet blows,
But I – I am first in the battle,"
  Said our Lady of the Snows.

A nation spoke to a Nation,
  A Throne sent word to a Throne:
"Daughter am I in my mother's house,
  But mistress in my own,
The gates are mine to open,
  As the gates are mine to close,
And I abide by my Mother's House,"
  Said our Lady of the Snows.

4.24 *Queen Victoria, "Proclamation to the Princes, Chiefs, and People of India" (Nov. 1, 1858)*[25]

In 1857 "native" sepoy soldiers rose against British rule in India, and, after the vast "mutiny" was repressed, the British government ended the administration of the subcontinent by the East India Company. The following royal proclamation was issued by the government in the name of Queen Victoria (1819–1901), who a few years later assumed the title "Empress" of India. The Indians continued to suffer from catastrophic famines and were not

[25] George Dodd, *The History of the Indian Revolt 1856–7–8* (London, 1859), 623–4.

granted representative government until well into the twentieth century. The British took aggressive steps to incorporate many semi-independent princely states directly under British rule. On the other hand, the presence of activist Christian missionaries was restricted. Indians were appointed to many administrative posts, and the princes were treated as authentic royalty by the viceroy in India and the queen in Britain.

Why might the British government recognize and preserve the dignity of the regional Indian rulers? Why did the government decide to restrict the spread of Christian missionaries in India? Why might the government have chosen to speak to the people of the Indian Empire through the mouthpiece of Queen Victoria?

. . . We hereby call upon all our [Indian] subjects . . . to be faithful and to bear true allegiance to us, our heirs and successors, and to submit themselves to the authority of those whom we may hereafter, from time to time, see fit to appoint to administer the government of our said territories, in our name and on our behalf. . . .

We hereby announce to the native princes of India, that all treaties and engagements made with them by or under the authority of the East India Company are by us accepted, and will be scrupulously maintained; and we look for the like observance on their part.

We desire no extension of our present territorial possessions; and, while we will permit no aggression upon our dominions or our rights to be attempted with impunity, we shall sanction no encroachment on those of others. We shall respect the rights, dignity, and honor of native princes as our own; and we desire that they, as well as our own subjects, should enjoy that prosperity and that social advancement which can only be secured by internal peace and good government. . . .

Firmly relying ourselves on the truth of Christianity, and acknowledging with gratitude the solace of religion, we disclaim alike the right and the desire to impose our convictions on any of our subjects. We declare it to be our royal will and pleasure that none be in any wise favored, none molested or disquieted, by reason of their religious faith or observances, but that all shall alike enjoy the equal and impartial protection of the law . . .

And it is our further will that, so far as may be, our subjects, of whatever race or creed, be freely and impartially admitted to offices in our service, the duties of which they may be qualified, by their education, ability, and integrity, duly to discharge.

We know, and respect, the feelings of attachment with which natives in India regard the lands inherited by them from their ancestors, and we desire to protect them in all rights connected therewith, subject to the equitable demands of the State; and we will that, generally, in framing and administering the law, due regard be paid to the ancient rights, usages, and customs of India.

4.25 J.A. Froude, Oceana or England and Her Colonies (1886)[26]

The celebrated and controversial historian J.A. Froude (1818–94) traveled extensively through the British Empire in the 1880s at a time when the "white" dominions were gathering strength and imperial rule was rapidly expanding across Africa. A number of British political and economic thinkers began to conceive of the empire as a way to sustain Britain's position as a great power in parity with the United States, already a strong competitor in size and strength, and, in the longer term, Russia after it became fully industrialized. The empire would allow Britain to retain its rank among these "continental" giants and also surpass its rival, Germany. The historian J.A. Froude commented on the positive attributes of empire.

What did he see as most valuable about the empire? What was his case for maintaining the empire? What would he have said about the non-white colonies? Was it wise for Britain keep those? Even though the empire did remain intact until 1947, by that date Britain had failed to hold its own as an equal partner with Russia and the USA. Why?

The situation has been extremely difficult. It cannot be wondered at, that when war followed on war in New Zealand and South Africa, and British money was spent, and British troops were employed in killing Maoris and Caffres who had done us no harm, and whose crime was believed by many of us to be no more than the possession of land which others coveted, public opinion at home grew impatient. Long bills for these wars appeared in the Budgets year after year. Political economists began to ask what was the use of colonies which contributed nothing to the Imperial exchequer, while they were a constant expense to the taxpayer. They had possessed a value once as a market for English productions, but after the establishment of free trade the world was our market. The colonies, as part of the world, would still buy from us, and would continue to do so, whether as British dependencies or as free. In case of war we should be obliged to defend them and to scatter our force in doing it. They gave us nothing. They cost us much. They were a mere ornament, a useless responsibility....

[Nonetheless] the returns of trade show in the first place that commerce follows the flag. Our colonists take three times as much of our productions in proportion to their numbers as foreigners take. The difference increases rather than diminishes, and the Australian, as a mere consumer, *is* more valuable to us than the American.... But more than this. It has become doubtful even to the political economist whether England can trust entirely to free trade and

[26] James Anthony Froude, *Oceana or England and Her Colonies* (London, 1886), 5–6, 13–14.

Figure 4.1 "Queen Victoria and her Indian servant Hafiz Abdul Karim," photograph (c.1890), by Hills & Saunders, carbon print, July 1893, 18 in. × 23 5/8 in. (457 mm × 600 mm). © National Portrait Gallery, London. NPG P51/digital image no 22505.

Queen Victoria (document 4.24) was made "Empress" of India in 1876, and she took a keen interest in the subcontinent. Her Indian servant, known as "the Munshi," was a great favorite. How did the queen choose to portray herself in this photograph? Why might she have wanted the Indian man to be included? How was he presented to the viewer? How did race and rank interact in this image?

competition to keep the place which she has hitherto held. Other nations press us with their rivalries. Expenses increase, manufactures languish or cease to profit. Revenue, once so expansive, becomes stationary. "Business" may, probably will, blaze up again, but the growth of it can no longer be regarded as constant, while population increases and hungry stomachs multiply, requiring the three meals a day whatever the condition of the markets. Hence those among us who have disbelieved all along that a great nation can venture its whole fortunes safely on the power of underselling its neighbors in calicoes and iron-work no longer address a public opinion entirely cold. It begins to be admitted that were Canada and South Africa and Australia and New Zealand members of one body with us, with a free flow of our population into them, we might sit secure against shifts and changes. In the multiplying number of our own fellow-citizens animated by a common spirit, we should have purchasers for our goods from whom we should fear no rivalry; we should turn in upon them the tide of our emigrants which now flows away, while the emigrants themselves would thrive under their own fig tree, and rear children with stout limbs and color in their cheeks, and a chance before them of a human existence. Oceana would then rest on sure foundations; and her navy – the hand of her strength and the symbol of her unity – would ride securely in self-supporting stations in the four quarters of the globe.

4.26 *Joseph Chamberlain, speech, "Want of Employment and the Development of Free Markets" (Jan. 22, 1894)*[27]

One of the most important supporters of empire, especially its expansion in Africa during the later nineteenth century, was the industrialist turned politician Joseph Chamberlain (1836–1914). He advocated a preferential imperial tariff union. He began as a Liberal but shifted to the Conservative Party after the Liberals adopted Home Rule for Ireland. He became Colonial Secretary in Lord Salisbury's government.

What did he see as the greatest advantage of empire? How did he look upon the character and rights of the indigenous populations of Africa and Asia? What was his opinion of those opposed to imperialism? Chamberlain was Colonial Secretary in the period running up to the Boer War and seems to have sanctioned the unprovoked attack on one of the Boer republics called the "Jameson Raid." He once said of imperialism: "you cannot have omelettes without breaking eggs." What would the earl of Morton (document 3.7) have said to Chamberlain?

. . . I am convinced that it is a necessity as well as a duty for us to uphold the dominion and empire which we now possess. (Loud cheers.) . . . I would never lose the hold which we now have over our great Indian dependency – (hear, hear) – by far the greatest and most valuable of all the customers we have or ever shall have in this country. For the same reasons I approve of the continued occupation of Egypt; and for the same reasons I have urged upon this Government, and upon previous Governments, the necessity for using every legitimate opportunity to extend our influence and control in that great African continent which is now being opened up to civilization and to commerce; and, lastly, it is for the same reasons that I hold that our navy should be strengthened – (loud cheers) – until its supremacy is so assured that we cannot be shaken in any of the possessions which we hold or may hold hereafter.

Believe me, if in any one of the places to which I have referred any change took place which deprived us of that control and influence of which I have been speaking, the first to suffer would be the working-men of this country. Then, indeed, we should see a distress which would not be temporary, but which would be chronic, and we should find that England was entirely unable to support the enormous population which is now maintained by the aid of her foreign trade. If the working-men of this country understand, as I believe they do – I am one of those who have had good reason through my life to rely upon their intelligence and shrewdness – if they understand their own interests, they will never lend any countenance to the doctrines of those politicians who never lose an opportunity of

[27] Joseph Chamberlain, *Foreign and Colonial Speeches* (London, 1897), 132–3, 135–6.

pouring contempt and abuse upon the brave Englishmen, who, even at this moment, in all parts of the world are carving out new dominions for Britain, and are opening up fresh markets for British commerce, and laying out fresh fields for British labor. (Applause.) . . .

I hold it to be our duty to the people [in Africa] for whom at all events we have for the time accepted responsibility, as well as to our own people, even at some cost of life, some cost of treasure, to maintain our rule and to established settled order, which is the only foundation for permanent prosperity. . . .

But I will go further than that. [The colonies in the interior of Africa] should be developed. . . . Unless we can reach a country by the sea we cannot obtain its products in a form or at a cost which would be likely to be of any use to us, nor can we get our products to them. . . . What we want is to give to [them] the means of communication by a railway from the coast which would bring to that population . . . our iron, and our cloths, and our cotton, and even our jewelry, because I believe that savages are not at all insensible to the delights of personal adornment. (Laughter.)

4.27 J.A. Hobson, Imperialism *(1902)*[28]

J.A. Hobson (1858–1940), a British economist, published his critique of imperialism in 1902. He began as a Liberal but moved to the Labour Party. Lenin eventually adopted his analysis of imperialism and suggested it was a product of the search for places to invest excess capital overseas. Hobson's thesis was often attacked by later historians but has recently found support in the work of P.J. Cain and A.G. Hopkins.[29] A central contradiction of the empire was despotism in the colonies and democracy at home. Hobson also was among the first to stress the danger of imperial rule to democracy in the mother country of an empire.

Did Hobson underestimate the force of nationalism? Was he able clearly to explain the mechanism that connects the ambitions of capitalists with the formation of state policy? Why has economic growth in advanced countries continued to expand after colonial empires were abandoned in the years following World War II?

The Economic Roots of Imperialism

. . . It is open to Imperialists to argue thus: "We must have markets for our growing manufactures, we must have new outlets for the investment of our surplus

[28] J.A. Hobson, *Imperialism: A Study* (London, 1902), 76–8, 82, 86, 98–9, 127–8, 133–4, 143, 145, 158–60.

[29] P.J. Cain and A.G. Hopkins, *British Imperialism: Innovation and Expansion, 1688–1914* and *British Imperialism: Crisis and Deconstruction, 1914–1990* (London, 1993).

capital and for the energies of the adventurous surplus of our population: such expansion is a necessity of life to a nation with our great and growing powers of production. An even larger share of our population is devoted to the manufactures and commerce of towns, and is thus dependent for life and work upon food and raw materials from foreign lands. In order to buy and pay for these things we must sell our goods abroad. During the first three-quarters of the nineteenth century we could do so without difficulty by a natural expansion of commerce with continental nations and our colonies, all of which were far behind us in the main arts of manufacture and the carrying trades. So long as England held a virtual monopoly of the world markets for certain important classes of manufactured goods, Imperialism was unnecessary. [After 1872] this manufacturing and trading supremacy was greatly impaired: other nations, especially Germany, the United States, and Belgium, advanced with great rapidity, and while they have not crushed or even stayed the increase of our external trade, their competition made it more and more difficult to dispose of the full surplus of our manufactures at a profit. The encroachments made by these nations upon our old markets, even in our own possessions, made it most urgent that we should take energetic means to secure new markets. These new markets had to lie in hitherto undeveloped countries, chiefly in the tropics, where vast populations lived capable of growing economic needs which our manufacturers and merchants could supply. Our rivals were seizing territories for similar purposes, and when they have annexed them closed them to our trade. The diplomacy and the arms of Great Britain had to be used in order to compel the owners of the new markets to deal with us . . . [and establish] protectorates or [annex colonies] . . . [In Britain] large savings are made which cannot find any profitable investment; they must find employment elsewhere, and it is to the advantage of the nation that they should be employed as largely as possible in lands where they can be utilized in opening up markets for British trade. . . .

It is this economic condition of affairs that forms the taproot of Imperialism. If the consuming public in this country raised its standard of consumption to keep pace with every rise of productive powers, there could be no excess of goods or capital clamorous to use Imperialism in order to find markets. . . .

This is the entire issue of empire. A people limited in number and energy and in the land they occupy have the choice of improving to the utmost the political and economic management of their own land . . . or they may proceed, like the slovenly farmer, to spread their power and energy over the whole earth, tempted by the speculative value or the quick profits of some new market, or else by mere greed or territorial acquisition, and ignoring the political and economic wastes and risks involved by this imperial career. . . .

. . . It is idle to attack Imperialism or Militarism as political expedients or policies unless the axe is laid at the economic root of the tree, and the classes for whose interest Imperialism works are shorn of the surplus revenues which seek this outlet.

Are any parts of Hobson's commentary tinged with racism? How important were imperial rivalries in causing the outbreak of World War I? What damage to democracy in Britain was due to holding an empire abroad? Did Britain become less democratic during the second half of the twentieth century? Could a few thousand retired imperial officers and businessmen change the political temper of English society?

The Political Significance of Imperialism

The present condition of the government under which the vast majority of our fellow-subjects in the Empire live is eminently un-British in that it is based, not on the consent of the governed, but upon the will of imperial officials; does indeed betray a great variety of forms, but they agree in the essential of un-freedom. Nor is it true that any of the more enlightened methods of administration we employ are directed towards undoing this character. Not only in India, but in the West Indies, and wherever there exists a large preponderance of colored population, the trend, not merely of ignorant, but of enlightened public opinion, is against a genuinely representative government on British lines. It is perceived to be incompatible with the economic and social authority of a superior race.

When British authority has been forcibly fastened upon large populations of alien race and color . . . we are obliged in practice to make a choice between good order and justice administered autocratically in accordance with British standards, on the one hand, and delicate, costly, doubtful, and disorderly experiments in self-government on British lines upon the other, and we have practically everywhere decided to adopt the former alternative. . . . It cannot be too clearly recognized that the old Liberal notion of our educating lower races in the arts of popular government is discredited . . .

Every one of the steps of expansion in Africa, Asia, and the Pacific have been accompanied by bloodshed; each imperialist Power keeps an increasing army available for foreign service; rectification of frontiers, punitive expeditions, and other euphemisms for war have been in incessant progress. The *Pax Britannica* [British Peace], always an impudent falsehood, has become a grotesque monster of hypocrisy. . . . Where thirty years ago there existed one sensitive spot in our relations with France, or Germany, or Russia, there are a dozen now . . .

It is not in the interest of the British people, either as producers of wealth or as tax-payers, to risk a war with Russia and France in order to join Japan in preventing Russia from seizing Korea; but it may serve the interests of a group of commercial politicians to promote this dangerous policy. The South African war [Boer War 1899–1902], openly fomented by gold speculators for their private purposes, will rank in history as a leading case of this usurpation of nationalism . . .

[Indigenous peoples are now used as mercenaries to fight our wars in the colonies.] It . . . proved [in the case of the Roman Empire] one of the most perilous devices of parasitism, by which a metropolitan population entrusts the defense of its lives and possessions to the precarious fidelity of conquered races, commanded by ambitious pro-consuls. . . .

This mode of militarism, while cheaper and easier in the first instance, implies less and less control from Great Britain. Though reducing the strain of militarism upon the population at home, it enhances the risks of wars, which become more frequent and more barbarous in proportion as they involve to a less degree the lives of Englishmen . . .

As the despotic portion of our Empire has grown in area, a larger and larger number of men, trained in the temper and methods of autocracy as soldiers and civil officials in our Crown colonies, protectorates, the Indian Empire, reinforced by numbers of merchants, planters, engineers, and overseers, whose lives have been those of a superior caste living an artificial life removed from all the healthy restraints of ordinary European society, have returned to this country, bringing back the characters, sentiments, and ideas imposed by this foreign environment. The South and South-West of England is richly sprinkled with these men, many of them wealthy, most of them endowed with leisure, men openly contemptuous of democracy, devoted to material luxury, social display, and the shallower arts of intellectual life. The wealthier among them discover political ambitions, introducing into our Houses of Parliament the coarsest and most selfish spirit of "Imperialism," using their imperial experience and connections to push profitable companies and concessions for their private benefits, and posing as authorities so as to keep the yoke of Imperialism firmly fixed upon the shoulders of the "nigger." The South African millionaire [such as Cecil Rhodes] is the brand most in evidence: his methods are the most barefaced, and his success, social and political, the most redoubtable. . . . Not a few [imperial ex-officials] enter our local councils, or take posts in our constabulary or our prisons: everywhere they stand for coercion and for resistance to reform. Could the incomes expended in the [counties around London] and other large districts of Southern Britain be traced to their sources, it would be found that they were in large measure wrung from the enforced toil of vast multitudes of black, brown, or yellow natives, by arts not differing essentially from those which supported in idleness and luxury imperial Rome.

The Origins of World War I

4.28 Norman Angell, The Great Illusion: A Study of the Relation of Military Power to National Advantage *(1910)*[30]

After the assassination by a Serbian terrorist of the Archduke Franz Ferdinand of Austria-Hungary in June 1914 a complex series of diplomatic misadventures eventually dragged all the major powers of Europe into what was known until

[30] Norman Angell, *The Great Illusion: A Study of the Relation of Military Power to National Advantage* (New York, 1913), ix.

1939 as "The Great War." Some observers saw it coming. Norman Angell (1872–1967), the economist and pacifist, published a book in 1910 titled *The Great Illusion* that spelled out the consequences of prewar trends.

Why did statesmen fail to see the problem and work to solve it? What impact might Social Darwinism have had on public opinion (see documents 6.14–17)? How would Froude and Chamberlain (documents 4.25 and 4.26) have responded?

What are the fundamental motives that explain the present rivalry of armaments in Europe, notably the Anglo-German? Each nation leads the need for defense; but this implies that someone is likely to attack, and has therefore a presumed interest in so doing. What are the motives which each State thus fears its neighbors may obey?

They are based on the universal assumption that a nation, in order to find outlets for expanding population and increasing industry, or simply to ensure the best conditions possible for its people, is necessarily pushed to territorial expansion and the exercise of political force against others . . . It is assumed that a nation's relative prosperity is broadly determined by its political power; that nations being competing units, advantage in the last resort goes to the possessor of preponderant military force, the weaker goes to the wall, as in the other forms of the struggle for life.

4.29 Sir Edward Grey to Sir Francis Bertie (July 31, 1914)[31]

The British government had kept secret the military aspects of its diplomatic understanding with France, the *Entente Cordiale*, first concluded in 1904. The German leadership, the British dominions, and Parliament were not properly informed. This led to some uncertainty in the mind of Sir Edward Grey (1862–1933), the foreign secretary, whether Parliament and even many members of the Cabinet would endorse a declaration of war should France be attacked by Germany. Hence historians have accused Grey of indecisiveness in his handling of the unraveling situation in July and early August 1914.

It is evident from this letter to Sir Francis Bertie, British Ambassador in Paris, however, that Grey did make it clear to the German government that vital British interests were engaged. Does this statement conclusively prove that Germany understood British intervention was inevitable should they attack France? Was Grey's statement strong enough to convince Germany of

[31] "'The White Paper' issued by the British Foreign Office 5 August 1914," *International Conciliation*, 83, Oct. 1914, 76–7.

Britain's determination to intervene on the side of France? Why had the Liberal government kept its military objectives secret?

M. Cambon [French ambassador to London] referred today to a telegram . . . from the French Ambassador in Berlin saying that it was the uncertainty with regard to whether we would intervene which was the encouraging element in Berlin, and that, if we would only declare definitely on the side of Russia and France, it would decide the German attitude in favor of peace. I said that it was quite wrong to suppose that we had left Germany under the impression that we would not intervene. I had refused overtures to promise that we should remain neutral. I had only definitely declined to say that we would remain neutral. I had even gone so far this morning as to say to the German Ambassador that, if France and Germany became involved in war, we should be drawn into it. That, of course, was not the same thing as taking an engagement to France, and I told M. Cambon of it only to show that we had not left Germany under the impression that we would stand aside.

4.30 *Sir Edward Grey, speech in the House of Commons (Aug. 3, 1914)*[32]

Sir Edward Grey addressed Parliament on the issuance of the German ultimatum to Belgium through which it intended to invade France. He placed before the Commons the choice of peace or war. He finally revealed the reliance of France on naval protection from Britain, which was a decisive issue, but placed more public emphasis on an 80-year-old treaty to protect the neutrality of Belgium, which was of less strategic importance but garnered huge public support.

How important was his fear of the "economic consequences" of losing trade with the combatants should Britain remain neutral in determining British policy? Would Britain have lost "respect" for not upholding an antique treaty concluded in a different era and a promise to France made without any consultation with the democratic institutions of the country?

What other policy is there before the House? There is but one way in which the Government could make certain at the present moment of keeping outside this war, and that would be that it should immediately issue a proclamation of unconditional neutrality. We cannot do that [cheers]; we have made a commitment to France, which I have read to the House, which prevents us from doing that. We have got the consideration of Belgium also which prevents us

[32] *Parliamentary Debates*, LXV, August 3, 1914, c. 1825.

from any unconditional neutrality, and without those conditions absolutely satisfied and satisfactory we are bound not to shrink from proceeding to the use of all the forces in our power. If we . . . have nothing to do with the matter . . . we should, I believe, sacrifice our respect and good name and reputation before the world, and should not escape the most serious and grave economic consequences.

HISTORIANS' DEBATES

What were the true intentions of the Whig aristocrats in passing the Reform Act of 1832?

Richard Brent, *Liberal Anglican Politics: Whiggery, Religion, and Reform, 1830–1841* (Oxford, 1987); Michael Brock, *The Great Reform Act* (London, 1973); John Cannon, *Parliamentary Reform, 1640–1832* (Cambridge, 1973); J.C.D. Clark, *English Society, 1688–1832: Religion, Ideology, and Politics during the Ancien Regime* (Cambridge, 2000); Joseph Hamburger, *James Mill and the Art of Revolution* (New Haven, 1963); Peter Mandler, *Aristocratic Government in the Age of Reform: Whigs and Liberals, 1830–1852* (Oxford, 1990); L.G. Mitchell, *Lord Melbourne 1779–1848* (Oxford, 1997); D.C. Moore, *The Politics of Deference: A Study of the Mid-Nineteenth Century English Political System* (Brighton, 1976); G.M. Trevelyan, *British History in the Nineteenth Century and After, 1782–1919* (New York, 1937); Ellis A. Wasson, *Whig Renaissance: Lord Althorp and the Whig Party* (New York, 1986).

Was the culture of imperialism "orientalist," that is, intent on subordinating the colonial peoples by "othering" them? This debate was prompted by Edward Said's creative but flawed book.

Edward Said, *Orientalism: Western Conceptions of the Orient* (New York, 1978); Sadiq Jalal al-'Azm, "Orientalism and Orientalism in Reverse," in *Forbidden Agendas: Intolerance and Defiance in the Middle East*, ed. Jon Rothschild (London, 1984); David Cannadine, *Ornamentalism: How the British Saw Their Empire* (Oxford, 2001); Linda Colley, *Captives: Britain, Empire, and the World, 1600–1850* (London, 2002); Anne McClintock, *Imperial Leather: Race, Gender, and Sexuality in the Colonial Contest* (London, 1995); J.M. MacKenzie, *Orientalism: History, Theory and the Arts* (Manchester, 1995); Dennis Porter, "*Orientalism* and Its Problems," in *The Politics of Theory*, ed. Francis Barker *et al.* (Colchester, 1983); R. Price, "One Big Thing: Britain, Its Empire, and Their Imperial Culture," *JBS* 45 (2006), 602–27; D.A. Washbrook, "Orients and Occidents: Colonial Discourse Theory and the Historiography of the British Empire," in *Oxford History of the British Empire*, volume 5, ed. Robin Winks (Oxford, 1999).

What forces led to the repeal of the Corn Laws? What were the motives of the parties for and against repeal?

L. Brown, *The Board of Trade and the Free-Trade Movement, 1830–42* (London, 1958); S. Fairlie, "The Nineteenth-Century Corn Law Reconsidered," *EcHR* 18 (1965), 562–75; N. Gash, *Sir Robert Peel: The Life of Sir Robert Peel after 1830*, 2nd ed. (London, 1986); W.D. Grampp, "How Britain Turned to Free Trade," *BHR* 61 (1987), 86–112; B. Hilton, *Corn, Cash and Commerce: The Economic Policies of the Tory Governments, 1815–30* (Oxford, 1977); A.C. Howe, "Free Trade and the City of London, c. 1820–1870," *History* 77 (1992), 391–410; G. Kitson Clark, "The Electorate and the Repeal of the Corn Laws," *TRHS* 1 (1951), 109–26; N. McCord, *The Anti-Corn Law League, 1838–46* (London, 1958); A.D. Macintyre, "Lord George Bentinck and the Protectionists: A Lost Cause?" *TRHS* 39 (1989), 141–65; David Spring, "Earl Fitzwilliam and the Corn Laws," *AHR* LIX

(1954), 287–304; R. Stewart, *The Politics of Protection: Lord Derby and the Protectionist Party, 1841–52* (Cambridge, 1971).

Who were the Chartists? Was the Chartist movement a failure? Why was it important?

Eugenio F. Biagini and Alastair J. Reid, eds., *Currents of Radicalism: Popular Radicalism, Organised Labour, and Party Politics in Britain, 1850–1914* (Cambridge, 1991); Asa Briggs, ed., *Chartist Studies* (London, 1959); James Epstein, *The Lion of Freedom: Feargus O'Connor and the Chartist Movement, 1832–1842* (London, 1982); Margot C. Finn, *After Chartism: Class and Nation in English Radical Politics, 1848–1874* (Cambridge, 1993); Gareth Stedman Jones, *Languages of Class: Studies in English Working Class History, 1832–1982* (Cambridge, 1983); John Savile, *1848: The British State and the Chartist Movement* (Cambridge, 1987); Dorothy Thompson, *The Chartists* (London, 1984); J.T. Ward, *Chartism* (London, 1973).

Was William Gladstone a great prime minister? What were his accomplishments and failures? How progressive was he?

Travis L. Crosby, *The Two Mr. Gladstones: A Study in Psychology and History* (New Haven, 1997); Roy Jenkins, *Gladstone* (London, 1995); Philip Magnus, *Gladstone: A Biography* (London, 1954); H.C.G. Matthew, *Gladstone*, 2 vols (Oxford, 1986–95); John Morley, *The Life of William Ewart Gladstone*, 3 vols (London, 1903); Richard Shannon, *Gladstone: Peel's Inheritor, 1809–1865* (London, 1982); Richard Shannon, *Gladstone: Heroic Minister, 1865–1898* (London, 1999); Peter Stansky, *Gladstone: A Progress in Politics* (New York, 1979).

How influential was Queen Victoria? What role did she play in national life?

Walter L. Arnstein, *Queen Victoria* (Basingstoke, 2003); David Cannadine, "The Last Hanoverian Sovereign? The Victorian Monarchy in Historical Perspective, 1688–1988," in *The First Modern Society: Essays in English History in Honour of Lawrence Stone*, ed. James Rosenheim (Cambridge, 1989); Carolly Erickson, *Her Little Majesty: The Life of Queen Victoria* (London, 1997); Frank Hardie, *The Political Influence of Queen Victoria* (London, 1935); William Kuhn, *Democratic Royalism: The Transformation of the British Monarchy, 1861–1914* (London, 1996); Elizabeth Longford, *Victoria R. I.* (London, 1964); Adrienne Munich, *Queen Victoria's Secrets* (New York, 1997); Frank Prochaska, *Royal Bounty: The Making of the Welfare Monarchy* (New Haven, 1995); Giles St. Aubyn, *Queen Victoria: A Portrait* (London, 1991); Lytton Strachey, *Queen Victoria* (London, 1922); Dorothy Thompson, *Queen Victoria: Gender and Power* (London, 1989); Richard Williams, *The Contentious Crown: Public Discussion of the British Monarchy in the Reign of Queen Victoria* (Aldershot, 1997).

Was Cecil Rhodes driven mainly by benevolent aspirations, desire for power, greed, or imperial arrogance? To what degree was he responsible for the racist regime in South Africa?

John Flint, *Cecil Rhodes* (London, 1976); J.G. Lockhart and C.M. Woodhouse, *Rhodes* (London, 1963); John Marlowe, *Cecil Rhodes: The Anatomy of Empire* (London, 1972); Brian Roberts, *Cecil Rhodes: Flawed Colossus* (London, 1987); Robert I. Rothberg and Miles F. Shore, *The Founder: Cecil Rhodes and the Pursuit of Power* (Oxford, 1988); Antony Thomas, *Rhodes* (London, 1997).

COUNTERFACTUALS TO CONSIDER

What if the Reform Bill of 1832 had not been passed? Would a revolution such as occurred in France in 1830 have taken place or would a strong conservative government have used military force successfully to suppress the middle and working classes and sustained an *ancien régime* state deep into the nineteenth century such as ruled in Prussia? What if a successful revolution had taken place in 1832?

What if Britain had declared neutrality in 1914? Would Germany have won a quick victory and dominated Europe in the twentieth century, leaving Britain in its wake? Or would a whale and elephant scenario reminiscent of the Franco-British rivalry of the eighteenth century have developed?

CHAPTER FIVE

Economy and Society

Increased economic productivity began in England in the seventeenth century. Initially manufacturing was geographically tied to sources of raw materials and energy (water power). Businesses began to shift in the later eighteenth century to locations where steam engines could be introduced (near coal) and ports that could easily carry large outputs away to markets. Steam power brought large factories and the development of the factory system with low wages, long hours, dangerous conditions, and new discipline. Large concentrations of people were gathered in "shock" cities such as Manchester. Here wealth accumulated rapidly but living conditions for workers were poor. Slums arose and epidemic diseases spread. Unprecedented problems produced increasingly radical changes in the way of life for most British people. At the same time rural life was traditional, and the social order remained hierarchical while at the same time it continued to absorb newcomers rapidly.

Many observers tried to understand the dynamics of capitalism, sought amelioration for the suffering, and advocated routes to prosperity and success. Capitalism offered ever-increasing prosperity to many but could it ever be fair? How could society balance liberty and equality?

As you read the documents in this chapter, consider the following questions:

- What was the "Industrial Revolution" and what were its consequences?
- In what ways did continuity prevail in the face of rapid changes in British society during the nineteenth century?
- What were the character and consequences of the debate over the development of capitalism?

Sources and Debates in Modern British History: 1714 to the Present, First Edition. Edited by Ellis Wasson.

Published 2012 by Blackwell Publishing Ltd.

Industrialization

5.1 *Arnold Toynbee,* Lectures on the Industrial Revolution of the Eighteenth Century in England *(1884)*[1]

The historian Arnold Toynbee (1852–83) first popularized the term and concept of an "industrial revolution." This argument imposes a premodern and modern division upon historical analysis. His ideas were subsequently challenged, and our present understanding of economic growth is much more nuanced. We understand that it took place over a much broader time span, and that full industrialization did not come until well into the nineteenth century. Nonetheless, most historians find the concept of an "industrial revolution" impossible to live without.

To what degree does Toynbee's analysis match our present understanding of industrialization? To what degree were his ideas compatible with Marxist theory? With Adam Smith (document 2.10)? Are there factors that Toynbee neglected? Unlike most other sources in this book, Toynbee's analysis is not contemporaneous with the events he was describing. However, he was born and raised in the era when Britain first became a fully industrialized nation. Can his ideas be seen as an account by an eyewitness? Is his "discovery" of an industrial revolution comparable in type and importance to Adam Smith's economic theories? If not, why not?

Coming to the facts of the Industrial Revolution, the first thing that strikes us is the far greater rapidity which marks the growth of population. Before 1751 the largest decennial increase, so far as we can calculate from our imperfect materials, was 3 percent. For each of the next three decennial periods the increase was 6 percent; then between 1781 and 1791 it was 9 percent, between 1791 and 1801, 11 percent; between 1801 and 1811, 14 percent; between 1811 and 1821, 18 percent....

Next we notice the relative and positive decline in the agricultural population. In 1811 it constituted 35 percent. Of the whole population of Great Britain; in 1821, 33 percent; in 1831, 28 percent. And at the same time its actual numbers have decreased. ... Contemporaneously with this change, the center of density of population has shifted from the Midlands to the North; ...

An agrarian revolution plays as large a part in the great industrial change of the end of the eighteenth century as does the revolution in manufacturing industries ... The destruction of the common field system of cultivation; the enclosure, on a large scale, of common and waste lands; and the consolidation of small farms into large. ...

[1] Arnold Toynbee, *Lectures on the Industrial Revolution of the 18th Century in England: Popular Addresses, Notes, and other Fragments* (London, 1902), 87–8, 90–1, 93.

Passing to manufactures, we find here the all-prominent fact to be the substitution of the factory for the domestic system, the consequence of mechanical discoveries of the time. Four great inventions altered the character of the cotton manufacture: the spinning-jenny, patented by Hargreaves in 1770; the water-frame, invented by Arkwright the year before; Crompton's mule introduced in 1779, and the self-acting mule, first invented by Kelly in 1792, but not brought into use till Roberts improved it in 1825. But in 1769 – the year in which Napoleon and Wellington were born – James Watt took out his patent for the steam-engine. Sixteen years later it was applied to the cotton manufacture. . . . The most famous invention of all, and the most fatal to domestic industry, the power-loom, though also patented by Cartwright in 1785, did not come into use for several years . . . In fifteen years the cotton trade trebled itself. . . . Meanwhile, the iron industry had been equally revolutionized by the invention of smelting by pit-coal brought into use between 1740 and 1750, and by the application in 1788 of the steam-engine to blast furnaces. . . .

A further growth of the factory system took place independent of machinery, and owed its origin to the expansion of trade, an expansion which was itself due to the great advance made at this time in the means of communication. The canal system was being rapidly developed throughout the country. . . .

The new class of great capitalist employers made enormous fortunes, they took little or no part personally in the work of their factories, their hundreds of workmen were individually unknown to them; and as a consequence, the old relations between masters and men disappeared, and a "cash nexus" was substituted for the human tie. The workmen on their side resorted to combination, and Trades-Unions began a fight which looked as if it were mortal enemies rather than joint producers. The misery which came upon large sections of the working people at this epoch was often, though not always, due to a fall in wages . . . They suffered likewise from the conditions of labor in the factory system, from the rise of prices, especially from the high price of bread before the repeal of the corn laws, and from those sudden fluctuations of trade, which, ever since production has been on a large scale, have exposed them to recurrent periods of bitter distress. The effects of the Industrial Revolution prove that free competition may produce wealth without producing well being.

5.2 *Andrew Ure,* The Philosophy of Manufactures *(1835)*[2]

Andrew Ure (1778–1857) was a professor of applied science at Glasgow University. He saw industrialization as a triumph of civilization and human ingenuity, and defended the factory system vigorously. He pointed out that an industrialized economy rewarded workers better than a purely agricultural one.

Why did people enthusiastically support the factory system? Why did they resist government regulation? Did Ure's background affect his outlook? What

[2] Andrew Ure, *The Philosophy of Manufactures* (London, 1835), 6–7, 20, 23.

did he mean by "unfailing wages"? Factory workers were subject to frequent layoffs and extended periods of unemployment. Is it likely that they had "nearly nothing to do at all"? Were factory owners who adopted improved machinery doing so for "philanthropic" reasons?

This island is pre-eminent among civilized nations for the prodigious development of its factory wealth, and has been therefore long viewed with a jealous admiration by foreign powers. . . .

The blessings which physio-mechanical science has bestowed on society, and the means it has still in store for ameliorating the lot of mankind, have been too little dwelt upon; while, on the other hand, it has been accused of lending itself to the rich capitalists as an instrument for harassing the poor . . . It has been said, for example, that the steam-engine now drives the power-looms with such velocity as to urge on their attendant weavers at the same rapid pace; but that the hand-weaver, not being subjected to this restless agent, can throw his shuttle and move his treddles at his convenience. There is, however, this difference in the two cases, that in the factory, every member of the loom is so adjusted, that the driving force leaves the attendant nearly nothing at all to do, certainly no muscular fatigue to sustain, while it procures for him good, unfailing wages, besides a healthy workshop *gratis*: whereas the non-factory weaver, having everything to execute by muscular exertion, finds the labor irksome, makes in consequence innumerable short pauses, separately of little account, but great when added together; earns therefore proportionally low wages, while he loses his health by poor diet and the dampness of his hovel. . . .

The constant aim and effect of scientific improvement in manufactures are philanthropic . . .

The principle of the factory system then is, to substitute mechanical science for hand skill, and the partition of a process into its essential constituents, for the division or graduation of labor among artisans. . . .

It is, in fact, the constant aim and tendency of every improvement in machinery to supersede human labor altogether, or to diminish its cost, by substituting the industry of women and children for that of men; or that of ordinary laborers for trained artisans.

5.3 *Robert Southey,* Sir Thomas More or Colloquies on the Progress and Prospects of Society *(1831)*[3]

Not all contemporaries welcomed the new economic system, even if it increased national power and wealth. The Romantic poet Robert Southey (1774–1843)

[3] Robert Southey, *Sir Thomas More or Colloquies on the Progress and Prospects of Society* (London, 1831), 166, 170.

used a fictional dialogue between himself and the ghost of the Tudor politician and author of *Utopia*, Sir Thomas More, to critique industrialization. He said of industrial buildings, that in his view disfigured the pristine countryside, "Time will not mellow them; nature will neither clothe nor conceal them; and they will remain always as offensive to the eye as to the mind."[4]

Was Southey's assessment of factories accurate? What were his objections to child labor? How would Adam Smith (document 2.10) respond to government legislation to protect children from such labor? Why did "Romantic" poets despise the Industrial Revolution?

Sir Thomas More comments: Yonder children are on the way to a manufactory, where they pass six days out of the seven, from morning till night. Is it likely that the little they learn at school on the seventh (which ought to be their day of recreation as well as rest), should counteract the effects of such an education, when the moral atmosphere wherein they live and move and have their being, is as noxious to the soul, as the foul and tainted air which they inhale is to their bodily constitution? . . .

What shall we say of a system which in its direct consequences debases all who are engaged in it? A system that employs men unremittingly in pursuits unwholesome for the body, and unprofitable for the mind, . . . a system in which the means are so bad, that any result would be dearly purchased at such an expense of human misery and degradation, and the end so fearful, that the worst calamities which society has hitherto endured may be deemed light in comparison with it?

5.4 *Peter Gaskell,* The Manufacturing Population of England *(1833)*[5]

In the 1830s parliamentary commissions investigated factory conditions, which prompted increased regulation, especially of child labor. Other evidence was gathered and published by men such as Dr Peter Gaskell (1805–41). His inaccurate descriptions of a happier, preindustrial world misled Friedrich Engels (document 5.8) in his book on the industrialized proletariat.[6]

How would you assess the conditions in the factories? Was life likely to have been different for farm laborers or shop workers? Considering how little physicians actually knew about effective medical treatment in the nineteenth century, how much credence should we give this account? Why would a middle-class professional care about or object to factory conditions? What might Gaskell have suggested to improve the situation?

[4] T.B. Macaulay, "Southey's Colloquies on Society," *Edinburgh Review* 50 (Jan. 1830), 540.

[5] P. Gaskell, *The Manufacturing Population of England* (London, 1833), 161–2, 202–3.

[6] *The Condition of the Working Class in England*, trans. W.O. Henderson and W.H. Chaloner (Stanford, 1968), xi.

Any man who has stood at twelve o'clock at the single narrow doorway, which serves as the place of exit for the hands employed in the great cotton mills, must acknowledge that an uglier set of men and women, of boys and girls, taking them in a mass, it would be impossible to congregate in a smaller compass. Their complexion is sallow and pallid – with a peculiar flatness of feature, caused by the want of a proper quantity of adipose substance to cushion out the cheeks. Their stature low – the average height of four hundred men, measured at different times and different places, being five feet six inches. Their limbs, slender, and playing badly and ungracefully. A very general bowing of the legs. Great numbers of girls and women walking lamely or awkwardly, with raised chests and spinal flexures. Nearly all have flat feet, accompanied with a down-tread, differing very widely from the elasticity of action in the foot and ankle, attendant upon perfect formation. Hair thin and straight – many of the men having but little beard, and that in patches of a few hairs ... A spiritless and dejected air, a sprawling and wide action of the legs ...

Factory labor is a species of work, in some respects singularly unfitted for children. Cooped up in a heated atmosphere, denied the necessary exercise, remaining in one position for a series of hours, one set or system of muscles alone called into activity, it cannot be wondered at that its effects are injurious to the physical growth of a child. Where the bony system is still imperfect, the vertical position it is compelled to retain, influences its direction; the spinal column bends beneath the weight of the head, bulges out laterally, or is dragged forward by the weight of the parts composing the chest, the pelvis yields beneath the opposing pressure downwards, and the resistance given by the thigh bones; its capacity is lessened, sometimes more and sometimes less; the legs curve, and the whole body loses height, in consequence of this general yielding and bending of parts.

5.5 *George Smith, autobiography (event in 1830s, pub. 1871)*[7]

During the Industrial Revolution the majority of child laborers did not work in factories. They were to be found in greater numbers in places such as mines, brickyards, farms, shops, and small family businesses. Many were servants or chimney sweeps. Most of these forms of employment were unregulated, and children were grossly exploited, their health and lives often endangered. George Smith (1831–95) describes a typical experience. It was not until 1871 that legislation was passed to regulate child labor with significant effect. Although attempts had been made to protect children used as chimney sweeps, it was not until 1875 that actual regulation occurred in that trade.

[7] George Smith, *The Cry of the Children from the Brick-yards of England*, 6th ed. (London, 1879), 6.

Why would a child's parents allow such treatment to continue? Why was the government reluctant to intervene? What would Adam Smith (document 2.10) have said about regulating child labor?

When a child of about seven years of age I was employed by a relative to assist him in making bricks. It is not my wish to say anything against him; but, like most of his class at that time, and like many even now, he thought kicks and blows formed the best means of obtaining the maximum of work from a lad. And as if these were not enough, excessively long hours of work were added.

At nine years of age my employment consisted in continually carrying about forty pounds of clay upon my head, from the clay heap to the table on which the bricks were made. When there was no clay, I had to carry the same weight of bricks. This labor had to be performed, almost without intermission, for thirteen hours daily. Sometimes my labors were increased by my having to work all night at the kilns.

The result of the prolonged and severe labor to which I was subjected, combined with the cruel treatment experienced by me at the hands of the adult laborers, are shown in marks that are borne by me to this day. On one occasion I had to perform a very heavy amount of labor. After my customary day's work I had to carry 1,200 nine-inch bricks from the maker to the floors on which they were placed to harden. The total distance thus walked by me that night was not less than fourteen miles, seven miles of which I traversed with eleven pounds weight of clay in my arms, besides lifting the unmade clay and carrying it some distance to the maker. The total quantity of clay thus carried by me was five and a half tons. For all of this labor I received sixpence! The fatigue thus experienced brought on a serious illness, which for several weeks prevented me from resuming work.

5.6 *Patience Kershaw, testimony before the Parliamentary Committee on Mines (1841–42)*[8]

Coal mining had been undertaken in Britain for many centuries, but the amount produced surged dramatically as the steam engine and new iron-making processes created a huge appetite for the resource. Coal was also used as the main means of heating houses in a country with a rapidly expanding population. Steam-driven pumps and elevators made it possible to dig deeper and deeper, and railways delivered coal cheaply and quickly throughout the country. The following extract comes from testimony by a 17-year-old girl to Lord Ashley's (1801–85) parliamentary investigation (1841–42) into working conditions in the mines.

[8] *Parliamentary Papers*, 1842, XV–XVII, Appendix 1; Appendix 2.

Why would a poor family have so many children? Why didn't she move from her job in the pits to a mill? Did the state of dress and relationship between the men and girl accord with general assumptions about Victorian morality? What were the long-term effects of such labor in the mines on the health of men and women?

My father has been dead about a year; my mother is living and has ten children, five lads and five lasses; the oldest is about thirty, the youngest is four; three lasses go to the mill; all the lads are colliers, two [cutters at the coal face] and three [coal wagon pullers] ...

All my sisters have been [wagon pullers], but three went to the mill. Alice went because her legs swelled from [wagon pulling] in cold water when she was hot. I never went to day-school; I go to Sunday-school, but I cannot read or write; I go to pit at five o'clock in the morning and come out at five in the evening; I get my breakfast of porridge and milk first; I take my dinner with me, a cake, and eat it as I go; I do not stop or rest any time for the purpose; I get nothing else until I get home, and then have potatoes and meat, not every day meat. I [pull the wagons full of coal] in the clothes I have now got on, trousers and ragged jacket; the bald place upon my head is made by thrusting the [wagons]; my legs have never swelled, but sister's did when she went to the mill; I [pull the wagons] a mile and more under ground and back; they weigh three hundred pounds; I pull 11 a day; I wear a belt and chain at the workings to get the [wagons] out; the [cutters] that I work for are naked except their caps; they pull off all their clothes; I see them at work when I go up; sometimes they beat me, if I am not quick enough, with their hands; they strike me upon my back; the boys take liberties with me; sometimes they pull me about; I am the only girl in the pit; there are about 20 boys and 15 men; all the men are naked; I would rather work in mill than in coal-pit.

5.7 Prince Albert, memorandum on Sir Robert Peel's program of economic and social reform (Dec. 25, 1845)[9]

Prince Albert (1819–61) increasingly took on the role of policy advisor to his wife Queen Victoria and consulted regularly with senior politicians. In this document he laid out the plans the prime minister, Sir Robert Peel, who the Prince greatly admired, had for the next session of Parliament. Peel was preparing to end protective tariffs on wheat, even though a majority of members of his own party strongly supported their retention.

9 *Letters of Queen Victoria: A Selection from Her Majesty's Correspondence*, first series (1837–61), ed. A.C. Benson and Viscount Esher, 3 vols (London, 1907), II, 78–9.

How would you characterize Peel's program? Was he really working for the benefit of the whole nation? What role did he see the state playing in the preservation of social stability? Why might the prince have supported this program?

Sir Robert has *an immense scheme in view*; he thinks he shall be able to remove the contest entirely from the dangerous ground upon which it has got – that of a war between the manufacturers, the hungry and the poor against the landed proprietors, the aristocracy, which can only end in the ruin of the latter; he will not bring forward a measure upon the Corn Laws, but a much more comprehensive one. He will deal with the whole commercial system of the country. He will adopt the principle of the [Anti-Corn Law] League, *that of removing all protection and abolishing all monopoly*, but not in favor of one class and as a triumph over another, but to the benefit of the nation, farmers as well as manufacturers. He would begin with cotton, and take in all the necessaries of life and corn amongst them. . . . A great calamity must be foreseen, when the innumerable rail-roads now in progress shall have been terminated, which will be the case in a few years. This will throw an enormous laboring population suddenly out of employment. There might be a law passed which would provide employment for them, and improve the agriculture and production of the country, by enabling the State to advance money to the great proprietors for the improvements of their estates, which they could not obtain otherwise without charging their estates beyond what they already have to bear.

Urban and Rural Life and Employment during Industrialization

5.8 *Friedrich Engels,* The Condition of the Working-Class in England in 1844 *(1844)*[10]

Friedrich Engels (1820–95), a German manufacturer, was a close observer of the living conditions in big British cities in the mid-nineteenth century (Figure 5.1). In spite of his capitalist credentials, he became close to Karl Marx and was co-author of the *Communist Manifesto* (1848).

Is selfish egotism a characteristic of modern cities? Do people become more isolated in an urban setting? What causes slums to develop? What would Engels have proposed as a solution? How might his Marxist ideology have skewed his vision of urban life?

10 Frederick Engels, *The Condition of the Working-Class in England in 1844* (London, 1892), 23–6.

After roaming the streets of the capital a day or two, making headway with difficulty through the human turmoil and the endless lines of vehicles, after visiting the slums of the metropolis, one realizes for the first time that these Londoners have been forced to sacrifice the best qualities of their human nature, to bring to pass all the marvels of civilization which crowd their city; that a hundred powers which slumbered within them have remained inactive, have been suppressed in order that a few might be developed more fully and multiply through union with those of others. The very turmoil of the streets has something repulsive, something against which human nature rebels. The hundreds of thousands of all classes and ranks crowding past each other, are they not all human beings with the same qualities and powers, and with the same interest in being happy? And have they not, in the end, to seek happiness in the same way, by the same means? And still they crowd by one another as though they had nothing in common, nothing to do with one another, and their only agreement is the tacit one, that each keep to his own side of the pavement, so as not to delay the opposing streams of the crowd, while it occurs to no man to honor another with so much as a glance. The brutal indifference, the unfeeling isolation of each in his private interest, becomes the more repellent and offensive, the more these individuals are crowded together, within a limited space. And, however much one may be aware that this isolation of the individual, this narrow self-seeking, is the fundamental principle of our society everywhere, it is nowhere so shamelessly barefaced, so self-conscious as just here in the crowding of the great city. The dissolution of mankind into monads, of which each one has a separate principle, the world of atoms, is here carried out to its utmost extreme. . . .

What is true of London, is true of Manchester, Birmingham, Leeds, is true of all great towns. Everywhere barbarous indifference, hard egotism on one hand, and nameless misery on the other, everywhere social warfare, every man's house in a state of siege, everywhere reciprocal plundering under the protection of the law, and all so shameless, so openly avowed that one shrinks before the consequences of our social state as they manifest themselves here undisguised, and can only wonder that the whole crazy fabric still hangs together. . . .

Every great city has one or more slums, where the working-class is crowded together. True, poverty often dwells in hidden alleys close to the palaces of the rich; but, in general, a separate territory has been assigned to it, where, removed from the sight of the happier classes, it may struggle along as it can. These slums are pretty equally arranged in all the great towns of England, the worst houses in the worst quarters of the towns; usually one or two-storied cottages in long rows, perhaps with cellars used as dwellings, almost always irregularly built. These houses of three or four rooms and a kitchen form, throughout England, some parts of London excepted, the general dwellings of the working-class. The streets are generally unpaved, rough, dirty, filled with vegetable and animal refuse, without sewers or gutters, but supplied with foul, stagnant pools instead. Moreover, ventilation is impeded by the bad, confused method of building of the whole quarter, and since many human beings here live crowded into a small space, the atmosphere that prevails in these working-men's quarters may readily be imagined.

Figure 5.1 "Wentworth Street, Whitechapel," by Gustav Doré (1872). Photo © Duncan Walker/iStockphoto.

This view of a street in the "East End" of London portrays one of the worst slums in the city where poverty, disease, crime, and illiteracy entrapped hundreds of thousands of people. Yet London was also the grandest and richest city in the world and the capital of the greatest empire that there had ever been. What can one tell about the lives of the people portrayed in this engraving? What might prosperous citizens of the "West End" have said about the condition of the poor? How would most of these Londoners have made a living?

5.9 *John Robertson, letter printed in the* Report of the Select Committee on Health of Towns *(Apr. 8, 1840)*[11]

A surgeon, John Robertson, provided evidence to one of the numerous reports of committees established in the nineteenth century to gather information and propose legislation relating to the changes in society precipitated by industrialization.

[11] *Reports from Select Committees of the House of Commons, and Evidence Communicated to the Lords on Health of Towns*, 9 vols, 1840, XI, 222, Appendix 2.

What responses were likely to be evoked by these conditions from the comfortable middle classes? Why did local governments fail to regulate the development of housing and sanitation conditions? Who might have dominated local government boards in big manufacturing cities? Would workers have been able to afford housing built with better materials spread out over larger areas of land?

So long as this and other great manufacturing towns were multiplying and extending their branches of manufacture and were prosperous, every fresh addition of operatives found employment, good wages, and plenty of food; and so long as the families of working people are well fed, it is certain they maintain their health in a surprising manner, even in cellars and other close buildings. Now, however, the case is different. Food is dear, labor scarce, and wages in many branches very low; consequently, as might be expected, disease and death are making unusual havoc. In the years 1833, 1834, 1835, and 1836 (years of prosperity), the number of fever cases admitted to the Manchester House of Recovery amounted only to 1,685 or 421 per annum; while in the two pinching years, 1838 and 1839, the number admitted was 2,414 or 1,207 per annum. It is in such a depressed state of the manufacturing districts as at present exists that unpaved and badly sewered streets, narrow alleys, close, unventilated courts and cellars, exhibit their malign influence in augmenting the sufferings which that greatest of all physical evils, want of sufficient food, inflicts on young and old in large towns, but especially on the young.

Manchester has no public park or other grounds where the population can walk and breath fresh air. . . . Every advantage of this nature has been sacrificed to the getting of money in the shape of ground-rents.

5.10 *George Eliot (Mary Anne Evans),* Felix Holt: the Radical *(1866)*[12]

Poverty was everywhere. It was present both in towns and in rural areas, which were becoming more comingled in the North and the Midlands during the first half of the nineteenth century. The novelist George Eliot (1819–80), who grew up in the Midlands in the countryside that she describes here, gives an account of a journey through the region in the early 1830s.

What effects did the industrializing cities have on the countryside? What continuities survived from earlier times? Was Eliot sympathetic to such changes? What might the poor one day demand their rulers to do? Can fiction convey an accurate picture of the geography and economy of a society? Did the time gap of 30 years between when Eliot wrote and the period she was describing affect her accuracy?

[12] George Eliot, *Felix Holt: The Radical*, new ed. (Edinburgh, 1866), 5–7.

The district [consisted of] of clean little market-towns without manufactures, of fat livings, an aristocratic clergy, and low poor-rates. But as the day wore on the scene would change: the land would begin to be blackened with coal-pits, the rattle of handlooms to be heard in hamlets and villages. Here were powerful men walking queerly with knees bent outward from squatting in the mine, going home to throw themselves down in their blackened flannel and sleep through the daylight, then rise and spend much of their high wages at the ale-house . . .; here the pale eager faces of handloom-weavers, men and women, haggard from sitting up late at night to finish the week's work, hardly begun till the Wednesday. Everywhere the cottages and the small children dirty, for the languid mothers gave their strength to the loom . . . The gables of Dissenting chapels now made a visible sign of religion, and of a meeting-place to counter-balance the ale-house, even in the hamlets . . . The breath of the manufacturing town, which made a cloudy day and a red gloom by night on the horizon, diffused itself over all the surrounding country, filling the air with eager unrest. Here was a population not convinced that old England was as good as possible; here were multitudinous men and women aware that their religion was not exactly the religion of their rulers, who might therefore be better than they were, and who, if better, might alter many things which now made the world perhaps more painful than it need be, and certainly more sinful. Yet there were the grey steeples too, and the churchyards, with their grassy mounds and venerable headstones, and fine old woods covering a rising ground, or stretching far by the roadside, allowing only peeps at the park and mansion which they shut in from the working-day world. In these midland districts the traveler passed rapidly from one phase of English life to another: after looking down on a village dingy with coal-dust, noisy with the shaking of looms, he might skirt a parish all of fields, high hedges, and deep-rutted lanes; after the coach had rattled over the pavement of a manufacturing town, the scene of riots and trades-union meetings, it would take him in another ten minutes into a rural region, where the neighborhood of the town was only felt in the advantages of a near market for corn, cheese, and hay . . . The busy scenes of the shuttle and the wheel, of the roaring furnace, of the shaft and the pulley, seemed to make but crowded nests in the midst of the large-spaced, slow-moving life of homesteads and far-away cottages and oak-sheltered parks. . . . It was easy for the traveler to conceive that town and country had no pulse in common . . .

5.11 Report of the Royal Commission on Labour *(1894)*[13]

Between 1892 and 1894 a royal commission collected information and opinions about relations between employees and employers and about labor

[13] *Fifth and Final Report of the Royal Commission on Labour, Part I, Parliamentary Papers,* 1894, XXXV, 33–4.

conditions. The distinguished economist Alfred Marshall (1842–1924) contributed heavily to the project.

Assess the validity of the arguments made by the manufacturers and trade unionists. Which arguments are most persuasive for each case? Would it have been better for the government to set wages and working conditions? How could that have been accomplished fairly?

The employers who have given evidence have usually recognized a legitimate province for trade unions in bargaining as to wages and hours and watching over the general interests of their members, and admitted that strong organizations, acting within those limits, tend on the whole to improve industrial relations, and to make their members act in a better informed way and a more reasonable spirit. But the view has also been put forward, even by those who hold these opinions, that the action and rules of trade unions have been in some respects prejudicial to the efficiency of production and to the industrial prosperity of the country.

The allegations upon this point are as follows: –

1. The trade unions have a growing tendency to interfere with details of business . . .
2. The trade unions often misjudge the true position of affairs, and by ill-timed and excessive demands . . . discourage enterprise and further investment of capital . . .
3. That though organizations may tend to diminish the frequency of industrial conflicts, they extend their range . . .
4. That workmen with a powerful union behind them are apt to become too confident as to their position . . .
5. That the action of trade unions has a tendency to bring about a uniformity of wages and hours . . . [and thus] are reducing workmen to a dead level of enterprise, discouraging work of more than average merit, and taking away from individual workmen the motive power of ambition and self-interest. . . .
6. That trade unions injure trades by the rigidity of their rules. . . .

The representatives of trade unions claim that, even supposing it to be possible to prove some drawbacks, the existence of these societies is essential to preserve the independence of workmen and to protect their interests. . . . The actions of trade unions has secured improved wages, hours and conditions of labor not only directly for organized workmen, but indirectly for those not organized. . . .

They deny, then, that these organizations take away the motive of self-interest and therefore diminish the energy of the individual workman, but they allege that, in the interests of large bodies of workmen, it is necessary to some extent to restrain by rules the natural desire of the individual workman to work overtime, for the sake of higher wages, and other modes by which he might seek to benefit himself at the cost of his fellow workmen as well as his own health and strength, or that of his offspring. . . . They allege that the action of strong trade unions is beneficial even to employers by preventing them from destroying each other through unlimited competition.

5.12 Sydney Smith, essay on modern innovations (1839)[14]

Sydney Smith (1771–1845) was an Anglican cleric of advanced political views and great wit. Indeed, he could be so outrageously funny that none of his friends in government ever dared promote him to a high ecclesiastical office. He moved in aristocratic Whig circles and helped in 1802 to found the great literary and political journal the *Edinburgh Review.* In this passage he comments with a firm belief in the goodness of advancement and reform on the changes that had taken place during his lifetime.

What significant changes in the economy and society during his lifetime did Smith neglect to mention? Of those he did mention, which was the most important? Were the changes he mentioned more numerous and dramatic than those of the previous century or the century after his death? Why is it sometimes difficult to identify the significance of changes until long after they were introduced?

It is of some importance at what period a man is born. A young man, alive at this period, hardly knows to what improvements of human life he has been introduced; and I would bring before his notice the following eighteen changes which have taken place in England since I first began to breathe in it the breath of life – a period amounting now to nearly seventy-three years.

Gas was unknown: I groped about the streets of London in all but utter darkness of a twinkling oil lamp, under the protection of watchmen in their grand climacteric, and exposed to every species of depredation and insult.

I have been nine hours in sailing from Dover to Calais [crossing the English Channel] before the invention of steam. It took me nine hours to go from Taunton to Bath, before the invention of railroads, and I now go in six hours from Taunton to London! In going from Taunton to Bath, I suffered between 10,000 and 12,000 severe contusions, before stone-breaking Macadam [a road improver whose name is still used to describe paving] was born.

I have paid £15 in a single year for repairs of carriage-springs on the pavement of London; and I now glide without noise or fracture, on wooden pavements.

I can walk, by the assistance of the police, from one end of London to the other, without molestation; or, if tired, get into a cheap and active cab, instead of those cottages on wheels, which the hackney coaches were at the beginning of my life.

I had no umbrella! They were little used, and very dear. There were no waterproof hats, and *my* hat was often reduced by rains into its primitive pulp.

14 *The Works of the Rev. Sydney Smith,* 3rd ed. (London, 1845), III, 457–8.

I could not keep my smallclothes [underwear; elastic had still to be invented] in their proper place, for braces [suspenders] were unknown. If I had the gout, there was no colchicum. If I was bilious, there was no calomel. If I were attacked by ague, there was no quinine. There were filthy coffee-houses instead of elegant clubs. Game could not be bought [all game belonged to the landowners on whose property it was caught or killed]. Quarrels about uncommuted tithes [a tax on farmers to support Anglican clergy and churches particularly offensive to Dissenters and Roman Catholics] were endless. The corruption of Parliament, before Reform, infamous. There were no banks to receive the savings of the poor. The Poor Laws were gradually sapping the vitals of the country; and, whatever miseries I suffered, I had no post to whisk my complaints for a single penny to the remotest corners of the empire; and yet, in spite of all these privations, I lived on quietly, and am now ashamed that I was not more discontented, and utterly surprised that all these changes and inventions did not occur two centuries ago.

I forgot to add that, as the basket of stage-coaches, in which luggage was then carried, had no springs, your clothes were rubbed all to pieces; and even in the best society one third of the gentlemen at least were always drunk.

Social Position and Money

5.13 *Jane Austen,* Mansfield Park *(1814)*[15]

The novelist Jane Austen (1775–1817) had an acute sensitivity to the gradations of the social order and the nature of early nineteenth-century society. This passage features Miss Crawford, who came from a well-heeled but rootless family, and Edmund Bertram, younger son of a rich and titled landowner destined for a clerical life in the Church of England as vicar of a family "living" (appointed by the owner of the parish, his father), a post that would support him in comfort. The eldest sons of landed families inherited the entire estate (primogeniture), obliging daughters to find husbands and younger sons to join a profession or go into business.

Why might Miss Crawford look down on a clerical life? Why did Edmund Bertram see it as an attractive option? What value might a family gain by having the right to appoint one of its members to be the vicar of a parish on their estate?

Miss Crawford began with, "So you are to be a clergyman, Mr. Bertram. This is rather a surprise to me."

"Why should it surprise you? You must suppose me designed for some profession, and might perceive that I am neither a lawyer, nor a soldier, nor a sailor."

15 Jane Austen, *Mansfield Park*, 3 vols (London, 1814), I, 189–91, 194.

"Very true; but, in short, it had not occurred to me. And you know there is generally an uncle or a grandfather to leave a fortune to the second son."

"A very praise-worthy practice," said Edmund, "but not quite universal. I am one of the exceptions, and *being* one, must do something for myself."

"But why are you to be a clergyman? I thought *that* was always the lot of the youngest, where there were many to choose before him."

"Do you think the church itself never chosen then?"

"*Never* is a black word. But yes, in the *never* of conversation which means *not very often*, I do think it. For what is to be done in the church? Men love to distinguish themselves, and in either of the other lines, distinction may be gained, but not in the church. The clergyman is nothing."

". . . A clergyman cannot be high in state or fashion. . . . But I cannot call that situation nothing, which has charge of all that is of first importance to mankind, individually or collectively considered, temporally and eternally – which has the guardianship of religion and morals . . ."

"I am just as much surprised now as I was at first that you should intend to take [holy] orders. You really are fit for something better. Come, do change your mind. It is not too late. Go into the law."

5.14 *Alexis de Tocqueville,* Journeys to England and Ireland *(May 11, 1835)*[16]

The French politician, aristocrat, and social observer Alexis de Tocqueville (1805–59), author of the brilliant *Democracy in America* (1835–40), traveled extensively in England during the 1830s and analyzed the structure of society. De Tocqueville used the word "rich" more in the French context than the English. Aristocratic fortunes were much more modest in France than in England. By rich he meant prosperous or of independent means, not necessarily the possession of a great fortune.

De Tocqueville saw money, not inherited position, as the dominant source of "power, reputation and glory" in England. Did this make England a more fair and just society than a place where only those born to high rank had such advantages? What made the legal system biased against the poor? Why did de Tocqueville fail to discuss gradations of wealth among the rich?

The whole of English society is based on privileges of money. Demonstration of this:

A man must be rich to be a [Cabinet] Minister, since the style of living expected from him runs him into expenses much greater than what he receives from the State, which is obvious when one thinks of the lavish political world in which he must live.

[16] Alexis de Tocqueville, *Journeys to England and Ireland*, ed. J.P. Mayer (New York, 1968), 77–8.

A man must be rich to get into the House of Commons because election expenses are immense.

A man must be rich to be a Justice of the Peace, Lord Lieutenant, High Sheriff, Mayor, or Overseer of the Poor as these duties are unpaid.

A man must be rich to be a barrister or a judge because the education necessary to enter these professions costs a lot.

A man must be rich to be a clergyman again because the necessary education is expensive.

A man must be rich to be a litigant since one who cannot give bail must go to prison. There is not a country in the world where justice, that first need of peoples, is more the privilege of the rich. Apart from the Justices of the Peace there is no tribunal for the poor man.

Finally, to gain that wealth which is the key to all the rest, the rich man again has great advantages since he can easily raise capital and find opportunities to increase his own wealth or to enrich his relations.

Why should one be surprised at this people's cult of money? Money is the hallmark not of wealth alone, but of power, reputation and glory. So where the Frenchman says: "he has 100,000 francs of income", the Englishman says, "He is worth £5,000 a year."

Manners go even further than the laws in this direction; or rather it is the laws that have molded manners.

Intelligence, even virtue, seem of little account without money. Everything worthwhile is somehow tied up with money. It fills all the gaps that one finds between men, but nothing will take its place.

The English have left the poor but two rights: that of obeying the same laws as the rich, and that of standing on an equality with them if they can obtain equal wealth. But those two rights are more apparent than real, since it is the rich who make the laws and who create for their own or their children's profit, the chief means of getting wealth.

5.15 John Binny, "Thieves and Swindlers" (1862)[17]

Prostitution was a major source of employment for women in Victorian London. The number of people involved is hard to establish, but it was large. This passage is taken from a series of accounts collected by the first important survey of poverty in London, edited by Henry Mayhew (1812–87). Here the upper end of the trade consisting of women who catered to the well-to-do of the West End is described.

What led most women to become prostitutes? What would happen to these women if they became diseased or old? What sort of men might make use of

[17] Henry Mayhew, *London Labour and the London Poor: Those That Will Not Work, volume 4* (London, 1862), 357.

their services? Does the large number of prostitutes raise questions about the nature of Victorian masculinity, social conventions, marriage, home life, and attitudes toward women? What role did class play?

They consist of the better educated and more genteel girls, some of them connected with respectable middle-class families. We do not say they are well-educated and genteel, but either well-educated or genteel. Some of these girls have a fine appearance, and are dressed in high style, yet are poorly educated, and have sprung from an humble origin. Others who are more plainly dressed, have had a lady's education, and some are not so brilliant in their style, who have come from a middle-class home. Many of these girls have at one time been milliners or sewing girls in genteel houses in the West-end, and have been seduced by shopmen, or by gentlemen of the town, and after being ruined in character, or having quarreled with their relatives, may have taken to a life of prostitution; others have been waiting maids in hotels, or in service in good families, and have been seduced by servants in the family, or by gentlemen in the house, and betaken themselves to a wild life or pleasure. A considerable number have come from the provinces to London, with unprincipled young men of their acquaintance, who after a short time have deserted them, and some of them have been enticed by gay gentlemen of the West-end, when on their provincial tours. Others have come to the metropolis in search of work, and been disappointed. After spending the money they had with them, they have resorted to the career of a common prostitute. Others have come from provincial towns, who had not a happy home, with a stepfather or stepmother. Some are young milliners and dressmakers at one time in business in town, but being unfortunate, are now walking the Haymarket. In addition to these, many of them are [mistresses] turned away or abandoned by the persons who supported them, who have recorse to a gay life in the West-end.

5.16 *Jack London,* The People of the Abyss *(1904)*[18]

The American journalist and writer Jack London (1876–1916) dressed up as a working man and did some investigative reporting in the East End (a working-class district) of London in 1902. He discovered the importance of appearance as a class identifier. Then he met a couple of men trying to find a bed in a poorhouse (shelters operated under the authority of the Poor Law) in London. They were skilled workers: a man who had managed a horse-drawn cart and a carpenter. They were among tens of thousands of people seeking assistance, and often not finding it, on any given day.

[18] Jack London, *The People of the Abyss* (New York, 1904), 13–15, 77–83.

Was Jack London's American background likely to affect the way he saw the English? As a writer needing to make his living by selling books, might London be tempted to sensationalize his findings through exaggeration or concentrating only on the worst aspects of the life that he observed? Do clothes act as class indicators today? How efficient was the poor relief system? Explain the reasoning behind the regulations in the poorhouses.

Clothes and class

No sooner was I out on the streets than I was impressed by the difference in status effected by my clothes. All servility vanished from the demeanor of the common people with whom I had contact. Presto! In the twinkling of an eye, so to say, I had become one of them. My frayed and out-at-elbows jacket was the badge and advertisement of my class, which was their class. ... The man in corduroy and dirty neckerchief no longer addressed me as "sir" or "governor." It was "mate" now.... Governor! It smacks of mastery, and power, and high authority – the tribute of a man who is under to the man on top, delivered in the hope that he will let up a bit and ease his weight, which is another way of saying that it is an appeal for alms. ...

Other changes I discovered were wrought in my condition by my new garb. In crossing crowded thoroughfares I found I had to be, if anything, more lively in avoiding vehicles, and it was strikingly impressed upon me that my life had cheapened in direct ratio to my clothes. ... At railway stations, a third-class ticket was now shoved out at me as a matter of course. ...

The Poor House

The Carter was hard put to keep the pace at which we walked (he told me he had eaten nothing that day), but the Carpenter, lean and hungry, his grey and ragged overcoat flapping mournfully in the breeze, swung on a long and tireless stride ... Both kept their eyes upon the pavement ... and every now and then one or the other would stoop and pick something up ...

From the slimy, spittle-drenched sidewalk, they were picking up bits of orange peel, apple skin, and grape stems, and, they were eating them. The pits of greengage plums they cracked between their teeth for the kernels inside. They picked up stray bits of bread the size of peas, apple cores so black and dirty one would not take them to be apple cores, and these things these two men took into their mouths, and chewed them, and swallowed them; and this, between six and seven o'clock in the evening of August 20, year of our Lord 1902, in the heart of the greatest, wealthiest, and most powerful empire the world has ever seen.

... [The Carpenter said] "I go to the [workhouse] for a bed. Must be there by two or three in the afternoon or I won't get in. ... What chance does that give me to look for work? S'pouse I do get into the [place]. Keep me in all day to-morrow, let me out mornin' o' next day. What then? The law sez I can't get in another [workhouse] that night less'n ten miles distant. Have to hurry an' walk to be there that same day. What chance does that give me to look for a job?"

... I asked them what I might expect in the way of treatment, if we succeeded in getting into the Poplar Workhouse ... Having taken a cold bath on entering, I would be given for supper six ounces of bread and "three parts of skilly." "Three parts" means three-quarters of a pint, and "skilly" is a fluid concoction of three quarters of oatmeal stirred into three buckets and a half of hot water.

... [In the morning] "Then you've got your task, pick four pounds of oakum, or clean an' scrub, or break ten to eleven hundredweight o' stones. I don't have to break stones; I'm past sixty you see." ...

"Then comes dinner," he went on. "Eight ounces of bread, one and a arf ounces of cheese, an' cold water. Then you finish your task an' 'ave supper, same as before ... Then to bed, six o'clock, an' next mornin' you're turned loose, provide you've finished your task."

5.17 *Samuel and Sarah Adams,* The Complete Servant *(1825)*[19]

In the mid-nineteenth century more than a million people worked as domestic servants in England and Wales. The household of a substantial landed family would contain the following list of servants, ranked here by annual wage (most servants were also provided with housing, food, and uniforms). Wages were higher both for the most skilled jobs and those that brought the servants most closely into contact with the landowner and his family. The list contains 27 servants. In addition such families would employ "beaters" during shoots to drive game, perhaps a skeleton staff at a London house and at a second country house, governesses and tutors for children, and additional staff at seasonal events during the year. A large fox-hunting establishment would involve additional grooms. A middle-range middle-class family might employ three or more servants, a great aristocratic household over 100. In large houses a number of servants were needed to take care of the needs of the other servants.

Why were so many servants necessary? Which servants could be dispensed with and which ones were necessary to operate even an ordinary middle-class home? What gave employers power over their employees other than wages? Would work be harder in a large or a small household? Where did servants stand in the social structure? Above factory workers? Below craftsmen? At the bottom of the scale?

19 Samuel and Sarah Adams, *The Complete Servant* (London, 1825), 7. I have rearranged the order of the list.

Male French cook	80 guineas[20]
Head gamekeeper	70 guineas with house, food, fuel
Under gamekeeper	52 guineas
Butler	50
Head gardener	40 guineas with house, food, fuel
Female teacher	30 guineas
Assistant gardener	30
Coachman	28
Housekeeper (female)	24
Footman	24
Lady's maid	20
Head nurse	20
Under footman	20
Upper housemaid	15
Under housemaid	14
Kitchen maid	14
Upper laundry maid	14
Lady's groom	12
Second nurse	10
Under laundry maid	10
Still-room maid	9
Scullion	9
Dairy maid	8
Nursery maid	7
Second dairy maid	7
Groom	liveries and gratuity
Nursery room boy	clothes and gratuity

Economic Theory

5.18 David Ricardo, On the Principles of Political Economy and Taxation *(1817)*[21]

David Ricardo (1772–1823) was a successful banker and stockbroker and later Member of Parliament. Influenced by the work of Adam Smith (document 2.10) and Thomas Malthus (documents 2.9 and 2.11), he saw labor as a commodity. His theory of wages was known as the "iron law" due to its rigid structure and cruel implications. The ideas of early "classical" economists long restrained politicians from interfering with the mechanics of the economy.

[20] A guinea was 21 shillings (one pound, one shilling).
[21] *The Works of David Ricardo*, ed. J.R. McCulloch (London, 1888), 50–1, 54, 57–8.

What influence of Smith and Malthus can be discerned in Ricardo's ideas? Who would have been most likely to embrace this philosophy, a manufacturer or a worker? Does the modern "welfare state" accord with Ricardo's views on the Poor Law? Even in Ricardo's day the economy suffered boom and bust cycles. What would he have proposed to do for the unemployed who could not find another job during a depression?

The market price of labor is the price which is really paid for it, from the natural operation of the proportion of the supply to the demand; labor is dear when it is scarce, and cheap when it is plentiful. . . .

It is when the market price of labor exceeds its natural price, that the condition of the laborer is flourishing and happy, that he has it in his power to command a greater proportion of the necessaries and enjoyments of life, and therefore to rear a healthy and numerous family. When, however, by the encouragement which high wages give to the increase of population, the number of laborers is increased, wages again fall to their natural price, and indeed from a re-action sometimes fall below it.

When the market price of labor is below its natural price, the condition of the laborers is most wretched: then poverty deprives them of those comforts which custom renders absolute necessaries. It is only after their privations have reduced their number, or the demand for labor has increased, that the market price of labor will rise to its natural price, and that the laborer will have the moderate comforts which the natural rate of wages will afford. . . .

In the natural advance of society, the wages of labor will have a tendency to fall, as far as they are regulated by supply and demand; for the supply of laborers will continue to increase at the same rate, whilst the demand for them will increase at a slower rate. . . .

These, then, are the laws by which wages are regulated, and by which the happiness of far the greatest part of every community is governed. Like all other contracts, wages should be left to the fair and free competition of the market, and should never be controlled by the interference of the legislature.

The clear and direct tendency of the poor laws, is in direct opposition to these obvious principles: it is not, as the legislation benevolently intended, to amend the condition of the poor, but to deteriorate the condition of both poor and rich; instead of making the poor rich, they are calculated to make the rich poor; and whilst the present laws are in force, it is quite in the natural order of things that the fund for the maintenance of the poor should progressively increase, till it has absorbed all the net revenue of the country, or at least so much of it as the state shall leave to us, after satisfying its own never failing demands for the public expenditure. . . .

The nature of the evil points out the remedy. By gradually contracting the sphere of the poor laws; by impressing on the poor the value of independence, by teaching them that they must look not to systematic or casual charity, but to their own exertions for support, that prudence and forethought are neither unnecessary nor unprofitable virtues, we shall by degrees approach a sounder and more healthful state.

5.19 *Edward Edwards, "The Influence of Free Trade upon the Condition of the Labouring Classes,"* Blackwood's Edinburgh Magazine *(Apr. 27, 1830)*[22]

The "classical" economists were high priests of laissez-faire and open markets (see document 2.10). "Free trade" gradually carried all before it as the nineteenth century progressed, but a powerful protectionist element always remained active. This passage from the Tory *Blackwood's Edinburgh Magazine* was published in 1830. The "last stand" of the protectionists took place in 1845 when they were defeated over repeal of the Corn Laws.

Who would you expect to be opposed to free trade? What economic interests were endangered by laissez-faire? Who benefited from free trade? Why was Britain able to create a genuine free trade system in the second half of the nineteenth century? Why would a party led by aristocrats and supported by great landowners have been sympathetic to the plight of the poor who suffered because of the depression in wages caused by a free market?

There is indeed nothing in the conduct of the advocates of Free Trade so deserving of reprehension, as the hypocritical pretences with which they attempt to disguise or conceal the real object of their measures. If we credit their professions, this amiable and enlightened tribe of philosophers has nothing in view but the common good, and the improvement of the condition of the industrious classes. There is, however, room to think, that they overestimate the ignorance and blindness of the community. . . . Recent and dear bought experience has taught the working classes, that the free competition of [imported products made or harvested by] foreign labor *must* diminish the compensation which they can expect to receive for their toil. The artisans and mechanics of this country have probably by this time become pretty well convinced, that the importation and consumption of the produce of foreign labor has no tendency to ameliorate their condition, and that they at least form no portion of that public whom the Free Trade system is said to benefit.

22 "The Influence of Free Trade upon the Condition of the Labouring Classes," *Blackwood's Edinburgh Magazine*, Apr. 27, 1830, 561.

5.20 *Friedrich Engels, "A Fair Day's Wage for a Fair Day's Work" (May 1881)*[23]

Friedrich Engels (see document 5.8), the friend and associate of Karl Marx, lived and worked in Manchester. He wrote extensively about the relationship between capital and labor.

Why might Engels have called political economy a "science"? According to Engels, what made the competition between labor and capital inherently unfair? What might he have proposed to correct this imbalance? What steps were taken in Victorian Britain to rectify it?

A fair day's wage for a fair day's work? But what is a fair day's wage, and what is a fair day's work? How are they determined by the laws under which modern society exists and develops itself? For an answer to this we must not apply to the science of morals or of law and equity, nor to any sentimental feeling of humanity, justice, or even charity. What is morally fair, what is even fair in law, may be far from being socially fair. Social fairness or unfairness is decided by one science alone – the science which deals with the material facts of production and exchange, the science of political economy.

Now what does political economy call a fair day's wage and a fair day's work? Simply the rate of wages and the length and intensity of a day's work which are determined by competition of employer and employed in the open market. And what are they, when thus determined?

A fair day's wage, under normal conditions, is the sum required to procure to the laborer the means of existence necessary, according to the standard of life of his station and country, to keep himself in working order and to propagate his race. The actual rate of wages, with the fluctuations of trade, may be sometimes above, sometimes below this rate; but, under fair conditions, that rate ought to be the average of all oscillations.

A fair day's work is that length of working day and that intensity of actual work which expends one day's full working power of the workman without encroaching upon his capacity for the same amount of work for the next and following days. . . .

As, according to political economists, wages and working days are fixed by competition, fairness seems to require that both sides should have the same fair start on equal terms. But that is not the case. The Capitalist, if he cannot agree with the Laborer, can afford to wait, and live upon his capital. The workman cannot. He has but wages to live upon, and must therefore take work when, where, and at what terms he can get it. The workman has no fair start. He is fearfully

[23] Friedrich Engels, "A Fair Day's Wage for a Fair Day's Work," *The Labour Standard: An Organ of Industry*, May 7, 1881.

handicapped by hunger. Yet, according to the political economy of the Capitalist class, that is the very pink of fairness. . . .

If trade is bad [laborers] may starve, beg, steal, or go to the workhouse; if trade is good they are ready at hand to expand production; and until the very last man, woman or child of this army of reserve shall have found work – which happens in times of frantic over-production alone – until then will its competition keep down wages, and by its existence alone strengthen the power of Capital in its struggle with Labor. In the race with Capital, Labor is not only handicapped, it has to drag a cannon-ball riveted to its foot. Yet this is fair according to Capitalist political economy.

5.21 *Richard Cobden, speech (Jan. 16, 1846)*[24]

Richard Cobden (1804–65), a Manchester manufacturer, became a great advocate of free trade, which he saw not merely as an economic advancement but as a means of destroying aristocratic power. He helped found and lead the Anti-Corn Law League. He was as much or more interested in moral issues as in economic ones.

Why might he have thought free trade would produce world peace and brotherhood? Why would it destroy the aristocracy? Was free trade likely to diminish the conflict between labor and capital or reduce patriotic feelings? How do you explain the fact that Karl Marx believed a communist revolution would produce the same outcome of international peace and brotherhood as Cobden's unleashed capitalism?

I look farther; I see in the Free-Trade principle that which shall act on the moral world as the principle of the gravitation of the universe, – drawing men together, thrusting aside the antagonism of race, and creed, and language, and uniting us in the bonds of eternal peace . . .. I believe that the effect will be to change the face of the world, so as to introduce a system of government entirely distinct from that which now prevails. I believe that the desire and the motive for large and mighty empires; for gigantic armies and great navies . . . will die away; I believe that such things will cease to be necessary, or to be used when man becomes one family, and freely exchanges the fruits of his labor with his brother man.

24 Richard Cobden, *Speeches on Questions of Public Policy*, ed. John Bright and James E. Thorold Rogers (London, 1878), 187.

5.22 *Samuel Smiles,* Self-Help *(1859)*[25]

At the heart of mid-nineteenth-century Liberalism was the belief in self-reliance. No one articulated the view better than Samuel Smiles (1812–1904), a Scot of humble origins who became a successful journalist. He was an advocate of "classical" economic thinking, free trade, and self-help. His book was one of the great bestsellers in modern British history. Though most popular with the middle classes, many working-class men and women strongly endorsed Smiles's vision of the path to respectability. They rejected both Tory paternalism and state-sponsored social welfare.

Why was this doctrine most appealing to members of the middle classes? Why did it appeal to working men and women? How accurate do you believe his assessment is? Could his own rise from poverty have influenced his philosophy?

"Heaven helps those who help themselves," is a well-worn maxim, embodying in a small compass the results of vast human experience. The spirit of self-help is the root of all genuine growth in the individual; and, exhibited in the lives of many, it constitutes the true source of national vigor and strength. Help from without is often enfeebling in its effects, but help from within invariably invigorates. Whatever is done for men or classes, to a certain extent takes away the stimulus and necessity of doing for themselves; and when men are subjected to over-guidance and over-government, the inevitable tendency is to render them comparatively helpless. . . .

The value of legislation as an agent in human advancement has usually been much overestimated. . . .

National progress is the sum of individual industry, energy, and uprightness, as national decay is of individual idleness, selfishness, and vice. . . . The highest patriotism and philanthropy consist, not so much in altering laws and modifying institutions, as in helping and stimulating men to elevate and improve themselves by their own free and independent action. . . .

Any class of men that lives from hand to mouth will ever be an inferior class. They will necessarily remain impotent and helpless, hanging on to the skirts of society, the sport of times and seasons. Having no respect for themselves, they will fail in securing the respect of others. . . .

"The world," once said Mr. Cobden [see document 5.21], "has always been divided into two classes, – those who saved, and those who have spent, – the thrifty and the extravagant. The building of all the houses, the mills, the bridges, and the ships, and the accomplishment of all other great works which have rendered man civilized and happy, has been done by the savers, the thrifty; and those who have wasted their resources have always been the slaves."

[25] Samuel Smiles, *Self-Help*, ed. Ralph Lytton Bower (New York, 1904), 7–8, 177.

5.23 Robert Giffen, "The Liquidations of 1873–1876," The Fortnightly Review (1877)[26]

The Victorian economy was dynamic, but growth came in bursts followed by recessions and depressions – boom and bust. Capitalism seemed to be inherently unstable. More and more the financial markets of the world were interlocked. While most owners of property could weather these storms with relative ease, working people, who lived on modest wages from week to week, could not. In the following passage a financial journalist, Robert Giffen (1837–1910), who worked as an editor at the *Economist* and the *Times*, describes the depression of 1873 to 1876. Giffen was one of the most distinguished statisticians of his age and became director general of the Board of Trade.

What would Giffen think of Adam Smith (document 2.10), David Ricardo (document 5.18), and Samuel Smiles (document 5.22)? How did being part of an instant global economy (due to the telegraph and undersea cables) change the British economy? How did it affect working people?

An impression prevails that the present stagnation of trade is unprecedented in intensity and duration, and that it is likely to be permanent. A similar impression has often been found to prevail at such times …

… What we are first struck with, in a general survey of the last three or four years, is the universality of the depression. Almost every civilized country has been affected. The beginning was in 1873, with the great Vienna panic and crash in May of that year – a crash which was accompanied by immense agitation throughout Germany and in England, and the occurrence of incidents on almost every European Bourse which only stopped short of panic. Next came a great panic and crash in the autumn of 1873 in the United States … This was accompanied by a renewal of agitation in England, as well as generally on the Continent … The following year was comparatively quiet, but it was marked by great monetary disturbances in South America, and by a great fall in prices both at home, on the Continent, and in the United States. …

This universality, on a comparison with former periods of crisis, may be in fact apparent only, arising from the greatly increased facilities of observation at the present day. … But it is also true that commercial relations are themselves far more extended than was the case before railways and telegraphs. … The London money market appears to be the great equalizer of markets, because it receives the shock of every important business event throughout the world, and transmits the shock of what it feels to every other center.

26 Robert Giffen, "The Liquidations of 1873–1876," *The Fortnightly Review*, n.s., vol. 22, no. 130 (Oct. 1, 1877), 510–12.

5.24 *L.T. Hobhouse,* Liberalism *(1911)*[27]

Liberalism changed character during the course of the nineteenth century (see documents 4.19 and 4.20). Early Liberals were determined supporters of laissez-faire. By the first decade of the twentieth century they were constructing the foundations of the welfare state. The following passage written in 1911 by L.T. Hobhouse (1884–1929), an Oxford academic and editor of the *Manchester Guardian*, attempted to reconcile these positions.

How would Conservatives view state intervention? Did their views, like the Liberals', change over the course of the nineteenth century? Why did Liberalism transform itself?

Apart from monopolies, industry was shackled in the earlier part of the modern period by restrictive legislation in various forms, by navigation laws, and by tariffs. In particular, the tariff was not merely an obstruction to free enterprise, but a source of inequality as between trade and trade. Its fundamental effect is to transfer capital and labor from the objects on which they can be most profitably employed in a given locality, to objects on which they are less profitably employed, by endowing certain industries to the disadvantage of the general consumer. Here, again, the Liberal movement is at once an attack on an obstruction and on an inequality. In most countries the attack has succeeded in breaking down local tariffs and establishing relatively large Free Trade units. It is only in England, and only owing to our early manufacturing supremacy, that it has fully succeeded in overcoming the Protective principle, and even in England the Protectionist reaction would undoubtedly have gained at least a temporary victory but for our dependence on foreign countries for food and the materials of industry. The most striking victory of Liberal ideas is one of the most precarious. At the same time, the battle is one which Liberalism is always preferred to fight over again. It has led to no back stroke, no counter-movement within the Liberal ranks themselves.

It is otherwise with organized restrictions upon industry. The old regulations, which were quite unsuited to the conditions of the time, either fell into desuetude during the eighteenth century, or were formally abolished during the earlier years of the industrial revolution. For a while it seemed as though wholly unrestricted industrial enterprise was to be the progressive watchword, and the echoes of that time still linger. But the old restrictions had not been formally withdrawn before a new process of regulation began. The conditions produced by the new factory system shocked the public conscience; and as early as 1802 we find the first of a long series of laws, out of which has grown an industrial code that year by year follows the life of the operative, in his relations with his employer, into more minute detail. The first stages of this movement were contemplated with doubt and distrust by many

[27] L.T. Hobhouse, *Liberalism* (London, 1911), 15–16.

men of Liberal sympathies. The intention was, doubtless, to protect the weaker party, but the method was that of interference with freedom of contract. Now the freedom of the sane adult individual – even such strong individualists as Cobden recognized that the case of children stood apart – carried with it the right of concluding such agreements as seemed best to suit his own interests, and involved both the right and the duty of determining the lines of his life for himself. Free contract and personal responsibility lay close to the heart of the whole Liberal movement. Hence the doubts felt by so many Liberals as to the regulation of industry by law. None the less, as time has gone on, men of the keenest Liberal sympathies have come not merely to accept but eagerly to advance the extension of public control in the industrial sphere, and of collective responsibility in the matter of the education and even the feeding of children, the housing of the industrial population, the care of the sick and aged, the provision of the means of regular employment. On this side Liberalism seems definitely to have retraced its steps, and we shall have to inquire closely into the question whether the reversal is a change of principle or of application.

HISTORIANS' DEBATES

Optimists and pessimists joust in the "standard of living" controversy. At what point did the working class genuinely begin to benefit from the Industrial Revolution?

The original debate was launched by E.J. Hobsbawm, "The British Standard of Living, 1790–1850," *EcHR* 10 (1957), 46–68, and Robert M. Hartwell, "The Rising Standard of Living in England, 1800–1850," *EcHR* 13 (1961), 397–416; Robert M. Hartwell, "The Standard of Living. An Answer to the Pessimists," *EcHR* 16 (1963), 135–46; E.J. Hobsbawm, "The Standard of Living During the Industrial Revolution. A Discussion," *EcHR* 16 (1963), 119–34; T.S. Ashton, *The Industrial Revolution, 1760–1830*, rev. ed. (London, 1968); T.S. Ashton, "The Standard of Life of the Workers in England, 1790–1830," in *Capitalism and the Historians*, ed. F.A. Hayek, rev. ed. (Chicago, 1962); F.W. Botham and E.H. Hunt, "Wages in Britain during the Industrial Revolution," *EcHR* 40 (1987), 380–99; Nicholas Crafts, "Some Dimensions of the 'Quality of Life' during the British Industrial Revolution," *EcHR* 50 (1997), 617–39; Charles Feinstein, "Pessimism Perpetuated: Real Wages and the Standard of Living in Britain During and After the Industrial Revolution," *JEH* 58 (1998), 625–58; Roderick Floud, Kenneth Wachter, and Annabel Gregory, *Height, Health, and History: Nutritional Status in the United Kingdom, 1750–1980* (Cambridge, 1990); Joel Mokyr, *The Enlightened Economy: An Economic History of Britain 1700–1850* (New Haven, 2009); P. Scholliers, ed., *Real Wages in Nineteenth and Twentieth Century Europe: Historical and Comparative Perspectives* (Oxford, 1989); L.D. Schwarz, "The Standard of Living in the Long Run: London, 1700–1860," *EcHR* 38 (1985), 24–41; Simon Szreter and Graham Mooney, "Urbanization, Mortality, and the Standard of Living Debate," *EcHR* 51 (1998), 84–112; Arthur J. Taylor, ed., *The Standard of Living in Britain in the Industrial Revolution* (London, 1975); E.P. Thompson, *The Making of the English Working Class* (London, 1963); G. Nicholas von Tunzelmann, "The Standard of Living Debate and Optimal Economic Growth," in *The Economics of the Industrial Revolution*, ed. Joel Mokyr (Totowa, NJ, 1985); J.E. Williams, "The British Standard of Living, 1750–1850," *EcHR* 19 (1966), 581–606.

Why was imposing government regulation on child labor, working conditions, safety, and hours in the factories controversial?

Per Bolin-Hort, *Work, Family, and the State: Child Labour and the Organization of Production in the British Cotton Industry, 1780–1920* (Lund, 1989); Hugh Cunningham, *The Children of the Poor: Representations of Childhood since the Seventeenth Century* (Oxford, 1991); Cecil Driver, *Tory Radical: The Life of Richard Oastler* (New York, 1946); Robert Gray, *The Factory Question and Industrial England, 1830–1860* (Cambridge, 1996); J.L. Hammond and Barbara Hammond, *The Town Labourer*, ed. John Lovell (London, 1978); Ursula Henriques, *Before the Welfare State: Social Administration in Early Industrial Britain* (London, 1979); Eric Hopkins, *Childhood Transformed: Working-Class Children in Nineteenth-Century England* (Manchester, 1994); Pamela Horn, *Children's Work and Welfare, 17801–1880s* (London, 1994); Sara Horrell and Jane Humphries, "'The Exploitation of Little Children': Child Labour and the Family Economy in the Industrial Revolution," *EEH* 32 (1995), 485–516; J. Humphries, "Protective Legislation, the Capitalist State and Working-Class Men: The Case of the 1842 Mines Regulation Act," *FR* 7 (1981), 1–31; Clark Nardinelli, *Child Labour and the Industrial Revolution* (Bloomington, 1990); R.E. Peacock, "The Successful Prosecution of the Factory Acts, 1833–1855," *EcHR* 37 (1984), 197–210; E.P. Thompson, *The Making of the English Working Class* (London, 1963); M. Valverde, "'Giving the Female a Domestic Turn': The Social, Legal and Moral Regulation of Women's Work in British Cotton Mills, 1820 to 1850," *JSH* 21 (1988), 619–34; Stewart Angus Weaver, *John Fielden and the Politics of Popular Radicalism, 1832–1847* (Oxford, 1987).

When did the working class and working-class vs. middle-class consciousness emerge?

Craig Calhoun, *The Question of Class Struggle: Social Foundations of Popular Radicalism during the Industrial Revolution* (Chicago, 1982); John Foster, *Class Struggle and the Industrial Revolution: Early Industrial Capitalism in Three English Towns* (London, 1974); E.J. Hobsbawm, *Labouring Men: Studies in the History of Labour* (London, 1964); Gareth Stedman Jones, *Languages of Class: Studies in English Working Class History, 1832–1982* (Cambridge, 1983); Patrick Joyce, *Visions of the People: Industrial England and the Question of Class, 1840–1914* (Cambridge, 1991); Harold Perkin, *The Origins of Modern English Society 1780–1880* (London, 1969); Richard Price, *Labour in British Society: An Interpretive History* (London, 1986); E.P. Thompson, *The Making of the English Working Class* (London, 1963); James Vernon, *Politics and the People: A Study in English Political Culture, c. 1815–1867* (Cambridge, 1993); Dror Wahrman, *Imagining the Middle Class: The Political Representation of Class in Britain, c. 1780–1840* (Cambridge, 1995).

What were the dominant cultural values of the eighteenth- and nineteenth-century economy? Was it a "refined" "gentlemanly capitalism" that merged the values of the landed elite and London financiers or industrial entrepreneurship?

P.J. Cain and Anthony G. Hopkins, *British Imperialism: Innovation and Expansion* (Harlow, 1993); Martin J. Daunton, "Gentlemanly Capitalism and British Industry 1820–1914," *P&P* 122 (1989), 119–58; W.D. Rubinstein and M. Daunton, "Debate: 'Gentlemanly Capitalism' and British Industry 1820–1914," *P&P* 132 (1991), 150–87; Donald C. Coleman, "Gentlemen and Players," *EcHR* 26 (1973), 92–116; Deirdre McCloskey, *The Bourgeois Virtues: Ethics for an Age of Commerce* (Chicago, 2006); David Sunderland, *Social Capital, Trust and the Industrial Revolution, 1780–1880* (London, 2007); F.M.L. Thompson, *Gentrification and the Enterprise Culture: Britain 1780–1980* (Oxford, 2001); Ellis Wasson, "The Penetration of New Wealth into the English Governing Class from the Middle Ages to the First World War," *EcHR* 51 (1998), 25–48; Martin Wiener, *English Culture and the Decline of the Industrial Spirit, 1850–1980*, 2nd ed. (Cambridge, 2004).

Did the New Poor Law make a difference or was it merely a modest modification of the Old Poor Law? Were the poor abandoned or was reform a real step toward ending poverty?

M. Blaug, "The Myth of the Old Poor Law and the Making of the New," *JEH* 23 (1963), 151–84; G.R. Boyer, *An Economic History of the English Poor Law, 1750–1850* (Cambridge, 1990); Mitchell Dean, *The Constitution of Poverty: Toward a Genealogy of Liberal Governance* (London, 1991); P. Dunkley, *The Crisis of the Old Poor Law in England, 1795–1834* (New York, 1982); Derek Fraser, *The Evolution of the British Welfare State*, rev. ed. (London, 1984); Derek Fraser, ed., *The New Poor Law in the Nineteenth Century* (New York, 1976); Gertrude Himmelfarb, *The Idea of Poverty: England and the Early Industrial Age* (New York, 1984); Stephen King, "Poor Relief and English Economic Development Reappraised," *EcHR* 50 (1997), 360–8; Lynn Hollen Lees, *The Solidarities of Strangers: The English Poor Laws and the People, 1700–1948* (Cambridge, 1998); P. Mandler, "The Making of the New Poor Law Redivivus," *P&P* 117 (1987), 131–57; J.D. Marshall, *The Old Poor Law, 1795–1834* (London, 1968); G.W. Oxley, *Poor Relief in England and Wales, 1601–1834* (Newton Abbot, 1974); J. S. Taylor, "The Mythology of the Old Poor Law," *JEH* 29 (1969), 292–7; D. Thomson, "The Decline of Social Welfare: Falling State Support for the Elderly since Early Victorian Times," *AS* 4 (1984), 451–82; Karel Williams, *From Pauperism to Poverty* (London, 1981).

COUNTERFACTUALS TO CONSIDER

What if industrialization had stalled, perhaps because the elite had refused to enact free trade and renovate the economic system? Would Britain have sunk to the rank of a second-rate power, lost India, and never acquired the rest of its empire? Would its people have starved?

What if the Liberal Party had embraced full-blown socialism? Progressive economic and social reforms would have occurred earlier and perhaps the socialism of twentieth-century Britain would have been more radical.

CHAPTER SIX

Culture and Identity

The dialogue between men and women about gender roles took on new intensity during the nineteenth century. Some women became more assertive; some men began to acknowledge inequality between the sexes as unjust, although many men and women preferred paternalism or separate spheres. The logic of liberty and equality, however, made it increasingly hard to defend the status quo. Religion and science were not necessarily incompatible, but many people began to think that something like a zero sum game existed between them. The advance of science seemed to threaten traditional religious beliefs, and, as secularism advanced, religious practice, if not faith, retreated. Many people were made more and more unsettled or pessimistic by ideas of materialism and relativism emanating from the new science. During the second half of the nineteenth century a scientific revolution was underway that would reinvent the way men and women perceived the physical world and their place in it. Many people looked at the technological, economic, scientific, cultural, and political achievements of Victorian Britain and concluded that European civilization was superior to any other in the world due to the process of natural selection discovered by Charles Darwin. Some concluded this gave them a right, even a duty, to rule the globe and that warfare was a natural and healthy means for advancing human wellbeing.

During the 1840s the Irish people suffered a natural catastrophe unprecedented in its scale and horror in modern European history since the Thirty Years War. The Great Famine further deepened a divide between the English and the Irish that was already impelled forward by economic and political oppression, new concepts of nationalism, and other forces that had emerged during the eighteenth century. Ireland also became more deeply divided within itself.

Sources and Debates in Modern British History: 1714 to the Present, First Edition. Edited by Ellis Wasson.

Published 2012 by Blackwell Publishing Ltd.

As you read the documents in this chapter, consider the following questions:

- What role did British society offer to women in the nineteenth century and how did women respond to their circumstances?
- What problems relating to society and life interested Victorian thinkers, and what conclusions did they come to?
- What were the most important characteristics of British and Irish identities in the nineteenth century? How and why did they differ?

Women

6.1 *Samuel Bamford,* Passages in the Life of a Radical and Early Days *(1819)*[1]

The memoirs of the radical Samuel Bamford (see document 4.3) recounted his activities at public meetings agitating for reform during the period of severe unrest in 1819. Many radical groups and trades unions paid scant attention to female participation or rights. However, women had begun to take an active role in public life during the later eighteenth century in the slave abolition movement, and this continued in support of other causes in the following century.

What does this passage tell us about men and women's ideas about female participation in public life? How do you account for the fact that women were not accorded much prominence in the Chartist movement, which failed to call for female suffrage? Nor were trades unions very interested in promoting the welfare of female workers. Why? Why were religious and charitable institutions more ready to welcome female participation and leadership?

Numerous meetings [took place] in various parts of the country. . . . I, in the course of an address, insisted on the right, and the propriety also, of females who were present at such assemblages voting by a show of hand for or against resolutions. This was a new idea; and the women, who attended numerously . . ., were mightily pleased with it. The men being nothing dissentient, when the resolution was put the women held up their hands amid much laughter; and ever from that time females voted with the men at the Radical meetings. I was not then aware that the new impulse thus given to political movement would in a short time be applied to charitable and religious purposes. But it was so; our females voted at every subsequent meeting; it became the practice, female unions were formed, with their chairwomen, committees, and other officials; and from us the

[1] Henry Dunckley, *Bamford's Passages in the Life of a Radical and Early Days* (London, 1893), II, 141–2.

practice was soon borrowed, very judiciously no doubt, and applied in a greater or less degree to the promotion of religious and charitable institutions.

6.2 *Daniel O'Connell, speech in the House of Commons (June 3, 1833)*[2]

Daniel O'Connell (1775–1847, see document 6.22) was the leading Irish nationalist politician of the first half of the nineteenth century. He spoke to the House of Commons about the anti-slavery petitions submitted to Parliament largely signed by women in 1833. Why did O'Connell assume the slave abolition movement was a cause likely to attract women's interest? Would he have welcomed women becoming active in other political movements such as the fight for Irish Home Rule, women's suffrage, and female members of Parliament?

. . . He would say – and he cared not who the person was of whom he said it – he would say, that that person had had the audacity to taunt the maids and matrons of England with the offence of demanding that their fellow-subjects in another clime should be emancipated. He would say nothing of the bad taste and the bad feeling which such a taunt betrayed – he would merely confine himself to the expression of an opinion, in which he was sure that every Member of that House would concur with him, namely, that if ever the females had a right to interfere, it was upon that occasion. Assuredly, the crying grievance of slavery must have sunk deep into the hearts, and strongly excited the feelings of the British nation, before the females of this country could have laid aside the retiredness of their character to come forward and interfere in political matters . . . and, he hesitated not to say, that the man, whoever he might be, who had taunted the females of Great Britain with having petitioned Parliament – the man who could do that, was almost as great a ruffian as the wielder of the cart-whip.

6.3 *Caroline Sheridan Norton,* The Separation of Mother and Child by the Law of "Custody of Infants," Considered *(1838)*[3]

Caroline Norton (1808–77) had her three sons taken away from her by an abusive, drunkard husband. Her response was a successful campaign to persuade Parliament to enact a child custody law giving rights to mothers, which it did in 1839. After their separation her husband confiscated her

[2] *Parliamentary Debates*, XVIII, June 3, 1833, 309.

[3] Caroline Sheridan Norton, *The Separation of Mother and Child by the Law of "Custody of Infants," Considered* (London, 1838), 1–2, 24.

earnings as an author as his rightful property. Her response was to run up bills, and she then directed tradesmen who wished to collect their money to him. She was also an advocate of divorce reform.

On what basis did Norton make her case? Did the response to her campaign suggest changing attitudes among men toward women's rights or merely an adjustment to the system to punish unworthy men?

The custody of legitimate children, is held to be the right of the Father *from the hour of their birth*: to the utter exclusion of the Mother, whose separate claim has no legal existence, and is not recognized by the Courts. No circumstance can modify or alter this admitted right of the father: though he should be living in open adultery, and his wife legally separated from him on that account. He is responsible to no one for his motives, should he desire entirely to exclude his wife from all access to her children . . . the construction of the law being, that [the courts] have no power to interfere with the exercise of the Father's right. . . .

The Father's right is absolute and paramount and can no more be affected by the Mother's claim, than if she had no existence. . . .

Surely in this country, where hatred of all oppression is made a national boast, where if a master were to strike his footboy, an action would lie for assault and damages – where even offensive and violent language subjects a man to a penalty; in this country, and at this time, when all liberal opinions are encouraged and fostered, it is a strange and crying shame, that the only despotic right an Englishman possesses is to wrong the mother of his children!

6.4 *Mrs John Sandford,* Woman in Her Social and Domestic Character *(1837)*[4]

Many women supported the subordination of their own sex. Mrs John Sandford (1797–1853, née Elizabeth Poole) wrote an advice book for women asserting their inferiority to males. Due to the existing system of morality, women had more to lose than men and were likely to defend conventional gender relations, which many female authors did. Her support for a purely domestic role for women was popular, and her book went through many editions.

What would Mrs Sanford have regarded as the principal tasks of women? Why was she concerned about changes taking place and can you account for the change? Why would she have argued that those responsibilities were critical to society? Would she have supported women becoming leaders of

[4] Mrs John Sandford, *Woman in Her Social and Domestic Character* (London, 1831), 1–2, 13, 63, 84, 169.

philanthropic efforts? What would she have said about the education of women? Taking into consideration her views, how do you account for her publishing a book? Who was likely to buy it?

The sentiment for women has undergone a change. The romantic passion, which once almost deified her, is on the decline; and it is by intrinsic qualities that she must now inspire respect. . . .

A really sensible woman feels her dependence. She does what she can, but she is conscious of inferiority, and therefore grateful for support. She knows she is the weaker vessel, and that it is as such that she should receive honor; and, in this view, her weakness is an attraction, not a blemish. . . .

Nature has assigned her a subordinate place, as well as subordinate powers; and it is far better that she should feel this, and should not arrogate the superiority of the other sex, whilst she claims the privileges of her own.

The character of woman, though inferior, is not less interesting than that of man. On the contrary, her very defects render her an object of solicitude; and if they disqualify her for some situations, they help to point out those for which she is really fitted. . . .

Want of judgment is, indeed, one of the most common defects in female character, and it is in discernment, rather than in capacity, that the inferiority of women consists. She chose wrong at first [a reference to Adam and Eve], and liability to error seems entailed upon her. It is where judgment is required that she is most apt to fail. . . .

A woman must be domestic. Her heart must be at home. She must not be on the look-out for excitement of any kind, but must find her pleasure as well as her occupation in the sphere which is assigned to her.

6.5 *John Stuart Mill,* The Subjection of Women *(1869)* [5]

The greatest political philosopher of Victorian Britain was John Stuart Mill (1806–73). He was the son of James Mill, an author of considerable distinction in his own right and disciple of Bentham. Mill the younger produced many remarkable works including a gripping autobiography. He became an early champion of women's rights and proposed in 1867, as a Member of Parliament, that female suffrage be enacted. He argued in 1869, in a book written with his stepdaughter Helen Taylor, that male dominance was illiberal and that women were not innately inferior to men.

Compare and contrast this excerpt with that written by Mary Wollstonecraft (document 3.14). Why did the movement to achieve equality

[5] John Stuart Mill, *The Subjection of Women*, 2nd ed. (New York, 1911), 1, 9–10, 28–9, 32–3.

for women choose the electoral franchise as its goal? Why did the movement only gain significant support and attention during the second half of the nineteenth century? How did Mill account for women accepting subordination?

The principle which regulates the existing social relations between the two sexes – the legal subordination of one sex to the other – is wrong in itself, and now one of the chief hindrances to human improvement; and . . . it ought to be replaced by a principle of perfect equality, admitting no power or privilege on the one side, nor disability on the other. . . .

In the first place, the opinion in favor of the present system, which entirely subordinates the weaker sex to the stronger, rests upon theory only; for there never has been trial made of any other: as that experience, in the sense in which it is vulgarly opposed to theory, cannot be pretended to have pronounced any verdict. And in the second place, the adoption of this system of inequality never was the result of deliberation, or forethought, or any social ideas, or any notion whatever of what conduced to the benefit of humanity or the good order of society. It arose simply from the fact that from the very earliest twilight of human society, every woman (owing to the value attached to her by men, combined with her inferiority in muscular strength) was found in a state of bondage to some man. . . .

But, it will be said, the rule of men over women differs from all these others in not being a rule of force: it is accepted voluntarily; women make no complaint, and are consenting parties to it. In the first place, a great number of women do not accept it. Ever since there have been women able to make their sentiments known by their writings (the only mode of publicity which society permits them), an increasing number of them have recorded protests against their present social condition: and recently many thousands of them, headed by the most eminent women known to the public, have petitioned Parliament for their admission to the parliamentary suffrage. The claim of women to be educated as solidly, and in the same branches of knowledge, as men is urged with growing intensity, and with a great prospect of success; while the demand for their admission into professions and occupations hitherto closed against them becomes every year more urgent. Though there are not in this country, as there are in the United States, periodical Conventions and an organized party to agitate for the Rights of Women, there is a numerous and active Society organized and managed by women, for the more limited object of obtaining the political franchise. . . .

When we put together three things – first, the natural attraction between opposite sexes; secondly, the wife's entire dependence on the husband, every privilege and pleasure she has being wither his gift, or depending entirely on his will; and lastly, that the principal object of human pursuit, consideration, and all objects of social ambition, can in general be sought or obtained by her only through him, it would be a miracle if the object of being attractive to men had not become the polar star of feminine education and formation of character. And this great means of influence over the minds of women having been acquired, an instinct of selfishness made men avail themselves of it to the utmost as a means of holding women in subjection, by representing to them meekness, submissiveness, and resignation of all individual will into the hands of a man, as an essential part of sexual attractiveness. Can it be doubted that any of the other yokes which mankind have succeeded in breaking would have subsisted till now if the same means had existed, and had been as sedulously used to bow down their minds to it?

6.6 *William Gladstone, second Midlothian speech (Nov. 26, 1879)*[6]

During his celebrated sequence of speeches of the "Midlothian Campaign" in November 1879 Gladstone (see documents 4.13 and 4.19) articulated many of the core attitudes of Victorian Liberalism. In this passage in which he laid down the idea that foreign policy was above all a moral issue (he was attacking Disraeli over the Ottoman atrocities in Bulgaria) he also revealed his conception of women's role in society.

What does it tell us about late Victorian society that a political leader making a campaign speech felt obliged specifically to address the women in the audience? What did Gladstone assume was the correct role for women in politics? What is the tone of this passage? Would he have supported the enfranchisement of women?

With regard to the special occasion which has brought us here to-night, I understand it to be your wish that I should use some words addressed to the particular share that ladies, and that women, may be thought to have in the crisis to-day. I use the expression women with greater satisfaction than the former one which I uttered, the name of ladies; because it is to them, not only in virtue of a particular station, not only by reason of their possessing a greater portion of the goods of life than may have been granted to the humbler classes of society, that I appeal. I appeal to them in virtue of the common nature which runs through us all. And I am very glad, sir, that you have introduced to us with a special notice the factory girls of the place, who on this occasion have been desirous to testify their kindly feelings. . . .

I speak to you, ladies, as women; and I do think and feel that the present political crisis has to do not only with human interests at large, but especially with those interests which are most appropriate, and ought to be most dear, to you. The harder and sterner, and drier lessons of politics are little to your taste. You do not concern yourselves with abstract propositions. It is that side of politics, which is associated with the heart of man, that I must call your side of politics.

6 William Gladstone, *Political Speeches in Scotland, November and December 1879* (London, 1879), 89–90.

6.7 *Beatrice Potter Webb,* Women and the Factory Acts, Fabian Tract No. 67 *(1896)*[7]

Beatrice Potter Webb (1858–1947) became a social scientist and Fabian (see document 4.21) socialist. Along with her husband she helped found the London School of Economics (LSE) in 1895. The suffragettes, who placed the equal treatment of men and women in the political arena as their highest priority, came into conflict with those, like Webb, who wanted to protect women from excessive hours and physical endangerment in the workplace.

Why did the suffragettes ignore the problems confronted by women doing manual labor? Why did the trades unions give women little support in the workplace? Would Webb have been in favor of giving women the vote? How did her belief in socialism affect her attitude toward the suffragettes?

The discussions on the Factory Act of 1895 raised once more all the old arguments about factory legislation, but with a significant new cleavage. This time legal regulation was demanded, not only by all the organizations of working women whose labor was affected, but also by, practically, all those actively engaged in Factory Act administration. The four women Factory Inspectors unanimously confirmed the opinion of their male colleagues. Of all the classes having any practical experience of Factory legislation, only one – that of the employers – was ranged against the Bill, and that not unanimously. But the employers had the powerful aid of most of the able and devoted ladies who have usually led the cause of women's enfranchisement, and whose strong theoretic objection to Factory legislation caused many of the most important clauses in the Bill to be rejected. . . .

Unfortunately, working women have less power to obtain legislation than middle-class women have to obstruct it.

. . . We are so accustomed, in the middle-class, to see men and women engaged in identical work, as teachers, journalists, authors, painters, sculptors, comedians, singers, musicians, medical practitioners, clerks, or what not, that we almost inevitably assume the same state of things to exist in manual labor and manufacturing industry. But this is far from being the case. . . . There is no more chance of our having our houses built by women than of our getting our floors scrubbed by men. And even in those industries which employ both men and women, we find them sharply divided in different departments, working at different processes, and performing different operations.

[Moreover] women are far more helpless in the labor market, and much less able to enforce their own common rule by trade unionism.

7 Mrs Sidney [Beatrice Potter] Webb, *Women and the Factory Acts, Fabian Tract No. 67* (London, 1896), 3–15.

JUSTICE.

Figure 6.1 "Victorian Era: Justice," *Punch*, Jan. 30, 1901. Britannia wields a sword to protect non-European women from their men. Punch Cartoon Library 1857.09.12.109. Reproduced with Permission of Punch Ltd, www.punch.co.uk

In this cartoon "Justice"/"Britannia" is illustrated protecting Asian women from their own men. Many ambiguities arise in the engraving. Both "Justice" and "Britannia" were, of course, women, as was the queen-empress of the Victorian empire. The "white" race is portrayed as superior to a darker-skinned race because they are protecting women, even if the latter are darker-skinned ones. What does the artist intend to convey? What did he unintentionally tell us about the British and their empire and their attitudes toward women? How would Social Darwinists (documents 6.14–17) view this picture?

6.8 E. Sylvia Pankhurst, The Suffragette *(1910)*[8]

Many women sacrificed comfort, dignity, and even their lives for the cause of gaining female suffrage. Others committed acts of terror including the destruction of property and attempted assassinations. In 1910 Lady Constance

8 E. Sylvia Pankhurst, *The Suffragette: The History of the Women's Militant Suffrage Movement 1905–1910* (London, 1912), 483–7.

Lytton (1869–1923), a member of an important aristocratic family, deliberately provoked mistreatment by the authorities after hunger strikes by imprisoned suffragettes were met with forced feeding. The suffragette movement was supported by activists from among all classes in society. This account was written by Sylvia Pankhurst (1882–1960), the daughter of the most celebrated leader of the movement, Emmeline Pankhurst.

What was the purpose of this publication? Do you think it gives an accurate account of what happened? Why was an aristocratic person chosen as a subject to write about? Why would a Liberal government minister respond to her protest as he did?

Now Lady Constance Lytton, in spite of her fragile constitution and the [heart] disease from which she suffered, again determined to place herself beside the women in the fighting ranks who were enduring the greatest hardship . . . [In front of a prison where suffragettes were being held] Lady Constance called the people to follow her to its gates, and demand the release of the tortured women. Then she moved forward and, as she had foreseen, she was immediately placed under arrest . . .. Lady Constance had disguised herself by cutting her hair, wearing spectacles, and dressing herself in poor plain garments, and now she gave Jane Warton, seamstress, as her name and occupation. Next morning she was sentenced to fourteen days' hard labor without the option of a fine . . . On arriving at the prison . . . they made the usual claim to be treated as political prisoners, and, on this being refused, signified their intention of refusing to conform to any of the prison rules. Thereupon they were forcibly stripped by the wardresses and dressed in prison clothes. A five o'clock, on Tuesday, the doctor entered Lady Constance Lytton's cell with four wardresses and the forcible feeding apparatus. Then, without testing her heart or feeling her pulse, though she had not been medically examined since entering the prison, he ordered that she should be placed in position. . . . The doctor then produced a wooden and a steel gag and told her that he would not use the latter, which would hurt, unless she resisted him; but, as she would not unlock her teeth, he threw the milder wooden instrument aside and pried her mouth open with the steel one. Then the stomach tube was forced down and the whole hateful feeding business was gone through. "The reality surpassed all that I had anticipated," she said. "It was a living nightmare of pain, horror and revolting degradation. The sense is of being strangled, suffocated by the thrust down of the large rubber tube, which arouses great irritation in the throat and nausea in the stomach. The anguish and effort of retching whilst the tube is forcibly pressed back into the stomach and the natural writhing of the body restrained, defy description. I forgot what I was in there for, I forgot women, I forgot everything, except my own sufferings, and I was completely overcome by them." The doctor, annoyed by her one effort to resist, affected to consider her distress assumed, and struck her contemptuously on the cheek as he rose to leave . . . When she was fed the second time the vomiting was more excessive and the doctor's clothes suffered. He was angry and left the cell hastily, saying, "You did that on purpose. If you do it again tomorrow I shall feed you twice."

... The third time she was fed she vomited continuously, but the doctor kept pouring in more food until she was seized with a violet fit of shivering. Then he became alarmed. He hastily told the wardresses to lay her on the floor and called in his assistant to test her heart, but, after a brief and superficial investigation, it was pronounced "quite sound" and the pulse "steady."

... [After her release] Lady Constance Lytton now sent a careful statement to Mr. Gladstone [William Gladstone's son, the home secretary] asserting that forcible feeding was performed with unnecessary cruelty and without proper care. He declared that all her charges were unfounded, and the visiting magistrates, having held a one-sided enquiry into the matter, announced that the regulations had been carried out with the greatest care and consideration.

Victorian Thinkers

6.9 *John Stuart Mill,* Considerations on Representative Government *and* On Liberty *(1859 and 1861)*[9]

Over the course of his life Mill (see document 6.5) gradually moved from the laissez-faire utilitarianism of his father to more collectivist Liberalism heading toward socialism. What were Mill's greatest concerns about liberty? How can his emphasis on liberty be reconciled with state intervention to reduce poverty? Are his ideas too unrealistic to be implemented? Is it possible to defend effectively against popular hostility to unconventional ideas or activities? Does Mill's emphasis on individualism undermine society's ability to cooperate in the face of modern challenges such as global warming? How might a Marxist or Conservative have responded to Mill?

Considerations on Representative Government

One of the greatest dangers, therefore, of democracy, as of all other forms of government, lies in the sinister interest of the holders of power: it is the danger of class legislation, of government intended for (whether really effecting it or not) the immediate benefit of the dominant class, to the lasting detriment of the whole. And one of the most important questions demanding consideration, in determining the best constitution of a representative government, is how to provide efficacious securities against this evil.

[9] John Stuart Mill, *Considerations on Representative Government* (London, 1861), 127–30 and *On Liberty* (London, 1865), 2–8.

If we consider as a class, politically speaking, any number of persons who have the same sinister interest, – that is, whose direct and apparent interest points towards the same description of bad measures – the desirable object would be that no class, and no combination of classes likely to combine, should be able to exercise a preponderant influence in the government. A modern community, not divided within itself by strong antipathies of race, language, or nationality, may be considered as in the main divisible into two sections, which, in spite of partial variations, correspond on the whole with two divergent directions of apparent interest. Let us call them (in brief general terms) laborers on the one hand, employers of labor on the other: including however along with employers of labor, not only retired capitalists, and the possessors of inherited wealth, but all that highly paid description of laborers (such as the professions) whose education and way of life assimilate them with the rich, and whose prospect and ambition it is to raise themselves into that class. With the laborer, on the other hand, may be ranked those smaller employers of labor, whose interest, habits, and educational impressions, are assimilated in wishes, tastes, and objects to the laboring classes; comprehending a large proportion of petty tradesmen. In a state of society thus composed, if the representative system could be made ideally perfect, and if it were possible to maintain it in that state, its organization must be such, that these two classes, manual laborers and their affinities on one side, employers of labor and their affinities on the other, should be, in the arrangement of the representative system, equally balanced, each influencing about an equal number of votes in Parliament: since, assuming that the majority of each class, in any difference between them, would be mainly governed by their class interests, there would be a minority of each in whom that consideration would be subordinate to reason, justice, and the good of the whole; and this minority of either, joining with the whole of the other, would turn the scale against any demands of their own majority which were not such as ought to prevail. The reason why, in any tolerably constituted society, justice and the general interest mostly in the end carry their point, is that the separate and selfish interests of mankind are almost always divided; some are interested in what is wrong, but some, also, have their private interest on the side of what is right: and those who are governed by higher considerations, though too few and weak to prevail alone, usually after sufficient discussion and agitation become strong enough to turn the balance in favor of the body of private interests which is on the same side with them. The representative system ought to be so constituted as to maintain this state of things: it ought not to allow any of the various sectional interests to be so powerful as to be capable of prevailing against truth and justice and the other sectional interests combined.

On Liberty

The will of the people, moreover, practically means the will of the most numerous or the most active *part* of the people; the majority, or those who succeed in making themselves accepted as the majority; the people, consequently, *may* desire to oppress a part of their number; and precautions are as much needed against this as against any other abuse of power. The limitation, therefore, of the power of government over individuals loses none of its importance when the holders of power are regularly accountable to the community, that is, to the strongest party therein. . . . "The tyranny of the majority" is now generally included among the evils against which society requires to be on its guard.

Like other tyrannies, the tyranny of the majority was at first, and is still, vulgarly, held in dread, chiefly as operating through the acts of the public authorities. But reflecting persons perceive that when society is itself the tyrant – society collectively, over the separate individuals who compose it – its means of tyrannizing are not restricted to the acts which it may do by the hands of its political functionaries. Society can and does execute its own mandates: and if it issues wrong mandates instead of right, or any mandates at all in things with which it ought not to meddle, it practices social tyranny more formidable than many kinds of political oppression, since, though not usually upheld by such extreme penalties, it leaves fewer means of escape, penetrating much more deeply into the details of life, and enslaving the soul itself. Protection, therefore, against the tyranny of the magistrate is not enough: there needs protection also against the tyranny of the prevailing opinion and feeling; against the tendency of society to impose, by other means than civil penalties, its own ideas and practices as rules of conduct on those who dissent from them; to fetter the development, and, if possible, prevent the formation, of any individuality not in harmony with its ways, and compel all characters to fashion themselves upon the model of its own. . . .

Though this proposition is not likely to be contested in general terms, [but] . . . where to place the limit – how to make the fitting adjustment between individual independence and social control – is a subject on which nearly everything remains to be done. All that makes existence valuable to anyone, depends on the enforcement of restraints upon the actions of other people. Some rules of conduct, therefore, must be imposed, by law in the first place and by opinion on many things which are not fit subjects for the operation of the law. What these rules should be, is the principal question in human affairs. . . .

Whenever there is an ascendant class, a large portion of the morality of the country emanates from its class-interests, and its feelings of class superiority. . . .

In England, from the peculiar circumstances of our political history, though the yoke of opinion is perhaps heavier, that of law is lighter than in most other countries in Europe; and there is considerable jealousy of direct interference, by the legislative or executive power, with private conduct; not so much from any just regard for the independence of the individual, as from the still subsisting habit of looking on the government as representing an opposite interest to the public. The majority have not yet learned to feel the power of the government their power, or its opinions their opinions. When they do so, individual liberty will probably be as much exposed to invasion from the government, as it already is from public opinion. But, as yet, there is a considerable amount of feeling ready to be called forth against any attempt of the law to control individuals in things in which they have not hitherto been accustomed to be controlled by it. . . . Some, whenever they see any good to be done, or evil to be remedied, would willingly instigate the government to undertake the business; while others prefer to bear almost any amount of social evil, rather than add one to the departments of human interests amenable to government control. . . .

The object of this Essay is to assert one very simple principle . . . That principle is, that the sole end for which mankind are warranted, individually or collectively, in interfering with the liberty of action of any of their number, is self-protection. That the only purpose for which power can be rightfully exercised over any member of a civilized community, against his will, is to prevent harm to others. His own good, either physical or moral, is not sufficient warrant. . . . The only part of the conduct of anyone, for which he is amenable to society, is that which concerns others. In the part which merely concerns himself, his independence is, of right, absolute. Over himself, over his own body and mind, the individual is sovereign.

This, then, is the appropriate region of human liberty. It comprises, first, the inward domain of consciousness; demanding liberty of conscience, in the most comprehensive sense; liberty of thought and feeling; absolute freedom of opinion and sentiment on all subjects, practical or speculative, scientific, moral, or theological. The liberty of expressing and publishing opinions may seem to fall under a different principle, since it belongs to that part of the conduct of an individual which concerns other people; but, being almost of as much importance as the liberty of thought itself, and resting in great part on the same reasons, is practically inseparable from it. Secondly, the principle requires liberty of tastes and pursuits; of framing the plan of our life to suit our own character; of doing as we like, subject to such consequences as may follow: without impediment from our fellow creatures, so long as what we do does not harm them, even though they should think our conduct foolish, perverse, or wrong. Thirdly, from this liberty, within the same limits, of combination among individuals; freedom to unite, for any purpose not involving harm to others; the persons combining being supposed to be of full age, and not forced or deceived.

No society in which these liberties are not, on the whole, respected, is free, whatever may be its form of government. . . .

There is . . . in the world at large an increasing inclination to stretch unduly the powers of society over the individual, both by the force of opinion and even by that of legislation; and as the tendency of all the changes taking place in the world is to strengthen society, and diminish the power of the individual; this encroachment is not one of the evils which tend spontaneously to disappear, but, on the contrary, to grow more and more formidable. The disposition of mankind, whether as rulers or as fellow-citizens, to impose their own opinions and inclinations as a rule of conduct on others, is so energetically supported by some of the best and some of the worst feelings incident to human nature, that it is hardly ever kept under restraint by anything but want of power.

6.10 *John Henry Newman,* Apologia pro Vita Sua *(1864–5)*[10]

Victorian intellectuals continued to consider religion a central aspect of life and civilization. John Henry Newman (1801–90), an Oxford academic and Anglican clergyman who converted to Roman Catholicism in 1845 and later became a cardinal, was one of the leaders of the "Oxford Movement." He listed his three key propositions in his celebrated book *Apologia pro Vita Sua,* in which he attempted to identify the principles that led to his conversion. In some respects a throwback to the Romantics, he believed "rationalism is the great evil of the day."

How did Newman view his own time? Why might he have been brought up to be prejudiced against Roman Catholics? Were his arguments likely to persuade rationalists? Why might he have been reluctant to announce his conversion publicly?

1. First was the principle of dogma: my battle was with liberalism; by liberalism I meant the anti-dogmatic principle and its developments. This was the first point on which I was certain. . . . I have changed in many things: in this I have not. From the age of fifteen, dogma has been the fundamental principle of my religion. I know no other religion. . . . Religion, as a mere sentiment, is to me a dream and a mockery. As well can there be filial love without the fact of a father, as devotion without the fact of a Supreme Being. . . .

2. Secondly, I was confident in the truth of a certain definite religious teaching, based upon this foundation of dogma; viz., that there was a visible Church with sacraments and rites which are the channels of invisible grace. . . .

3. But now, as to the third point on which I stood in 1833, and which I have utterly renounced and trampled upon since, my view then of the Church of Rome; – I will speak about it as exactly as I can. When I was young, as I have said already, and after I was grown up, I thought the Pope to be Antichrist. . . . I thought the Church of Rome was bound up with the cause of Antichrist by the Council of Trent [1545–63; shaped the Counter-Reformation]. When it was that in my deliberate judgment I gave up the notion altogether in any shape, that some special reproach was attached to her name, I cannot tell; but I had a shrinking from renouncing it, even when my reason so ordered me, from a sort of conscience or prejudice, I think up to 1843.

[10] John Henry Newman, *Apologia pro Vita Sua,* new ed. (London, 1904), 30–3.

6.11 *Alfred Russel Wallace,* Darwinism *(1889)*[11]

Alfred Russel Wallace (1823–1913) independently developed a theory of survival of the fittest while the biologist Charles Darwin (1809–82) was working on his theory of evolution. He became an important interpreter of Darwinism. Many people were troubled by the implicit challenge to the biblical story of creation.

Why might Darwinism have been almost universally accepted in Britain and Western Europe by 1914 but still encounter serious resistance in the United States? Why can one argue that Darwin was the most influential Englishman of the nineteenth century?

The point I wish especially to urge is this. Before Darwin's work appeared, the great majority of naturalists, and almost without exception the whole literary and scientific world, held firmly to the belief that *species* were realities, and had not been derived from other species by any process accessible to us . . . and to have originated by some totally unknown process so far removed from ordinary reproduction that it was usually spoken of as "special creation." There was, then no question of the origin of families, orders, and classes, because the very first step of all, the "origin of species," was believed to be an insoluble problem. But now this is all changed. The whole scientific and literary world, even the whole educated public, accepts, as a matter of common knowledge, the origin of species from other allied species by the ordinary process of natural birth. The idea of special creation or any altogether exceptional mode of production is absolutely extinct! . . . And this vast, this totally unprecedented change in public opinion has been the result of the work of one man, and was brought about in the short space of twenty years! This is the answer to those who continue to maintain that the "origin of species" is not yet discovered; that there are still doubts and difficulties; that there are divergencies of structure so great that we cannot understand how they had their beginning. We may admit all this, just as we may admit that there are enormous difficulties in the way of a complete comprehension of the origin and nature of all parts of the solar system and of the stellar universe. But we claim for Darwin that he is the Newton of natural history, and that, just so surely as that the discovery and demonstration by Newton of the law of gravitation established order in place of chaos and laid a sure foundation for all future study of the starry heavens, so surely has Darwin, by his discovery of the law of natural selection and his demonstration of the great principle of the preservation of useful variations in the struggle for life, not only thrown a flood of light on the

[11] Alfred Russel Wallace, *Darwinism: An Exposition of the Theory of Natural Selection* (London, 1901), 8–9.

process of development of the whole organic world, but also established a firm foundation for all future study of nature.

6.12 *Charles Darwin,* On the Origin of Species *(1859)*[12]

Charles Darwin's *On the Origin of Species* is one of the most important books published in English in the nineteenth century. His theory of evolution reshaped natural science and, more broadly, the way human beings perceive existence. His ideas moved the modern world toward a more materialist conception of life. Everything from nationalism to Marxism owes something to this reconfiguration of mankind's view of itself. Darwin's work was perceived by some Christians as a direct challenge to religion, but to many people his discoveries did not seem aimed at anything other than the expansion of human knowledge.

How did Malthus's thought (documents 2.9 and 2.11) influence Darwin? To what degree was Darwin's work a product of the Enlightenment? Can Darwinian theory be reconciled with Christianity? Could Adam Smith's ideas (document 2.10) about the market have influenced Darwin? Discuss examples of the influence of Darwin on the modern world.

The Struggle for Existence amongst all organic beings throughout the world, which inevitably follows from the high geometrical ratio of their increase, will be considered. This is the doctrine of [Thomas Robert] Malthus, applied to the whole animal and vegetable kingdoms. As many more individuals of each species are born than can possibly survive; and as, consequently, there is a frequently recurring struggle for existence, it follows that any being, if it vary however slightly in any manner profitable to itself, under the complex and sometimes varying conditions of life, will have a better chance of surviving, and thus be *naturally selected.* From the strong principle of inheritance, any selected variety will tend to propagate its new modified form. . . .

All that we can do, is to keep steadily in mind that each organic being is striving to increase in a geometrical ratio: that each at some period of its life, during some season of the year, during each generation or at intervals, has to struggle for life and to suffer great destruction. When we reflect on this struggle, we may console ourselves with the full belief that the war of nature is not incessant, that no fear is felt, that death is generally prompt, and that the vigorous, the healthy, and the happy survive and multiply.

12 Charles Darwin, *On the Origin of Species* (London, 1902), 4, 72.

6.13 *Charles Darwin,* The Descent of Man *(1871)*[13]

Darwin went on in a subsequent book, *The Descent of Man,* to link man to lower animals, which caused a considerable stir. What was Darwin's evidence to support his theories? What was Darwin's view of nature? Was Darwinism a challenge to Marxism? How would Cardinal Newman (document 6.10) have argued against Darwin?

The main conclusion here arrived at, and now held by many naturalists who are well competent to form a sound judgment, is that man is descended from some less highly organized form. The grounds on which this conclusion rests will never be shaken, for the close similarity between man and the lower animals in embryonic development, as well as in innumerable points of structure and constitution, both of high and the most trifling importance, – the rudiments which he retains, and the abnormal reversions to which he is occasionally liable, – are facts which cannot be disputed. They have long been known, but until recently they told us nothing with respect to the origin of man. Now when viewed by the light of our knowledge of the whole organic world, their meaning is unmistakable. The great principle of evolution stands up clear and firm, when these groups of facts are considered in connection with others, such as the mutual affinities of the members of the same group, their geographical distribution in past and present times, and their geological succession. . . .

I am aware that the conclusions arrived at in this work will be denounced by some as highly irreligious; but he who denounces them is bound to show why it is more irreligious to explain the origin of man as a distinct species by descent from some lower form, through the laws of variation and natural selection, than to explain the birth of the individual through the laws of ordinary reproduction. The birth both of the species and of the individual are equally parts of that grand sequence of events, which our minds refuse to accept as the result of blind chance. The understanding revolts at such a conclusion, whether or not we are able to believe that every slight variation of structure, – the union of each pair in marriage, – the dissemination of each seed, – and other such events, have all been ordained for some special purpose . . .

The main conclusion arrived at in this work, namely that man is descended from some lowly-organised form, will, I regret to think, be highly distasteful to many. But there can hardly be a doubt that we are descended from barbarians . . . He who has seen a savage in his native land will not feel much shame, if forced to acknowledge that the blood of some more humble creature flows in his veins. For my own part I would as soon be descended from that heroic little monkey, who

[13] Charles Darwin, *The Descent of Man and Selection in Relation to Sex,* new ed. (New York, 1897), 606–7, 613, 618–19.

braved his dreaded enemy in order to save the life of his keeper, or from that old baboon, who descending from the mountains, carried away in triumph his young comrade from a crowd of astonished dogs – as from a savage who delights to torture his enemies, offers up bloody sacrifices, practices infanticide without remorse, treats his wives like slaves, knows no decency, and is haunted by the grossest superstitions.

Social Darwinism

6.14 *Herbert Spencer,* Social Statistics *(1896)*[14]

Darwin's theory of evolution was influential in the thinking of many writers about economics, society, and politics, often entwined with the ideas of Adam Smith (document 2.10), T.R. Malthus (documents 2.9 and 2.11), David Ricardo (document 5.18), and other laissez-faire thinkers. Herbert Spencer (1820–1903), an early sociologist, was particularly important. He developed the idea of "survival of the fittest" some years before Darwin published *On the Origin of Species*, and the biologist actually adopted it in his own work. However, "Social Darwinists," as they were called, carried the originator's ideas into realms that he had not suggested or wanted to go including the justification of eugenics, racism, imperialism, unregulated capitalism, patriarchy, and the glorification of war. Here Spencer comments on both state and private efforts to help the poor.

Explain the links between "classical" economics and Social Darwinism. How would Victorian religious leaders have responded to Spencer's arguments? Why did Social Darwinism fail to block both Conservatives and Liberals from enacting humane legislation and the rise of the welfare state? Darwin put emphasis on the sociability of animal societies and the fact that as organisms become more complex mutual concern and cooperation increases, which helps shape morality. What would a "Social Darwinist" have said about the importance of morality and cooperation versus competition? How would Whitbread and Pitt (document 2.8) have responded to Spencer? Engels (document 5.20)? L.T. Hobhouse (document 5.24)?

Pervading all Nature we may see at work a stern discipline which is a little cruel that it may be very kind. That state of universal warfare maintained throughout the lower creation, to the great perplexity of many worthy people, is at bottom the most merciful provision which the circumstances admit of. It is much better that the ruminant animal, when deprived by age of the vigor which

[14] Herbert Spencer, *Social Statistics*, abridged and revised ed. (New York, 1899), 149–51, 154–5.

made its existence a pleasure, should be killed by some beast of prey, than that it should linger out a life made painful by infirmities, and eventually die of starvation. By the destruction of all such, not only is existence ended before it becomes burdensome, but room is made for a younger generation capable of the fullest enjoyment; and, moreover, out of the very act of substitution happiness is derived for a tribe of predatory creatures. Note, further, that their carnivorous enemies . . . also weed out the sickly, the malformed, and the least fleet or powerful. . . .

Meanwhile, the well-being of existing humanity and the unfolding of it into this ultimate perfection, are both secured by that same beneficial though severe discipline to which the animate creation at large is subject. It seems hard that an unskillfulness, which with all its efforts he cannot overcome, should entail hunger upon the artisan. It seems hard that a laborer, incapacitated by sickness from competing with his stronger fellows, should have to bear the resulting privations. It seems hard that widows and orphans should be left to struggle for life and death. Nevertheless, when regarded not separately but in connection with the interests of universal humanity, these harsh fatalities are seen to be full of beneficence which brings to early graves the children of diseased parents, and singles out the intemperate and the debilitated as the victims of an epidemic. . . .

. . . We must call those spurious philanthropists who, to prevent present misery, would entail greater misery on future generations. That rigorous necessity which, when allowed to operate, becomes so sharp a spur to the lazy and so strong a bridle to the random, these paupers' friends would repeal, because of the wailings it here and there produces. Blind to the fact that under the natural order of things society is constantly exerting its unhealthy, imbecile, slow, vacillating, faithless members, these unthinking, though well-meaning, men advocate an interference which not only stops the purifying process, but even increases the vitiation – absolutely encourages the multiplication of the reckless and incompetent by offering them an unfailing provision, and *dis*courages the multiplication of the competent and provident by heightening the difficulty of maintaining a family. . . .

. . . By suspending the process of adaptation, a poor-law increases the distress to be borne at some future day; and here we shall find that it also increases the distress to be borne now. For be it remembered that of the sum taken in any year to support paupers, a large portion would otherwise have gone to support laborers employed in new productive works – land-drainage, machine-building, &c. An additional stock of commodities would by-and-by have been produced, and the number of those who go short would consequently have been diminished. Thus the astonishment expressed by some that so much misery should exist, notwithstanding the distribution of fifteen millions [pounds] a year by endowed charities, benevolent societies, and poor-law unions, is quite uncalled for; seeing that the larger the sum gratuitously administered, the more intense will shortly become the suffering.

6.15 *Herbert Spencer,* The Man versus the State *(1884)*[15]

Herbert Spencer argued that "all socialism involves slavery." Social Darwinists became fierce advocates of individualism and unrestrained capitalist competition. Why did Spencer object to state interference with free competition between individuals? How would Marxists, who claimed a "scientific" basis for their rationalist and materialist ideas, have responded to Spencer's arguments? John Stuart Mill (document 6.9)? R.H. Tawney (document 8.5)?

It is a matter of common remark, often made when a marriage is impending, that those possessed by strong hopes habitually dwell on the promised pleasures and think nothing of the accompanying pains. A further exemplification of this truth is supplied by these political enthusiasts and fanatical revolutionists. Impressed with the miseries existing under our present social arrangements, and not regarding these miseries as caused by the ill-working of a human nature but partially adapted to the social state, they imagine them to be forthwith curable by this or that rearrangement. Yet, even did their plans succeed it could only be by substituting one kind of evil for another. A little deliberate thought would show that under their proposed arrangements their liberties must be surrendered in proportion as their material welfares were cared for.

For no form of co-operation, small or great, can be carried on without regulation, and an implied submission to the regulating agencies . . . so that each would stand toward the governing agency in the relation of slave to master.

The services of each will belong to the aggregate of all; and for these services, such returns will be given as the authorities think proper. So that even if the administration is of the beneficent kind intended to be secured, slavery, however mild, must be the outcome of the arrangement.

. . . The function of Liberalism in the past was that of putting a limit to the powers of kings. The function of true Liberalism in the future will be that of putting a limit to the powers of Parliaments.

6.16 *Karl Pearson,* National Life from the Standpoint of Science *(1900)*[16]

The professor of mathematics and statistician Karl Pearson (1857–1936) embraced imperialism as an expression of natural selection and asserted what he called this "scientific view" in a lecture delivered in 1900. Not surprisingly, he also advocated eugenics.

15 Herbert Spencer, *Social Statistics together with The Man versus the State* (New York, 1899), 328–30, 411.

16 Karl Pearson, *National Life from the Standpoint of Science*, 2nd ed. (London, 1905), 21, 23–5.

Ruling an empire, of course, required big government expenditure and large numbers of officials. How would Pearson have defended such expansion of government to Spencer (documents 6.14 and 6.15)? Did Spencer and Pearson accept traditional morality or the idea of human rights as developed during the Enlightenment?

How many centuries, how many thousand of years, have the Kaffir or the Negro held large districts in Africa undisturbed by the white man? Yet their intertribal struggles have not yet produced a civilization in the least comparable with the Aryan [a term used by racial theorists to describe "superior" Europeans]. Educate and nurture them as you will, I do not believe that you will succeed in modifying the stock. History shows me one way, and one way only, in which a high state of civilization has been produced, the struggle of race with race, and the survival of the physically and mentally fitter race. If you want to know whether the lower races of man can evolve a higher type, I fear the only course is to leave them to fight it out among themselves . . .

The only healthy alternative [to the white man living alongside an inferior race] is he should go and completely drive out the inferior race. That is practically what the white man has done in North America . . .. I venture to assert, then, that the struggle for existence between white and red man, painful and even terrible as it was in its details, has given us a good far outbalancing its immediate evil. In place of the red man, contributing practically nothing to the work and thought of the world, we have a great nation, mistress of many arts, and able, with its youthful imagination and fresh, untrammeled impulses, to contribute much to the common stock of civilized man . . .

6.17 J.E.C. Welldon, Recollections and Reflections *(1915)*[17]

The British elite raised athletic pursuits to a central place in the education of their children, teaching them the subtle and elegant game of cricket and the more ferocious rugby (a game named after a famous boarding school where it was invented). Intensely competitive sports were seen as the best possible training for those to be sent out to rule the empire. The Reverend J.E.C. Welldon (1854–1937), headmaster of Harrow where the young Winston Churchill was one of his pupils, wrote the following account of an incident at the school. He later became Bishop of Calcutta in India where his zeal to convert the natives to Christianity led to his ouster by more pragmatic officials.

[17] J.E.C. Welldon, *Recollections and Reflections* (London, 1915), 144.

Why might members of the British ruling class have encouraged their children to play violent sports and actively promote ideas of racial superiority? A number of elite Egyptian and Indian boys were educated at Harrow – most famously, Jawaharlal Nehru, the first prime minister of India after independence. Why would such a school that educated many British aristocrats admit dark-skinned members of subject peoples?

One remarkable instance of fighting at Harrow, if only one, I still recall. Among my pupils there was an Egyptian boy of high rank, who was admitted to the school, I think, at the instance of [the senior British administrator there], as it was judged on political grounds to be important that his education should take place in England rather than in France. One morning this boy appeared in school with two black eyes. I wrote to his house-master, asking him, if possible, to find out who had been fighting with the Egyptian boy. After some inquiry, he sent me as the culprit, the last boy whom I should have suspected of an aggressive pugilism. I said to him, "B—, you have been fighting. Have you any excuse to give? You know fighting is an offense against school rules. What do you mean by giving that boy two black eyes?" He hesitated a moment, then he raised his eyes and said apologetically, "Please sir, sir, he said something bad about the British race." The only possible reply which I could make was: "That is enough, my boy; you may go."

6.18 *Thomas H. Huxley, "Evolution and Ethics" (1893)*[18]

Thomas Huxley (1825–95) became an important supporter of Darwin in the early days after the publication of *On the Origin of Species*, famously debating Bishop Wilberforce at Oxford in 1860. He was skeptical, however, about the capacity of scientific theory to explain all aspects of society. How effective are Huxley's arguments in countering those of the Social Darwinists? What would he have said to Pearson (document 6.16)?

. . . The most obvious attribute of the cosmos is its impermanence. It assumes the aspect not so much of a permanent entity as of a changeful process, in which naught endures save the flow of energy and the rational order which pervades it.

. . . The propounders of what are called the "ethics of evolution," when the "evolution of ethics" would usually better express the object of their speculations, adduce a number of more or less interesting facts and more or less sound arguments, in favor of the origin of the moral sentiments, in the same way as other

[18] Thomas H. Huxley, "Evolution and Ethics," *The Popular Science Monthly*, XLIV (Nov. and Dec. 1893), 21, 187–8.

natural phenomena, by a process of evolution. I have little doubt, for my own part, that they are on the right track; but as the immoral sentiments have no less been evolved, there is so far, as much natural sanction for the one as for the other. The thief and the murderer follow nature just as much as the philanthropist. Cosmic evolution may teach us how the good and the evil tendencies of man may have come about; but, in itself, it is incompetent to furnish any better reason why what we call good is preferable to what we call evil than we had before. Some day, I doubt not, we shall arrive at an understanding of the evolution of the aesthetic faculty; but all the understanding in the world will neither increase or diminish the force of the intuition that this is beautiful and that is ugly.

There is another fallacy which appears to me to pervade the so-called "ethics of evolution." It is the notion that because, on the whole, animals and plants have advanced in the perfection of organization by means of the struggle for existence and the consequent "survival of the fittest"; therefore men in society, men as ethical beings, must look to the same process to help them towards perfection. I suspect that this fallacy has arisen out of the unfortunate ambiguity of the phrase "survival of the fittest." "Fittest" has a connotation of "best"; and about "best" there hangs a moral flavor. In cosmic nature, however, what is "fittest" depends on the conditions. Long since, I ventured to point out that if our hemisphere were to cool again, the survival of the fittest might bring about, in the vegetable kingdom, a population of more and more stunted and humbler and humbler organisms, until the "fittest" that survived might be nothing by lichens, diatoms, and such microscopic organisms as those which give red snow its color; while, if it became hotter, the pleasant valleys of the Thames . . . might be uninhabitable by any animated beings save those that flourish in a tropical jungle. They, as the fittest, the best adapted to the changed conditions, would survive.

British Identities

6.19 *Alexis de Tocqueville,* Journeys to England and Ireland *(May 30, 1835)*[19]

Alexis de Tocqueville (see document 5.14) was a French aristocrat who traveled extensively through England and Ireland in the 1830s. He married an English woman. Though not as insightful as his observations on America, his reflections on England were penetrating and based on a wide range of acquaintance and interviews. Were the qualities de Tocqueville noted unique to England? How did they affect society and social relations? Were they exclusively traits of the upper and middle classes?

[19] Alexis de Tocqueville, *Journeys to England and Ireland*, ed. J.P. Mayer (New York, 1968), 74–5.

I see many things in this country which I cannot yet completely understand, among others this:

Two spirits which, if not altogether contrary, are at least very diverse, seem to hold equal sway in England.

The one prompts people to pool their efforts to attain ends which in France we would never think of approaching in this way. There are associations to further science, politics, pleasure, business ...

The other prompts each man and each association to keep all advantages as much as possible to themselves, to close every possible door that would let any outsider come in or look in. ...

I cannot completely understand how "the spirit of association" and "the spirit of exclusion" both came to be so highly developed in the same people, and often to be so intimately combined. Example a club; what better example of association than the union of individuals who form the club? What more exclusive than the corporate personality represented by the club? The same applies to almost all civil and political associations, the corporations ... See how families divide up when the birds are able to leave the nest!

On reflection I incline to the view that the spirit of individuality is the basis of the English character. Association is a means suggested by sense and necessity for getting things unattainable by isolated effort. But the spirit of individuality comes in on every side; it recurs in every aspect of things. Perhaps one may suggest that it has indirectly helped the development of the other spirit by inspiring every man with greater ambitions and desires than one finds elsewhere. That being so, the need to club together is more generally felt, because the urge to get things is more general and stronger .... I suppose that if the French could become more enlightened than they are, they would take to clubbing together more naturally than the English.

6.20 Charles Astor Bristed, Five Years in an English University *(1852)*[20]

Charles Astor Bristed (1820–74) was a wealthy American educated at Yale who spent five years as a student at Cambridge University in the 1840s. Here he compares the English and American ways of life.

Did this passage apply only to the English educated elite, or was it characteristic of the whole population? How accurate do you think Bristed's description is? How do de Tocqueville (document 6.19) and Bristed differ or share opinions? Were outside observers liable to be more accurate than English ones? How were the characteristics of British society observed by Bristed likely to shape society?

[20] Charles Astor Bristed, *Five Years in an English University*, 2nd ed. (New York, 1852), 32–3, 346.

One of the first things which surprises a young man from our Atlantic cities on visiting England, is the inferiority of the English in certain refinements of civilization – in which he was prepared to find them infinitely superior. It is with no small astonishment that the New Yorker, or Philadelphian, or Bostonian finds it almost impossible to get clothes made to fit in England; nor, while doing justice to the mutton and ale of the country, is he less disappointed to find that there is no variety – the eternal steak, chops and potatoes, and big joints everywhere; and that the national taste in wine is of the most barbarous description, most of the fluid consumed under that honorable appellation being half brandy. Moreover, having usually mixed more with Frenchmen, Spaniards, and Germans, and speaking what he knows of their languages more fluently than the Englishman of the same age, he has a decided advantage when any native of the Continent happens to be present, or when Continental matters are under discussion. . . . More than one [English] youth who thought to astonish the American savage by a display of the mysteries of civilization, was rather astonished in his turn at my summary condemnation of English tailors and cooks, and my ostentatious learning in French wines and dishes. . . .

The moral education of English boys is very much neglected, especially that part of education which consists in example and in removing temptation out of their way rather than debarring them from it. . . . If boys can be made *manly*, that is to say, courageous, honest, and tolerably truthful, the formation of habits of purity and self-denial is altogether a secondary matter. Grown people, old, grey-headed men, encourage boys to drink, and talk before them as the fastest [most stylish and fashionable] specimen of Young America would not talk before his younger brother. A stranger . . . could not but remark the progress made in vice at an early age by the inmates of a public [private boarding] school, and the trouble which a conscientious teacher has with them in combating the fearful delusion, evidently derived not merely from practice, but from the admitted theory of their elders, that indulgence in sensual vices is not incompatible with a Christian life.

6.21 Reports of the Commissioners of Inquiry into the State of Education in Wales (1848)[21]

Religious Dissent became the dominant cultural and social force in shaping the Welsh national identity in the eighteenth and nineteenth centuries. Methodism was particularly important. Nonconformity was a direct challenge to the rule of the Anglican landed elite and the authority of the established Church. On the other hand, Dissenting Sunday schools discouraged vice and encouraged industriousness, respect for superiors, and strong community values.

[21] *Reports of the Commissioners of Inquiry into the State of Education in Wales* (London, 1848), I, 5–6.

What is the tone of the author of the report? What purposes other than religious worship did Nonconformist churches provide for the Welsh? Why might a member of the English ruling elite have mixed feelings about the situation? What were the most important differences between the English and Welsh?

The universality of these schools, and the large proportion of persons attending them who take part in their government, have very generally familiarized the people with some of the more ordinary terms and methods of organization such as *committee*, *secretary* and so forth.

These schools satisfy the gregarious sociability which animates the Welsh towards each other. . . . Every man, woman and child feels comfortably at home in them. It is all among neighbors and equals. Whatever ignorance is shown here, whatever mistakes are made, whatever strange speculations are started, there are no superiors to smile and open their eyes. . . . Whatever Sunday-schools may be as places of instruction, they are real fields of mental activity. The Welsh working-man rouses himself for them. Sunday is to him more than a day of bodily rest and devotion. It is his best chance, all the week through, of showing himself in his own character. He marks his sense of it by a suit of clothes regarded with a feeling hardly less sabbatical than the day itself. I do not remember to have seen an adult in rags in a single Sunday-school throughout the present district. There always seemed to me better dressed on Sundays than the same classes in England.

Irish Identities

6.22 *Daniel O'Connell, speech at the Hill of Tara (Aug. 15, 1843)*[22]

Daniel O'Connell (see document 6.2) was known to the Irish as "The Liberator" for his part in forcing the British government to concede political rights to Catholics in 1829. He went on to lead a campaign to repeal the Union of 1801 between Great Britain and Ireland and to reestablish a parliament in Dublin. In the 1840s he held a series of monster rallies culminating in the one at Tara, the seat of the ancient high kings of Ireland, where perhaps as many as a million people came to hear him speak.

Was O'Connell correct to say that Parliament had no authority to enact the Union? On what foundation did he base his claim for disengaging with Great Britain? Was this speech likely to convince the British government, queen, or people?

[22] Leopold Wagner, ed., *Modern Political Orations* (New York, 1896), 42–3.

On this spot I have a most important duty to perform. I here protest, in the name of my country and in the name of God, against the unfounded and unjust Union. My proposition to Ireland is that the Union is not binding on her people. It is void in conscience and in principle . . . Neither the English nor the Irish Legislature was competent to pass that Act, and I arraign it on these grounds. One authority alone could make that Act binding, and that was the voice of the people of Ireland. . . .

I need not detain you by quoting authorities to show the invalidity of the Union. I am here the representative of the Irish nation, and in the name of that moral, temperate, virtuous, and religious people, I proclaim the Union a nullity.

6.23 *George Moore,* Parnell and His Island *(1887)*[23]

In 1855 a Guinness of the famous brewing family purchased a 30,000 acre estate in the west of Ireland, an area that was still suffering from the after-effects of the Great Famine. His son, the first Lord Ardilaun (1840–1915), transformed the existing house into a gigantic fortress in the medieval style in the late 1870s on the eve of the Land War and nationalist agitation for Home Rule. During the violent 1880s two of his bailiffs were assassinated. Ardilaun did not descend from the Anglo-Irish Ascendancy but from a native family that had converted to Protestantism. He was an Irish industrialist building himself a house fit for membership in the landowning elite. This description appeared in a book by George Moore (1852–1933), a Roman Catholic writer from a gentry family who was nearly ruined financially by his tenants refusing to pay their rents. He converted to Protestantism and moved to England.

Why did Lord Ardilaun choose a medieval style of architecture for his new house? What is the tone of Moore's observations? How might his background have affected his views? What does the passage tell us about Irish society in the 1870s and 1880s?

. . . We grow gradually conscious of certain changes in the aspect of the country: it seems more orderly, and it wears an air of well-to-do-ness that we had not before observed. The rickety walls built out of loose round stones piled one on the top of the other have disappeared and are replaced by handsome stone and mortar walls; and the cottages of the peasants are less dirty, and here and there the landscape is marked by small cleanly-slated houses. . . . Below us, falling in sweet inclining plain, a sea of green turf flows in and out of stone walls and occasional clumps of trees down to the rocky promontories, the reedy reaches and the long curved woods which sweep about the castle . . . that Lord Ardilaun has built on this beautiful Irish land. There it stands on that green headland with the billows

[23] George Moore, *Parnell and His Island* (London, 1887), 176–83.

of a tideless sea, lashing about its base; and oh! The towers and battlements rising out of the bending foliage of ten thousand trees . . .

We are still two miles from our destination, and as we advance signs of wealth and industry increase. We pass large roads, domain walls in process of construction, and a large archway upon which at least a hundred men are at work . . . On either side of us the park now spreads. Through the hillocks hundreds and hundreds of fallow deer move away at our approach, and over the crest of a hill the broad bluff red deer raise their antlered heads and gaze at us as steadfastly as lions . . .

After a week spent in the thin, mean poverty of the north-west, amid the sadness of ruined things, this strangely beautiful castle renders me singularly happy. . . . Here we are almost shut out of the storm and gloom of crime and poverty that enfolds the land, but even here the shadow of murder and outrage falls across our way. For as we sit at breakfast we hear the smothered detonation of the dynamite exploding in the huge moat which our host is having cut through the solid rock, and sometimes small splinters of stone strike the windows. Fifty or sixty men are engaged upon this work; and after breakfast, as we walk down the grounds, we examine this new fortification, which when finished will separate the castle from the mainland. It is thirty feet deep by twenty feet wide.

"You see," says our host, "I have a taste for the picturesque. The moat will be protected by battlements, and cannon will be placed at convenient distances. I shall be able to defend myself in case of invasion, and as the drawbridge will be raised nightly it will be difficult for the dynamiters to get at me."

6.24 Michael Davitt, speech, "The Land League Proposal," Manchester (May 21, 1882)[24]

Michael Davitt (1846–1906) led the Land League which responded to agricultural distress and attacked the established system of land ownership in Ireland. The following extract comes from his "Land League Proposal" of 1882.

Why did Davitt call the Liberal prime minister William Gladstone a Whig? What did he see as the cause and solution of the Anglo-Irish conflict? Why was land so important to the Catholic peasantry?

If the Land League is to be prevented from succoring the evicted, if every channel of political effort not favorable to Whig legislation on the land question is to be closed up, then, indeed, will the whole situation be surrendered to the secret movement, and *lex talionis* become the only refuge for despair. As the moral

[24] D.B. Cashman, *Life of Michael Davitt* (Glasgow, c.1882), 166–7.

responsibility of the outrage epidemic of the past twelve months must, in my humble opinion, rest upon the Whig Administration for its coercive incitation to vengeance, so must the crimes that will follow additional coercion be placed at the same door. If Mr. Gladstone is earnest in his efforts to put down crime, let him go to the source of all agrarian outrage, and remove Irish landlordism from Ireland (Cheers). If he be determined to put down secret societies, let him remove from the government of Ireland what makes English rule detested and English law distrusted – let him sweep away Dublin Castle [the seat of the British administration] – (loud cheers) – and show that he can repose the same confidence in Ireland that has now been abused in Canada (Cheers). If he believes that peace will be restored in Ireland while landlords have power to evict and the Castle power to trample upon every political opponent and every vestige of liberty, he has read the history of the Anglo-Irish difficulty to no purpose. As well might the doctor dream of restoring to health and vigor a patient in whose sensitive flesh the instrument that made the wound lies unremoved.

6.25 *William Gladstone, speech in the House of Commons (Apr. 1886)*[25]

In the mid-1880s Gladstone (see documents 4.13, 4.19, and 6.6) came to the conclusion that granting the Irish a separate parliament in Dublin to manage their own internal affairs (Home Rule) was the only solution to the problems created by nationalist aspirations. This decision split the Liberal Party, and Gladstone failed to achieve his goal.

How did Gladstone account for the hostility in Anglo-Irish relations? Why did he call nationalism "local patriotism"? Why was his solution for Ireland different than for Scotland? Would Gladstone's concession have satisfied Michael Davitt (document 6.24)?

. . . Law is discredited in Ireland, and discredited in Ireland upon this ground especially – that it comes to the people of that country with a foreign aspect, and in a foreign garb. Those coercion bills of ours, of course, for it has become a matter of course, I am speaking of the facts and not of the merits, these coercion bills are stiffly resisted by the Members who represent Ireland in Parliament. The English mind, by cases of this kind and by the tone of the Press towards them, is estranged from the Irish people and the Irish mind is estranged from the people of England and Scotland . . .

. . . The case of Ireland, though she is represented here not less fully than England or Scotland, is not the same as that of England and Scotland. England, by her own strength, and by her vast majority in this House, makes her own laws just

[25] William E. Gladstone, *Speeches on the Irish Question in 1886*, rev. ed. (Edinburgh, 1886), 7–10, 51.

as independently as if she were not combined with two other countries. . . . Scotland, wisely recognized by England, has been allowed and encouraged in this House to make her own laws as freely and effectually as if she had a representation six times as strong. The consequence is that the mainspring of law in England is felt by the people to be English; the mainspring of law in Scotland is felt by the people to be Scotch; but the mainspring of law in Ireland is not felt by the people to be Irish, and I am bound to say – truth extorts from me an avowal – that it cannot be felt to be Irish in the same sense as it is English and Scotch. . . .

Something must be done, something is imperatively demanded from us to restore to Ireland the first conditions of civil life – the free course of law, the liberty of every individual in the exercise of every legal right, the confidence of the people in the law, and their sympathy with the law, apart from which no country can be called, in the full sense of the word, a civilized country, nor can there be given to that country the blessings which it is the object of civilized society to attain. . . .

I hold that there is such a thing as local patriotism, which, in itself, is not bad, but good. The Welshman is full of local patriotism, the Scotchman is full of local patriotism; the Scotch nationality is as strong as it ever was, and should the occasion arise, which I believe it never can, it will be ready to assert itself as in the days of Bannockburn. I do not believe that the local patriotism is an evil. I believe it is stronger in Ireland even than in Scotland. Englishmen are eminently English, Scotchmen are profoundly Scotch; and, if I read Irish history aright, misfortune and calamity have wedded her sons to her soil. The Irishman is more profoundly Irish; but it does not follow that, because his local patriotism is keen, he is incapable of Imperial patriotism.

6.26 Douglas Hyde, speech, "The Necessity for De-Anglicising Ireland" (Nov. 25, 1892)[26]

Douglas Hyde (1860–1949) was born into an Ascendancy family, the son of a Protestant clergyman. He became, however, an ardent nationalist and hoped to strengthen Irish culture by reviving the Gaelic language. He founded the Gaelic League in 1893 and served as President of Ireland from 1938 to 1945.

Was it illogical for the Irish to adopt English as a language? Were the mass of the Irish people "classically learned"? Was his proposal for change realistic? Can history's clock be turned backwards?

If we take a bird's-eye view of our island today, and compare it with what it used to be, we must be struck by the extraordinary fact that the nation which once was, as

[26] Douglas Hyde, *Revival of Irish Literature and Other Addresses*, ed. Lady Gregory (London, 1894), 117.

everyone admits, one of the most classically learned and cultivated nations in Europe, is now one of the least so . . .

I shall endeavor to show that this failure of the Irish people in recent times has been largely brought about by the race diverging during this century from the right path, and ceasing to be Irish without becoming English. I shall attempt to show that with the bulk of the people this change took place recently, much more recently than most people imagine, and is, in fact, still going on. I should also like to call attention to the illogical position of men who drop their own language to speak English, of men who translate their euphonious Irish names into English monosyllables, of men who read English books, and know nothing about Gaelic literature, nevertheless protesting as a matter of sentiment that they hate the country which at every hand's turn they rush to imitate.

I wish to show you that in Anglicizing ourselves wholesale we have thrown away with a light heart the best claim we have upon the world's recognition of us as a separate nationality.

6.27 "Solemn League and Covenant" (Sept. 28, 1912)[27]

Protestants in the northern Irish province of Ulster, who considered themselves "British," were bitterly opposed to Home Rule. Although they formed a majority of the population in their own region, a democratically elected parliament for all of Ireland would have placed them in a comparatively small minority. They feared "Rome" rule by the Catholic Irish nationalist majority and roused themselves to a fever pitch of opposition as the Home Rule legislation moved toward implementation in 1914. More than 250,000 people signed the Solemn League and Covenant in September 1912, and the eventual total of subscribers reached nearly half a million. Rifles were imported from abroad, and Ulster moved toward civil war.

Why would people whose ancestors had lived in Ireland for as long as 300 years see themselves as British, not Irish? Why did they dread Irish Nationalist rule? Most of those who signed the Covenant were working- or middle-class men. Yet they were pledging to defend the continued rule of a small elite of landed aristocrats and business magnates. Why? What would have happened if civil war had broken out in the fall of 1914? How would Michael Davitt (document 6.24) or Douglas Hyde (document 6.26) have responded to their fears?

Being convinced in our conscience that Home Rule would be disastrous to the material well-being of Ulster as well as to the whole of Ireland, subversive of our civil and religious freedom, destructive of our citizenship and perilous to the unity

[27] *Evening Post* LXXXIV (Sept. 30, 1912), 7.

of the Empire, we whose names are underwritten, men of Ulster, loyal subjects of the King, humbly relying on the God whom our fathers in days of stress and trial confidently trusted, do hereby pledge ourselves in solemn covenant throughout this our time of threatened calamity to stand by one another in defending for ourselves and our children our cherished position of equal citizenship in the United Kingdom and in using all means which may be found necessary to defeat the present conspiracy to set up a Home Rule Parliament in Ireland. In the event of such a Parliament being forced upon us, we further solemnly mutually pledge ourselves to refuse to recognize its authority.

HISTORIANS' DEBATES

To what degree were nineteenth-century women confined to the domestic sphere? When and for how long was the concept of separate spheres for men and women the prevailing view? Only for the middle class?

Leonore Davidoff and Catherine Hall, *Family Fortunes: Men and Women of the English Middle Class, 1780–1850* (London, 1987); Deborah Gorham, *The Victorian Girl and the Feminine Ideal* (Bloomington, 1982); David R. Green and Alastair Owens, "Gentlewomanly Capitalism? Spinsters, Widows and Wealth Holding in England and Wales, c. 1800–1960," *EcHR* 56 (2003), 510–36; Peter Groenewgen, ed., *Feminism and Political Economy in the Victorian Economy* (Brookfield, 1994); Susan Kingsley Kent, *Sex and Suffrage in Britain, 1860–1914* (Princeton, 1987); Rosalind K. Marshall, *Virgins and Viragos: A History of Women in Scotland from 1080 to 1980* (London, 1983); Nicola Phillips, *Women in Business, 1700–1850* (Woodbridge, 2006); June Purvis, ed., *Women's History: Britain 1850–1945* (New York, 1995); Robert B. Shoemaker, *Gender in English Society, 1650–1850: The Emergence of Separate Spheres?* (London, 1998); Martha Vicinus, ed., *Suffer and Be Still: Women in the Victorian Age* (Bloomington, 1972); Amanda Vickery, "Golden Age to Separate Spheres? A Review of the Categories and Chronology of English Women's History," *HJ* 36 (1993), 383–414.

Did women leave the workforce as industrialization progressed? Did a male-dominated "breadwinner–homemaker household" emerge in the nineteenth century, refreshing patriarchy among working families and encouraging the domestication of the wife?

Joyce Burnette, *Gender, Work, and Wages in Industrial Revolution Britain* (New York, 2008); Edward Cadbury and M. Cecile Matheson, *Women's Work and Wages: A Phase of Life in an Industrial City* (London, 1980); Anna Clark, *The Struggle for the Breeches: Gender and the Making of the British Working Class* (Berkeley, 1995); Colin Creighton, "The Rise of the Male Breadwinner Family. A Reappraisal," *CSSH* 38 (1996), 310–37; Sarah Horrell and Jane Humphries, "Women's Labour Force Participation and the Transition to the Male-Breadwinner Family, 1790–1865," *EcHR* 48 (1995), 89–117; Sarah Horrell and Jane Humphries, "The Origins and Expansion of the Male Breadwinner Family. The Case of Nineteenth-Century Britain," in Angelique Janssens, ed., *IRSH* 42 (1997), *Supplement 5: The Rise and Decline of the Male Breadwinner Family?* 25–65; Hilary Land, "The Family Wage," *FR* 6 (1980), 55–77; Stephan Nicholas and Deborah Oxley, "The Living Standards of Women during the Industrial Revolution, 1795–1820," *EcHR* 46 (1993), 723–49; L. Orem, "The Welfare of Women in Labouring Families. England, 1860–1950," in *Clio's Consciousness Raised: New Perspectives on the History of Women,* ed. Mary S. Hartman and Lois Banner (New York, 1974); Ivy Pinchbeck, *Women Workers and the Industrial Revolution,*

1750–1850 (London, 1930); Sonya O. Rose, *Limited Livelihoods: Gender and Class in Nineteenth-Century England* (London, 1992); Wally Seccombe, "Patriarchy Stabilized. The Construction of the Male Breadwinner Wage Norm in Nineteenth-Century Britain," *SH* 11 (1986), 53–76; K.D. M. Snell, *Annals of the Labouring Poor: Social Change and Agrarian England 1660–1900* (Cambridge, 1985); Pat Thane, "Women and the Poor Law in Victorian and Edwardian England," *HW* 6 (1978), 29–51; Janet Thomas, "Women and Capitalism. Oppression or Emancipation?" *CSSH* 30 (1988), 534–49; Louise Tilly, "Women, Women's History, and the Industrial Revolution," *SR* 61 (1994), 115–37; Deborah Valenze, *The First Industrial Woman* (Oxford, 1995).

Why did the Irish starve during the Great Famine of the 1840s, and what more could the British government have done to relieve the distress?

Austin Bourke, *The Visitation of God?: The Potato and the Great Irish Famine,* ed. Jacqueline Hill and Cormac Ó Gráda (Dublin, 1993); Kenneth H. Connell, *The Population of Ireland, 1750–1845* (Oxford, 1950); James S. Donnelly, Jr., *A New History of Ireland under the Union I, 1801–1870,* ed. W.E. Vaughan (Oxford, 1989); Christine Kinealy, *The Great Calamity: The Irish Famine, 1845–1852* (Dublin, 1994); Joel Mokyr, *Why Ireland Starved: A Quantitative and Analytical History of the Irish Economy* (London, 1983); Cormac Ó Gráda, *Ireland before and after the Famine: Explorations in Economic History, 1800–1925,* 2nd ed. (Manchester, 1993); Cormac Ó Gráda, *The Great Irish Famine* (Dublin, 1989); Cathal Poirteir, ed., *The Great Irish Famine* (Dublin, 1995).

What drove the Home Rule movement: economic factors, the assertion of national identity, a political campaign for full independence, religious identity?

Paul Bew, *Land and the National Question in Ireland, 1858–1882* (Dublin, 1978); Paul Bew, *Ideology and the Irish Question: Ulster Unionism and Irish Nationalism, 1912–1916* (Oxford, 1994); D. George Boyce and Alan O'Day, eds., *The Making of Modern Irish History: Revisionism and the Revisionist Controversy* (London, 1996); R.V. Comerford, *The Fenians in Context: Irish Politics and Society, 1848–1882* (Dublin, 1985); George Dangerfield, *The Strange Death of Liberal England* (London, 1935); K. Theodore Hoppen, *Elections, Politics, and Society in Ireland, 1832–1885* (Oxford, 1984); T.A. Jenkins, Gladstone, *Whiggery, and the Liberal Party, 1874–1886* (Oxford, 1988); F. S.L. Lyons, *Ireland since the Famine* (London, 1971); F.S.L. Lyons, *Culture and Anarchy in Ireland, 1890–1939* (Oxford, 1979); Oliver MacDonagh, *Ireland: The Union and Its Aftermath,* rev. ed. (London, 1977); Nicholas Mansergh, *The Irish Question, 1840–1921* (London, 1965); H.C.G. Matthew, *Gladstone,* 2 vols. (Oxford, 1986–95); Alan O'Day, *Irish Home Rule, 1867–1921* (Manchester, 1998); Patrick O'Farrell, *Ireland's English Question: Anglo-Irish Relations, 1534–1970* (London, 1971); James O'Shea, Priest, *Politics, and Society in Post-Famine Ireland* (Dublin, 1983).

The ideas of John Stuart Mill have been upheld as visionary, but others see amorality, relativism, and even totalitarian tendencies. How should we view Mill's ideas?

Stefan Collini, *Public Moralists: Political Thought and Intellectual Life in Britain, 1850–1930* (Oxford, 1991); Maurice Cowling, *Mill and Liberalism,* 2nd ed. (Cambridge, 1990); Gertrude Himmelfarb, *On Liberty and Liberalism: The Case of John Stuart Mill* (New York, 1974); Michael St. John Packe, *The Life of John Stuart Mill* (London, 1954); John M. Robson, *The Improvement of Mankind: The Social and Political Thought of John Stuart Mill* (Toronto, 1968); Bernard Semmel, *John Stuart Mill and the Pursuit of Virtue* (New Haven, 1984); James Fitzjames Stephen, *Liberty, Equality, Fraternity* (Chicago, 1991 [1873]); William Thomas, *Mill* (Oxford, 1985).

COUNTERFACTUALS TO CONSIDER

What if Home Rule had been enacted in 1886? Would Ireland and Britain have moved progressively toward a more unified culture and identity? Would Ireland have developed a stronger economy? On the other hand, what if Home Rule had been, as intended, enacted in 1914? Would civil war have broken out in Ireland? Would Ulster have become an independent dominion? Would the British state have sided with the Roman Catholic majority and crushed the Protestants in the North?

Part III

The Twentieth Century

CHAPTER SEVEN

State and Empire

Two great wars shaped the course of twentieth-century British history. The loss of life was horrific, and the economic, political, social, and cultural dislocations caused by the conflicts were immense. It is not necessarily clear, however, whether one war or the other had a greater effect. The interwar years have been called "the Age of Anxiety." Why? There were many good reasons not to confront Hitler and avoid World War II, but the towering figure of Winston Churchill emerged to challenge the British people to take the hard course. He also helped shape (not always intentionally) the postwar confrontation with communism and the unraveling of empire. Why did he gradually lose control of events? The postwar era produced the welfare state (see Chapter 8) and imperial retreat. Britons struggled with their diminished role in the world, and their special relationship with the United States that was both their salvation and a bond that was unequal and uneasy. At the end of the twentieth century Britain was still divided about what its role in Europe and the world should be and whether further "decline" had been staunched or was incipient.

It is fascinating to trace the relationship between Britain and Iraq across the twentieth century. The territory was captured from the Ottomans during World War I, and acquired as a "mandate" from the League of Nations. The new technology of air power was used to suppress dissent there, but control slipped away in the 1950s. The British were no longer able to project power successfully in the Middle East. In 1990 and 2003, however, the British army returned, in alliance with the Americans, yet again invading Iraq. Is this story mere accident and happenstance or a model of British imperial history in the twentieth century?

Sources and Debates in Modern British History: 1714 to the Present, First Edition. Edited by Ellis Wasson

Published 2012 by Blackwell Publishing Ltd.

As you read the documents in this chapter, consider the following questions:

- What impact did World Wars I and II have on British society?
- What were the problems and ideological shifts necessary to address those effects that confronted the British political system?
- How did the disappearance of the British Empire and rise of the Commonwealth affect Britain?

World War I

7.1 *Laurence Binyon, "For the Fallen" (Sept. 1914)*[1]

The glorification of patriotic death was a common theme during the war, and, despite those who protested against what they saw as useless slaughter, remained so after the conflict was over. Public opinion shifted, but not always in a uniform or predictable way. Laurence Binyon (1869–1943) wrote "For the Fallen" soon after the outbreak of war when cavalry units were being readied to ride directly to Berlin and men hurried to join the army so as not to miss the "show," which was expected to be over by Christmas. Why might many civilians, especially those who lost husbands or brothers, have continued to believe in the spirit of noble individual sacrifice even after the war was over?

With proud thanksgiving, a mother for her children,
   England mourns for her dead across the sea.
Flesh of her flesh they were, spirit of her spirit,
   Fallen in the cause of the free.

Solemn the drums thrill: Death august and royal
   Sings sorrow up into immortal spheres.
There is music in the midst of desolation
   And a glory that shines upon our tears.

They went with songs to the battle, they were young,
   Straight of limb, true of eye, steady and aglow.
They were staunch to the end against odds uncounted,
   They fell with their faces to the foe.

They shall grow not old, as we that are left grow old:
   Age shall not weary them, nor the years condemn.
At the going down of the sun and in the morning
   We shall remember them.

1 Laurence Binyon, *The Winnowing Fan* (New York, 1915), 28–9.

7.2 *Robert Graves,* Goodbye to All That *(1929)*[2]

Robert Graves (1895–1985), the poet and writer, went directly from secondary school into the trenches where he became a captain in the Royal Welch Fusiliers. He published this memoir of his experiences in 1929, one of the best accounts of the war written in English.

What was trench warfare like according to Graves? The officers were still almost exclusively drawn from the upper and middle classes while the soldiers were mostly working class. How might class backgrounds have affected their service in the trenches? The British army never experienced any serious mutinies or refusals to obey orders between 1914 and 1918. What kept up morale up and willingness to fight in the face of such experiences?

Having now been in the trenches for five months, I had passed my prime. For the first three weeks, an officer was of little use in the front line; he did not know his way about, had not learned the rules of health and safety, or grown accustomed to recognizing degrees of danger. Between three weeks and four weeks he was at his best, unless he happened to have any particular bad shock or sequence of shocks. Then his usefulness gradually declined as neurasthenia developed. At six months he was still more or less all right; but by nine or ten months, unless he had been given a few weeks' rest on a technical course, or in a hospital, he usually became a drag on the other company officers. After a year or fifteen months he was often worse than useless. Dr. W.H.R. Rivers told me later that the action of one of the ductless glands – I think the thyroid – caused this slow general decline in military usefulness, by failing at a certain point to pump its sedative chemical into the blood. . . .

Officers had a less laborious but more nervous time than the men. There were proportionately twice as many neurasthenic cases among officers as among men, though a man's average expectancy of trench service before getting killed or wounded was twice as long as an officer's. Officers between the ages of twenty-three and thirty-three could count on a longer useful life than those older or younger. I was too young. Men over forty, though not suffering from want of sleep so much as those under twenty, had less resistance to sudden alarms and shocks. The unfortunates were officers who had endured two years or more of continuous trench service. In many cases they became dipsomaniacs. I knew three or four who had worked up to the point of two bottles of whisky a day before being lucky enough to get wounded or sent home in some other way. A two-bottle company commander of one of our line battalions is still alive who, in three shows running, got his company needlessly destroyed because he was no longer capable of taking clear decisions.

[2] Robert Graves, *Goodbye to All That* (Harmondsworth, 1960), 143–4.

7.3 "The Balfour Declaration" (Nov. 2, 1917)[3]

Arthur Balfour (1848–1930), as foreign secretary, made a bid to win support from Jews in both Germany and the United States by writing to the British Zionist leader Lord Rothschild to offer the prospect of a homeland in Palestine, which had recently been captured by British troops from the Ottoman Turks. This promise, however, did not entirely accord with secret arrangements made with the French (the Sykes–Picot Agreement of 1916), nor with imperial policy between 1919 and 1947.

Why might Balfour have wanted support from German and American Jews? Why might the British government have failed to fulfill the promise made by Balfour in 1917? Was anti-Semitism likely to have been a factor in government policy? How was it possible to respect the rights of the native Arab inhabitants while establishing a Zionist state in Palestine?

Dear Lord Rothschild,

I have much pleasure in conveying to you, on behalf of His Majesty's Government, the following declaration of sympathy with Jewish Zionist aspirations which have been submitted to, and approved by, the Cabinet: "His Majesty's Government view with favor the establishment in Palestine of a National Home for the Jewish people, and will use their best endeavours to facilitate the achievement of this object, it being clearly understood that nothing shall be done which may prejudice the civil and religious rights of existing non-Jewish communities in Palestine, or the rights and political status enjoyed by Jews in any other country." I shall be grateful it you would bring this declaration to the knowledge of the Zionist Federation.

Yours sincerely, Arthur James Balfour

7.4 Deaths in World War I (1914–19)[4]

A total of approximately 9,700,000 military deaths took place during World War I. In some cases, such as the American army, a substantial number of losses were due to the great influenza epidemic of 1918 or other factors not directly related to military action. Many millions more were injured, blinded, lost limbs, and so on. Millions of civilians also died in the Russian civil war and during the breakup of the German and Ottoman Empires.

[3] *The Times*, Nov. 9, 1917.

[4] For a list of the main sources for World War I casualty data, see: www.Wikipedia.org, "World War I casualties". Figures are rounded.

What observations can you make about the proportionate deaths among the great powers? Compare the deaths among men from each of the "white" dominions of the British Empire. Who made the greatest sacrifices? The vast majority of casualties occurred in the European theater. Is it appropriate to call this conflict a "world war"? Why would Australia or New Zealand send so many of their young men to war when Germany, and still less Austria or Turkey, posed no significant threat to their security? What contribution did India make, and why would Indian soldiers have been willing to volunteer to fight in Europe or the Middle East? What are the implications for work, population growth, the economy, and social stability of these deaths? Long-term effects?

	Population in millions	Military & civilian deaths	Deaths as a % of population	Military wounded
Allies				
UK	45.4	994,000	2.19%	1,663,000
Canada	7.2	66,000	0.93%	149,000
Australia	4.5	61,000	1.38%	152,000
N. Zealand	1.1	18,000	1.64%	41,000
India	315.1	74,000	0.02%	69,000
France	39.6	1,697,000	4.29%	1,260,000
Italy	35.6	1,240,000	3.48%	953,000
Russia	175.1	3,311,000	1.89%	4,950,000
USA	92.0	117,400	0.13%	205,000
Central Powers				
Germany	64.9	2,476,000	3.82%	4,247,000
Austria-Hung.	51.4	1,567,000	3.05%	3,620,000
Ottoman Empire	21.3	2,921,000	13.72%	400,000

World War II and the Cold War

7.5 Neville Chamberlain, speech in the House of Commons (Oct. 6, 1938)[5]

From 1933 the German dictator Adolf Hitler (1889–1945) moved to reverse the Versailles settlement of 1919. In 1935 he restored military conscription, in 1936 he remilitarized the Rhineland, and in 1938 he absorbed Austria into his

5 *Parliamentary Debates*, vol. 339, Oct. 6, 1938, c. 545–52.

new empire. Later in that year he demanded reincorporation of 2.8 million "Sudeten" Germans and their land into the Reich, which meant detaching territory assigned to Czechoslovakia by the Versailles peace treaty and denuding the Prague government of virtually all its military defenses. Neither the Tory prime minister, Stanley Baldwin (1867–1947), nor his successor in 1937, Neville Chamberlain (1869–1940), attempted to stop the German advance and made limited efforts to rearm Britain. This policy came to be called "Appeasement" (Figure 7.1). In 1938 at a conference in Munich, Germany, Chamberlain along with the French agreed not to oppose Hitler's invasion of the Sudetenland. Chamberlain broadcast to the nation on September 27, 1938 during the negotiations leading to the Munich agreement, noting that his government had no intention of going to war on behalf of a central European power about whom most British people knew nothing. On returning from Munich with what he called "peace in our time," he spoke to the House of Commons.

Why was Chamberlain ready to accept Hitler's breach of the Versailles settlement? How did he excuse his failure to defend Czechoslovakia? Why was he not more alert to the untrustworthy nature of the Nazi regime? Why were most British people relieved by the achievement of an agreement at Munich? To what degree did the foreign policy positions taken by Italy, France, Russia, and the United States in the 1930s help shape British policy? What made it difficult for Britain to rearm?

When war starts . . . in the very first hour, before any professional soldier, sailor, or airman has been touched, it will strike the workman, the clerk, the man-in-the-street or in the 'bus, and his wife and children in their homes. As I listened, I could not help being moved, as I am sure everybody was who heard the hon. Member for Bridgeton (Mr. Maxton) when he began to paint the picture which he himself had seen and realized what it would mean in war – people burrowing underground, trying to escape from poison gas, knowing that at any hour of the day or night death or mutilation was ready to come upon them. Remembering that the dread of what might happen to them or to those dear to them might remain with fathers and mothers for year after year – when you think of these things you cannot ask people to accept a prospect of that kind; you cannot force them into a position that they have got to accept it; unless you feel yourself, and can make them feel, that the cause for which they are going to fight is a vital cause – a cause that transcends all the human values, a cause to which you can point, if some day you win the victory, and say, "That cause is safe."

Since I first went to Berchtesgaden [Hitler's residence] more than 20,000 letters and telegrams have come to No. 10 Downing Street. Of course, I have only been able to look at a tiny fraction of them, but I have seen enough to know that the people who wrote did not feel that they have such a cause for which to fight, if they were asked to go to war in order that the Sudeten Germans might not join the Reich. That is how they are feeling. That is my answer to those who say that we should have told Germany weeks ago that, if her army crossed the border of Czechoslovakia, we should be at war with her. We had no treaty obligations and no legal obligations to Czechoslovakia and if we had said that, we feel that we should have received no support from the people of this country. . . .

As regards future policy, it seems to me that there are really only two possible alternatives. One of them is to base yourself upon the view that any sort of friendly relations, or possible relations, shall I say, with totalitarian States are impossible, that the assurances which have been given to me personally are worthless, that they have sinister designs and that they are bent upon the domination of Europe and the gradual destruction of democracies. Of course, on that hypothesis, war has got to come, and that is the view – a perfectly intelligible view – of a certain number of hon. and right hon. Gentlemen in the House. . . .

If the view which I have been describing is the one to be taken, I think we must inevitably proceed to the next stage – that war is coming, broadly speaking the democracies against the totalitarian States – that certainly we must arm ourselves to the teeth, that clearly we must make military alliances with any other Powers whom we can get to work with us, and that we must hope that we shall be allowed to start the war at the moment that suits us and not at the moment that suits the other side. That is what the right hon. Gentlemen call collective security. Some hon. Members opposite [Labour Party] will walk into any trap if it is only baited with a familiar catchword and they do it when this system is called collective security. But that is not the collective security we are thinking of or did think of when talking about the system of the League of Nations. That was a sort of universal collective security in which all nations were to take their part. This plan may give you security; it certainly is not collective in any sense. It appears to me to contain all the things which the party opposite used to denounce before the War – entangling alliances, balance of power and power politics. If I reject it, as I do, it is not because I give it a label; it is because, to my mind, it is a policy of utter despair. . . .

. . . Does the experience of the Great War and of the years that followed it give us reasonable hope that, if some new war started, that would end war any more than the last one did? No. I do not believe that war is inevitable . . . What is the alternative to this bleak and barren policy of the inevitability of war? In my view it is that we should seek by all means in our power to avoid war, by analyzing possible causes, by trying to remove them, by discussion in a spirit of collaboration and good will. I cannot believe that such a program would be rejected by the people of this country, even if it does mean the establishment of personal contact with dictators, and of talks man to man on the basis that each, while maintaining his own ideas of the internal government of his country, is willing to allow that other systems may suit better other peoples. . . .

One good thing, at any rate, has come out of this emergency through which we have passed. It has thrown a vivid light upon our preparations for defense, on their

Figure 7.1 "Which backbone shall I lay out this morning, My Lord?" Cartoon by David Low, *Evening Standard*, Aug. 1, 1938. British Cartoon Archive, University of Kent, www.cartoons.ac.uk / *Evening Standard.*

Lord Halifax was foreign secretary in Neville Chamberlain's government. He was not as wholly committed to "appeasement" as Chamberlain and emerged as the chief alternative candidate to Churchill for prime minister in May 1940 but stood aside. What does the cartoonist think about "appeasement"? How is the aristocracy portrayed in this illustration? Did this cartoon reflect popular opinion at the time of the Munich Crisis in 1938?

strength and our weakness. I should not think we were doing our duty if we had not already ordered that a prompt and thorough inquiry should be made to cover the whole of our preparations, military and civil, in order to see, in the light of what has happened during these hectic days, what further steps may be necessary to make good our deficiencies in the shortest possible time.

7.6 Winston S. Churchill, speech in the House of Commons (Oct. 5, 1938)[6]

Winston S. Churchill (1874–1965) was one of the few public figures to raise his voice in opposition to the policy of appeasement. He shrewdly predicted the imminent extinction of Czechoslovakia, which Hitler soon devoured a few months after Munich despite his promises otherwise. Churchill's denunciation of the Munich agreement found little support in 1938, but

6 *Parliamentary Debates*, vol. 339, Oct. 5, 1938, c. 360–73.

would help make him prime minister in 1940. Only Hitler's unprovoked invasion of Poland in September 1939 opened Chamberlain's eyes to the untrustworthiness and depravity of the Nazi regime.

What were Churchill's reasons for believing the Munich agreement was a disaster? How did Churchill account for Britain's unpreparedness to meet the challenge of Nazi aggression? What policy did Churchill advocate and why? Would you agree with the argument that the Appeasers were responsible for World War II because they encouraged Hitler to believe they would never stand up to his demands and that assumption led him to attack Poland?

I will begin by saying what everybody would like to ignore or forget but which must nevertheless be stated, namely, that we have sustained a total and unmitigated defeat, and that France has suffered even more than we have ...

The utmost my right hon. Friend the Prime Minister ... has been able to gain from Czechoslovakia in the matters which were in dispute has been the German dictator, instead of snatching his victuals from the table, has been content to have them served to him course by course ...

And I will say this, that I believe the Czechs, left to themselves and told they were going to get no help from the Western Powers, would have been able to make better terms than they have got – they could hardly have worse – after all this tremendous perturbation ...

All is over. Silent, mournful, abandoned, broken, Czechoslovakia receded into the darkness. She has suffered in every respect by her association with the Western democracies and with the League of Nations, of which she has always been an obedient servant. She has suffered in particular from her association with France, under whose guidance and policy she has been actuated for so long. ...

I venture to think that in future the Czechoslovak State cannot be maintained as an independent entity. You will find that in a period of time which may be measured by years, but may be measured only by months, Czechoslovakia will be engulfed by the Nazi regime. Perhaps they may join it in despair or in revenge. At any rate, that story is over and told. But we cannot consider the abandonment and ruin of Czechoslovakia in the light only of what happened last month. It is the most grievous consequence which we have yet experienced of what we have done and of what we have left undone in the last five years – five years of futile good intention, five years of eager search for the line of least resistance, five years of uninterrupted retreat of British power, five years of neglect of our air defenses. Those are the features which I stand here to declare and which marked an improvident stewardship for which Great Britain and France have dearly to pay. We have been reduced in those five years from a position of security so overwhelming and so unchallengeable that we never cared to think about it. We have been reduced from a position where the very word "war" was considered one which would be used only by persons qualifying for a lunatic asylum. We have been reduced from a position of safety and power – power to do good, power to be generous to a beaten foe, power to make terms with Germany, power to give her proper redress for her grievances, power to stop her arming if we chose, power to take any step in strength or mercy or justice which we thought right – reduced in five years from a position safe and unchallenged to where we stand now.

When I think of the fair hopes of a long peace which still lay before Europe at the beginning of 1933 when Herr Hitler first obtained power, and of all the opportunities of arresting the growth of the Nazi power which have been thrown away, when I think of the immense combinations and resources which have been neglected or squandered, I cannot believe that a parallel exists in the whole course of history. So far as this country is concerned the responsibility must rest with those who have the undisputed control of our political affairs. They neither prevented Germany from rearming, nor did they rearm ourselves in time . . . They neglected to make alliances and combinations which might have repaired previous errors, and thus they left us in the hour of trial without adequate national defense or effective international security. . . .

We are in the presence of a disaster of the first magnitude which has befallen Great Britain and France. Do not let us blind ourselves to that. It must now be accepted that all the countries of Central and Eastern Europe will make the best terms they can with the triumphant Nazi Power. The system of alliances in Central Europe upon which France has relied for her safety has been swept away, and I can see no means by which it can be reconstituted. . . .

Many people, no doubt, honestly believe that they are only giving away the interests of Czechoslovakia, whereas I fear we shall find that we have deeply compromised, and perhaps fatally endangered, the safety and even the independence of Great Britain and France . . . The Prime Minister desires to see cordial relations between this country and Germany. There is no difficulty at all in having cordial relations with the German people. Our hearts go out to them. But they have no power. You must have diplomatic and correct relations, but there can never be friendship between the British democracy and the Nazi Power, that Power which spurns Christian ethics, which cheers its onward course by a barbarous paganism, which vaunts the spirit of aggression and conquest, which derives strength and perverted pleasure from persecution, and uses, as we have seen, with pitiless brutality the threat of murderous force. That Power cannot ever be the trusted friend of the British democracy . . .

And do not suppose that this is the end. This is only the beginning of the reckoning. This is only the first sip, the first foretaste of a bitter cup which will be proffered to us year by year unless by a supreme recovery of moral health and martial vigor, we arise again and take our stand for freedom as in olden time.

7.7 *Winston S. Churchill, speeches in the House of Commons (1940)*[7]

In the wake of the German "blitzkrieg" against the Low Countries and France in April 1940 the Chamberlain government collapsed and Churchill (document 7.6) became prime minister. One of his signal accomplishments was to rally the British people and to persuade the political elite to continue the war in the face of almost overwhelming odds. His sequence of speeches in 1940 are unparalleled in British history. They were originally delivered in the House of Commons and then broadcast to the nation in shortened versions on the radio.

What arguments did Churchill make to justify continuing the war against Germany? What aspects of the tone and style of the words and sentences contributed to the persuasiveness of his analysis? In what ways did he invoke a moral argument for British victory?

May 13, 1940

I would say to the House, as I said to those who have joined this Government: "I have nothing to offer but blood, toil, tears and sweat."

We have before us an ordeal of the most grievous kind. We have before us many, many long months of struggle and of suffering. You ask, what is our policy? I can say: It is to wage war, by sea, land and air, with all our might and with all the strength that God can give us; to wage war against a monstrous tyranny, never surpassed in the dark, lamentable catalogue of human crime. That is our policy. You ask, what is our aim? I can answer in one word: It is victory, victory at all costs, victory in spite of all terror, victory, however long and hard the road may be; for without victory, there is no survival. Let that be realized; no survival for the British Empire, no survival for all that the British Empire has stood for, no survival for the urge and impulse of the ages, that mankind will move forward towards its goal. But I take up my task with buoyancy and hope. I feel sure that our cause will not be suffered to fail among men. At this time I feel entitled to claim the aid of all, and I say, "Come then, let us go forward together with our united strength."

June 4, 1940

Even though large tracts of Europe and many old and famous states have fallen or may fall into the grasp of the Gestapo and all the odious apparatus of Nazi rule, we hall not flag or fail. We shall go on to the end. We shall fight in France, we shall

[7] *Parliamentary Debates*, vol. 360, May 13, 1940, c. 1502; vol. 361, Jun. 4, 1940, c. 796; vol. 361, Aug. 20, 1940, c. 1159, 1163–4, 1170–1.

fight on the seas and oceans, we shall fight with growing confidence and growing strength in the air. We shall defend our island, whatever the cost may be. We shall fight on the beaches, we shall fight on the landing-grounds, we shall fight in the fields and in the streets, we shall fight in the hills. We shall never surrender; and even if, which I do not for a moment believe, this island or a large part of it were subjugated and starving, then our Empire beyond the seas, armed and guarded by the British Fleet, would carry on the struggle, until, in God's good time, the New World, with all its power and might, steps forth to the rescue and liberation of the Old.

August 20, 1940

Almost a year has passed since the war began, and it is natural for us to focus, I think, to pause on our journey at this milestone and survey the dark, wide field. . . .

. . . The British nation and the British Empire finding themselves alone, stood undismayed against disaster. No one flinched or wavered; nay, some who formerly thought of peace, now think only of war. Our people are united and resolved, as they have never been before. Death and ruin have become small things compared with the shame of defeat or failure in duty. We cannot tell what lies ahead. It may be that even greater ordeals lie before us. We shall face whatever is coming to us. We are sure of ourselves and of our cause and here then is the supreme fact which has emerged in these months of trial. . . .

I hope – indeed I pray – that we shall not be found unworthy of our victory if after toil and tribulation it is granted to us. For the rest, we have to gain the victory. That is our task. . . .

For my own part, looking out upon the future, I do not view the process with any misgivings. I could not stop it if I wished; no one can stop it. Like the Mississippi, it just keeps rolling along. Let it roll. Let it roll on full flood, inexorable, irresistible, benignant, to broader lands and better days.

7.8 Winston S. Churchill, "Iron Curtain" speech at Westminster College, Fulton, Missouri (Mar. 5, 1946)[8]

In 1946 Winston Churchill, no longer prime minister but still leader of the Conservative Party, delivered the iconic speech of the Cold War, as it took shape between the USSR and the West in the later 1940s. He spoke at the invitation of President Harry Truman (1884–1972) at a college in the latter's home state.

8 *Congressional Record*, 79th Congress, 2nd session, Appendix, vol. 92-Part 9, March 6, 1946, 1145–7.

How did Churchill address the problem of the decline in British power after the war? What policy did Churchill propose as the means to deal with the Soviet Union? What did Churchill mean by the "special relationship"? What is it about Churchill's rhetoric that makes his case seem so persuasive?

The United States stands at this time at the pinnacle of world power. It is a solemn moment for the American democracy. For with primacy in power is also joined an awe-inspiring accountability to the future. As you look around you, you feel not only the sense of duty done but also you feel anxiety lest you fall below the level of achievement. Opportunity is here now, clear and shining for both our countries. To reject it or ignore it or fritter it away will bring upon us all the long reproaches of the after-time. It is necessary that constancy of mind, persistency of purpose, and the grand simplicity of decision shall guide and rule the conduct of the English-speaking people in peace as they did in war. . . .

We cannot be blind to the fact that the liberties enjoyed by individual citizens throughout the United States and the British Empire are not valid in a considerable number of countries, some of which are very powerful. In these States control is enforced upon the common people by various kinds of all-embracing police governments . . . The power of the state is exercised without restraint, either by dictators or by compact oligarchies operating through a privileged party and a political police. It is not our duty at this time, when difficulties are so numerous, to interfere forcibly in the internal affairs of countries which we have not conquered in war, but we must never cease to proclaim in fearless tones the great principles of freedom and the rights of man which are the joint inheritance of the English-speaking world and which, through Magna Carta, the Bill of Rights, the habeas corpus, trial by jury, and the English common law find their most famous expression in the American Declaration of Independence.

All this means that the people of any country have the right and should have the power, by constitutional action, by free, unfettered elections, with secret ballot, to choose or change the character or form of government under which they dwell, that freedom of speech and thought should reign; that courts of justice, independent of the executive, unbiased by any party, should administer laws which have received the broad assent of large majorities or are consecrated by time and custom. Here are the title deeds of freedom, which should lie in every cottage home. Here is the message of the British and American peoples to mankind. Let us preach what we practice – let us practice what we preach . . .

Neither the sure prevention of war, nor the continuous rise of world organization, will be gained without what I have called the fraternal association of the English-speaking peoples. This means a special relationship between the British Commonwealth and Empire and the United States. . . .

A shadow has fallen upon the scenes so lately lightened by the Allied victory. Nobody knows what Soviet Russia and its Communist international organization intends to do in the immediate future, or what are the limits, if any, to their expansive and proselytizing tendencies. I have a strong admiration and regard for the valiant Russian people and for my wartime comrade, Marshal Stalin. . . .

We understand the Russian need to be secure on her western frontiers by the removal of all possibility of German aggression. We welcome Russia to her rightful place among the leading nations of the world. . . . It is my duty however, for I am sure you would wish me to state the facts as I see them to you, to place before you certain facts about the present position in Europe.

From Stettin in the Baltic to Trieste in the Adriatic, an iron curtain has descended across the continent. Behind that line lie all the capitals of the ancient states of central and eastern Europe. Warsaw, Berlin, Prague, Vienna, Budapest, Belgrade, Bucharest and Sofia, all these famous cities and the populations around them lie in what I must call the Soviet sphere, and all are subject, in one form or another, not only to Soviet influence but to a very high, and in many cases, increasing measure of control from Moscow. . . .

The Russian-dominated Polish Government has been encouraged to make enormous and wrongful inroads upon Germany, and mass expulsions of millions of Germans on a scale grievous and undreamed-of are now taking place. The Communist parties, which were very small in all these eastern states of Europe, have been raised to preeminence and power far beyond their numbers and are seeking everywhere to obtain totalitarian control.

Except in the British Commonwealth and in the United States, where Communism is in its infancy, the Communist parties or fifth columns constitute a growing challenge and peril to Christian civilization. . . .

. . . I repulse the idea that a new war is inevitable, still more that it is imminent. It is because I am sure that our fortunes are still in our own hands and that we hold the power to save the future, that I feel the duty to speak out now that I have the occasion and the opportunity to do so. I do not believe that Soviet Russia desires war. . . .

From what I have seen of our Russian friends and allies during the war, I am convinced that there is nothing they admire so much as strength, and there is nothing for which they have less respect than for weakness. For that reason the old doctrine of a balance of power is unsound. We cannot afford, if we can help it, to work on narrow margins, offering temptations to a trial of strength. If the western democracies stand together in strict adherence to the principles of the United Nations Charter, their influence for furthering those principles will be immense and no one is likely to molest them. If, however, they become divided or falter in their duty and if these all-important years are allowed to slip away, then indeed catastrophe may overwhelm us all.

Let no man underrate the abiding power of the British Empire and Commonwealth. Because you see the 46,000,000 in our island harassed about their food supply, of which they grew only one half, even in war time, or because we have difficulty in restarting our industries and export trade after 6 years of passionate war effort, do not suppose that we shall not come through these dark years of privation as we have come through the glorious years of agony, or that half a century from now you will not see seventy or eighty millions of Britons spread about the world and united in defense of our traditions, our way of life, and of the world causes we and you espouse. . . . If all British moral and material forces and convictions are joined with your own in fraternal association, the highroads of the future will be clear, not only for us but for all, not only for our time but for a century to come.

Party Ideologies

7.9 Conservative Party Manifesto (1979)[9]

The 1970s in Britain were difficult years. At times the country seemed to become ungovernable. Inflation was rampant and the unions were in open conflict with both businesses and the government. Onto that scene arrived a new and dynamic figure, Margaret Thatcher (b.1925), who promised order and prosperity. The Conservative Party manifesto for the general election in 1979 that swept her to victory laid out a road map of her plan of attack.

Some of the language is coded or deliberately misleading. For example, getting people to buy the homes provided by the state was supposed to "support family life." In fact it was to create a larger property-owning lower middle class that would vote Conservative and cut taxes. Can you identify other masked agenda items? How would a Labour supporter have replied to Thatcher's proposals? What in this agenda might appeal to people who had previously voted Labour? To what degree did Thatcher carry out her promises?

This election is about the future of Britain – a great country which seems to have lost its way. . . .

Today, this country is faced with its most serious problems since the Second World War. What has happened to our country, to the values we used to share, to the success and prosperity we once took for granted?

During the industrial strife of last winter, confidence, self-respect, common sense, and even our sense of common humanity were shaken. At times this society seemed on the brink of disintegration. . . .

[The Labour Government] have made things worse in three ways. First, by practicing the politics of envy and by actively discouraging the creation of wealth, they have set one group against another in an often bitter struggle to gain a larger share of a weak economy.

[9] "1979 Conservative Party General Election Manifesto," www.conservative-party.net.

Second, by enlarging the role of the State and diminishing the role of the individual, they have crippled the enterprise and effort on which a prosperous country with improving social services depends.

Third, by heaping privilege without responsibility on the trade unions, Labour have given a minority of extremists the power to abuse individual liberties and to thwart Britain's chances of success. One result is that the trade union movement, which sprang from a deep and genuine fellow-feeling for the brotherhood of man, is today more distrusted and feared than ever before.

It is not just that Labour have governed Britain badly. They have reached a dead-end. The [radical] nature of their Party now prevents them from governing successfully in a free society and a mixed economy. . . .

Our five tasks are:

1. To restore the health of our economic and social life, by controlling inflation and striking a fair balance between the rights and duties of the trade union movement.
2. To restore incentive so that hard work pays, success is rewarded and genuine new jobs are created in an expanding economy.
3. To uphold Parliament and the rule of law.
4. To support family life, by helping people to become home-owners, raising the standards of their children's education, and concentrating welfare services on the effective support of the old, the sick, the disabled and those who are in real need.
5. To strengthen Britain's defenses and work with our allies to protect our interests in an increasingly threatening world.

7.10 Tony Blair, Speech to the Labour Party annual conference (Oct. 2, 2001)[10]

Tony Blair (b.1953), more than any other single person, created the "New Labour" Party. He moved to eliminate the commitment to "socialism" in Labour's declaration of principles and shifted the party's direction in a moderate, centrist, social democratic direction. In this speech he explains some of the reasons for doing so.

Some argue that New Labour was more about becoming "electable" than about principle, and some see it as a betrayal of traditional Labour values and ideas. How was New Labour different from traditional Labour? How was New Labour different from the early twentieth-century Liberal Party (documents 4.20 and 5.24), Margaret Thatcher's (document 7.9) ideas, or from the post-Thatcher Conservative Party?

10 "Tony Blair's speech," www.guardian.co.uk, Oct. 2, 2001.

What is the answer to Britain's future? Not each person for themselves, but working together as a community to ensure that everyone, not just the privileged few get the chance to succeed.

This is an extraordinary moment for progressive politics. Our values are the right ones for this age: the power of community, solidarity, the collective ability to further the individual's interests.

People ask me if I think ideology is dead. My answer is: in the sense of rigid forms of economic and social theory, yes. The 20th century killed those ideologies and their passing causes little regret. But, in the sense of a governing idea in politics, based on values, no. The governing idea of modern social democracy is community. Founded on the principles of social justice. That people should rise according to merit not birth; that the test of any decent society is not the contentment of the wealthy and strong, but the commitment to the poor and weak.

But values aren't enough. The mantle of leadership comes at a price: the courage to learn and change; to show how values that stand for all ages, can be applied in a way relevant to each age.

Our politics only succeed when the realism is as clear as the idealism. This party's strength comes from the journey of change and learning we have made.

We learnt that however much we strive for peace, we need strong defense capability where a peaceful approach fails. We learnt that equality is about equal worth, not equal outcomes.

Today our idea of society is shaped around mutual responsibility; a deal, an agreement between citizens not a one-way gift, from the well-off to the dependent.

Our economic and social policy today owes as much to the liberal social democratic tradition of Lloyd George, Keynes and Beveridge as to the socialist principles of the 1945 Government.

Just over a decade ago, people asked if Labour could ever win again. Today they ask the same question of the Opposition. Painful though the journey of change has been, it has been worth it, every stage of the way. On this journey, the values have never changed. The aims haven't. Our aims would be instantly recognizable to every Labour leader from Keir Hardie onwards. But the means do change.

The journey hasn't ended. It never ends. The next stage for New Labour is not backwards; it is renewing ourselves again. Just after the election, an old colleague of mine said: "Come on Tony, now we've won again, can't we drop all this New Labour and do what we believe in?" I said: "It's worse than you think. I really do believe in it." . . .

Economic competence is the pre-condition of social justice. We have legislated for fairness at work, like the minimum wage which people struggled a century for. But we won't give up the essential flexibility of our economy or our commitment to enterprise. Why? Because in a world leaving behind mass production, where technology revolutionizes not just companies but whole industries, almost overnight, enterprise creates the jobs people depend on.

Why? Because in the new markets countries like Britain can only create wealth by brain power not low wages and sweatshop labor. We have cut youth unemployment by 75 per cent.

But more than any government before us . . . we refuse to pay [welfare] benefits to those who refuse to work. Why? Because welfare that works is welfare that helps people to help themselves.

The graffiti, the vandalism, the burnt out cars, the street corner drug dealers, the teenage mugger just graduating from the minor school of crime: we're not old fashioned or right-wing to take action against this social menace.

We're standing up for the people we represent, who play by the rules and have a right to expect others to do the same.

The European Union

7.11 Enoch Powell, speech in the House of Commons (Oct. 28, 1971)[11]

Many reasons were offered for opposing British entry into the European Economic Community (EEC), later the European Union (EU). Some feared severing ties with the Commonwealth or breaking up the "Special Relationship" with the United States. Others worried about European socialism creeping into British government. Perhaps the most visceral and serious objection had to do with loss of sovereignty. The Conservative MP Enoch Powell (1912–98) predicted trouble ahead in this speech in 1971 when the principal activities of the EEC were still economic. The tradition in British politics had been that Parliament was supreme, and now the country was moving in a direction where that would no longer be true.

Why was the supremacy of Parliament important? What troubled Powell about the commitment to Europe? What benefits would the economic union and later the political union bring that might offset loss of sovereignty? Can loss of sovereignty actually take place if countries are able withdraw from the community? What strengths did Britain bring to the union?

The unique character of the decision proposed to the House, which involves a cession by the House – initially perhaps minor, but destined to grow – of its present sovereignty, of its present ultimate sovereignty, and requires from the people a commitment to merge themselves and their destinies with those of the countries of the adjacent Continent.

I do not think the fact that this involves a cession – and a growing cession – of Parliament's sovereignty can be disputed. Indeed, I notice that those who are the

11 *Parliamentary Debates*, vol. 818, Oct. 28, 1971, c. 2186–7.

keenest proposers of British entry are the most ready to confess – not to confess, but to assert – that of course this involves by its very nature a reduction of the sovereignty of the House. Nevertheless, it is worth while reminding the House that the advice which it was given by the Lord Chancellor [the chief legal official in Britain]: "The constitutional innovation would lie in the acceptance in advance as part of the law of the United Kingdom of provisions to be made in the future by instruments issued by the Community institutions" – then follow these words – "a situation for which there is no precedent in this country." It is an unprecedented act of renunciation which this House is called upon to make. No wonder, then, that it should be a condition for that that it should have our full-hearted consent. . . .

For legal purposes we ought to regard this as an irrevocable commitment. But leaving that on one side, this is a step which by its very nature makes no sense unless it is intended to be irrevocable or irreversible. This is not the kind of community, nor are these the kind of grounds, of which one can say that we will enter into it but that if we do not like it we shall be off like a shot. What we are asked for in this House and in this country is an intention, an irrevocable decision, gradually to part with the sovereignty of this House and to commit ourselves to the merger of this nation and its destinies with the rest of the Community.

7.12 Lord Kingsland, speech in the House of Lords (Nov. 3, 1997)[12]

Lord Kingsland (1942–2009) was a Conservative politician who favored membership in the European Union. However, as a lawyer, he had doubts about the enactment of the 1998 Human Rights Act introduced by the Labour Party. The constitutional historian Vernon Bogdanor calls the Act the "cornerstone of the new constitution."[13] Until 1998 Britain did not have legislation guaranteeing protection to individuals against the rule of the majority. Parliament exercised unlimited powers. Unlike most EU member states Britain did not incorporate the Union's Convention on Human Rights into its own system of laws because that would have infringed parliamentary supremacy, although in 1966 British subjects had been granted the right to appeal to the European Court at Strasbourg. From 1998 British courts were empowered to decide whether British law contravened the Convention, which fundamentally changed the position of judges in their relationship with Parliament, for they could now oblige the legislature to revise laws incompatible with the Convention. Many people continue to urge enactment of a British Bill of Rights so that no ambiguities can remain about the protection of individual human rights.

12 *Parliamentary Debates*, vol. 582, Nov. 3, 1997, c. 1234–8.
13 Vernon Bogdanor, *The New British Constitution* (Oxford, 2009), 53.

Why was Kingsland concerned about the Human Rights Act? Why might some people oppose guaranteeing human rights irrevocably? To what degree was the issue a concern about European versus British law as opposed to changes in the British constitution?

If the Bill becomes law it will be a defining moment in the life of our constitution. Perhaps the only other examples this century of such defining moments were the passage of the Parliament Acts of 1911 and 1949. As your Lordships are acutely aware, they had a dramatic effect on the balance of power between your Lordships' House and another place [House of Commons].

If this Bill reaches the statute book it will have an equally defining influence on the balance of power between the legislature and the judiciary. Whatever the inherent merits of its contents, I hope that your Lordships, in formulating your amendments, will be aware of how deep are the implications for that relationship. They lie at the heart of the doctrine of the separation of powers in our constitution, which has been the hallmark of our liberties throughout the centuries. . . .

There are many obvious reasons for wanting incorporation [of the European Convention on Human Rights into British Law]. Many people believe it hypocritical that we send our citizens to Strasbourg to obtain rights to which they are not entitled at home. We know that the convention is judge-driven and we often find that the judges in the court in Strasbourg – brilliant and well-meaning lawyers though they are – lack an understanding of our constitutional ways which are, after all, unique.

Furthermore, the number of countries which have become part of the convention has expanded rapidly in recent years. Often the senior judges from those countries who will sit in Strasbourg have little experience of the jurisprudence of a free society. Until recently the jurisprudence in their countries has frequently been rubber stamping an order of the local commissar. [The latter was] the man who counted. Therefore, in that context, putting the interpretation of the convention in the hands of our own judges has its attractions.

It is also a fact that, for a long time, where there has been ambiguity about a domestic statute and where one acceptable interpretation would be in accordance with the convention, our judges have given our statutes that interpretation. Therefore, to some degree the process of incorporation is already occurring. . . .

What is the doctrine of the separation of powers in our country? It is that judges do not interfere with the parliamentary process on the one hand and Parliament does not interfere with the judicial process on the other. That principle has stood us in enormously good stead, certainly since the Glorious Revolution more than 300 years ago. To the extent that the judges are not reflecting the jurisprudence of the convention but stating their own view about what the convention says, they are in breach of that doctrine. They are initiating new legislation. . . .

Empire to Commonwealth

7.13 The Statute of Westminster (1931)[14]

Although Canada, Australia, and other "white" dominions had in large measure achieved self-government before World War I, and southern Ireland soon thereafter, an imperial conference in 1926 laid the groundwork for full independence. This policy was given legislative force by the "Statute of Westminster" enacted by the British Parliament in 1931. The king and his successors remained sovereigns of all the "white" colonies with the exception of South Africa after 1961.

Did the Empire have any continued importance after 1931? Why might the "white" colonies have declared war on Germany shortly after Britain did so in 1939?

And whereas it is in accord with the established constitutional position that no law hereafter made by the Parliament of the United Kingdom shall extend to any of the said Dominions as part of the law of that Dominion otherwise than at the request and with the consent of that Dominion.

... The Dominion of Canada, the Commonwealth of Australia, the Dominion of New Zealand, the Union of South Africa, the Irish Free State and Newfoundland have severally requested and consented to the submission of a measure to the Parliament of the United Kingdom for making such provision with regard to the matters aforesaid ...

7.14 The Atlantic Charter (Aug. 14, 1941)[15]

Winston S. Churchill (documents 7.6, 7.7, and 7.8) and US President Franklin D. Roosevelt (1882–1945) met at sea off the coast of Newfoundland in August 1941 and jointly issued the following declaration. Churchill was desperate to achieve America's entry into the war and was ready to promise virtually anything to achieve that end. Roosevelt could not persuade his own people or Congress that the European war was crucial to American security, but he agreed to lay out a series of promises reminiscent of Wilson's Fourteen Points in an attempt to focus his country on the need to safeguard democracy.

Why might Churchill have been reluctant to subscribe to some of the points in the Charter? With respect to the third pledge, Churchill argued in the House

[14] 22 Geo. V, c. 4, 13–17.

[15] www.nato.int, last updated May 15, 2009.

of Commons that it only applied to the countries conquered by the Nazis or Communists in Europe. Was his argument convincing in terms of the British Empire? What were the long-term implications of the Charter for the British Empire? What was Roosevelt hoping to achieve through the Charter?

1. [The United States and Great Britain] seek no aggrandizement, territorial or other.
2. They desire to see no territorial changes that do not accord with the freely expressed wishes of the peoples concerned.
3. They respect the right of all peoples to choose the form of government under which they will live; and they wish to see sovereign rights and self government restored to those who have been forcibly deprived of them.
4. They will endeavor, with due respect for their existing obligations, to further the enjoyment by all States, great and small, victor or vanquished, of access, on equal terms, to the trade and to the raw materials of the world which are needed for their economic prosperity.
5. They desire to bring about the fullest collaboration between all nations in the economic field with the object of securing, for all, improved labor standards, economic advancement and social security.
6. After the final destruction of the Nazi tyranny, they hope to see established a peace which will afford to all nations the means of dwelling in safety within their own boundaries, and which will afford assurance that all the men in all the lands may live out their lives in freedom from fear and want.
7. Such a peace should enable all men to traverse the high seas and oceans without hindrance.
8. They believe that all of the nations of the world, for realistic as well as spiritual reasons must come to the abandonment of the use of force. Since no future peace can be maintained if land, sea or air armaments continue to be employed by nations which threaten, or may threaten, aggression outside of their frontiers, they believe, pending the establishment of a wider and permanent system of general security, that the disarmament of such nations is essential. They will likewise aid and encourage all other practicable measures which will lighten for peace-loving peoples the crushing burden of armament.

7.15 Clement Attlee, memorandum to the Cabinet on Indian Policy (Jan. 4, 1947)[16]

The Government of India Act in 1935 had finally set the British government on the road to granting Indian self-government. The postwar Labour

[16] Great Britain, National Archives, CAB/129/16.

administration was determined on full independence both on principle and as a matter of facing reality. Britain no longer had the military or economic strength to hold on to such a vast realm. Ironically, the problem that stood in the way of seeking this outcome was the division among Indian leaders over whether to continue as a single state or separate into a Muslim Pakistan and a Hindu India. Prime minister Clement Attlee (1883–1967) laid out the issues for his Cabinet.

Is it fair to say that Hitler was the man most responsible for the independence of India and the breakup of the British Empire? Why might the United States also have put pressure on the British to withdraw? Were the British responsible for the divisions within Indian society that made the attainment of a peaceful resolution to the crisis of 1947 impossible? Did the British cut and run too quickly? Why might Attlee have chosen a member of the royal family (Earl Mountbatten, Prince Louis of Battenberg, 1900–79) to serve as the viceroy in charge of the final negotiations for independence? Why did the Labour government decide not to grant independence to the British colonies in Africa at the same time as India was freed?

The declaration of the prime minister of 15th March last which met with general approval in Parliament and the country, made it clear that it was for the Indian people themselves to choose their future status and constitution and that in the opinion of His Majesty's Government the time had come for responsibility for the government of India to pass into Indian hands.

The Cabinet Mission which was sent to India last year spent over three months in consultation with Indian leaders in order to help them to agree upon a method for determining the future constitution of India, so that the transfer of power might be smoothly and rapidly effected. It was only when it seemed clear that without some initiative from the Cabinet Mission agreement was unlikely to be reached that they put forward proposals themselves.

These proposals, made public in May last, envisaged that the future constitution of India should be settled by a Constituent Assembly composed . . . of representatives of all communities and interests in British India and other Indian [princely] states. . . .

His Majesty's Government desire to hand over their responsibility to authorities established by a constitution approved by all parties in India, but unfortunately there is at present no clear prospect that such a constitution and such authorities will emerge. The present state of uncertainty is fraught with danger and cannot be indefinitely prolonged. His majesty's Government wish to make it clear that it is their definite intention to effect the transference of power in India by a date not later than the middle of 1948.

7.16 The London Declaration (1949)[17]

After World War II India and then other former "non-white" colonies gained independence but chose either to retain King George VI (1895–1952), and after 1952 Queen Elizabeth II (b.1926), as their monarch or to voluntarily join a new post-imperial organization called the Commonwealth. The Empire was reconfigured by a conference in London held in April 1949 when the king took the title Head of the Commonwealth. Today the queen leads the organization that includes one-third of the world's population.

Why might India and other former colonies have decided to retain the monarch as the leader of the Commonwealth? Why did former colonies once forcibly held under British rule choose voluntarily to retain association with other former members of the Empire and the United Kingdom itself?

The Governments of the United Kingdom, Canada, Australia, New Zealand, South Africa, India, Pakistan and Ceylon, whose countries are united as Members of the British Commonwealth of Nations and owe a common allegiance to the Crown, which is also the symbol of their free association, have considered the impending constitutional changes in India.

. . . The Government of India have . . . declared and affirmed India's desire to continue her full membership of the Commonwealth of Nations and her acceptance of The King as the symbol of a free association of its independent nations and as such the Head of the Commonwealth. . . .

Accordingly the United Kingdom, Canada, Australia, New Zealand, South Africa, India, Pakistan and Ceylon hereby declare that they remain united as free and equal members of the Commonwealth of Nations, freely co-operating in the pursuit of peace, liberty, and progress.

7.17 Gamal Abdel Nasser, speech (Sept. 15, 1956)[18]

Britain granted independence to Egypt after the war, but its "puppet" king was overthrown in 1952. Later a military officer, Gamal Abdel Nasser (1918–70), became dictator. In 1956 he seized control of the Suez Canal, a key shipping channel, ownership of which recently had been relinquished by the British and French. In this speech he justified his actions and appealed for support from the Arab world. He became a hero to many people in countries

[17] *The Times*, Apr. 28, 1949, 4.

[18] "Speech of Gamal Abdel Nasser, 15 Sept. 1956," in *The Suez Problem*, July 26– Sept. 22, US Department of State Publication, No. 6392, Washington, DC, GPO, 1956, 345–51.

that had suffered under imperialism or still lived in colonies. An attempt to repossess that canal by military force organized by prime minister Anthony Eden (1897–1977) foundered when the United States forced the French, Israelis, and British to withdraw by threatening severe economic sanctions. British public opinion was deeply, even bitterly divided by Eden's policy.

What was Nasser's strategy to resist British imperialism? Why did the British have to back down? What were the consequences of this humiliating disaster in the short and long term? Why did the United States break with its Cold War allies in order to support Nasser?

In these decisive days in the history of mankind, these days in which truth struggles to have itself recognized in international chaos where powers of evil domination and imperialism have prevailed Egypt stands firmly to preserve her sovereignty. Your country stands solidly and staunchly to preserve her dignity against imperialistic schemes of a number of nations who have uncovered their desires for domination and supremacy.

... I am speaking in the name of every Egyptian Arab and in the name of all free countries and of all those who believe in liberty and are ready to defend it. I am speaking in the name of principles proclaimed by these countries in the Atlantic Charter. But they are now violating these principles and it has become our lot to shoulder the responsibility of reaffirming and establishing them anew ...

... By stating that by succeeding, Abdel Nasser would weaken Britain's stand against Arab nationalism, Eden is in fact admitting his real objective is not Abdel Nasser as such but rather to defeat Arab nationalism and crush its cause. Eden speaks and finds his own answer. A month ago he let out the cry that he was after Abdel Nasser. Today the Egyptian people are fully conscious of their sovereign rights and Arab nationalism is fully awakened to its new destiny ...

7.18 Harold Macmillan, speech to the South African Parliament (Feb. 3, 1960)[19]

The Conservative prime minister, Harold Macmillan (1894–1986), delivered what became known as the "Wind of Change" speech to an unconvinced and unhappy white supremacist legislature at Cape Town, South Africa in February 1960. His assessment was correct, but the South African regime decided to break its ties with the Commonwealth and stand alone against the tide of African nationalism. Britain followed Macmillan's course and freed all of its remaining African colonies in short order.

19 *The Times*, Feb. 4, 1960, 15.

Why was South Africa different than Britain's other colonies in Africa? What role did the Cold War play in the decolonization process? Was it the main reason for Britain's retreat from empire? What other forces were at work? Could more skilled statecraft and more effective modernization of industry have prevented the loss of the Empire?

In the twentieth century, and especially since the end of the war, the processes which gave birth to the nation-states of Europe have been repeated all over the world. We have seen the awakening of national consciousness in peoples who have for centuries lived in dependence on some other power. . . .

The most striking of all the impressions I have formed since I left London a month ago is the strength of this African consciousness. In different places it may take different forms, but it is happening everywhere. The wind of change is blowing through the continent.

Whether we like it or not, this growth of national consciousness is a political fact. We must all accept it as a fact. . . .

As I see it, the great issue in this second half of the twentieth century is whether the uncommitted peoples of Asia and Africa will swing to the east or to the west. Will they be drawn into the Communist camp? Or will the great experiments in self-government that are now being made in Asia and Africa, especially within the Commonwealth, prove so successful, and by their example so compelling, that the balance will come down in favor of freedom and order and justice?

The struggle is joined and it is a struggle for the minds of men. What is now on trial is much more than our military strength or our diplomatic and administrative skill. It is our way of life.

The uncommitted nations want to see before they choose. What can we show them to help them choose aright? Each of the independent members of the Commonwealth must answer that question for itself.

7.19 Sir Alec Douglas-Home, speech in the House of Commons (July 22, 1970)[20]

Sir Alec Douglas-Home (1903–95), formerly fourteenth earl of Home and prime minister 1963–4, was serving as foreign secretary in a Tory government when he gave this speech defending the decision to sell arms to South Africa. That country was ruled by a ruthless white minority government that discriminated heavily against the black and mixed-race majority of the population. Most Commonwealth countries condemned the regime.

[20] *Parliamentary Debates*, vol. 804, July 22, 1970, c. 581–6.

The Conservatives in Britain wanted the UK economy to profit from the arms sales and believed engagement was better than isolation.

Is there a distinction between trading with a dictatorial regime and selling them weapons? How could the Labour Party justify trading with a racist regime? How did Douglas-Home justify the decision of his government? What effect might Britain's policy have had on the Commonwealth as a whole?

On what, in relation to South Africa, do both sides of the House agree? We agree that it is abhorrent to build a society on color discrimination. We agree, however, that force cannot be used to change the policies of apartheid. Both parties reject an embargo on trade. In fact, under the last [Labour] Government our trade with South Africa increased very largely. [Interruption.] Hon. Members must face this. There are £1,000 million investments by this country in South Africa, and there is £300 million of trade each way.

The question I put to right hon. Gentlemen opposite [Labour leaders] is this. Do they think that that does not strengthen South Africa? Of course increasing trade with South Africa strengthens South Africa. One of the arguments against the sale of arms to South Africa is that it strengthens the South African nation, giving them more power against their neighbors. But all the time this has been happening through increased trade, and right hon. and hon. Members opposite have welcomed it. Indeed, the right hon. Gentleman went further than any Conservative Government in this direction. [Labour prime minister Harold Wilson] authorized the Atomic Energy Authority to place a plant in South-West Africa for the manufacture of uranium. . . . I can recognize very well the position of the hon. Member for Ebbw Vale [Michael Foot, future leader of the Labour Party], and others who take the line that the boycott is right, that to apply sanctions against South Africa is right, and that not to co-operate with South Africa is right. I can recognize that as a moral stance, and indeed I think that I can recognize boycott as perhaps a Christian attitude. It is possible to say that something is so evil that you will have nothing to do with it. I can recognize that. If force is ruled out, however – and war will not solve the problem of apartheid – there is another and I suggest just as moral and just as Christian way – by contact, to convince by example. There is strong evidence to show that the trouble with South Africa is because South Africa is so isolated from every other country in the world, and the greater the isolation the more stubborn her doctrine of apartheid becomes. It is not without interest that it is under the impact of modern industrial organization that the rigid rules of apartheid are found impossible to sustain. I therefore uphold the proposition on moral grounds that South Africa should not be ostracized and put in Coventry but that her territory should be opened up to the civilizing influences of the outside world. It is one or the other – [Interruption.] – the Leader of the Opposition continues to mutter.

This is a serious argument between two moral propositions. It will come to a choice. It will be one or the other. It will either end by boycott, sanctions and probably inevitably by war, or it will end by contact, by example and reconciliation between the white populations of Africa who have ruled successfully ever since. I find, therefore, the policy of the boycotters credible but wrong, but I see nothing to be said for the pretence of the Socialist Front Bench as they have conducted their policy with South Africa during the past six years.

7.20 Paddy Ashdown, The Ashdown Diaries *(July 9 and 11, 1996)*[21]

In 2007 a statue of Nelson Mandela (b.1918), the black nationalist leader in South Africa and first African president of that country, was erected in Parliament Square in London, a green across from the House of Commons used to honor the likes of Abraham Lincoln and Winston Churchill. His struggle against, and long imprisonment by, a ruthless apartheid regime and role as president of a new multiracial South Africa that reentered the Commonwealth under his leadership is deeply admired in Britain. There are many contradictions in his relationship with the old imperial state, not the least being his encounters with Queen Elizabeth II, which became warm and frequent. He called her simply "my friend Elizabeth." As Head of the Commonwealth, the monarch does not act directly under the advice of the British prime minister, which on several occasions has led to complications and tension, especially over the question of sanctions against the white regime in South Africa, which Margaret Thatcher did not support and which the rest of Commonwealth did. There is little doubt that the queen and Thatcher disagreed over this policy. This passage from the diary of the leader of the Liberal Democratic Party, Paddy Ashdown (b.1941), captures some of the contradictions implicit in the post-imperial legacy. He describes a triumphal visit by Mandela to London in July 1996.

Why might Nelson Mandela and Queen Elizabeth II become good friends? Why would the British erect a statue to honor Mandela, who had been a communist and an advocate of violent overthrow of a regime that had once been part of the Empire? How do the British now regard their past as imperialists?

I walked down into Westminster Hall for Mandela's address to the joint Houses [of Parliament]. It was packed. Fifteen hundred people, or so. The Westminster Hall is magnificent on these occasions: red carpet, arc lights, the Royal Heralds . . .

21 Paddy Ashdown, *The Ashdown Diaries*, Vol. 1: *1988–1997* (London, 2000), 444–6. The order of the last paragraph has been rearranged.

[Mandela] emerged into the arc lights after the fanfare, and I immediately thought of the prisoner in [Beethoven's opera] *Fidelio* emerging blinking into the sunlight. He looked immensely calm. He had difficulty with the steps because of the damage done to his ankles by the chains in prison . . .

Mandela spoke for surprisingly long. There was real tension at the beginning of his speech, in which he didn't flinch from saying that we had a bad colonial record in South Africa. But real warmth at the end, when he went through the people who had maintained faith with the blacks in South Africa . . .

[Later] the queen and Mandela came in. All I could see was two grizzled heads as they moved among the crowd, one short with wavy hair and the other taller with crinkly hair. But they seemed to move perfectly together. From their body language, they really seemed to like each other.

I noticed that during lunch they were leaning towards each other like an elderly couple who had known each other all their lives. I found it very affecting: the queen with all her background of pomp and this frail ex-prisoner who was now recognized as one of the really great men of our time. . . .

At the state dinner for him at Buckingham Palace this evening Mandela wore a black shirt without a tie. He looked splendid and somehow quite formal enough, even among the tails and medals. Wonderful grace in the face. I kept watching him while the queen was speaking and the pipers were marching around after dinner. Yet he still does not look nearly as old as his years. How very curious to see this grizzled head and black face full of humility and grace against the crimson backdrop of the British throne.

7.21 Tony Blair, speech to the Labour Party annual conference (Oct. 2, 2001)[22]

The Labour prime minister Tony Blair (see document 7.10) spoke to his party conference only a few weeks after the destruction of the World Trade Center in New York on September 11 in which several hundred British subjects had been killed. He had flown to Washington shortly after the attack to meet with George W. Bush and sat in the gallery of the House of Representatives to show solidarity while the president addressed Congress and the nation. Such gestures harked back to the Churchill/Roosevelt days of World War II. Blair gave unswerving support to Bush during the wars in Afghanistan and Iraq. Many believe Blair's premiership will be judged harshly by history due to his decisions over Iraq. This speech lays out quite early his unwavering advocacy for the American wars and the policy of international intervention and regime change.

22 "Tony Blair's Speech," www.guardian.co.uk (Oct. 2, 2001).

Although there was widespread sympathy in Britain for the USA after September 11, and NATO broadly supported intervention in Afghanistan to retaliate against Osama bin Laden, Blair's steely commitment to the war on terror quickly made his own party uncomfortable. What arguments does he use to try to bring them along with him? Why might many people on the left be opposed to military interventions abroad, especially in a former British imperial possession such as Iraq? How might the European and the non-European world view Blair's speech? Blair hoped that he could gain influence in Washington to help shape and restrain the excesses of American foreign policy. In this he failed. Why?

In retrospect, the Millennium marked only a moment in time. It was the events of September 11 that marked a turning point in history, where we confront the dangers of the future and assess the choices facing humankind. It was a tragedy. An act of evil. From this nation, goes our deepest sympathy and prayers for the victims and our profound solidarity with the American people. We were with you at the first. We will stay with you to the last. . . .

Be in no doubt: Bin Laden and his people organized this atrocity. The Taliban aid and abet him. He will not desist from further acts of terror. They will not stop helping him. Whatever the dangers of the action we take, the dangers of inaction are far, far greater. . . .

The action we take will be proportionate; targeted; we will do all we humanly can to avoid civilian casualties. But understand what we are dealing with. Listen to the calls of those passengers on the planes. Think of the children on them, told they were going to die. Think of the cruelty beyond our comprehension as amongst the screams and the anguish of the innocent, those hijackers drove at full throttle planes laden with fuel into buildings where tens of thousands worked. They have no moral inhibition on the slaughter of the innocent. If they could have murdered not 7,000 [the total was later found to be less than 3,000] but 70,000 does anyone doubt they would have done so and rejoiced in it?

There is no compromise possible with such people, no meeting of minds, no point of understanding with such terror. Just a choice: defeat it or be defeated by it. And defeat it we must. . . .

Those that finance terror, those who launder their money, those that cover their tracks are every bit as guilty as the fanatic who commits the final act. . . .

People say: we are only acting because it's the USA that was attacked. Double standards, they say. But when Milosevic [president of Serbia] embarked on the ethnic cleansing of Muslims in Kosovo, we acted. The skeptics said it was pointless, we'd make matters worse, we'd make Milosevic stronger and look what happened, we won, the refugees went home, the policies of ethnic cleansing were reversed and one of the great dictators of the last century, will see justice in this century [he was eventually arrested and stood trial at the International

Court at the Hague]. And I tell you if Rwanda happened again today as it did in 1993, when a million people were slaughtered in cold blood, we would have a moral duty to act there also. We were there in Sierra Leone when a murderous group of gangsters threatened its democratically elected Government and people.

HISTORIANS' DEBATES

Were the British troops on the Western Front 1914–18, led by Sir Douglas Haig and other generals, "lions led by donkeys"?

Alan Clark, *The Donkeys* (London, 1961); Duff Cooper, *Haig*, 2 vols (London, 1935–36); Martin Gilbert, *The Somme* (New York, 2006); Paddy Griffith, *Battle Tactics of the Western Front: The British Army's Art of Attack, 1916–1918* (New Haven, 1994); Gerard de Groot, *Douglas Haig, 1861–1928* (London, 1988); Basil H. Liddell Hart, *A History of the First World War* (London, 1970); Hubert C. Johnson, *Breakthrough! Tactics, Technology, and the Search for Victory on the Western Front in World War I* (Novato, CA, 1994); J.H. Johnson, *Stalemate! The Great Trench Warfare Battles of 1915–1917* (London, 1995); John Keegan, *The First World War* (London, 1998); James Marshall-Cornwall, *Haig as Military Commander* (New York, 1973); Robin Prior and Trevor Wilson, *Command on the Western Front: The Military Career of Sir Henry Rawlinson, 1914–18* (Oxford, 1992); Simon Robbins, *British Generalship during the Great War: The Military Career of Sir Henry Horne* (Burlington, VT, 2010); Hew Strachan, *The First World War* (New York, 2004); John Terraine, *Douglas Haig, the Educated Soldier* (London, 1963); Denis Winter, *Haig's Command: A Reassessment* (London, 1991).

To what degree were the bitter feelings felt by many people on the left toward prime minister Ramsay MacDonald justified? Did he betray the Labour Party?

David Marquand, *Ramsay MacDonald* (London, 1977); Austen Morgan, *J. Ramsay MacDonald* (Manchester, 1987); Kenneth O. Morgan, *Labour People: Leaders and Lieutenants from Hardie to Kinnock*, rev. ed. (Oxford, 1992); C.L. Mowat, "Ramsay MacDonald and the Labour Party," in *Essays in Labour History 1886–1923*, ed. Asa Briggs and John Savile (London, 1971); Benjamin Sacks, *J. Ramsay MacDonald in Thought and Action* (Albuquerque, 1952); Robert Skidelsky, *Politicians and the Slump: The Labour Government of 1929–1931* (London, 1967); L. MacNeill Weir, *The Tragedy of Ramsay MacDonald: A Political Biography* (London, 1938); Chris Wrigley, "James Ramsay MacDonald 1922–1931," in *Leading Labour: From Kier Hardie to Tony Blair*, ed. Kevin Jeffrerys (London, 1999).

How harshly should history judge Neville Chamberlain and his pursuit of the policy of "appeasement"? Has the benefit of hindsight led to an unfair judgment?

Sidney Aster, "'Guilty Men': The Case of Neville Chamberlain," in *Paths to War: New Essays on the Origins of the Second World War*, ed. Robert Boyce and Esmonde M. Robertson (New York, 1989); "Cato," *Guilty Men* (London, 1940); John Charmley, *Chamberlain and the Lost Peace* (London, 1989); David Dutton, *Neville Chamberlain* (London, 2001); Keith Feiling, *Life of Neville Chamberlain* (London, 1946); Larry William Fuscher, *Neville Chamberlain and Appeasement: A Study in the Politics of History* (New York, 1982); Duncan Keith-Shaw, *Prime Minister Neville Chamberlain* (London, 1939); Frank McDonagh, *Neville Chamberlain, Appeasement and the British Road to War* (Manchester, 1998); R.A.C. Parker, *Chamberlain and Appeasement: British Policy and the Coming of the Second World War* (New York, 1993).

Was the strategic bombing offensive against Germany during World War II immoral and/or ineffective?

Paul Addison and Jeremy A. Crang, eds., *Firestorm: The Bombing of Dresden 1945* (London, 2006); Paul Brickhill, *The Dam Busters*, rev. ed. (London, 1999); British Bombing Survey Unit, *The Strategic Air War against Germany, 1939–1945: The Official Report* (London, 1998); Stephen A. Garrett, *Ethics and Airpower in World War II: The British Bombing of German Cities* (New York, 1993); A.C. Grayling, *Among the Dead Cities: Was the Allies' Bombing of Civilians in World War II a Necessity or a Crime?* (London, 2006); Arthur T. Harris, *Bomber Offensive* (London, 1947); Max Hastings, *Bomber Harris: His Life and Times* (London, 2001); Charles Messenger, *"Bomber" Harris and the Strategic Bombing Offensive, 1939–1945* (London, 1984); Richard Overy, *Why the Allies Won* (London, 1995); Henry Probert, *Bomber Harris: His Life and Times* (London, 2001); Dudley Saward, *Bomber Harris: The Story of Marshal of the Royal Air Force, Sir Arthur Harris* (London, 1984); Frederick Taylor, *Dresden: Tuesday February 13, 1945* (New York, 2005); Charles Webster and Noble Frankland, *The Strategic Air Offensive against Germany, 1939–1945* (London, 1961).

Was the postwar consensus shaped by Liberal thinking in the 1920s, by the experience of the slump in the 1930s, or by the unity that emerged during the war? Or did it really exist at all?

Paul Addison, *The Road to 1945: British Politics and the Second World War*, 2nd ed. (London, 1992); Alan Booth, *British Economic Policy, 1931–1949: Was There a Keynesian Revolution?* (London, 1989); Peter Clarke, *The Keynesian Revolution in the Making, 1924–1936* (Oxford, 1988); Elizabeth Durbin, *New Jerusalems: The Labour Party and the Economics of Democratic Centralism* (London, 1985); B. Harrison, "The Rise, Fall and Rise of Political Consensus in Britain since 1940," *History* 84 (1999), 301–24; Kevin Jefferys, *The Churchill Coalition and Wartime Politics, 1940–1945* (Manchester, 1991); Harriet Jones and Michael Kandiah, eds., *The Myth of Consensus: New Views on British History, 1945–1964* (New York, 1996); Keith Middlemas, *Politics in Industrial Society: The Experience of the British System since 1911* (London, 1979); Daniel Ritschel, *The Politics of Planning in Britain in the 1930s* (Oxford, 1997); Neil Rollings, "Poor Mr. Butskell: A Short Life, Wrecked by Schizophrenia," *TCBH* 5 (1994), 183–205.

What was the significance of the Suez Crisis? Did it have lasting consequences?

David Carlton, *Anthony Eden: A Biography* (London, 1981); Randolph S. Churchill, *The Rise and Fall of Anthony Eden* (London, 1959); David Dutton, *Anthony Eden: A Life and Reputation* (New York, 1997); Anthony Eden, *Full Circle: The Memoirs of the Rt Hon Sir Anthony Eden* (London, 1960); Robert Rhodes James, *Anthony Eden* (New York, 1987); Keith Kyle, *Suez* (London, 1990); Richard Lamb, *The Failure of the Eden Government* (London, 1987); Selwyn Lloyd, *Suez 1956: A Personal Account* (London, 1978); Louise Richardson, *When Allies Differ: Anglo-American Relations during the Suez and Falklands Crises* (New York, 1996).

Historians differ about the strength and significance of the "special relationship" between Britain and the United States. How important was the alliance to the United States? To Britain? How did the relationship change over time?

Terry H. Anderson, *The United States, Great Britain, and the Cold War 1944–1947* (Columbia, 1981); John Baylis, *Anglo-American Defence Relations, 1939–1980: The Special Relationship* (New York, 1981); Duncan Campbell, *The Unsinkable Aircraft Carrier: American Military Power in Britain* (London, 1984); Alan P. Dobson, *The Politics of the Anglo-American Economic Special Relationship 1940–1987* (New York, 1988); Simon Duke, *United States Defence Bases in the United Kingdom: A Matter for Joint Decision?* (London, 1987); John Dumbrell, *A Special Relationship: Anglo-American Relations in the Cold War and After* (London, 2001); Robert M. Hathaway, *Great*

Britain and the United States: Special Relations since World War II (Boston, 1990); William Roger Louis and Hedley Bull, eds., *The "Special Relationship": Anglo-American Relations since 1945* (Oxford, 1986); W. Scott Lucas, *Divided We Stand: Britain, the US, and the Suez Crisis* (London, 1991); Richard E. Neustadt, *Alliance Politics* (New York, 1970); Ritchie Ovendale, *Britain, the United States, and the Transfer of Power in the Middle East, 1945–1962* (Leicester, 1996); Henry Butterfield Ryan, *The Vision of Anglo-America: The US–UK Alliance and the Emerging Cold War, 1943–1945* (Cambridge, 1987); Geoffrey Smith, *Reagan and Thatcher* (London, 1990).

Major constitutional changes have taken place in the last few decades. What led to these changes? Do these changes constitute a "new" constitution?

L.S. Amery, *Thoughts on the Constitution* (London, 1947); Vernon Bogdanor, *The New British Constitution* (Oxford, 2009); Vernon Bogdanor, *Proportional Representation: Which System?* (London, 1992); Robert Brazier, *Constitutional Reform* (Oxford, 1991); Peter Hennessy, *The Hidden Wiring: Unearthing the British Constitution* (London, 1995); Nevil Johnson, *In Search of the Constitution: Reflections on State and Society in Britain* (Oxford, 1977); A.S. King, *The British Constitution* (Oxford, 2009); Philip Norton, *The Constitution in Flux* (Oxford, 1982); Brian Sedgemore, *The Secret Constitution: An Analysis of the Political Establishment* (London, 1980); W.J. Stankiewicz, ed., *British Government in an Era of Reform* (London, 1976).

COUNTERFACTUALS TO CONSIDER

What if Germany had successfully invaded in 1940? Would Britain have become a vassal state or would it have allied with Hitler to achieve global domination under a reactionary regime?

What if the political and social order had disintegrated in the 1970s? Would a revolution have occurred? Who would have emerged as the new dominant force in British society?

What if Britain had struggled to hold on to its empire as vigorously or even more forcefully than France and Portugal? What would the economic consequences for Britain have been? How would the world be different today?

CHAPTER EIGHT

Economy and Society

The British government emerged from World War I with huge debts, and it was virtually bankrupted by World War II. Although the economy did not reach the depths of depression experienced in America in the 1930s, unemployment was a serious problem. The suffering of the unemployed brought into question both the morality and the viability of the capitalist system. Liberals gradually, and Labour more enthusiastically, called for widespread intervention by the state in the economy and amelioration of social ills. After World War II something close to a consensus among the political parties sustained a mixed economy until the 1980s. Like capitalism, the welfare state brought its own set of problems, the unraveling of which continues in the twenty-first century.

Despite the onrush of scientific and technological change and the leftward advance of politics, traditional elements in British society remained strong. Continuity in the constitution and the social hierarchy were striking characteristics of twentieth-century Britain. Ironically, for example, as power slipped away from the House of Lords the quality of the debate there continued to improve and earn widespread attention. The monarchy was probably never more widely respected in its modern history than at the death of George VI in 1952. How do you account for the survival of tradition and deference in an increasingly democratic society?

As you read the documents in this chapter, consider the following questions:

- What problems confronted the British economy in the twentieth century?
- How did British writers, thinkers, and politicians react to the moral problems inherent in capitalism?
- What is the purpose of the welfare state and what have been its successes and failures?

Sources and Debates in Modern British History: 1714 to the Present, First Edition. Edited by Ellis Wasson.

Published 2012 by Blackwell Publishing Ltd.

Traditional Society

8.1 *Tables of General Precedence (1915)*[1]

In the first few decades of the twentieth century Britain was still a hierarchical and deferential society with a functioning hereditary aristocracy. Victory in World War I actually enhanced the prestige of the traditional structures of landed and military authority, although radically increased levels of taxation led to large sales of land. Many great landowners, however, remained rich, influential, and engaged in local and national politics through to World War II. The table of precedence, although based on ancient usage, parliamentary statutes, and royal warrants (used to this day at both political and social ceremonies and events and by which means every member of the social and political elite can be assigned an exact place in the hierarchy), had begun to detach itself from the realities of how power was distributed. A separate table of precedence existed for Scotland (in which the Lord High Commissioner to the General Assembly of the Church of Scotland ranked immediately after the king) and Ireland (where the number two spot was held by the viceroy).

What anomalies in terms of the power and prestige of political offices appear in the rankings? Why were there separate tables for Scotland and Ireland? Why was there a separate table for women? What purpose might these tables have served and why were they continued even when out of kilter with reality?

Precedence in England

The King
The Prince of Wales
The King's younger sons, grandsons, brothers, uncles, and nephews
Archbishop of Canterbury [primate of the Church of England]
Lord Chancellor [head of the legal profession and member of the Cabinet]
Archbishop of York [number two in the Anglican Church]
The Prime Minister
Lord President of the Council [politician and member of the Cabinet]
Lord Privy Seal [same as above]
Lord Great Chamberlain [courtier and hereditary office divided between two titled families]
Earl Marshal [courtier, hereditary office held by the dukes of Norfolk]
Lord Steward of the Household [courtier]
Lord Chamberlain [courtier but also censor of plays produced in London]
Master of the Horse [courtier]

[1] *Debrett's Peerage, Baronetage, Knightage, and Companionage*, ed. Arthur G.M. Hesilrige (London, 1915), xxii–xxviii. I have compressed some aspects of these tables.

Dukes of England, Scotland, Great Britain, Ireland, and the United Kingdom [by date of creation]
Eldest sons of dukes of the blood royal [if not princes in their own right]
Marquesses [in order like the dukes]
Eldest sons of dukes [bore a "courtesy" title of marquess or earl but had no seat in the House of Lords]
Earls [in order like the dukes]
Younger sons of dukes of the blood royal
Marquesses' eldest sons [held courtesy titles such as earl or viscount]
Dukes' younger sons [first name preceded by the title "Lord"]
Viscounts [in order like the dukes]
Earls' eldest sons [held courtesy titles such as viscount or baron]
Marquesses' younger sons [first name preceded by the title "Lord"]
Bishops of London, Durham, and Winchester
English bishops in order of consecration
Irish bishops consecrated prior to disestablishment [1869]
Secretaries of State [senior Cabinet members] if of baronial rank
Barons [in order like the dukes] followed by judges who sat in the House of Lords for life
Speaker of the House of Commons
Treasurer of the Household [courtier]
Comptroller of the Household [courtier]
Vice Chamberlain of the Household [courtier]
Secretaries of State [senior Cabinet members] if commoners
Viscounts' eldest sons [held courtesy titles of baron]
Earls' younger sons [first name preceded by "the honorable"]
Barons' eldest sons [first name preceded by "the honorable"]
Knights of the Garter if commoners [almost always peers, usually great landowners, names followed by the initials KG]
Privy Councilors [Cabinet members and politicians who had held senior political appointments, names followed by the initials PC]
Chancellor of the Exchequer [finance minister]
Chancellor of the Duchy of Lancaster [a minister without portfolio]
Lord Chief Justice of England [most senior judge]
Master of the Rolls [senior judge]
Lord Justices of Appeal
Judges of the High Court of Justice
Viscounts' younger sons [first name preceded by "the honorable"]
Barons' younger sons [first name preceded by "the honorable"]
Sons of judicial peers
Baronets by date of patent [hereditary knights but with no seat in the House of Lords]
Knights of the other major orders [Bath, Star of India, St Michael and St George, etc.]
Knights
Commanders of the Royal Victorian Order [for personal service to the King]
Judges of County Courts of England, Wales, and Ireland
Serjeants-at-Law [legal officials]
Masters in Chancery [legal officials]
Masters in Lunacy [legal officials]

Companions of the various orders of knighthood [but who did not get the title "Sir"]
Members of the Royal Victorian Order 4th class
Companions of the Distinguished Service Order and Imperial Service Order
Gentlemen of the Privy Chamber
Eldest sons of the younger sons of peers
Eldest sons of Knights of the Garter
Eldest sons of knights of other orders
Members of the Royal Victorian Order 5th class
Younger sons of baronets
Esquires
Younger sons of knights
Gentlemen who possessed coats of arms
[Everybody else]

Ladies

The Queen
The Queen Mother
Princess of Wales
King's daughters [often the eldest held the courtesy title "Princess Royal"]
Wives of the King's younger sons
King's granddaughters
Wives of the King's grandsons
The King's sisters
Wives of the King's brothers
The King's aunts
Wives of the King's uncles
The King's nieces
Wives of the King's nephews
Daughters of the Princess Royal
Duchesses of England, Scotland, Great Britain, Ireland, and the United Kingdom
[And so on]

8.2 Conservative Cabinet formed by Andrew Bonar Law (1922)

The composition of Bonar Law's (1858–1923) Cabinet in 1922 was not unlike many ministries of the eighteenth and nineteenth centuries: a mixture of established aristocracy and gentry, some of ancient lineage and some more recently risen but already rich and titled. Only one authentically self-made man was part of this government, with a smattering of members of the upper middle class to accompany him. Four were authentic magnates whose wealth and ancestry stretched back into the Middle Ages. Three-quarters of the Cabinet were from substantial landed families, recognizably part of the ruling elite that had governed Britain and Ireland for centuries. Churchill's caretaker government of 1945, though only briefly in office, was almost equally blue-blooded. Both ministries contained more men from "governing" families than that of Pitt the Younger in the first decade of the nineteenth century or Gladstone in the 1870s.[2]

What does the composition of this government suggest about the influence of the old landed elite in postwar British society? Was it relevant that the prime minister did not come out of the top drawer? Subsequent Conservative premiers (Churchill, Eden, Macmillan, Home, and Cameron) *were* members of the old ruling class. Were such men equipped to manage a modern industrial state and world empire? In what ways might continuity have been an advantage? How do you account for the close interrelationship between business and landed wealth reflected in this Cabinet? What is the significance of that intimacy?

Prime Minister: Andrew Bonar Law

The son of a Presbyterian minister of modest means born in Canada and partly raised in Scotland with roots in Ulster. He was a self-made businessman and politician.

Lord Chancellor: the first Viscount Cave

Son of a London merchant and MP. Although he rose through the law to a viscountcy, his fortune at death was modest compared to a person of similar background and career a century earlier.

Lord President: the fourth marquess of Salisbury

His ancestor, Lord Burleigh, was the great minister who served Queen Elizabeth I in the later sixteenth century. His father the third marquess was a political titan, three times prime minister between 1885 and 1902. The family elected the first of dozens of MPs in 1504 and had sat in the House of Lords from 1571 with multiple branches gaining vast estates and numerous titles. The Salisbury line owned 20,000 acres of land and several great houses. Every marquess of Salisbury in the twentieth century sat as an MP before inheriting the title, and all but one served in the Cabinet, the last leaving office in 1997.

Chancellor of the Exchequer: Stanley Baldwin

The Baldwins made their money in the iron and steel industry during the eighteenth century and gradually moved into the gentry in the nineteenth century. Their

[2] Ellis Wasson, *Born to Rule: British Political Elites* (Stroud, 2000), 47–8.

business was worth more than a million pounds by 1900. They elected four MPs between 1880 and 1947. Stanley Baldwin was sent to Harrow and Trinity College, Cambridge, worked in the business, lived as a country gentleman, and went on to become prime minister and cap his career with an earldom in 1937.

Home Secretary: W.C. Bridgeman

W.C. Bridgeman was a grandson of the earl of Bradford. The family elected their first of over a dozen MPs in 1640 and succeeded by marriage to the estates of the Newport family, which had sent MPs to Westminster from 1380 onwards. The Newports gained a barony in 1640 and the Bridgemans an earldom in 1694. They owned over 20,000 acres in the nineteenth century and still ranked among the 400 richest Britons in the 1990s.

Foreign Secretary: the first Marquess Curzon

The Curzons acquired the estate in Derbyshire, which they still own today, before 1150. Their first of a dozen MPs was elected in 1379. At least one member of the family sat in the House of Commons in every century from the fourteenth to the twentieth. They became baronets in 1636 and entered the House of Lords in 1761. In the later nineteenth century they owned 15,000 acres and one of the most beautiful Georgian country houses in Britain.

Colonial Secretary: the ninth duke of Devonshire

The first of dozens of Cavendish MPs was elected in 1379. The fourth duke served as prime minister in the eighteenth century and the eighth duke was the senior leader of the Liberal Party second only to Gladstone and would have become prime minister had he not left the party over Home Rule. The family sat in the House of Lords from 1605. In the later nineteenth century they owned nearly 200,000 acres in England and Ireland. In the 1990s at least 70,000 acres remained, and they were still among the richest people in Britain. The eleventh duke served as a minister in his uncle, Harold Macmillan's government (1962–64).

Secretary for War: the seventeenth earl of Derby

The Stanleys were among the richest and most ancient aristocratic families in Britain. The first notable member of the family emerged in the mid-twelfth century. The first of many MPs was elected in 1407. They became barons in 1456 and earls of Derby in 1485. Members of the family figure in Shakespeare's plays and the fourteenth earl was prime minister while his son the fifteenth earl served as foreign secretary in the same Cabinet. Two of the seventeenth earl's sons served in the same Cabinet in 1938. They continued to hold senior political posts until 1945. In the late nineteenth century they owned nearly 70,000 acres, of which at least 30,000 are still in their hands today. They were popularly known as "Kings of Lancashire" due to their enormous influence in that county.

Secretary for India: the second Viscount Peel

The Peels became immensely rich as factory owners during the early stages of the Industrial Revolution and gained a baronetcy in 1800. The second baronet was one of the great prime ministers of the nineteenth century. Family members served regularly in the Cabinet until 1931. Fourteen Peels served in the House of Commons between 1790 and 1922, and the family gained membership in the House of Lords in 1895 and an earldom in 1929. The first Viscount Peel was Speaker of the House of Commons from 1884 to 1895. The family estates, divided among a number of branches, totaled over 25,000 acres in the later nineteenth century.

Secretary for Scotland: the first Viscount Novar

Lord Novar (created a viscount in 1920) descended from an ancient Scottish family, the Munros of Novar in Ross-shire, resident there since at least the thirteenth century. The family elected a number of MPs and owned 25,000 acres in the later nineteenth century. He married a daughter of the marquess of Dufferin.

First Lord of the Admiralty: L.S. Amery

Amery's father was in the Indian civil service and well enough placed to arrange for his son to attend Harrow and Oxford. Amery declined a peerage so as not to close off his own son's career in the Commons. The latter was made a life peer in 1992 and left an estate of over £4 million.

President of the Board of Trade: Sir Philip Lloyd-Graeme (Cunliffe-Lister)

Sir Philip Lloyd-Graeme was born into a gentry family. His wife succeeded to the Cunliffe-Lister estates (earl of Masham), and he took her name. The Cunliffes were Liverpool merchants and gentry in the seventeenth century and elected several MPs. A younger son invented a railway airbrake in 1848, later a wool-combing machine, and then became a silk-plush manufacturer. The fortune made in industry was invested in an estate that made the family the largest landowners in North Yorkshire, reaching 34,000 acres in the later nineteenth century. This branch of the family elected three MPs between 1832 and 1935 and gained a peerage in 1891.

Minister of Agriculture: Sir Robert Sanders

Robert Sanders was the son of a lawyer of gentry background and educated at Harrow and Oxford, where he spent a good deal of time fox-hunting. Although he prepared for the bar, he spent his life as a Tory squire and politician. He continued to hunt regularly while serving in the Cabinet. He was made a baron in 1929.

President of the Board of Education: Edward Wood

The Woods were launched by a fortune made in the China trade in the eighteenth century, and they gained a baronetcy in 1784. An estate of over 10,000 acres was acquired by the early nineteenth century. Discovery of a large coal seam on their property made them very rich. Four members of the family served in the House of Commons between 1829 and 1979. They entered the House of Lords in 1866, and Edward Wood became earl of Halifax in 1944 after a distinguished career as viceroy of India and foreign secretary. He was the alternative candidate for the premiership in May 1940, giving way to Winston Churchill.

Minister of Labour: Sir A. Montague-Barlow

Barlow was the son of a senior Anglican cleric and a country gentleman's daughter. He rose to a baronetcy through law and politics.

Minister of Health: Sir Arthur Griffith-Boscawen

The Griffiths were gentry by the mid-seventeenth century. In 1830 they inherited a large estate in Wales through marriage to a Boscawen heiress. The Boscawens had emerged in the fourteenth century, elected 16 MPs between 1646 and 1841, and gained a peerage in 1720. Their estates totaled 30,000 acres in the later nineteenth century.

Capitalism at Bay

8.3 *Pilgrim Trust Report,* Men Without Work *(1938)*[3]

The Pilgrim Trust was a charitable organization founded by a rich American in 1930.

This passage reports the results of research funded by the Trust on joblessness during an extended period of unemployment and economic depression during the 1920s and 1930s (Figure 8.1).

What is rationalization? What was more serious: the economic or the psychological damage caused by prolonged unemployment? Why was there no general strike in the 1930s? What can a capitalist society do to solve long-term unemployment?

[3] *Men Without Work: A Report Made to the Pilgrim Trust* (Cambridge, 1938), 144–9.

Figure 8.1 London's Great Sunday Food Convoy being guarded by armored cars and troops during the General Strike, 1926. Hulton Archive/Getty Images 3314013.

The General Strike brought Britain to a standstill in 1926. Food and other vital resources had to be moved under military or police protection, although relatively few outbreaks of serious violence occurred. Why did financial turmoil, mass unemployment, and gross inequality fail to precipitate revolution in Britain during the 1920s and 1930s? What made conditions for the working class endurable? What is the demeanor in this photograph of the working-class crowd lining the streets?

One of the main differences between the "working" classes and the "middle" classes is the difference of security. This is probably a more important distinction than income level. If working men and women seem to be unduly anxious to make their sons and daughters into clerks [white-collar workers], the anxiety behind it is not for more money but for greater security. Rightly or wrongly, they feel that a black-coated worker has a more assured position. The semi-skilled man is at the mercy of rationalization.

A week's notice may end half a lifetime's service, with no prospects, if he is elderly, but the dole [unemployment relief payments], followed by a still further reduction in his means of livelihood when the old age pension comes. . . . For months and indeed often for years [laid-off] men go on looking for work, and the same is true for many casual laborers. There were in the sample old men who have not a remote chance of working again but yet make it a practice to stand every morning at six o'clock at the works gates in the hope that perhaps they may catch the foreman's eye. There were young men who said that they could never settle to anything, but must be out all day, every day, looking for work. . . . When a man is thrown out of employment the first thing that he wants is work, and very few of those who have a good employment history can settle down to accept the fact of unemployment till they have been out of work for months.

But when a man who has had perhaps ten years' steady employment is thrown on the streets, to look for work effectively is not always easy. A large number of the sample cases had lost good jobs at the time of the [depression], when there was nothing else to be had. They had gone round from one works to another with hundreds of others all desperately anxious to secure employment, and failure after failure had gradually "got them down." The restlessness of which many wives spoke to tells its own tale: "Now he's out of work he don't seem to be able to settle down to anything." When a man is out of work, anxiety is part of a vicious circle, and the more he worries, the more he unfits himself to work.

There were other symptoms of this nerviness. The high proportions of instances in which married men were living apart from their wives is certainly in some degree to be explained by it. Among many of the families visited, tension between man and wife was apparent. Thus we saw a man of 25 in Liverpool, who had had previously to 1935 a certain amount of work as a builder's laborer. At the time of the visit his wife was 19; they had been married when she was 16. The first child had died the day after it was born and the mother had suffered from anaemia and kidney trouble at the time. There was another baby a few months old, which was taken to hospital with pneumonia the night before the visit occurred. The man gave the impression of one who had been not unhappy for a time lounging, but was now getting to the end of his tether. Speaking of his wife, he said: "She's always crying. But crying don't make things no better": and the early marriage, poverty, illness, and finally the quarrel seemed to summarize in a single instance several of the worst features of the situation of the long unemployed. . . .

The depression and apathy which finally settles down in many of the homes of these long-unemployed men lies at the root of most of the problems which are connected with unemployment. It is one of the reasons why they fail to get back to work. It is one of the reasons why the majority of them "have not the heart" for clubs or activities of other kinds, and it is one of the reasons why their homes seem so poverty-stricken. . . . Such a simultaneous onset of physical and psychological hardship can hardly help having serious results.

8.4 Lord Hugh Cecil, Conservatism *(1912)*[4]

Lord Hugh Cecil (1869–1956) was a younger son of the Victorian prime minister the third marquess of Salisbury. The Cecil family was the most relentlessly active British political family of the twentieth century and devoted to the cause of Conservatism. They were also devout Anglicans. Lord Hugh's brother was a bishop.

How might Cecil's aristocratic background have influenced his view of religion, politics, and the middle classes? What was his view of capitalism? What solution did he propose to reduce the suffering produced by capitalism?

[4] Lord Hugh Cecil, *Conservatism* (London, 1912), 89–91.

It cannot be denied that there is strong ground for Christians to censure the existing organization of commerce and industry. The competitive system is certainly not a Christian system. The governing motive of those who are engaged in industry or commerce is self-interest, not love, and Christianity indisputably requires that the mutual relations of all men shall be controlled by love. To buy as cheaply and sell as dearly as possible; to obtain labor at as low a wage as it can be got; to work only as much as is necessary to obtain employment; to strive, whether as employer or employed, to gain for oneself at the expense of others; these are not acts characteristic of Christianity. They are not immoral in the sense of transgressing any of the principles of the Ten Commandments: they are not dishonest or violent, but they are self-interested. They essentially belong to a system of morals lower than that which is revealed in the New Testament. This ought to be remembered by good men who are from time to time pained at features in industrial life which are shocking to their consciences. We are often told, we have recently been told by a great many ministers of religion, that the poverty and misery of large numbers of people in this country is a scandal to Christianity. And this is true. But it is strange that the scandal should occasion so much surprise. A system of which the mainstream is self-interest cannot be expected to result in consequences which are acceptable to the Christian conscience. . . .

So far, then, there seems an apparent case, not indeed for the adoption of Socialism, but for getting rid of the competitive system and substituting something better. But what is the mischief at the root of the competitive system? It is important to consider this, for unless the root of the evil be taken away, we may be sure that we shall not mend what is wrong though we may change the particular manifestation of it. The evil root is plain enough. It is that men are guided by self-interest. If Christianity is to reform the social system, it can only effectually do it by inducing people to substitute love for self-interest. Nothing is more certain than that the mechanism of human society will only express human character; it will not regenerate it. Character will transform the social system, but it takes something more vivifying than a social system to transform character. Accordingly unless there is prospect of such an improvement in human nature as the general substitution of love for self-interest, we may be sure at the outset that no change of social or political machinery will redeem society.

8.5 R.H. Tawney, Equality *(1931)*[5]

R.H. Tawney (1880–1962) was a historian and Christian socialist. He focused on economic history and was hostile to capitalism. He questioned the social morality of the existing political and economic basis of society of which he was a determined critic.

5 R.H. Tawney, *Equality*, 4th ed. (London, 1952), 57–8, 63–4.

Did Tawney share the same view of human nature as Lord Hugh Cecil (document 8.4)? What would he have said in response to Cecil? How did his background affect his views? What was his analysis of capitalism and socialism? Why did he think inequality was so hard to eradicate in Britain?

To criticize inequality and to desire equality is not, as is sometimes suggested, to cherish the romantic illusion that men are equal in character and intelligence. It is to hold that, while their natural endowments differ profoundly, it is the mark of a civilized society to aim at eliminating such inequalities as have their source, not in individual differences, but in its own organization, and that individual differences, which are a source of social energy, are more likely to ripen and find expression if social inequalities are, as far as practicable, diminished. And the obstacle to the progress of equality is something simpler and more potent than finds expression in the familiar truism that men vary in their mental and moral as well as in their physical characteristics, important and valuable though that truism is as a reminder that different individuals require different types of provision. It is that habit of mind which thinks it, not regrettable, but natural and desirable, that different sections of a community should be distinguished from each other by sharp differences of economic status, of environment, of education and culture and habit of life. It is the temper which regards with approval the social institutions and economic arrangements by which such differences are emphasized and enhanced, and feels distrust and apprehension at all attempts to diminish them.

The institutions and policies in which that temper has found expression are infinite in number. At one time it has coloured the relations between the sexes; at another, those between religions; at a third, those between members of different races. But in communities no longer divided by religion or race, and in which men and women are treated as political and economic equals, the divisions which remain are, nevertheless, not insignificant. The practical form which they most commonly assume – the most conspicuous external symptom of difference of economic status and social position – is, of course, a graduated system of social classes, and it is by softening or obliterating, not individual differences, but class gradations, that the historical movements directed towards diminishing inequality have attempted to attain their objective. It is, therefore, by considering the class system that light upon the problem of inequality is, in the first place at least, to be sought, and it is by their attitude to the relations between classes that the equalitarian temper and philosophy are distinguished from the opposite. . . .

England is peculiar in being marked to a greater degree than most other communities, not by a single set of class relations, but by two, of which one is the product of the last century of economic development, and the other, though transformed by that development and softened by the social policy of the democratic era, contains, nevertheless, a large infusion of elements which descend from the quite different type of society that existed before the rise of the great industry. It is the combination of both – the blend of a crude plutocratic reality with the sentimental aroma of an aristocratic legend – which gives the English class system its particular toughness and cohesion. It is at once as businesslike as Manchester and as gentlemanly as Eton; if its hands can be as rough as those of Esau, its voice is as mellifluous as that of Jacob. It is a god with two faces and a thousand tongues, and, while each supports its fellow, they speak in different accents and appeal to different emotions. Revolutionary logic, which is nothing if not rational, addresses its shattering syllogisms to the one, only to be answered in terms of polite evasion by the other. It appeals to obvious economic grievances, and is baffled by the complexities of a society in which the tumultuous impulses of economic self-interest are blunted and muffled by the sedate admonitions of social respectability.

War and Civilian Life

8.6 *James Lees-Milne,* Another Self *(event Apr. 1941, pub. 1970)*[6]

The Blitz (bombing raids by the German air force) hit London hard in 1940–41 and again in 1944–45. Almost 70,000 British civilians were killed in the war during air raids and ordinary life was severely disrupted, to say nothing of the economic and cultural damage. This is a description of one raid in April 1941 written by a soldier visiting London with a friend on leave. They were lodged in a hotel in the center of the West End near Piccadilly Circus. The East End, inhabited by the working class, suffered equally devastating and more frequent attacks.

What is the tone of Lees-Milne's description? In what ways was ordinary life in the city disrupted? What effect might such raids have had on civilian morale?

The raid getting worse we took a room on the fifth floor. There were nine floors in the hotel, and all the rooms on the lower were already taken. . . . The bombs were hailing, swishing down on all sides so that sleep was out of the question. The explosions and the rattle of retaliatory gunfire were deafening. We dressed again and went downstairs [to the basement shelter]. . . . As we passed through the entrance hall we saw slices of thick plate glass strewn upon the carpets. The revolving doors had blown in.

Less than twenty minutes later the first bomb hit the hotel. The building shivered and a fine dry dust filled the air and made people sneeze. . . . A second bomb fell on the hotel with a loud repercussion. It was like a thunder clap above our heads. I was pitched off my chair. While the foundations rocked and swayed there was time to screw my body like a hedgehog into a protective ball against the masonry crumbling, rumbling down the marble staircase. . . .

At five o'clock the all-clear sounded . . .. Piccadilly resembled a giant skeleton asleep upon an ice flow. The eye sockets of the houses looked reproachfully at the dawn. Like lids, torn blinds and curtains fluttered from every window. . . . On

[6] James Lees-Milne, *Another Self* (London, 1970), 148–52.

pavement and street a film of broken glass crunched under the feet like the jagged crystals of slush icicles. One had to take care that they did not clamber over the edge of one's shoes. The contents of shop windows were strewn over the pavements among the broken glass. Silk shirts and brocaded dressing-gowns fluttered upon area railings. The show case of a jeweler's window had sprinkled tray-loads of gold watches and bracelets as far as the curb of the street. I stooped to pick up a handful of diamonds and emeralds – and chuck them back into the shop before they got trodden on, or looted.

The sky had the gunmetal solidity of sky before a snowstorm. Cinders showered upon our hair, faces and clothes. On all sides columns of smoke sprang from raging fires, the glint of whose flames could be seen above the rooftops. . . . I was reminded of [the diarist] Pepys's description of the Great Fire of London in 1666, "a most horrid malicious bloody flame, not like the fine flame of an ordinary fire." . . .

Tongues of flame [from a ruptured gas line] were belching from craters in the road. We could not walk down Jermyn Street which was blocked by rubble from collapsed houses. Here I noticed the stripped, torn trunk of a man on the pavement. Further on I picked up what looked like a mottled, spread leaf of a plane tree. It was a detached hand with a signet ring on the little finger. . . .

The fire in Christie's was wonderful and awful. The façade still stood and the empty windows revealed a turgid golden tissue of flame. . . . The pale windows of Arthur's Club in St. James's Street were aglow with the reflection of yet another fire. . . . The attics of Bridgewater House were burning. The flames were smashing the windows with a horsewhip crack from inside, licking the outside walls and trying to fold their thongs round the chimneystacks. . . . My face and hair were scorched by another furnace across the road, a magnificent and sad spectacle. A sooty brick Georgian house in a silent corner of its own was turned into a devilish cauldron. A deep bow front with balconies acted like an enormous grate. The draught through the empty windows blew the fire into a ball of seething worms. The roof had gone and one long, thick, blackened beam raised a charred arm rhythmically up and down across the skyline, as though imprecating a dying curse upon our civilization; after a while it withdrew, leaving one calcined finger pointing threateningly. The finger too disappeared into the cauldron.

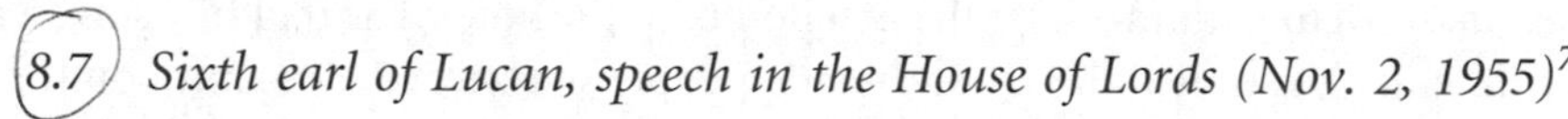

8.7 Sixth earl of Lucan, speech in the House of Lords (Nov. 2, 1955)[7]

The sixth earl of Lucan (1898–1964) was a Labour Party peer who had served as Deputy Director of Ground Defense in the Air Ministry during World War II. With the advent of the hydrogen bomb (far more powerful than the atomic ones dropped on Hiroshima and Nagasaki in 1945), he raised the question of what would happen to civil society if the Cold War got hot.

[7] *Parliamentary Debates*, vol. 194, Nov. 2, 1955, c. 211–12.

Was there anything other than retaliation in kind that the government could do to ward off such a massively destructive attack? What would happen in the aftermath of nuclear war? Would Britain come to an end as the people knew it? What moral questions are raised in the face of such destructive power? Why did the government fail to implement a nationwide construction campaign to build shelters?

The problem of nuclear warfare has been widely discussed in the Press and in many publications which have come from the United States. A number of varying estimates of the likely damage has been made, but it seems that the following is roughly the effect that is to be expected from an attack on this country by nuclear weapons. A bomb exploded over London would destroy all buildings, other than those specially strengthened, within a radius of five miles. It would severely damage all buildings within a radius of fifteen miles. It would cause fatal burns to persons in the open up to twelve miles away. It would cause fires in buildings up to the same distance. Finally, it would contaminate by radioactive fallout an area extending some 200 miles down wind on a width of about 40 miles – that is, some 8,000 square miles would be covered. The fall-out would be fatal to human beings and animals caught unprotected in the open and exposed for a certain period to the rays. The length of fatal exposure would, of course, vary with the distance from the point of explosion, known as "ground zero". The "Statement on Defence" [issued by the government] was guilty of no exaggeration when it said that such weapons would cause destruction, human and material on an unprecedented scale.

There are two measures which, in conjunction, could reduce the loss of life in such conditions. One is the digging of underground shelters. It appears that underground shelter gives a fair degree of protection against radioactivity anywhere except in the immediate vicinity of the explosion. Against the fall-out we are told that trenches with a small amount of head cover will give adequate protection; but one has only to think of the populations of our big cities spending a night in slit trenches in the countryside to realize that such a policy is quite impracticable. Then there is the question of the provision, or the strengthening, of basement and underground rooms in existing or new buildings. We should like to know what is the policy of Her Majesty's Government. Are they going to urge that all new construction should contain underground rooms to provide shelter?

The Welfare State

8.8 *Sir William Beveridge,* Social Insurance and Allied Services *(1942)*[8]

William H. Beveridge (1879–1963) was a British economist commissioned to study postwar social requirements. He went well beyond his brief and

8 Sir William Beveridge, *Social Insurance and Allied Services: Report* (London, 1942), 6–8, 17, 170.

laid out a plan that became the basis of the welfare state in Britain in the second half of the twentieth century. It is worth noting, however, that Beveridge was a Liberal, not a socialist. He was anxious to preserve as much individual liberty as possible while extending the safety net of social welfare. His plan incorporated insurance contributions by recipients to avoid the idea of state charity.

What passages reflect Beveridge's reluctance fully to embrace socialism? What did he mean by the report proposing a "British revolution"? Is it possible to build a welfare state without instituting a sense of entitlement that undermines individualism? How would Lord Hugh Cecil (document 8.4) and R.H. Tawney (document 8.5) have responded to Beveridge? How could a war-ravaged, bankrupt Britain afford to accomplish what Beveridge recommended? What specific proposals were implemented to address want, disease, ignorance, and squalor? Why has the United States been slower than Britain in implementing the welfare state?

... Three guiding principles may be laid down at the outset.

The first principle is that any proposals for the future, while they should use to the full experience gathered in the past, should not be restricted by consideration of sectional interests established in the obtaining of that experience. Now, when the war is abolishing landmarks of every kind, is the opportunity for using experience in a clear field. A revolutionary moment in the world's history is a time for revolutions, not for patching.

The second principle is that organization of social insurance should be treated as one part only of a comprehensive policy of social progress. Social insurance fully developed may provide income security; it is an attack upon the Want. But Want is one only of five giants on the road to reconstruction and in some ways the easiest to attack. The others are Disease, Ignorance, Squalor and Idleness.

The third principle is that social security must be achieved by co-operation between the State and the individual. The State should offer security for service and contribution. The State in organizing security should not stifle incentive, opportunity, responsibility: in establishing a national minimum, it should leave room and encouragement for voluntary action by each individual to provide more than that minimum for himself and his family. ...

Abolition of want requires, first, improvement of State insurance, that is to say provision against interruption and loss of earning power. ... None of the insurance benefits provided before the war were in fact designed with reference to the standards of the social surveys. Though unemployment benefit was not altogether out of relation to those standards, sickness and disablement benefit, old age pensions and widows' pensions were far below them, while workmen's compensation was below subsistence level for anyone who had family responsibilities or whose earnings in work were less than twice the amount needed for subsistence. To prevent interruption or destruction of earning power from leading to want, it is necessary to improve the present schemes of social insurance in three directions: by extension of scope to cover persons now excluded, by extension of purposes to cover risks now excluded, and by raising the rates of benefit. . . .

By a double re-distribution of income through social insurance and children's benefit allowances, want, as defined in the social surveys, could have been abolished in Britain before the present war. . . . The income available to the British people was ample for such a purpose. . . .

[This proposal] retains the contributory principle of sharing the cost of security between three parties – the insured person himself, his employer, if he has an employer, and the State. It retains and extends the principle that compulsory insurance should provide a flat rate of benefit, irrespective of earnings, in return for a flat contribution from all. . . . The scheme proposed here is in some ways a revolution, but in more important ways it is a natural development from the past. It is a British revolution. . . .

The Plan for Social Security is put forward as part of a general program of social policy. It is only one part of an attack upon [the] five giant evils . . . In seeking security not merely against physical want, but against all these evils [disease, ignorance squalor, and idleness] in all their forms, and in showing that security can be combined with freedom and enterprise and responsibility of the individual for his own life, the British community and those who in other lands have inherited the British tradition have a vital service to render to human progress.

8.9 Labour Party manifesto: "Let Us Face the Future: A Declaration of Labour Policy for the Consideration of the Nation" (1945)[9]

One goal of the Labour Party when it came to power at the end of World War II was to implement a wide array of welfare legislation (Figure 8.2). The other was to take into public ownership major industries such as fuel and power, transportation, and steel.

What grounds does the manifesto give for public ownership? What industries or commercial organizations were left out? How effective was the nationalization process? Why was privatization implemented by Margaret Thatcher (documents 7.9 and 8.12) and continued by the New Labour Party under Tony Blair (document 7.10)?

Industry in the Service of the Nation

By the test of war some industries have shown themselves capable of rising to new heights of efficiency and expansion. Others, including some of our older industries fundamental to our economic structure, have wholly or partly failed.

[9] "Let Us Face the Future: A Declaration of Labour Policy for the Consideration of the Nation" (London, 1945), 5–7.

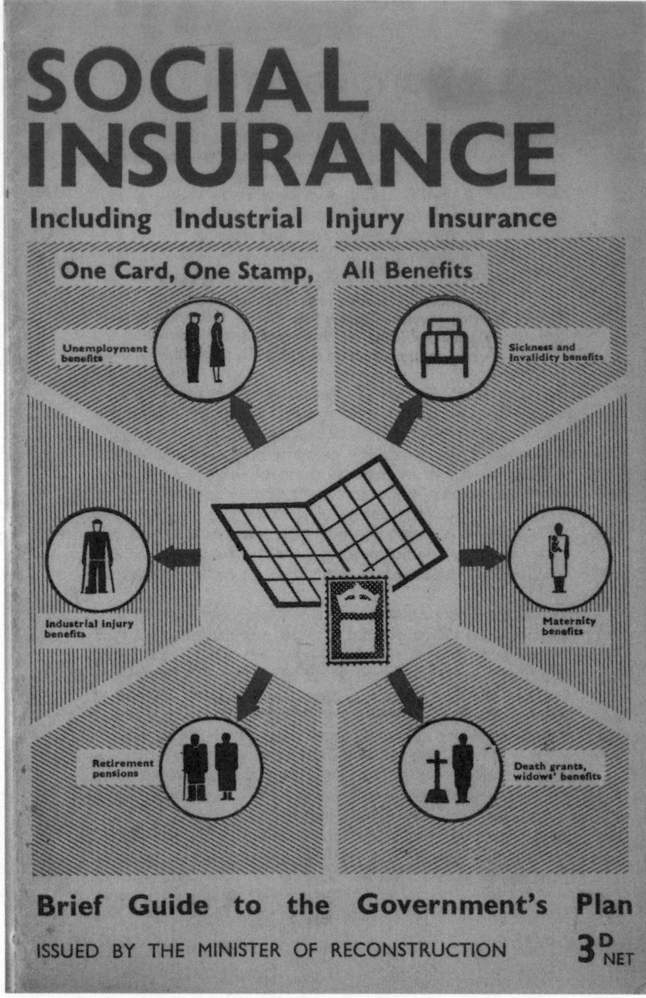

Figure 8.2 "*Social Insurance including industrial industry insurance ... Brief Guide to the Government's Plan*" (Ministry of Reconstruction, London, 1944). © The British Library Board, B.S.60/5.

The phrase "cradle to grave" was often applied to the provisions made for the people by the welfare state. To what degree does the program illustrated on the cover of this pamphlet accord with that concept? How might working-class people have reacted to this program? Middle-class people? The upper class? Are there elements of the welfare state not illustrated on this cover? What were they? Does the word "insurance" convey the idea of loss of independence or a free handout?

... Each industry must have applied to it the test of national service. If it serves the nation, well and good; if it is inefficient and falls down on the job, the nation must see that things are put right ...

The Labour Party is a Socialist Party, and proud of it. Its ultimate purpose at home is the establishment of the Socialist Commonwealth of Great Britain – free, democratic, efficient, progressive, public-spirited, its material resources organised in the service of the British people.

... There are basic industries ripe and over-ripe for public ownership and management in the direct service of the nation. There are many smaller businesses rendering good service which can be left to go on with their useful work.

There are big industries not yet ripe for public ownership which must nevertheless be required by constructive supervision to further the nation's needs and not to prejudice national interests by restrictive anti-social monopoly or cartel arrangements – caring for their own capital structures and profits at the cost of a lower standard of living for all.

In the light of these considerations, the Labour Party submits to the nation the following industrial programme:

1. *Public ownership of the fuel and power industries.*
[coal, gas, electricity]
2. *Public ownership of inland transport*
[rail, road, air, and canals]
3. *Public ownership of iron and steel*

These socialized industries, taken over on a basis of fair compensation, to be conducted efficiently in the interests of consumers, coupled with proper status and conditions for the workers employed in them ...

8.10 Rupert Speir, speech in the House of Commons (Mar. 4, 1960)[10]

Rupert Speir (1910–98), a Conservative MP, became well known for his campaigns to make life more pleasant for ordinary people. He fought tirelessly for control over litter and noise, two banes of life in the second half of the twentieth century. He had an inkling of the problems jet planes at airports would cause, but this did not reach epic proportions until decades after his bill for noise abatement was enacted in 1960. Today the London airports are among the most heavily used in the world and a constant source of noise pollution.

Why did it take an individual MP rather than the government to launch the fight against noise pollution? Who might have resisted such legislation? Who was most likely to support it? What other new factors diminished the quality of life in modern society? Is his intervention a contribution to the "nanny state," in which regulations proliferate in every direction to curb individual responsibility and freedom?

... I welcome the opportunity to make clear that my aim is to control, to curb, to restrict, and to reduce noise.

10 *Parliamentary Debates*, vol. 618, Mar. 4, 1960, c. 1571–3.

I believe that this can be done effectively and without any great difficulty or hardship to anyone by the means proposed in the Bill. To those who think that the provisions do not go far enough, that the measure is not sufficiently severe, that we have not faced the problem, I say that I believe that they are mistaken and that they under-estimate the powers which the Bill contains. Obviously, there are gaps, and some rather glaring ones, including aircraft, airports, railways, ice cream vendors. But I believe that the Bill, as drafted, will enable both local authorities and private individuals to take action in a simple, easy and cheap form if anyone causes excessive, unreasonable or unnecessary noise. . . . I consider that its provisions represent a happy compromise between the views of those who would go too far and those who think that not sufficient is being done.

It would be useless for Parliament to seek to intervene in such a complicated, difficult and universal problem if it were out of step with public opinion. But, judging from my postbag in recent months, I believe that we are supported by public opinion. . . . During recent months I have received dozens of letters from members of the public . . ., all urging that the Bill should find its way on to the Statute Book. I am pleased to say that I have not had a single letter against the idea behind the Bill. I therefore believe that we can count upon public support and sympathy.

The noises about which people have written complaining to me are not only legion, but extremely varied in character. I have had complaints of about seventy-five different kinds of noise. They are too many to mention here. Most of the letters I have received have been sensible letters, moderate in tone and some of them have been really very pathetic, showing that people were almost on the verge of a nervous breakdown because of various kinds of noise. I should say that without any doubt the chief cause of complaint in modern life is the unnecessary noise caused by motor-cycles, coupled, of course, with the noise from scooters, and mopeds.

That, undoubtedly, is the principal source of complaint at present, but it is closely followed by complaints about noisy wireless sets owned by neighbors, about the slamming of car doors, particularly in the early hours of the morning, about the barking of dogs, on which I have had a number of complaints, about the continuous ringing of burglar alarms, which are sometimes allowed to ring continuously through a weekend, and also about the chimes of ice cream vendors. These are a few of the many complaints I have received in recent months. . . .

8.11 C. Northcote Parkinson, Parkinson's Law *(1957)*[11]

The historian C. Northcote Parkinson (1909–93) made his name in 1957 with a small book about what he called "Parkinson's Law": work expands so as to fill the time available for its completion. His presentation was humorous but also

[11] C. Northcote Parkinson, *Parkinson's Law and Other Studies in Administration* (New York, 1969), 25–7.

telling. This phenomenon attracted special attention as the bureaucracy engendered by the welfare state burgeoned. In this passage he applied his "law" to the Colonial Office, which supervised the administration of the quickly disappearing empire. He noted that the staff of the office in 1935 was 372, in 1939 it had risen to 450, by 1943 it was 817, after the war in 1947 1139, and with India and Pakistan now independent, 1661 in 1954. From the 1940s onward ministries proliferated and bifurcated, producing tens of thousands of new bureaucrats, although the trend was reversed under Margaret Thatcher (document 7.9).

What was Parkinson's explanation for why his law operated? What forces acted to increase the number of bureaucrats? Were either the Tory or Labour parties more responsible for this increase? What can be done about it? How does it affect the cost and efficiency of government?

This department's responsibilities was far from constant during these twenty years. The colonial territories were not much altered in area or population between 1935 and 1939. They were considerably diminished by 1943, certain areas being in enemy hands. They were increased again in 1947, but have since then shrunk steadily from year to year as successive colonies achieve self-government. It would be rational to suppose that these changes in the scope of Empire would be reflected in the size of its central administration. But a glance at the figures is enough to convince us that the staff totals represent nothing but so many stages in an inevitable increase. And this increase, although related to that observed in other departments, has nothing to do with the size – or even the existence – of the Empire. . . .

Dealing with the problem of pure staff accumulation, all our researches so far completed point to an average increase [across various government departments] of 5.75 per cent per year. This fact established, it now becomes possible to state Parkinson's Law in mathematical form: In any public administrative department not actually at war, the staff increase may be expected to follow this formula –

$$x = \frac{2km + 1}{n}$$

k is the number of staff seeking promotion through the appointment of subordinates; *l* represents the difference between the ages of appointment and retirement; *m* is the number of man hours devoted to answering minutes within the department; and *n* is the number of effective units being administered. *x* will be the number of new staff required each year. Mathematicians will realize, of course, that to find the percentage increase they must multiply *x* by 100 and divide by the total of the previous year, thus:

$$\frac{100\,(2km + 1)}{yn}\%$$

where y represents the total original staff. This figure will invariably prove to be between 5.17 per cent and 6.56 per cent, irrespective of any variation in the amount of work (if any) to be done.

... It would probably be premature to attempt at this stage any inquiry into the quantitative ratio that should exist between the administrators and the administered. Granted, however, that a maximum ratio exists, it should soon be possible to ascertain by formula how many years will elapse before that ratio, in any given community, will be reached. The forecasting of such a result will have no political value. Nor can it be sufficiently emphasized that Parkinson's Law is a purely scientific discovery, inapplicable except in theory to the politics of the day. It is not the business of the botanist to eradicate the weeds. Enough for him if he can tell us just how fast they grow.

8.12 Margaret Thatcher, speech in the House of Commons (Jan. 16, 1979)[12]

What became known as the "English disease" afflicted Britain in the 1970s. Millions of days were lost to strikes. Both Labour and Conservative governments struggled with unions not only over pay but also power in the state. Gravediggers left bodies unburied, nurses left hospital patients unattended, the work week was reduced because not enough electricity was available to operate offices and factories. More than anyone else the Tory leader Margaret Thatcher (see document 7.9) transformed the situation. Here on the eve of winning office as the first female prime minister she lays out the nature of the crisis.

To what did Thatcher attribute the problem? Why did she criticize government-negotiated agreements about wage limits? What did she offer as a solution?

... We [are] in a position of grave trouble of crisis proportions – I should have thought that that was no longer in doubt ... a very grim picture indeed.

The Road Haulage Association confirms that picketing is affecting the supplies of essential goods. The Freight Transport Association also reports a new problem – shortage of diesel fuel, particularly in the South-West, because of picketing at the oil terminal at Avonmouth. British Rail reports quite simply: "There are no trains today."

The report from the Confederation of British Industry is that many firms are being strangled. There is a shortage of materials. They cannot move their own products. Exports are being lost. It says that secondary picketing, picketing of firms not in dispute, is very heavy all over the country. It is particularly affecting such items as packaging materials and sugar and all vital materials necessary if industry is

12 *Parliamentary Debates*, vol. 960, Jan. 16, 1979, c. 1524–8.

to keep going. Lay-offs known to the CBI are at least 125,000 already, and there are expected to be 1 million by the end of the week. There are telegrams and telexes from many companies saying that their exports are not being allowed through and that they might lose the orders for ever. . . .

The food industry in particular is shambolic. There is pressure on edible oils, yeast, salt, sugar and packaging materials. No maize came through Tilbury [port of London] yesterday. Associated Biscuits has already laid off 1500 people in Huyton and 400 in Southampton and will lay off more by the weekend. Cold stores are laying off people, and all large oil mills in Hull were picketed yesterday, except the one visited by BBC television. If that is not mounting chaos, it is difficult to see what is.

. . . We have had the bread strike, hospital strikes, strikes at old people's homes, and strikes in newspapers, broadcasting, airports and car plants. . . . Nearly half our factories had some form of industrial conflict, stoppages, overtime bans and go-slows in the past two years; and nearly one-third suffered from all-out strikes.

This is the picture in Britain today, and the troubles will not be over when the immediate strikes are settled. Not only are there more problems in the pipeline but many of the problems arising from the present strikes will carry on for very much longer than the strikes themselves. Many export orders might never be regained. . . .

Unlike the Prime Minister, we do not go around supporting strikes. . . . We never have and we never shall.

The Prime Minister's answer to all our troubles is a statistic – X per cent. This year it is to be 5 per cent. But we cannot have rigid pay policies for ever. That is not a possible way of conducting affairs in a free country which has a great deal of varied industry and where industry must always be changing to keep abreast of the times and one step ahead of competitors if we are to survive.

The right hon. Gentleman knows equally that the real problem is that we have lived through a long period of increasing trade union power. That period has been characterized by a series of what I would call package deals between the Government and the unions in which the Government have offered certain advantages in return for certain co-operation. The trouble has been that the advantages have tended to become permanent and enshrined in legislation, and the cooperation only temporary.

That time of mounting power for the trade unions has also been a period when we have seen increasing Left-wing militancy in control of the unions.

We have been through a period of increasing trade union power. The unions have had unique power and unique power requires unique responsibility. That responsibility has not been forthcoming. That is the reason for the position in which the country finds itself today – about which they can be no dispute.

HISTORIANS' DEBATES

What are the origins of the Welfare State? Was it an inevitable outcome of previous policies? Did it derive from a search for national efficiency or social control?

J. Brown and J.R. Hay in *The Origins of British Social Policy*, ed. Pat Thane (London, 1978); S. Koven and S. Michel, *Mothers of a New World: Maternalist Policies and the Origins of the Welfare State* (London, 1992); David Roberts, *Victorian Origins of the British Welfare State* (New Haven, 1960); G. Searle, *The Quest for National Efficiency* (Oxford, 1971); Pat Thane, "Histories of the Welfare State," in *Historical Controversies and Historians*, ed. William Lamont (London, 1998); Pat Thane, *The Foundations of the Welfare State*, 2nd ed. (Oxford, 1995).

Much emphasis has been placed on Britain's economic "decline" from the later nineteenth century onward and to the social, political, economic, and/or cultural forces to which it can be attributed.

Perry Anderson, *English Questions* (London, 1992); Correlli Barnett, *The Audit of War: The Illusion and Reality of Britain as a Great Nation* (London, 1986); P. Clarke and C. Trebilcock, eds., *Understanding Decline* (Cambridge, 1997); David Coates, *The Question of UK Decline: State, Society, and Economy* (London, 1994); David Coates and John Hillard, eds., *The Economic Decline of Modern Britain: The Debate between Left and Right* (Brighton, 1994); Nicholas Crafts, *Britain's Relative Economic Decline, 1870–1995: A Quantitative Perspective* (London, 1997); Michael Dintenfass, *The Decline of Industrial Britain, 1870–1980* (London, 1992); Bernard Elbaum and William Lazonick, eds., *The Decline of the British Economy* (Oxford, 1986); Richard English and Michael Kenny, eds., *Rethinking British Decline* (London, 2000); William P. Kennedy, *Industrial Structure, Capital Markets, and the Origins of British Economic Decline* (Cambridge, 1987); David S. Landes, *The Unbound Prometheus: Technological Change and Industrial Development in Western Europe from 1750 to the Present* (Cambridge, 1969); Robert Millward, "Productivity in the UK Services Sector: Historical Trends, 1865–1985 and Comparisons with the USA 1950–1985," *Oxford Bulletin of Economics and Statistics* 52 (1990), 423–36; Sidney Pollard, *Britain's Prime and Britain's Decline: The British Economy, 1870–1914* (London, 1989); Newton Scott and Dilwyn Porter, *Modernization Frustrated: The Politics of Industrial Decline in Britain since 1900* (London, 1988); Michael Shanks, *The Stagnant Society* (Harmondsworth, 1961); Andrew Shonfield, *British Economic Policy since the War* (Harmondsworth, 1958); F.M.L. Thompson, *Gentrification and the Enterprise Culture: Britain 1780–1980* (Oxford, 2001); J. Tomlinson, "Inventing 'Decline': The Falling Behind of the British Economy in the Post-War Years," *EcHR* 49 (1996), 731–57; Martin J. Wiener, *English Culture and the Decline of the Industrial Spirit, 1850–1980* (Cambridge, 1981).

What is the explanation for the divergence between Britain, on the one hand, and Germany and the United States, on the other, in industrial productivity?

S.N. Broadberry, *The Productivity Race: British Manufacturing in International Perspective, 1850–1990* (Cambridge, 1997); S.N. Broadberry, "Manufacturing and the Convergence Hypothesis: What the Long-run Data Show," *JEH* 53 (1993), 772–95; S.N. Broadberry and N.F.R. Crafts, "British Economic Policy and Industrial Performance in the Early Postwar Period," *BH* 38 (1996); Y. Cassis, *Big Business: The European Experience in the Twentieth Century* (Oxford, 1997); F. Dobbin, *Forging Industrial Policy: The United States, Britain and France in the Railway Age* (Cambridge, 1994); D. Edgerton and S. Horrocks, "British Industrial Research and Development before 1914," *EcHR* 47 (1984), 213–38; H.F. Gospel and C.R. Littler, eds., *Managerial Strategy and Industrial Relations: An Historical and Comparative Survey* (London, 1983); H.J. Habakkuk, *American and British Technology in the Nineteenth Century: The Search for Labour Saving Inventions* (Cambridge, 1962); N. Horn and J. Kocka, eds., *Law and the Formation of the Big Enterprise in the Nineteenth and Early Twentieth Centuries* (Göttingen, 1979); M.B. Rose, *Firms, Networks and Business Values: The British and American Cotton Industries since 1750* (Cambridge, 2000); N. Rosenberg, *Technology and American Economic Growth* (New York, 1972); C. Sabel and J. Zeitlin, "Historical Alternatives to Mass Production: Politics, Markets and Technology in Nineteenth Century Industrialisation," *P&P* 108 (1985), 133–76; C. Sabel and J. Zeitlin, eds., *World of*

Possibilities: Flexibility and Mass Production in Western Industrialization (Cambridge, 1997); B. Supple, "The Political Economy of Demoralization: The State and the Coalmining Industry in America and Britain between the Wars," *EcHR* 41 (1988), 566–91; G. Tweedale, *Sheffield Steel and America: A Century of Commercial and Technological Independence, 1830–1930* (Cambridge, 1987); S. Tolliday and J. Zeitlin, eds., *The Power to Manage? Employers and Industrial Relations in Comparative Historical Perspective* (London, 1981).

What was Benjamin Seebohm Rowntree's impact on the discussion of poverty in twentieth-century Britain?

Asa Briggs, *Social Thought and Social Action: A Study of the Work of Seebohm Rowntree 1871–1954* (London, 1961); B. Seebohm Rowntree, *Poverty: A Study of Town Life* (London, 1901); Sean Stitt and Diane Grant, *Poverty: Rowntree Revisited* (Aldershot, 1993); Peter Townsend, "The Meaning of Poverty," *BJS* 19 (1962), 210–27; Peter Townsend, *Poverty in the United Kingdom* (London, 1979); John Viet Wilson, "Seebohm Rowntree," in *Founders of the Welfare State*, ed. Paul Barker (London, 1984).

To what degree was World War I a watershed in terms of change in British society, particularly for women?

Gail Braybon, *Women Workers in the First World War: The British Experience* (London, 1981); Paul Fussell, *The Great War and Modern Memory* (New York, 1975); Margaret Randolph Higonnet *et al.*, eds., *Behind the Lines: Gender and the Two World Wars* (New Haven, 1987); Susan Kingsley Kent, *Making Peace: The Reconstruction of Gender in Interwar Britain* (Princeton, 1993); Arthur Marwick, *The Deluge: British Society and the First World War* (London, 1965); Arthur Marwick, *Women at War 1914–1918* (London, 1977); David Mitchell, *Monstrous Regiment: The Story of the Women of the First World War* (New York, 1965); John Turner, *British Politics and the Great War: Coalition and Conflict, 1915–1918* (New Haven, 1992); Trevor Wilson, *The Myriad of Faces: Britain and the Great War, 1914–1918* (Oxford, 1986); J.M. Winter, *The Great War and the British People* (London, 1985).

Did the traditional class structure of British society break down in the twentieth century? And if so, when? Are the traditional categories (classes) by which social structure is analyzed useful or relevant?

J. Benson, *The Rise of Consumer Society in Britain 1880–1980* (London, 1994); D. Cannadine, *Class in Britain* (London, 1998); R. Crompton, *Class and Stratification: An Introduction to Current Debates* (Cambridge, 1988); J.H. Goldthorpe, C. Payne, and C. Llewellyn, *Social Mobility and Class Structure in Modern Britain* (Oxford, 1987); P. Joyce, "The End of Social History?" *SH* 20 (1995), 73–91; R. McKibbin, *Classes and Cultures: England 1918–1951* (Oxford, 1998); R.E. Pahl, "Some Questions on the Adequacy of Sociological Theory on Urban and Regional Research," *IJURR* 12 (1988); H. Perkin, *The Rise of Professional Society: England since 1880* (London, 1990); A. Reid, "World War I and the Working Class in Britain," in *Total War and Social Change*, ed. A. Marwick (Basingstoke, 1988); J. Stevenson, *British Society 1914–45* (Harmondsworth, 1984).

COUNTERFACTUAL TO CONSIDER

What if Britain had taken the initiative in founding the European Union, perhaps in alliance with France? Would its economy have strengthened more rapidly? Could it have been more assertive in holding on to the Empire?

CHAPTER NINE

Culture and Identity

Women made important progress toward gender equality in the twentieth century, although in retrospect the rate of improvement was painfully slow. How could men still justify denying women under 30 the vote in 1918? Aspects of inequality hitherto not given much thought now became more prominent. Homosexuals had to wait until the 1960s for decriminalization of same-sex relationships, and they still lack full recognition as equal citizens in British society today. The retreat from empire led to increased immigration into Britain. People came from the West Indies, India, and Pakistan in large numbers. They were admitted in part due to continued delusions of imperial *noblesse oblige* and in part to fill jobs Britons were not doing. Traditional white Christian Britain began to experience serious trouble in digesting the newcomers. Racism, xenophobia, and a sense of economic rivalry all played a role in the unsettling process of absorption, recently made more acute by the rise of Islamic fundamentalism.

In 1922 southern Ireland parted ways with Britain after 800 years. The break was not a clean one, and the final process of creating a peaceful island is still a work in progress. In Wales and Scotland a demand for more autonomy led to more fragmentation within the archipelago. Will the United Kingdom stay united?

As you read the documents in this chapter, consider the following questions:

- How has the position of women and minorities changed over the course of the twentieth century?
- Can people who are not "normal" by the traditional definitions of twentieth-century Britain (gays, Muslims, Afro-Caribbeans) be successfully integrated into the society and culture?
- Is there a distinct identity for each nation in the archipelago?

Sources and Debates in Modern British History: 1714 to the Present, First Edition. Edited by Ellis Wasson.

Published 2012 by Blackwell Publishing Ltd.

Women

9.1 *Report of the War Cabinet Committee on Women in British Industry (1919)*[1]

Millions of men joined the military services during World War I. Many of their jobs were then filled by women. A Cabinet committee gathered data on women's contributions to the war effort and reported in 1919. The following extracts provide information on female employment during the period 1914–18.

During World War I what industries employed the largest proportion of women? To what degree did they contribute to the war effort? To what degree were their activities in the workplace likely to contribute to granting suffrage to women after the war? How likely were women to continue in such employment after demobilization of the armed forces?

In the second half of 1915 unemployed women were rapidly absorbed in munitions factories, and in January 1916, in industry proper the number of women had already increased by over a quarter of a million, of whom about one-half were employed in the Metal and Chemical trades. From this time onwards the figure of female employment rose steadily until in July, 1918, the total number of occupied women had, according to the Board of Trade figures, increased by 22 ½ per cent or from just under 6 million to nearly 7 1/3 million. . . .

. . . *Employment of Women during the War. Munition Metal Trades.* . . . The most important single trade was shell-making. The women were soon some 60 per cent of the workers, and made the shell throughout from the roughing and turning of the bodies to the final gauging of the completed shell. In general engineering shops and shipyards, foundries, gun and aircraft factories, women were introduced on most varieties of men's work – light laboring, turning, shaping, slotting, drawing, filing, grinding, punching, shearing, machine riveting, gear-cutting, crane-driving, assembling, dressing castings, soldering, welding – and were sometimes promoted as "fitters" and "turners" in the tool-room as "capstan lathe setters" and "tool setters". In some munition factories the men's work was almost entirely carried out by women. . . .

. . . *Hotels, Public Houses, &c.* Under this head the number of women increased by 21 per cent., or 39,000. In catering establishments women have been brought into all branches of the industry and into departments they have never previously entered. . . . Even establishments of the best class now employ women in occupations in which men were almost exclusively employed before the war. . ..

. . . *Teaching and other Professions.* The main fact with regard to the teaching profession in the war is that towards making good the loss of 22,000 men teachers,

[1] *Report of the War Cabinet Committee on Women in British Industry* (London, 1919), 80–1, 99, 102.

some 13,000 women were drawn into the service. The temporary displacement will probably accelerate the change in the proportion of the two sexes engaged which had been going on for some years before the war. . . .

. . . As an indirect result of the war and of the grant of the parliamentary suffrage to women some new professions are being opened to them. In January, 1918, the Society of Incorporated Accountants and Auditors obtained permission from the Chancery Court to alter their articles of association so as to permit of the admission of women as members. In March, 1918, a Bill to admit of women qualifying as Barristers and Solicitors passed the House of Lords.

9.2 *Representation of the People Act (1918)*[2]

In 1918 women were finally granted the vote, although only a limited category of them qualified. They had to wait until 1928 to be given completely equal representation with men. Why the delay for full eligibility? Why did the initial law require women to be at least 30 years of age to vote? Why the property qualifications? Why did the law get passed only in 1918?

Representation of the People Act, 1918

Part I, clause 4 (1) A woman shall be entitled to be registered as a parliamentary elector for a constituency . . . if she:

(a) has attained the age of thirty years; and
(b) is not subject to any legal incapacity; and
(c) is entitled to be registered as a local government elector in respect of the occupation in that constituency of land or premises (not being a dwelling-house) of a yearly value of not less than five pounds or of a dwelling-house, or is the wife of a husband entitled to be so registered.

9.3 *Marie Stopes,* Married Love *(1918)*[3]

Marie Stopes (1880–1958) caused a sensation with the publication of her book *Married Love* in 1918. Not only did she speak explicitly and in a progressive way about sexual relations, but also she advocated an equal partnership in marriage. She opened the first family planning clinic in Britain in 1921.

Why was there so much shocked reaction to Stopes's book? What conventions did she challenge? What did Stopes say about birth control? How did her work contribute to feminism as it developed later in the twentieth century?

[2] 8 Geo. V, c. 64.

[3] Marie Carmichael Stopes, *Married Love*, 7th ed. (New York, 1931), 7–8, 25–7, 111–14, 136.

The Heart's Desire

In the meantime, we *are* human. We each and all live our lives according to [chemical and physiological] laws, some of which we have begun to understand, many of which are completely hidden from us. The most complete human being is he or she who consciously or unconsciously obeys the profound physical laws of our being in such a way that the spirit receives as much help and as little hindrance from the body as possible. A mind and spirit finds its fullest expression thwarted by the misuse, neglect or gross abuse of the body in which it dwells. . . .

To use a homely simile – one might compare two human beings to two bodies charged with electricity to different potentials. Isolated from each other the electric forces within them are invisible, but if they come into the right juxtaposition the force is transmuted, and a spark, a glow of burning light arises between them. Such is love. . . .

Many writers, novelists, poets and dramatists have represented the uttermost tragedy of human life as due to the incomprehensible contrariness of the feminine nature. The kindly ones smile, perhaps a little patronizingly, and tell us that women are more instinctive, more childlike, less reasonable than men. The bitter ones sneer or reproach or laugh at this in women they do not understand, and which, baffling *their* intellect, appears to them to be irrational folly. . ..

Vaguely, perhaps, men have realized that much of the charm of life lies in the sex-*differences* between men and women; so they have snatched at the easy theory that women differ from themselves by being capricious. Moreover, by attributing to mere caprice the coldness which at times comes over the most ardent women, man was unconsciously justifying himself for at any time coercing her to suit himself.

Circumstances have so contrived that hitherto the explorers and scientific investigators, the historians and statisticians, the poets and artists have been mostly men. Consequently woman's side of the joint life has found little or no expression. Woman, so long coerced by economic dependence, and the need for protection while she bore her children, has had to be content to mold herself to the shape desired by man wherever possible, and she has stifled her natural feelings and her own deep thoughts as they welled up.

Most women have never realized intellectually, but many have been dimly half-conscious, that woman's nature is set to rhythms over which man has no more control than he has over the tides of the sea . . .

Children

It is utterly impossible, organized as our bodies are at present, for us to obey the dictates of theologians and refrain from the destruction of potential life. The germ-cells of the woman, though immeasurably less numerous than the male germ-cells (the sperm), yet develop uselessly over and over again in every celibate as well as in every married woman; while myriads of sperm-cells are destroyed even in the process of the act which does ensure fertilization of the woman by the single favored sperm. If the theologians really mean what they say, and demand the voluntary effort of complete celibacy from all men, save for the purpose of procreation, this will *not* achieve their end of preventing the destruction of all potential life; and the monthly loss of unfertilized egg-cell by women is beyond all efforts of the will to curb. Nature, not man, arranged the destruction of potential life against which ascetic Bishops rage.

If then, throughout the greater part of their lives the germinal cells of both sexes inevitably disintegrate without creating an embryo, there can be nothing wrong in selecting the most favorable moment possible for the conception of the first of these germinal cells to be endowed with the supreme privilege of creating a new life.

For many reasons it is more ideal to have children spontaneously and early; but if economic conditions are hard, as they often are in "civilized" life, it may be better to marry and defer the children rather than not to marry.

If the pair married very young, and before they could afford to support children, they might wait several years with advantage. . . .

There are many reasons, both for their own and for the child's sake, why the potential parents should take the wise precaution of delay, unless owing to special circumstances they cannot expect to live together uninterruptedly.

The child, conceived in rapture and hope, should be given every material chance which the wisdom and love of the parents can devise. And the first and *most* vital condition of its health is that the mother should be well and happy and free from anxiety while she bears it.

The tremendous and far-reaching effects of marriage on the woman's whole organism makes her less fitted to bear a child at the very commencement of marriage than later on, when the system will have adjusted itself to its new conditions. . . .

To those who protest that we have no right to interfere with the course of nature, one must point out that the whole of civilization, everything which separates man from animals, is an interference with what such people commonly call "nature." Nothing in the cosmos can be against nature, for it all forms part of the great processes of the universe.

9.4 *Enoch Powell, speech in the House of Commons (Mar. 26, 1975)*[4]

Enoch Powell (1912–98) was one of the leading Conservative politicians of his generation. He destroyed his own career by an extreme speech against allowing immigrants into the United Kingdom (see document 9.6). In the passage below he opposed a bill proposing anti-discrimination against women.

[4] *Parliamentary Debates*, vol. 899, Mar. 26, 1975, c. 539–44.

To what degree do you think Powell's ideas reflected male attitudes toward women in the 1970s? How can society reconcile the genuine differences between the sexes and the desire for individual freedom with the need to prevent discrimination based on gender, race, or sexual orientation? How do you account for the fact that even today women on average receive lower pay for the same work than men receive? Do free markets automatically guarantee liberty in non-economic spheres?

. . . Why refuse to recognize that there is an immense gradation, infinitely subtle, of the differences in the carrying out of a whole range of jobs according to whether it is a man or a woman who does so? This depends not only upon the nature of the job but upon the period of time for its performance – whether it is a matter of a short time, a year or a career which is envisaged – and varies almost invisibly with the changes in society, with the changes in qualifications and with the changes in industry. . . .

The Bill is a denial of the infinite differentiation of jobs and of those best fitted to perform them, . . . the differentiation of sex is all-pervasive and, in relation to different jobs and functions in society, confers – now in one direction, now in the other – more or less advantage and benefit on the way in which they are performed. Yet here is a Bill which sets out to eliminate the effects of that differentiation except where it is total or absolute. This is a defiance of reality. . . .

To some extent this measure was the foreseeable next stage of the equal pay legislation, which I also attacked and opposed at the time. If we seek to impose an equal price on essentially different items, goods or services, the next stage inevitably is that we are obliged to carry on and impose duress upon those who offer and those who invite services. So this Bill is, not solely but to a considerable extent, the logical consequence of the mistake which was made in legislating for equal pay.

It is in the context of pay that one can illustrate most simply what also applies to the whole range of opportunity. It is not possible for long or over a very wide area to pay different sums for services of the same value. It is simply impossible, because if services of the same value can be obtained under a different label more cheaply, those who so obtain them will drive out of the business of providing the goods or the services those who pay more than they need for a given quality of labor or of service. It is a process which works automatically and unobtrusively – not indeed perfectly, but it has the advantage that it works, and that it accommodates itself to all the changes and varieties of the real world.

What will happen is that this Bill, in its implementation, will introduce suspicion, discord, doubt and anxiety on the part of employer and employee. Wherever it is sought to be enforced there will be the intrusion of the law and of the investigatory powers of the commission into the affairs not merely of large firms but of all but the smallest.

There is a mania today in legislation for attacking discrimination, oblivious that all life is about discrimination, because all life is about differences. This Bill is a particularly heinous example of the follies into which governments and parliaments are led when they give heed to this fashionable but foolish craze.

Minorities and Immigration

9.5 Lord Soper, speech in the House of Lords (July 13, 1967)[5]

In 1954 the Conservative government commissioned a report on sexual offences, led by Sir John Wolfenden, which recommended decriminalizing homosexual relations in 1957. It was not until 1967, however, that legislation was at last enacted. In the debate in the House of Lords, Lord Auckland reflected a still widespread view when he called homosexuals "unfortunate people" who needed to be "cured" of their habits. Donald Soper (1903–98), a leading Methodist preacher, activist in the Campaign for Nuclear Disarmament, and influential leader on moral issues, supported the Sexual Offenses Bill.

Why might "Nonconformist" churches support tolerance of societal "deviance"? Why had society been unable to resolve the issue of whether homosexuality was innate or acquired behavior? What might account for the ten-year delay between the publication of the Wolfenden Report and action in Parliament? Why do many people continue to view homosexuals with hostility? What motivated those who favored greater tolerance? Wouldn't one expect Soper, as a clergyman, to condemn sexual relations outside marriage?

My Lords, one of the great effects, it seems to me, of the protracted debates in [the House of Commons] and here on this topic has been the tendency, at least, to education in many fields where before there was little but ignorance and prejudice. It may well be, as the last speaker has said, that this has tended in some cases to produce a coarsening of thought. But on the whole the evidence I would bring from the Free Churches [non-Anglican Protestant churches] is that the process has been to the good, and that since this question first appeared in headlines this process within the Free Churches has led to an almost total unanimity, so far as it is expressed in our affairs, that, on the whole, this Bill ought to be supported, and that in general it clarifies and expresses quite important moral issues.

It would seem to me, if I may say so with respect, that there is still some confusion in the minds of some people, perhaps even in your Lordships' House, as between homosexuality as a condition, an ineluctable condition, and

5 *Parliamentary Debates*, vol. 284, July 13, 1967, c. 1308–9.

homosexual practices as a way in which that condition expresses itself. I am quite sure that homosexuals, so far as I know them, are not aware that they are doing anything wrong or being evil because they feel these particular feelings and sustain these particular idiosyncrasies. And if it be argued that discipline is always required with regard to sexual matters, how much more, how much harder, is that discipline in the very often unrewarding and un-creating kind of environment in which a homosexual has to display that discipline, rather than in the far more natural and creative way in which the normal discipline has to be displayed!

But it would not be for me to deploy these arguments again, except to say – and in this respect I can speak for the Free Churches in this country – that I support this Bill on their behalf, and believe that it represents a necessary change in the law; that it represents a proper attitude to some aspects of homosexuality . . .

Since we speak frankly, or I hope we do, I suggest that there are homosexual practices which in the beginning, in the simpler expressions of physical affection as between homosexuals, are as natural and as innocuous in themselves as any practices as between a man and a girl. I cannot for the life of me (this is a purely personal observation) see that it is sinful for two men to hold hands, realizing as I do that that holding of hands may well be, at least in part, or involved in, a sexual behavior pattern. However, this is to raise highly controversial matters. What is, in my judgment, not controversial is that in this particular regard, certainly so far as I am concerned, to pass this Bill will remove a great deal of the terror, the fear, the unnatural hazards that affront so many good and decent homosexuals, and may be the beginning of other and better legislation to follow it, whereby the recovery of such people to what we call a normal pattern of life may be made easier. I support the Bill.

9.6 Enoch Powell, "Rivers of Blood" speech, Birmingham (Apr. 20, 1968)[6]

Immigration into Britain after World War II came mainly from "New Commonwealth" countries, especially the West Indies, India, and Pakistan. While there were 150,000 residents in Britain in 1981 from Australia, Canada, New Zealand, and South Africa, over 1,500,000 people came from the New Commonwealth, up from half a million in the years immediately before Enoch Powell's speech predicting such a trend.

Powell was a Conservative MP of great ability and fiery temperament. He was on his way to a distinguished career when he made this speech and was dismissed from the Shadow Cabinet by Ted Heath. He spent the rest of his career as an outsider. Powell began by quoting a constituent who claimed:

6 www.telegraph.co.uk Nov. 6, 2007.

"In this country in 15 or 20 years' time the black man will have the whip hand over the white man."

Why did most Conservatives distance themselves from Powell's statements? How could English people feel like a minority when immigrants themselves were still a small minority of the population? Was he wrong in his prediction of the expanding number of immigrants or about violence that would come? Was racial conflict inevitable?

In 15 or 20 years, on present trends, there will be in this country three and a half million Commonwealth immigrants and their descendants. . . .

There is no comparable official figure for the year 2000, but it must be in the region of five to seven million, approximately one-tenth of the whole population . . . Whole areas, towns and parts of towns across England will be occupied by sections of immigrant and immigrant-descended population. . . .

It is this fact which creates the extreme urgency of action now, of just that kind of action which is hardest for politicians to take, action where the difficulties lie in the present but the evils to be prevented or minimized lie several parliaments ahead. . . .

[The way to prevent the evil is] by stopping, or virtually stopping, further inflow, and by promoting the maximum outflow. . . .

[Yet] so insane are we that we actually permit unmarried persons to immigrate for the purpose of founding a family . . .

[Meanwhile white British people have] found themselves made strangers in their own country. They found their wives unable to obtain hospital beds in childbirth, their children unable to obtain school places, their homes and neighborhoods changed beyond recognition, their plans and prospects for the future defeated . . . The sense of being a persecuted minority which is growing among ordinary English people in the areas of the country which are affected is something that those without direct experience can hardly imagine. . . .

As I look ahead, I am filled with foreboding; like the Roman, I seem to see "the River Tiber foaming with much blood".

9.7 *John Rae,* Diary *(1975–83)*[7]

Westminster is one of Britain's celebrated "public" schools with a long line of famous alumni including John Locke, Jeremy Bentham, and Lord John Russell. In the 1970s its scholars were drawn largely from the new rich with business backgrounds and the upper levels of the traditional professional elite along with the occasional member of the royal family. These extracts are from

[7] John Rae, *The Old Boys' Network, A Headmaster's Diaries 1970–1986* (London, 2009), 73, 239–41.

the diary of Dr John Rae (1931–2006), a distinguished headmaster nationally known as a spokesman on education. In 1986 he appointed the first black pupil (a West Indian girl) to be head of the student body in the 450-year history of the school.

What do Rae's diary entries tell us about how British society was accommodating itself to immigration? Does his educational background and the elite nature of the school where tuition is very high make a difference in the attitudes of teachers and students toward immigrants and black people in general?

13 September 1975: This evening, I am disturbed to read a series of articles in the *Times Educational Supplement* arguing that as Britain is now multi-cultural schools should no longer pass on a mono-cultural tradition. What nonsense. If the history and literature of the country are watered down to suit ethnic minorities, the United Kingdom will be little more than a geographical expression. Happily, Westminster does not have to take any notice of this misguided idea.

19 October 1983: Frank Singer, the American English-Speaking Union [exchange] student, comes round for a talk. He likes Westminster . . . However, he says he is shocked by the open racism of some of the boys. Frank is Jewish and I ask whether the boys are anti-Semitic but he says no, the racism is directed against West Indian and Asian immigrants. He finds it all in marked contrast to the USA where – he says – that sort of blatant racism is a thing of the past. What he says does not altogether surprise me; racism is widespread among the English of all classes and schoolboys are less inhibited than their parents about expressing it or perhaps they are just less hypocritical.

16 November 1983: Horace Lashley comes to talk to the John Locke Society about his work for the Commission for Racial Equality. He makes a poor impression. He is from Trinidad [in the West Indies] and has lived most of his life in this country. He lectures the boys and girls on the failure of the British to recognize the passing of imperial status but the Empire means nothing whatsoever to them. Over lunch he is touchy because a girl says to him that black athletes are better sprinters because they have a lower center of gravity.

9.8 "*The Brixton Disorders, 10–12 April 1981,*" Report of an Inquiry by the Rt. Hon. The Lord Scarman *(1981)*[8]

The inquiry ordered by the government in the wake of serious riots in Brixton in south London in April 1981 was conducted by Lord Scarman (1911–2004). The looting and destruction had shocked the country, and drew sharp

[8] Lord Scarman, *The Brixton Disorders, 10–12 April 1981: Report of an Inquiry,* (London, 1981), 1–2, 73, 135–6.

attention to the racism inherent in British society aimed at minority groups with Asian and West Indian (usually African) backgrounds. The Brixton riots were provoked by discrimination against black people in employment, education, and in relations with the law, but immigrant populations from India and Pakistan also felt they were at a disadvantage in making a good life in British society.

How likely is it that a traditionally white-dominated society is going to make rapid strides toward multiculturalism? Was it race, poverty, religion, or culture that was the biggest problem?

Two views have been forcefully expressed in the course of the Inquiry as to the causation of the disorders. The first is: – oppressive policing over a period of years, and in particular the harassment of young blacks on the streets of Brixton. On this view, it is said to be unnecessary to look more deeply for an explanation of the disorders. They were "anti police". The second is that the disorders, like so many riots in British history, were a protest against society by people, deeply frustrated and deprived, who saw in a violent attack upon the forces of law and order their one opportunity of compelling public attention to their grievances. I have no doubt that each view, even if correct, would be an over-simplification of a complex situation.

... Nothing that I have heard or seen can excuse the unlawful behavior of the rioters. But the police must carry some responsibility for the outbreak of disorder. First, they were partly to blame for the breakdown in community relations. Secondly, there were instances of harassment, and racial prejudice among junior officers on the streets of Brixton which gave credibility and substance to the arguments of the police's critics. Thirdly, there was the failure to adjust policies and methods to meet the needs of policing a multi-racial society. The failures of the police, however, were only part of the story and arose in difficult circumstances. The community and community leaders in particular must take their share of the blame for the atmosphere of distrust and mutual suspicion between the police and the community which developed in Lambeth during the 1970s and reached its apogee in the weeks prior to the disorders. I hold it as a hopeful sign that in the closing stages of the Inquiry there was evidence of an apparent willingness on both sides to acknowledge past errors and to try to make a new start.

... Racial disadvantage is a fact of current British life. It was, I am equally sure, a significant factor in the causation of the Brixton disorders. Urgent action is needed if it is not to become an endemic, ineradicable disease threatening the very survival of our society.

... The police do not create social deprivation or racial disadvantage: they are not responsible for the disadvantages of the ethnic minorities. Yet their role is critical. If their policing is such that it can be seen to be the application to our new society of the traditional principles of British policing, the risk of unrest will diminish and the prospect of approval by all responsible elements in our ethnically diverse society will be the greater. If they neglect consultation and cooperation with the local community, unrest is certain and riot becomes probable.

A new approach is needed.

... The attack on racial disadvantage must be more direct than it has been. It must be co-ordinated by central government, who with local authorities must ensure that the funds made available are directed to specific areas of racial disadvantage. I have in mind particularly education and employment. A policy of direct co-ordinated attack on racial disadvantage inevitably means that the ethnic minorities will enjoy for a time a positive discrimination in their favour. But it is a price worth paying if it accelerates the elimination of the unsettling factor of racial disadvantage from the social fabric of the United Kingdom ...

9.9 *Lord Soper, speech in the House of Lords (Dec. 10, 1974)*[9]

In this speech Lord Soper (see document 9.5) addresses the teaching of public morality in schools. While nominally still a Christian country, church attendance in Britain dropped precipitously during the postwar era. Today less than 5% of English people attend a religious service weekly. Immigrants from Asia and Africa brought much greater religious diversity to British society.

What perspective would a Methodist bring to English life where an established Anglican church existed? How did Soper distinguish between public and private morality? What problems did he see in teaching "public" morality in schools? What was his assessment of the present state of religion and morality in Britain? What were Soper's views on non-Christian faiths?

... If we are not in a terminal condition of immorality, things are quite bad. ... There has been a progressive decline in religious belief, so that the trunk of the tree of morality has in very large degree been separated from the roots of theology in which alone I suspect it can finally be established and can fructify. ... There is a marked change from the emphasis upon morality as being a purely personal relationship between man and his neighbor or man and his God and the social morality which is a much more complex issue. ... There is a paradox, that many a sinful individual has contributed majestically to the general progress of humanity ... Therefore there is a difference between the piety which was regarded as the supreme expression of morality not so very long ago and the social content of that morality which in many cases, if not independent of the private moral behavior of those who agitate in the interests of that social morality, nevertheless does not determine it. In other words, those who think that social morality is the finer

[9] *Parliamentary Debates*, vol. 355, Dec. 10, 1974, c. 605–10.

breath and spirit of personal piety have a lot to learn about the way in which scoundrels can improve the society in which they live.

But I would submit to your Lordships that the greatest change that has taken place is that we now live in a multi-racial society, and there has come to all kinds of people who hitherto were ignorant of the facts, the awareness of the competitive social claims of other religions. . . . In a multi-racial society where there is the Hindu, the Brahmin, the Buddhist and the Islamic believer, the Humanist and the Communist – after all, Communism is one of the last of the heresies of the Christian faith – it is not surprising that to "railroad" people into an assumption that they can automatically see morality in terms of a Christian ethic is no longer tolerable and is an insult to other religions, since we do not hold in Christianity a monopoly of truth, let alone a monopoly of goodness. Here again is a problem for social morality which is comparatively new. There is one overarching problem in the field of social morality. . . . We live in a society in which the social morality of the necessity for the abhorrence of violence is as yet an unsolved problem. To put it crudely, a bomber who, in the midst of war, kills indiscriminately hundreds of children as well as adults in Dresden may well be decorated. A bomber who the other week threw his bomb into a public house in Birmingham is very properly execrated. There is a double standard in the field of violence to which we give our assent or withdraw our assent, and one of the greatest difficulties that confronts anybody who endeavors to teach the practice of moral values is that he is confronted with this double standard.

I am completely and utterly convinced that although we may be no worse than our fathers, we are certainly not morally adequate to stand up to the stresses which are greater than those which they had to confront. . . . We desperately need a recognition of the fundamental moral issues which belong to any society which can claim to be civilized. Christians cannot pretend that they have a monopoly of intelligence to find out what they are – Humanists or atheists. Of course the Jews and all kinds of other people from East and West are required in this adventure.

9.10 Ayatollah Ruhollah Khomeini, "The Fatwa on Salman Rushdie" (1989)[10]

On February 14, 1989 the Iranian Shiite leader Ayatollah Ruhollah Khomeini (1902–89) issued a "Fatwa" or religious injunction against the novelist Salman Rushdie for his characterization of the Prophet Mohammed in the book *The Satanic Verses.* Rushdie was a Cambridge-educated resident of Britain of Asian descent. Khomeini ordered British Muslims to kill the author. The British secret services took Rushdie under their protection and he was later awarded a knighthood. The incident brought into focus the contradictions

[10] en.wikipedia.org/wiki/The_Satanic_Verses_controversy (accessed July 7, 2011).

between modern British cultural values and law and those brought by some new immigrants and passed on to their children who had difficulty assimilating.

Is it possible to reconcile fundamentalist Islamic teaching and law with living in modern British society?

In the name of God the Almighty. We belong to God and to Him we shall return. I would like to inform all intrepid Muslims in the world that the author of the book *Satanic Verses*, which has been compiled, printed, and published in opposition to Islam, the Prophet, and the Qur'an, and those publishers who were aware of its contents, are sentenced to death. I call on all zealous Muslims to execute them quickly, where they find them, so that no one will dare to insult the Islamic sanctity. Whoever is killed on this path will be regarded as a martyr, God-willing.

In addition, if anyone has access to the author of the book but does not possess the power to execute him, he should point him out to the people so that he may be punished for his actions. May God's blessing be on you all. Rullah Musavi al-Khomeini.

9.11 The Governance of Britain *(2007)*[11]

Gordon Brown (b.1951), prime minister 2007–10, frequently expressed a concern that "British" values and citizenship be more actively promoted by the government. This may have been prompted both by a concern that an independent Scotland, where Labour electoral support was key to holding power in Parliament, might lead to his party's downfall and by the irruption of Islamic fundamentalism among young men raised in Britain from immigrant families. The government issued a proposal for reform in 2007.

What might prompt government concern about national unity and identity in the first decade of the twenty-first century? Can identity be taught in schools and at citizenship ceremonies? Why are the report's references only to "English" schools, yet it is "British" identity that is to be taught? Why might the report use the word "citizen" when the traditional term was "subject"?

In some London boroughs there are over 190 community languages spoken. Such diversity has had great benefits for the UK, not just economically, but also culturally, with recent surveys showing that foreign-born residents feel a strong attachment to this country. There is growing recognition of the need to ensure that

[11] *The Governance of Britain*, CM 7170, July 2007, paragraphs 125, 186, 191.

Britain remains a cohesive society, confident in its shared identity and secure in the face of the challenges it faces both at home and abroad. . . .

The Government has already improved a considerable range of measures aimed at raising the profile and meaning of citizenship, introducing language and Knowledge of Life tests for new applicants and starting the highly successful citizenship ceremonies which are organized in Town Halls across the country. . . .

But if there has been considerable advance in recent years in terms of the legal process of applying for citizenship, less attention has been paid to the nature of what it means to be a British citizen. There is a general lack of clarity about the rights and responsibilities that come with being granted British citizenship. The current entitlements and responsibilities are complex and confusing, and offer weak incentives to become British for long-term residents of other nationalities. . . .

The Government wants schools to be at the forefront of this and has brought in a new statutory duty for schools in England to promote community cohesion. The community cohesion duty will build on the excellent work many schools are already doing to promote greater unity and understanding across different communities. . . . This will give all young people the chance to foster a stronger sense of their own identity and what it means to be a British citizen.

British Identities

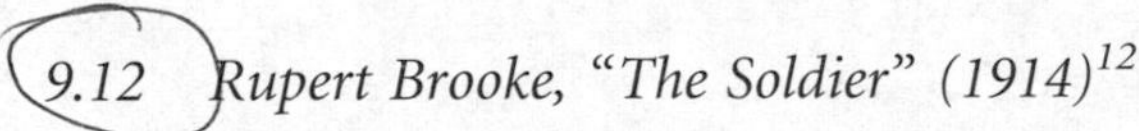

9.12 Rupert Brooke, "The Soldier" (1914)[12]

Most of the familiar poetry of World War I is at best ambiguous about the conflict if not outright condemnatory. There were, in fact, many patriotic poets and writers, although even their spirits were often muted as the terrible toll in lives lost mounted. The poet Rupert Brooke (1887–1915) was one of the last outstanding artists to celebrate English patriotism with undiminished fervor. This poem was written in 1914 after the outbreak of war. He died of illness while on active service as a soldier in the Mediterranean theater in April 1915.

What did "England" mean to Brooke? Was his vision of nationality in any way unique or distinctive from other nationalities in the British Isles?

The Soldier

If I should die, think only this of me:
  That there's some corner of a foreign field
That is forever England. There shall be
  In that rich earth a richer dust concealed;

[12] Rupert Brooke, *Collected Poems* (New York, 1915), 115.

A dust who England bore, shaped, made aware,
  Gave, once, her flowers to love, her ways to roam,
A body of England's, breathing English air,
  Washed by the rivers, blest by suns of home.
And think, this heart, all evil shed away,
  A pulse in the eternal mind, no less
Gives somewhere back the thoughts by England
  Given;
Her sights and sound; dreams happy as her day;
  And laughter, learnt of friends; and greatness,
In hearts at peace, under an English heaven.

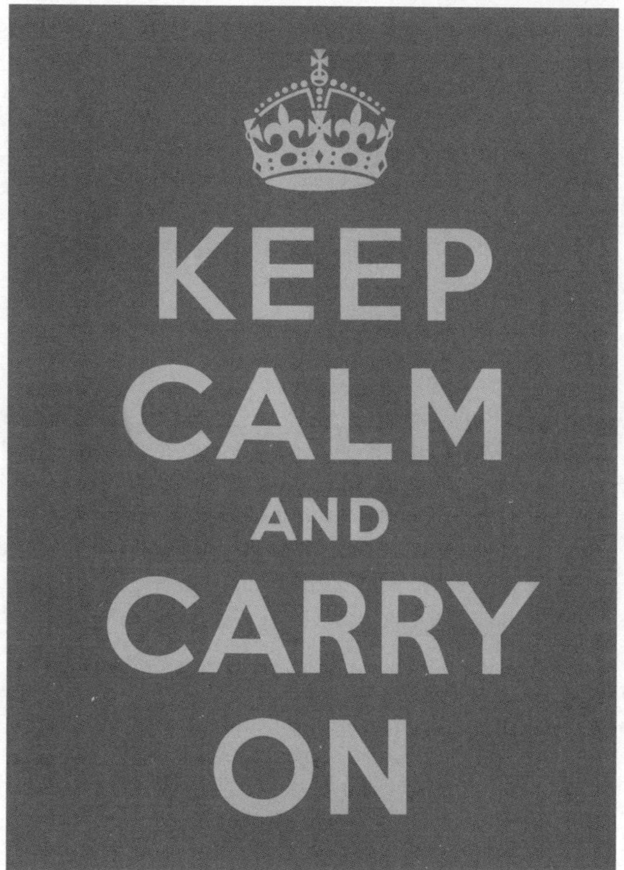

Figure 9.1 British World War II propaganda poster urging people to "Keep Calm and Carry On" – as relevant today as when first issued in 1939. © Rawdon Wyatt/Alamy B81MH6.

What might have motivated the government to issue such a poster? What does the poster tell us about British society in the 1940s? What did the government want the British people to think about themselves? Does the poster accurately reflect the feelings of the British people during the war?

9.13 *Robin Cook, "Chicken Tikka Masala" speech (Apr. 19, 2001)*[13]

Robin Cook (1946–2005) served as foreign secretary in Tony Blair's New Labour government until he resigned in protest against the Iraq War. He was a Scot who is perhaps best known for the following speech named after a popular British dish that derived from Indian cuisine. He made reference to the "cricket test" which some used to question the loyalty of British citizens of Asian or West Indian origin who sided with teams from their homelands in matches against England. The question of national identity became almost an obsession in Britain during the first decade of the twenty-first century.

Why might national identity become so debated in the early years of this century? Was Cook's Scottish background likely to affect his thinking or was it more a concern of a Labour Party official? It is all very well for him to point to invasions by Romans, Anglo-Saxons, Vikings, and Normans, but he does not really tackle the issue of racial difference. Why not? Are his arguments for diversity likely to convince xenophobic white working-class English people? What was his view of the "special relationship" with the United States likely to have been?

Sadly, it has become fashionable for some to argue that British identity is under siege, perhaps even in a state of terminal decline. The threat is said to come in three forms.

First, the arrival of immigrants who, allegedly, do not share our cultural values and who fail to support the England cricket team. . . .

Second, our continued membership of the European Union, which is said to be absorbing member states into a country called Europe.

Third, the devolution of power to Scotland, Wales and Northern Ireland, which is seen as a step to the break-up of the UK.

This evening, I want to set out the reasons for being optimistic about the future of Britain and Britishness. Indeed, I want to go further and argue that in each of the areas where the pessimists identify a threat, we should instead see developments that will strengthen and renew British identity.

The first element in the debate about the future of Britishness is the changing ethnic composition of the British people themselves. The British are not a race, but a gathering of countless different races and communities, the vast majority of which were not indigenous to these islands. In the pre-industrial era, when transport and communications were often easier by sea than by land, Britain was unusually open to external influence; first through foreign invasion, then, after Britain achieved naval supremacy, through commerce and imperial expansion. It is

[13] "Robin Cook's Chicken Tikka Masala Speech," www.guardian.co.uk, Apr. 19, 2001.

not their purity that makes the British unique, but the sheer pluralism of their ancestry. . . .

Today's London is a perfect hub of the globe. It is home to over 30 ethnic communities of at least 10,000 residents each. In this city tonight, over 300 languages will be spoken by families over their evening meal at home.

This pluralism is not a burden we must reluctantly accept. It is an immense asset that contributes to the cultural and economic vitality of our nation.

Legitimate immigration is the necessary and unavoidable result of economic success, which generates a demand for labor faster than can be met by the birth-rate of a modern developed country. Every country needs firm but fair immigration laws. There is no more evil business than trafficking in human beings and nothing corrodes social cohesion worse than a furtive underground of illegal migrants beyond legal protection against exploitation. But we must also create an open and inclusive society that welcomes incomers for their contribution to our growth and prosperity. . . .

Chicken Tikka Masala is now a true British national dish, not only because it is the most popular, but because it is a perfect illustration of the way Britain absorbs and adapts external influences. Chicken Tikka is an Indian dish. The Masala sauce was added to satisfy the desire of British people to have their meat served in gravy.

Coming to terms with multiculturalism as a positive force for our economy and society will have significant implications for our understanding of Britishness. The modern notion of national identity cannot be based on race and ethnicity, but must be based on shared ideals and aspirations. Some of the most successful countries in the modern world, such as the United States and Canada, are immigrant societies. Their experience shows how cultural diversity, allied to a shared concept of equal citizenship, can be a source of enormous strength. We should draw inspiration from their experience. . . .

[Secondly], to deny that Britain is European is to deny both our geography and our history. Our culture, our security, and our prosperity, are inseparable from the continent of Europe.

Underlying the anti-European case is the belief that there is an alternative future available to Britain. It used to be argued that the European Union is not Europe and that Britain could exist perfectly comfortably as one of a number of European countries maintaining a loose association with Brussels [capital of the EU]. But with the majority of non-EU states now clamoring for full membership, the changing geopolitics of Europe have consigned that argument to the past.

Some anti-Europeans now argue that Britain's destiny lies outside Europe, as part of the English-speaking world and as member of NAFTA [North American Free Trade Agreement]. Yet Britain trades three times more with the rest of the EU than we do with NAFTA. . . .

Britain is also a European country in the more profound sense of sharing European assumptions about how society should be organized. The last international survey of social attitudes put Britain squarely within the European mainstream on our approach to social justice and public service, such as health. . . .

The idea that the French, the Germans or the Spanish are attempting to erase their national identities by constructing a country called Europe is the mother of all Euromyths. On the contrary, our partners see their membership of a successful European Union as underwriting, not undermining, their assertion of national identity. . . .

The last of the three perceived threats to Britishness is the new flexibility in our modern constitution.

The devolution of power to Scotland, Wales and Northern Ireland will stand the test of time as one of this Government's most radical and significant achievements. The creation of a Scottish Parliament and Welsh Assembly allows both nations to choose the policies that are right for them through their own democratic structure. In Northern Ireland, devolution was needed for a different reason – to enable the communities of a divided society to share power and to work together to build a common future. . . .

Let us put to bed the scare stories about devolution leading to the Death of Britain. Devolution has been a success for Scotland and for Wales, but it has also been a success for Britain. The votes for devolution in the referendums were not votes for separation. They were votes to remain in the United Kingdom with a new constitutional settlement.

9.14 Fourth Lord Raglan, speech in the House of Lords (Nov. 26, 1958)[14]

Lord Raglan (1885–1964) was a soldier and scholar who descended from the dukes of Beaufort, long great landlords in Wales. He served as Lord Lieutenant of the Welsh border county of Monmouthshire. His attack on compulsory teaching of Welsh, a language he regarded as moribund, in schools caused a sensation in 1958 and helped mobilize the forces of Welsh nationalism in the following decades. Today over 1,000,000 people speak Welsh.

Why might an aristocrat denigrate the Welsh language? What was different about the situations of Ireland versus Wales? Why was the Welsh language so important to Welsh national identity? Why might Welsh nationalism only have become a viable political movement in the 1960s?

Though not a Welsh speaker, I shall now venture to say a few words about the Welsh language. The Welsh language is a very ancient language. I believe that it is a very difficult language, but it has a fine old literature. That literature flourished up to the end of the fifteenth century, by which time I should say that it compared very favorably, in quality and quantity, with that in English. But a Welshman, Henry VII, became King of England; the Welsh gentry flocked to London. Those

14 *Parliamentary Debates*, vol. 212, Nov. 26, 1958, c. 845–7.

who returned to Wales took to speaking English, so that the Welsh language gradually fell out of fashion and has been declining ever since.

Then, at the beginning of this century, under the influence of an incipient nationalism, there began a revival of the Welsh language. The language selected for this revival, as I understand it, was not the language that anybody now speaks. There are now at least two spoken languages in Wales, North Welsh and South Welsh, and I believe that those who speak one cannot understand those who speak the other. The language which was selected was the ancient literary Welsh, which I am told is nobody's native tongue and is not understood by ordinary Welsh speakers.

At the Census of 1951 . . . of the total population, 72 per cent. speak no Welsh and less than 2 per cent. speak no English. To say then that Welsh is the language of Wales seems to me quite ridiculous. There is no country in the world except Eire [Ireland] where so small a proportion of the inhabitants speak what is alleged to be the national language. . . .

It is clear that many people, many Welsh speakers, have migrated into the city, and they have not brought their children up to speak Welsh. Why should they, when there is no one they can speak it to, nothing they want to read in Welsh, and when the only time they hear Welsh spoken is during the very few seconds that elapse before a Welsh program starts on the wireless [radio], when somebody says "Welsh! switch it off"? "Switch it off: it's Welsh!" is a proverbial saying throughout Wales.

. . . As for books, quite a number of books are published in Welsh, and are dutifully bought by all the public libraries. It is very doubtful whether anyone reads them, however. Some years ago the librarian at Barmouth, a town in the heart of Welsh-speaking Wales, included in his annual report, which created some comment, mention of the fact that in the course of the whole year not a single Welsh book had been taken out of the library.

9.15 Gordon Brown, speech to the Fabian New Year Conference (Jan. 14, 2006)[15]

Gordon Brown (see document 9.11) was chancellor of the exchequer when he delivered the speech, and succeeded Tony Blair as prime minister the following year. One of his "signature" issues was renewing the British national identity. He hoped to identify the Labour Party with patriotism. Brown was right that the search for a "British" national day was difficult. St Andrew's Day in Scotland, St Patrick's Day in Ireland, and St David's Day in Wales have real resonance, much less so St George's Day in England. The Queen's Birthday in June is about as close as the British get to a national day of celebration, and it is

15 "Brown: The Future of Britishness," www.fabians.org.uk, Jan. 14, 2006.

a pretty low-key affair outside London and embassy parties abroad. The State Opening of Parliament might be more of a candidate, though some of its symbolism has long been inappropriate, it has a partisan political aspect, and it is not a holiday.

How might the fact that Brown was Scottish affect his views on national identity? To what degree was this an attempt to hijack patriotism for the Labour Party as opposed to a sincere appeal to British values? Based on your reading of this book, are there British values that are left out of Brown's speech? Does a somber memorial service to the war dead seem likely to serve as the equivalent of July 4th or Bastille Day? Are the values Brown discusses in any way unique to Britain? John Major, a retired Tory leader, responded to Brown by saying: "He seems not to mention that many of the actions of the present Government have ruptured Britishness by their own legislation."[16] To what might Major refer?

So what is it to be British? . . .

Even before America made it its own, I think Britain can lay claim to the idea of liberty. Out of necessity of finding a way to live together in a multinational state came the practice of toleration and then pursuit of liberty.

Voltaire said that Britain gave the world the idea of liberty. In the seventeenth century, Milton in "Paradise Lost" put it as "if not equal all, yet all equally free." Think of Wordsworth's poetry about the "flood of British freedom"; then Hazlitt's belief that we have and can have "no privilege or advantage over other nations but liberty"; right through to Orwell's focus on justice, liberty and decency defining Britain. We can get a Parliament from anywhere, said Henry Grattan, we can only get liberty from England.

So there is, as I have argued, a golden thread which runs through British history, that runs from that long ago day in Runnymede in 1215 [Magna Carta]; on to the Bill of Rights in 1689 where Britain became the first country to successfully assert the power of Parliament over the King; to not just one, but four great Reform Acts in less than a hundred years of the individual standing firm against tyranny and then an even more generous, expansive view of liberty the idea of government accountable to the people, evolving into the exciting idea of empowering citizens to control their own lives.

Just as it was in the name of liberty that in the 1800s Britain led the world in abolishing the slave trade [1807], something we celebrate in 2007, so too in the 1940s in the name of liberty Britain stood firm against fascism. . . .

But woven also into that golden thread of liberty are countless strands of common, continuing endeavor in our villages, towns and cities the efforts and popular achievements of ordinary men and women, with one sentiment in common, a strong sense of duty and responsibility: men and women who did

[16] "Brown Speech Promotes Britishness," BBC News, news.bbc.co.uk, Jan. 14, 2006.

not allow liberty to descend into a selfish individualism or into a crude libertarianism; men and women who, as is the essence of the labor movement, chose solidarity in preference to selfishness; thus creating out of the idea of duty and responsibility the Britain of civic responsibility, civic society and the public realm. . . .

The 20th century has given special place also to the idea that in a democracy where people have both political, social and economic rights and responsibilities, liberty and responsibility can only fully come alive if there is a Britain not just of liberty for all, and responsibility for all, but fairness for all.

Of course, the appeal to fairness runs through British history, from early opposition to the first poll tax in 1381 to the second [proposed by Margaret Thatcher]; fairness the theme from the civil war debates where Raineborough asserted that "the poorest he that is in England hath a life to live as the greatest he"; to the 1940s when Orwell talked of a Britain known to the world for its "decency."

Indeed a 2005 YouGov survey showed that as many as 90 per cent of the British people thought that fairness and fair play were very important or fairly important in defining Britishness. . . .

Take the NHS, like the monarchy, the army, the BBC, one of the great British institutions, what 90 per cent of British people think portrays a positive symbol of the real Britain, founded on the core value of fairness that all should have access to health care founded on need, not ability to pay. . . .

And so in this vision of a Britain of liberty for all, responsibility from all and fairness to all we move a long way from the old left's embarrassed avoidance of all explicit patriotism. Orwell correctly ridiculed the old left view for thinking that patriotism could be defined only from the right: as reactionary; patriotism as a defense of unchanging institutions that would never modernize; patriotism as a defense of deference and hierarchy; and patriotism as, in reality, the dislike of foreigners and self interested individualism. We now see that when the old left recoiled from patriotism they failed to understand that the values on which Britishness is based, liberty to all, responsibility by all, fairness for all, owe more to progressive ideas than to right wing ones. . . .

But think for a moment: what is the British equivalent of the US 4th of July, or even the French 14th of July for that matter? What I mean is: what is our equivalent for a national celebration of who we are and what we stand for? And what is our equivalent of the national symbolism of a flag in every garden? In recent years we have had magnificent celebrations of [the 60th anniversary of] VE Day, [the Queen's 50th] Jubilee and, last year [the 200th anniversary] Trafalgar Day. Perhaps Armistice Day [November 11th, commemorating the victories in World I and World War II] and Remembrance Sunday [when the Queen lays a wreath at the national war memorial in London, televised live and widely watched, in a memorial to the war dead] are the nearest we have come to a British day that is in every corner of our country commemorative, unifying, and an expression of British ideas of standing firm in the world in the name of liberty, responsibility and fairness.

9.16 The Governance of Britain *(2007)*[17]

As noted in document 9.11, in 2007 the Labour Party issued a report on the governance of Britain that indicated concern over the nature of the modern British identity. The concern was sparked both by immigration and by devolution. Conservatives, too, wondered about the nature of Britishness. Prime minister John Major had fallen back on George Orwell's description of "old maids bicycling to Holy Communion through the morning mist," but the phrase was part of a list of *English* characteristics that Orwell described as a "muddle": bitter beer, heavy coins, green grass, blatant advertisements, knobby faces, pubs, labor exchanges, red pillar mail boxes, and suet pudding.[18] Not the makings of a patriotic hymn. Even the socialist Orwell ended up using the lion and the unicorn from the royal coat of arms as his central image evoking Englishness.

Why might this document fail to mention the monarchy as a symbol of national identity while Orwell, writing 70 years earlier, did? What constitutes the core of "Britishness"? Why are the key beliefs of the society so hard to articulate and symbolize? Is Orwell's description of Englishness an idea the British nation could rally around? British patriotism in World War I and World War II proved more resilient and effective than that of any other European country, sustaining the military and the civilian population through tragic travails. What changed after 1945?

Parliament stands at the apex of the political system, the supreme legislative body of the United Kingdom. It is a major symbol of what it means to be British. . . .

Devolution does not cede ultimate sovereignty. The decisions Parliament takes have consequences for all the people of our nation. The great strength of our constitution is its effectiveness. It can accommodate difference and rough edges in support of wider goals of national unity, affiliation to the institutions of the state and the service of those institutions to the public. . . .

We can look to history to help us to define citizenship. We can learn much from countries that have a more clearly defined sense of citizenship, and what goes with it: notably from the United States, Canada, Australia and South Africa, and from those parts of Western Europe who have had to develop the idea of citizenship to survive as nations or, indeed, simply to be nations. . . .

French citizens have a clear understanding of their values of liberty, equality and fraternity. America has a strong national perception of itself as the "land of the free". But there is a less clear sense among British citizens of the values that

17 *The Governance of Britain*, CM 7170, July 2007, paragraphs 122, 183, 194, 196, Box 6, 204.

18 George Orwell, "The Lion and the Unicorn: Socialism and the English Genius," *The Collected Essays, Journalism and Letters of George Orwell, My Country Right or Left 1940–43*, volume 2, ed. Sonia Orwell and Ian Angus (New York, 1968), 57.

bind the groups and communities who make up the body of the British people. The principles of liberty, democracy, tolerance, free speech, pluralism, fair play and civic duty may be widely felt, but they are not fully articulated in ways that helps to define who we are and how we should behave. . . .

Shared values are the bedrock on which the elements of our nation are built. Our values are given shape and meaning by the institutions that people know and trust, from the [National Health Service] to Parliament. The symbols of the UK, and our rights, are among the most recognizable in the world. There are currently restrictions on flying the Union Flag. . . . The Government [is taking] new measures to change this. . . . While in other countries, such as France and the United States, the national flag is regarded as source of pride, in recent years the Union Flag has all too often become the preserve of political extremists, a symbol of discord rather than harmony. It is critical that this symbol is not hijacked by those who seek to work against the fundamental British values of tolerance and mutual respect. . . . At present there are only 18 fixed days each year on which the Union Flag may be flown on Government buildings in England. These restrictions are clearly tighter than those used in many other countries. The Government will therefore consult on altering the current guidance that prohibits the flying of the Union Flag from Government buildings for more than 18 set days in the year. . . .

[There is a need for a British Bill of Rights and Duties.] At the heart of British citizenship is the idea of a society based on laws which are made in a way that reflects the rights of citizens regardless of ethnicity, gender, class or religion. Alongside this sits the right to participate, in some way, in their making; the idea that all citizens are equal before the law and are entitled to justice and the protection of the law; the right of all citizens to associate freely; the right to free expression of opinion; the right to live without fear of oppression and discrimination; the idea that there is an appropriate balance to be drawn between the individual's right to freedom and the collective good of all and that, in the final analysis, the Government is accountable for its actions to the will of the people expressed in Parliament and through elections.

Irish Identities

9.17 Proclamation of the Republic (Easter Monday, Apr. 24, 1916)[19]

On Easter Monday 1916 a group of Irish Nationalists seized the Central Post Office building and other strategic points in Dublin and declared independence from Great Britain. It took a number of days for the army to suppress the rebellion and more than a dozen of the leaders were executed. Though doomed

[19] www.eirigi.org

to fail, and even unpopular with many Irish people, the event proved a pivotal point in the assertion of a free Irish identity.

Did the rebels speak for all Irish people? What gave them the idea that they could make their assertion of independence? How did they justify the violent overthrow of the existing government? Why did they desire a republic rather than the recreation of the ancient Gaelic monarchy?

Irishmen and Irishwomen: In the name of God and of the dead generations from which she receives her old tradition of nationhood, Ireland, through us, summons her children to her flag and strikes for her freedom.

... Having patiently perfected her discipline, having resolutely waited for the right moment to reveal itself, she now seizes that moment, and, supported by her exiled children in America and by gallant allies in Europe, but relying in the first on her own strength, she strikes in full confidence of victory.

We declare the right of the people of Ireland to the ownership of Ireland, and to the unfettered control of Irish destinies, to be sovereign and indefeasible. The long usurpation of that right by a foreign people and government has not extinguished the right ... In every generation the Irish people have asserted their right to national freedom and sovereignty; six times during the past three hundred years they have asserted it in arms. ...

The Irish republic is entitled to, and hereby claims, the allegiance of every Irishman and Irishwoman. The republic guarantees religious and civil liberty, equal rights and equal opportunities to all its citizens, and declares its resolve to pursue the happiness and prosperity of the whole nation and of all its parts, cherishing all the children of the nation equally, and oblivious of the differences carefully fostered by an alien government, which have divided a minority from the majority in the past.

9.18 Sir Roger Casement, speech from the dock at his trial for treason (1916)[20]

Sir Roger Casement (1864–1916), knighted for his services to humanity in bringing to light violations of human rights in African colonies, participated in the organization of the "Easter Rebellion" of 1916. He tried to recruit a pro-German unit to fight the British on the Western Front from among Irish prisoners of war. He arranged for the German government to land arms for the rebels on the Irish coast, although the British navy blocked this attempt. He was captured after landing in Ireland off a German submarine. Casement

[20] George H. Knott, ed., *Trial of Roger Casement* (Philadelphia, 1917), 198, 201.

was one of an impressive line of Irish Nationalists who had been born into the Protestant ruling class. He was hanged for treason on August 3, 1916.

How did Casement justify the need for Irish independence? Why might a Presbyterian sympathize with that aspiration? Did Casement take into account that Britain was at war with Germany in his call for freedom?

If true religion rests on love, it is equally true that loyalty rests on love. The law I am charged under has no parentage in love, and claims the allegiance of today on the ignorance and blindness of the past . . .

Loyalty is sentiment, not a law. It rests on love, not restraint. The Government of Ireland by England rests on restraint, and not on law; and since it demands no love, it can evoke no loyalty.

For if English authority be omnipotent – a power, as Mr. Gladstone phrased it, that reaches to the very ends of the earth – Irish hope exceeds the dimensions of that power, excels its authority, and renews with each generation the claims of the last. The cause that begats this indomitable persistency, the faculty of preserving through centuries of misery the remembrance of lost liberty – this surely is the noblest cause ever man strove for, ever lived for, ever died for.

9.19 "Oath of Allegiance" incorporated into the treaty creating a Free State in Ireland (1922)[21]

During the negotiations to establish an independent Irish dominion in 1922 the British offered one version of an "Oath to the Crown" and Eamon de Valera (1882–1975), head of the Irish free government, offered the following alternative version: "I . . . do solemnly swear true faith and allegiance to the constitution of the Free State, to the Treaty Association and recognize the King of Great Britain as head of the Associated States."[22] In the end an oath similar to the British version was accepted by the negotiating team and enacted by the Irish parliament. De Valera, however, refused to accept the new wording and led a rebellion by the Irish Republican Army against the newly independent state he had helped to create. The IRA was defeated, and de Valera eventually took the oath so that he could achieve office and then later abolish it.

What were the differences between the two versions? Why were such modest differences in wording worth dying for in the eyes of ardent Irish Nationalists? To what degree had republicanism become an inherent part of the Irish identity?

[21] Article 17 – Free State Constitution, 1922.

[22] Roy Foster, *Modern Ireland 1600–1972* (London, 1988), 505–6.

[British version]: I . . . do solemnly swear true faith and allegiance to the Constitution of the Irish Free State as by law established, and that I will be faithful to H[is] M[ajesty] King George V, his heirs and successors by law, in virtue of the common citizenship of Ireland with Great Britain and her adherence to and membership of the group of nations forming the British Commonwealth of Nations.

9.20 Sir Basil Brooke, 5th Baronet, speech in the Northern Irish Parliament (Apr. 24, 1934)[23]

Sir Basil Brooke, later Viscount Brookeborough (1888–1973), descended from a great landed family that gained their estates in Ireland in 1623. This dynasty elected six MPs and his uncle, Sir Alan Brooke, was Chief of the Imperial General Staff 1941–46, the supreme military commander of British forces in the defeat of Germany and Japan. Brooke became the leader of the Unionist Party and prime minister of Northern Ireland (1943–63). He fired all the Catholics working on his estates and explained why to the Northern Irish parliament.

How did Brooke justify the partition of Ulster from the rest of Ireland? Why might he have been prejudiced against Roman Catholics? How would Roman Catholics have responded to his leadership of the province?

There is, in fact, a Catholic political party, which ranges from what I might call benevolent nationalism to the extreme of the extreme. That is true, but the one plank in their platform is the destruction of Ulster as a unit and as a constitution. That is the policy, and it simply varies in method. Directly the hon. Gentlemen [Nationalist Party MPs] are attacked politically they play the old familiar game . . . and hang on to religion and say "You are treating us in a tyrannical manner; you are bigots" . . . May I explain what I mean by the word "disloyalist" . . . A disloyal man is a man who is scheming and plotting to destroy the country in which he lives. It does not mean a man who lives in that country and lives under the constitution but is opposed to the Government . . . but any man who is out to break up that constitution, which has been established by Great Britain, is to my mind disloyal. That is what I mean by disloyal . . . These gentlemen have been questioning . . . my urging that Roman Catholics – political Roman Catholics – should not be employed . . . What they [Nationalists] like to do is to employ all their own people of the same political faith, and leave our people to employ those they cannot employ themselves. There are three reasons to my mind why disloyalists should not be employed. Those who support the constitution, whether they agree with the policy of the present Government or not, should

[23] *Northern Ireland House of Commons Debates*, XVI, Apr. 24, 1934, c. 1114–2.

have the benefit of that constitution. Secondly every disloyalist allowed to come in is a potential voter for the destruction of this country. And, further, there is a grave danger in employing men who at the first opportunity will betray those who employ them . . .. I shall use all my energies and whatever powers I possess to defeat the aims of those who are out to destroy the constitution of Ulster be they Protestants or be they Roman Catholics.

9.21 Sir Edward Heath, speech in the House of Commons (June 8, 1993)[24]

Edward Heath (1916–2005) was Conservative prime minister 1970–74. The IRA (Irish Republican Army – a Nationalist terror organization) had recently carried out major attacks in London and elsewhere outside Ireland.

What solutions did Heath propose to the problem of terrorism in Northern Ireland? Why did he see the issues as particularly urgent in 1993? In his speech he suggested leaving some Unionist politicians out of peace negotiations and placed emphasis on relations with the Irish Republic. How might Northern Irish Protestants have reacted to his proposals? He praised the work of the army. How did the Roman Catholic community in Northern Ireland regard the troops? Why did he see the Northern Irish problem as vital to the whole United Kingdom? Were the events in Italy, Germany, and Spain to which he referred comparable to the situation in Ulster?

Next year, we shall have had 25 years of terrorism in the United Kingdom. It is now 20 years since I addressed the House on this subject and I want to do so again tonight in the light of the figure that I have just given. . . .

Let me make it plain at the beginning that I have the utmost admiration for the people of Northern Ireland. It is beyond my understanding how they can have put up with these conditions for this length of time. I have the greatest possible sympathy with them in the losses that they have sustained and the terrible life that they must live. That same sympathy goes to those now on the mainland [where several recent IRA bomb attacks had caused deaths and damage, including in the City of London], and all those elsewhere who are affected. That is the first thing that I want to make plain.

Secondly, I am in no way criticizing the work of Her Majesty's forces. As my right hon. and learned Friend the Secretary of State [for Northern Ireland] pointed out, wherever forces are deployed one finds occasional breaches of discipline. They are to be regretted, but I sometimes feel that there is so much emphasis on them that insufficient emphasis is laid on the good work that is being done

[24] *Parliamentary Debates*, vol. 226, June 8, 1993, c. 168–72.

by the forces, again in immensely difficult conditions. The same thing applies to the police. I have no criticism of them.

I must ask myself this question: at a time when other countries in Europe – to limit ourselves to that particular geographical area – have been able to deal with the problem, why have we failed? We have seen the most vicious forms of terrorism in Italy, with the Red Guards, in Germany, with the Red Army, in France and in Belgium, and they have got on top of it. In Spain, there have been periodic outbreaks, but they have been limited now to the Basque area. Why is it that those countries have been able to deal with this problem, but we have failed? We are entitled to ask that question.

The answer is that one can deal with terrorism only by being cleverer than the terrorists. That is absolutely basic. One has to be cleverer in intelligence, cleverer in action and cleverer politically. Again, to be perfectly blunt, we have failed in all three. That is why I want to get down to the basics; I do not believe that we can continue in this way. It is already being brought home to us here that the action in the City is damaging to our economic interests. Further action would be even more damaging.

This ought to be a major debate, but I have carefully calculated the number of those present and there are fewer than 5 percent of our Members here showing an interest in this matter which affects the whole of the United Kingdom. I ask myself – I do not wish to ask the House, because it might be embarrassing – whether, if the public relations representative of the IRA were in the Gallery, as for all I know he may be, he would say to his pals tonight, "My God, we are now in for a terrible time; with what those people are going to do to us, we shall be out of it." The answer is, not for a moment. He would go home and have a quiet drink and decide where to put the next bomb. This, I repeat, is why we have to get down to it.

Years ago, the other countries established official anti-terrorist bodies at the highest level, and that is why they have been successful. Those bodies took different forms, but we must have the same sort of thing if we are to be successful in dealing with this problem.

. . .

I believe that the Prime Minister must now lift the level above what it is today if we are to achieve results. This matter must be put in the hands of one very Senior Cabinet Minister whose sole purpose will be to deal with terrorism in the United Kingdom. . . .

It passes belief by most people who look at this, certainly from outside, how any group could have got together all the explosives that were planted in the City, let alone planted them there and arranged for the whole lot to go off – incidentally, doing £300 million of damage. Yet that is going on, and we do not know when and where the next explosion will be. That is intolerable after 25 years of trying to deal with this problem.

There are many things that could be done and ought to be done speedily once we get a supremo in charge. . . .

Politics and the military force go together. It is right that we should concentrate on politics, but we must also recognize that, until we begin to make serious progress against the terrorism, the politics will be more difficult. The more progress we make against the terrorism, the easier the political aspect will become. . . .

. . . We must have the best possible and closest relationship with the Republic of Ireland. I know that that will give offence, but it will have to be accepted. We shall not settle this problem until we have the closest possible relationship with Eire [Republic of Ireland]. We are in the same Community; we are both members. We have the same level playing fields in many different spheres. Why, then, can we not be together on this?

My impression, from the contacts that I have, is that the possibilities are becoming greater. There are changes coming about in the Eire constitution that we would not have dreamed of 20 years ago. We must use the situation to our advantage and have the closest possible relations with the Republic of Ireland.

9.22 Report of the International Body, *Northern Ireland (1996)*[25]

The British Government and the Republic of Ireland requested Senator George Mitchell (b.1933) of the United States, as an independent observer, to help get peace talks going in Northern Ireland. He was joined by General John de Chastelain of Canada and Harri Holkeri, former prime minister of Finland. Their report on the decommissioning of arms helped break the logjam that had held up negotiations. The Unionists demanded decommissioning of arms before talks began, the IRA only after they were concluded. Mitchell recommended that they start while the negotiations went forward.

What did Mitchell and his colleagues see as the biggest problem facing those ready to negotiate for peace? How could the obstacles be overcome? Why might an American, Canadian, and Finn be useful in the process of moving toward peace?

7. Our examination of the issues and of the facts, and the perspectives brought to us by those who briefed us or who made written representations to us, convince us that while there is no simple solution to the conflict in Northern Ireland, the factors on which a process for peace must be based are already known. . . .

. . .

10. For nearly a year and a half, the guns have been silent in Northern Ireland. The people want that silence to continue. They want lasting peace in a just society in which paramilitary violence plays no part. . . .

11. Notwithstanding reprehensible "punishment" killings and beatings, the sustained observance of the cease-fires should not be devalued. It is a significant

[25] Department of Foreign Affairs, Republic of Ireland, "Report of the International Body," www.dfa.ie, Jan. 22, 1996.

factor which must be given due weight in assessing the commitment of the paramilitaries to "work constructively to achieve" full and verifiable decommissioning.

12. Since the cease-fires, the political debate has focused largely on the differences that have prevented the commencement of all-party negotiations intended to achieve an agreed political settlement. This circumstance has obscured the widespread agreement that exists – so widespread that it tends to be taken for granted. In fact, members of both traditions may be less far apart on the resolution of their differences than they believe.

. . .

14. In paragraph five of the Communique we were asked "to provide an independent assessment of the decommissioning issue." It is a serious issue. It is also a symptom of a larger problem: the absence of trust. Common to many of our meetings were arguments, steeped in history, as to why the other side cannot be trusted. As a consequence, even well-intentioned acts are often viewed with suspicion and hostility.

15. But a resolution of the decommissioning issue – or any other issue – will not be found if the parties resort to their vast inventories of historical recrimination. Or, as it was put to us several times, what is really needed is the decommissioning of mind-sets in Northern Ireland.

HISTORIANS' DEBATES

To what degree did the suffragette movement contribute to achieving votes for women and were violence and militancy helpful to the campaign? What was the effect of enfranchisement?

Ian Christopher Fletcher, Laura E. Nym Mayhall, and Philippa Levine, eds., *Women's Suffrage in the British Empire: Citizenship, Nation, and Race* (London, 2000); Patricia Hollis, *Ladies Elect: Women in English Local Government, 1865–1914* (Oxford, 1987); Sandra Stanley Holton, *Feminism and Democracy: Women's Suffrage and Reform Politics in Britain, 1900–1918* (Cambridge, 1986); Helene Jones, *Women in British Public Life, 1914–1950: Gender, Power and Social Policy* (London, 2000); Jill Liddington and Jill Norris, *One Hand Tied behind Us: The Rise of the Women's Suffrage Movement* (London, 1978); David Mitchell, *The Fighting Pankhursts* (London, 1967); Martin Pugh, *The March of the Women: A Revisionist Analysis of the Campaign for Women's Suffrage, 1866–1914* (Oxford, 2000); Constance Rover, *Women's Suffrage and Party Politics in Britain, 1866–1914* (London, 1967); Ray Strachey, *The Cause: A Short History of the Women's Movement in Great Britain* (London, 1928).

What motivated postwar immigration into Britain? How successful was assimilation and integration? Did immigrants from different parts of the old empire have different experiences in Britain?

Beverly Bryan, Stella Dadzie, and Suzanne Scafe, *The Heart of the Race: Black Women's Lives in Britain* (London, 1985); Mary Chamberlain, *Narratives of Exile and Return* (London, 1997); Peter Fryer, *Staying Power: The History of Black People in Britain* (London, 1984); Paul Gilroy, *The Black Atlantic: Modernity and Double Consciousness* (London, 1993); Harry Goulbourne, *Race Relations in Britain since 1945* (London, 1998); Randall Hansen, *Citizenship and Immigration in Post-War*

Britain (Oxford, 2000); Dilip Hiro, *Black British, White British: A History of Race Relations in Britain*, 3rd ed. (London, 1991); Colin Holmes, *John Bull's Island: Immigration and British Society, 1871–1971* (Basingstoke, 1988); Zig Layton-Henry, *The Politics of Immigration: Immigration, "Race" and "Race Relations" in Post-War Britain* (Oxford, 1992); Tariq Modood and Richard Berthoud, *et al.*, *Ethnic Minorities in Britain: Diversity and Disadvantage* (London, 1997); Kathleen Paul, *Whitewashing Britain: Race and Citizenship in the Postwar Era* (Ithaca, 1997); Mike Phillips and Trevor Phillips, *Windrush: The Irresistible Rise of Multi-Racial Britain* (London, 1998); Ron Ramdin, *Reimaging Britain: Five Hundred Years of Black and Asian History* (London, 1999); James Walvin, *Passage to Britain: Immigration in British History and Politics* (Harmondsworth, 1984); Wendy Webster, *Imagining Home: Gender, "Race", and National Identity 1945–1964* (London, 1998); James Winston and Clive Harris, eds., *Inside Babylon: The Caribbean Diaspora in Britain* (London, 1993).

What role has the twentieth-century monarchy played in shaping national identity? Was Princess Diana a wronged woman and what was the significance of the outpouring of grief at her death?

Vernon Bogdanor, *The Monarchy and the Constitution* (New York, 1998); Sarah Bradford, *King George VI* (London, 1989); Tina Brown, *The Diana Chronicles* (New York, 2007); Beatrix Campbell, *Diana, Princess of Wales: How Sexual Politics Shook the Monarchy* (London, 1998); David Cannadine, "The Context, Performance, and Meaning of Ritual: The British Monarchy and the 'Invention of Tradition' c. 1820–1977," in *The Invention of Tradition*, ed. Eric Hobsbawm and Terence Ranger (Cambridge, 1983); Jonathan Dimbleby, *The Prince of Wales: A Biography* (London, 1994); Charles Douglas-Hume and Saul Kelly, *Dignified and Efficient: The British Monarchy in the Twentieth Century* (Brinkworth, 2000); William Kuhn, *Democratic Royalism: The Transformation of the British Monarchy, 1861–1914* (London, 1996); Kingsley Martin, *The Crown and the Establishment* (London, 1962); Mandy Merck, ed., *After Diana: Irreverent Elegies* (London, 1998); Tom Nairn, *The Enchanted Glass: Britain and Its Monarchy* (London, 1988); A. Olechnowicz, ed., *The Monarchy and the British Nation, 1780 to the Present* (Cambridge, 2007); Ben Pimlott, *The Queen: A Biography of Elizabeth II* (London, 1996); Frank Prochaska, *Royal Bounty: The Making of the Welfare Monarchy* (New Haven, 1995); Re:Public, eds., *Planet Diana: Cultural Studies and Global Mourning* (Sydney, 1997); Kenneth Rose, *King George V* (New York, 1984); Jon Savage, *England's Dreaming: Sex Pistols and Punk Rock* (London, 1991); David Sinclair, *Two Georges: The Making of the Modern Monarchy* (London, 1998).

What were the issues that divided the communities in Northern Ireland? Ethnic? Cultural? Tribal? Religious? British colonialism? Economic?

J. Bowyer Bell, *The Secret Army: The IRA*, 3rd ed. (Dublin, 1998); Steve Bruce, *God Save Ulster: The Religion and Politics of Paisleyism* (Oxford, 1986); Tim Pat Coogan, *The Troubles: Ireland's Ordeal 1966–1996 and the Search for Peace* (London, 1996); Michael Farrell, *Northern Ireland: The Orange State* (London, 1976); Rosemary Harris, *Prejudice and Tolerance in Ulster*, 2nd ed. (Manchester, 1972); Thomas Hennessy, *A History of Northern Ireland 1920–1996* (Dublin, 1997); James Louglin, *Ulster Unionism and British National Identity since 1885* (London, 1995); F.S.L. Lyons, *Culture and Anarchy in Ireland, 1890–1939* (Oxford, 1979); John McGarry and Brendan O'Leary, *Explaining Northern Ireland: Broken Images* (Oxford, 1995); David Miller, ed., *Rethinking Northern Ireland: Culture, Ideology, and Colonialism* (London, 1998); Fionnuala O'Connor, *In Search of a State: Catholics in Northern Ireland* (Belfast, 1993); Richard Rose, *Governing without Consensus: An Irish Perspective* (London, 1971); Joseph Ruane and Jenifer Todd, *The Dynamics of Conflict in Northern Ireland: Power, Conflict, and Emancipation* (Cambridge, 1996); A.T.Q. Stewart, *The Narrow Ground: The Roots of Conflict in Ulster*, rev. ed. (London, 1989); Tom Wilson, *Ulster: Conflict and Consent* (Oxford, 1989).

Some historians have argued that rise of new forms of popular culture and affordable material consumption undermined radicalism in working-class culture. A culture of consolation arose. Others see the changes as offering greater opportunity for creativity and self-expression.

A. Briggs, *The History of Broadcasting in the United Kingdom, II: The Golden Age of Wireless* (London, 1965); A. Davies, *Leisure, Gender and Poverty: Working-class Culture in Salford and Manchester, 1900–1939* (Milton Keynes, 1992); M. Frayn, "Festival of Britain," in *The Age of Austerity*, ed. P. French and M. Sissons (London, 1963); Richard Hoggart, *The Uses of Literacy* (London, 1957); Gareth Stedman Jones, "Working-class Culture and Working-class Politics in London, 1870–1914," *JSH* (1974), 460–508; R. McKibbin, *The Ideologies of Class: Social Relations in Britain, 1880–1950* (Oxford, 1990); J.J. Nott, *Music for the People: Popular Music and Dance in Interwar Britain* (Oxford, 2002); George Orwell, *The Road to Wigan Pier* (London, 1937).

COUNTERFACTUAL TO CONSIDER

What if Scotland had declared independence in 1997? Would England have lost its share of North Sea oil? Would Scotland have become a socialist polity?

Bibliography

Bibliographies

The Royal Historical Society bibliography of British and Irish history has recently been transferred to a limited access site www.brepolis.net, to which most research libraries subscribe. This is the most comprehensive bibliography of British history.

For Irish history, see also the site sponsored by the Royal Irish Academy at www.irishhistoryonline.ie

Oxford Bibliographies Online is a new project of the Oxford University Press. These are up to date and provide detailed guidance. Already up and running is the one on Atlantic History. In development is one on Victorian Literature. Future topics will almost certainly focus on other aspects of British history and culture. (See www.aboutobo.com)

William Matthews, *An Annotated Bibliography of British Diaries Written between 1442 and 1942* (Berkeley, 1950). British diaries and collections of correspondence constitute a rich seam of documentary history. Many have been published, however, after this volume came into print.

There are individual bibliographies assembled for many historical figures and time periods. To take a notable example, materials on Winston S. Churchill can be traced through: Ronald I. Cohen, *Bibliography of the Writings of Sir Winston Churchill* (2006); Eugene L. Rasor, *Winston S. Churchill, 1874–1965: A Comprehensive Historiography and Annotated Bibliography* (2000); and Curt J. Zoller, *Annotated Bibliography of Works about Sir Winston Churchill* (2004). Documents relating to Churchill can be found online at the Churchill Archive at Churchill College Cambridge (www.chu.cam.ac.uk/archives) and in a massive collection of companion volumes published to accompany the eight-volume official biography of Churchill by Randolph S. Churchill and Sir Martin Gilbert.

Sources and Debates in Modern British History: 1714 to the Present, First Edition. Edited by Ellis Wasson.

Published 2012 by Blackwell Publishing Ltd.

Start with the Royal Historical bibliography to track down specialized and annotated bibliographies.

Online Sources of Documents and Artifacts

This bibliography is a starting point. It would be impossible to list all relevant sites, partly because there are so many of them (often focused on a single author or specialized collection) and partly because the data being posted continues to expand exponentially. The big sites often have lists of links that are constantly updated. Specialized sites can often be of very high quality. See for example cain.ulst.ac.uk on the Northern Irish conflict. For Irish history in general, see irith.org, the site of Irish Resources in the Humanities. Many university libraries and history departments have established pages with many links to British history such as the University of Washington, Rutgers University, and the University of Southern California (college.usc.edu/history/ibis/links).

General Sites

British History Online. www.british-history.ac.uk. British History Online is a digital library focused on British history including political, social, and economic documents.

British Library. www.bl.uk. The British Library is the national library of the United Kingdom and one of the largest repositories in the world. The site has many digitized texts and resources.

British Library "Online Gallery." www.bl.uk/onlinegallery. A collection of over 30,000 items from the British national library, ranging from books to maps to the visual arts.

Bubl Link. http://bubl.ac.uk/link/b/britishhistory-general.htm. Contains many links to digital primary sources.

Connected Histories. www.connectedhistories.org. Integrated search access to 11 electronic resources containing millions of pages of records concerning British history 1500 to 1900. It includes Parliamentary Papers, British Newspapers 1600–1900, and many other valuable sites.

Euro Docs. http://eudocs.lib.byu.edu. Euro Docs is a site maintained by Brigham Young University. It has links for UK documents organized in three time periods between 1689 and the present.

Europeana. www.europeana.eu. A digitized archive of texts, images, audio, and video from European museums, libraries, archives, and audiovisual collections.

The European Library. www.theeuropeanlibrary.org. A catalog of the contents of major European libraries that provides links to digitized material and images and audio for Britain, Ireland, and European perspectives on Britain from the member states of the Council of Europe.

Imperial War Museum. www.iwmcollections.org.uk. The Imperial War Museum has many digitized items.

Institute of Historical Research. www.history.ac.uk/ihr/Resources. The Institute of Historical Research at the University of London provides a large number of links to various digitized collections.

Internet Archive. www.archive.org. Internet Archive is collecting a massive amount of information and cultural artifacts – books, music, film, etc. – which they are making available wherever possible. Unlike Google, it is a not-for-profit organization.

London Lives. www.londonlives.org. London Lives 1690–1800: Crime, Poverty and Social Policy in the Metropolis, has a searchable collection of over 240,000 manuscripts concerning everyday life in London.

Keele University. www.keele.ac.uk/depts/por/ukbase.htm. The School of Politics, International Relations and the Environment at Keele University maintains a vast list of links to all aspects of British political life. Much of the material is current, but many links contain historical documents and data, such as extensive material relating to election results.

MORI. www.ipsos-mori.com. The polling organization MORI has a research archive.

National Archives. www.nationalarchives.gov.uk. The British National Archives has a wide range of material of digitized material on its web archive.

National Library of Scotland. www.nls.uk/digital-gallery. National Library of Scotland has many links to various collections.

National Library of Wales. www.llgc.org.uk. The National Library of Wales has links to many documents.

The Victorian Research Web. http://victorianresearch.org. Has numerous links to other sites.

Webarchive.www.webarchive.org.uk The British Library supports this wide-ranging site that lists many links and contains textual and visual material.

In addition many articles in Wikipedia have links and footnotes that lead to documents.

Art

The National Gallery of Ireland. www.nationalgallery.ie. The National Gallery of Ireland in Dublin has an extensive collection of portraits and other artifacts.

The National Portrait Gallery. www.npg.org.uk. The National Portrait Gallery in London is a gateway to British history and has links to other sites including collections in Wales and Northern Ireland.

The National Portrait Gallery of Scotland. www.nationalgalleries.org. The National Portrait Gallery of Scotland in Edinburgh has a large collection.

The Tate Gallery. www.tate.org.uk. The Tate Gallery has a rich collection of British art.

VADS. http://vads.ac.uk. VADS is *the* online resource for visual arts. It has provided services to the academic community for 12 years and has built up a considerable portfolio of visual art collections comprising over 100,000 images that are freely available and copyright cleared for use in learning, teaching, and research.

The Yale Center for British Art. http://ycba.yale.edu. The Yale Center for British Art has important collections in many media.

Audio/Video

British Broadcasting Corporation. www.bbc.co.uk/archive. Contains many historic political speeches and much else of all kinds.

Pathé. www.britishpathe.com. Pathé has a large video archive of historical material.

YouTube. www.youtube.com. A vast range of material in visual and audio media now available relating to British history and society.

Cartoons and Prints

British Cartoon Archive. www.cartoons.ac.uk. Maintained at the University of Kent.

John Johnson Collection. http://vads.ahds.ac.uk/collections/JJPP.html. A large collection of political and satirical prints from the eighteenth to the twentieth century at the Bodleian Library Oxford University.

In addition there are collections held in great national repositories such as the British Library (www.imagesonline.bl.uk) and the Library of Congress (www.loc.gov/pictures).

Crime and Law

Blackstone's Commentaries. http://avalon.law.yale.edu/subject_menus/blackstone.asp. Blackstone's Commentaries on English law are available on this Yale Law School web site.

Old Bailey. www.oldbaileyonline.org. The proceedings of the Old Bailey (London) Criminal Court are online for 1674–1913, covering nearly 200,000 cases.

Victorian Crime and Punishment. http://vcp.e2bn.org. The Victorian Crime and Punishment web site has a number of databases relating to nineteenth-century crime.

Diaries

British and Irish Women's Diaries. http://alexanderstreet.com. A collection of 100,000 pages made available through this web site accessed through libraries.

Government

Hansard. http://hansard.millbanksystems.com. A digitized and searchable copy of the transcripts of debates in the House of Commons and the House of Lords 1803–2005.

Parliament. www.parliament.uk. The official site of the British Parliament. It has digitized archives on the site.

Royal Family. www.royal.gov.uk. The official site of the monarchy, which includes archival material. There is also a royal channel on YouTube.

Maps

Ordnance Survey. www.ordnancesurvey.co.uk. Digitized maps from the official map makers of the UK.

Vision of Britain through Time. http://vision.port.ac.uk. An academic site focused on historical maps, census data, and travel writing.

Material Culture

Science Museum. www.sciencemuseum.org.uk. The Science Museum has many of its objects relating to science and technology on digital display.

Victoria and Albert Museum. www.vam.ac.uk. The Victoria and Albert Museum holds a huge collection of items relating to British life, culture, and the arts.

In addition there are many local museums in Britain, country houses, and other collections with objects, pictures, books, etc., available online. See general sites for links.

Newspapers

British Newspapers. newspapers.bl.uk. The British Library online collection of over 2 million pages of newspapers 1800 to 1900.

The Illustrated London News. http://gale.cengage.co.uk/product-highlights/history/illustrated-london-news.aspx. *The Illustrated London News* Historical Archive, 1842–2003 is a magnificent source of both news and images reproduced in color covering 260,000 pages.

Most research libraries have the London *Times* and other papers in microform or access to them through searchable databases.

Population

Online Population Reports Website. www.histpop.org. Covers 1801 to 1937.

Texts of Books and Printed Material

Annual Register and the *Gentleman's Magazine.* www.bodley.ox.ac.uk. The Bodleian Library at Oxford has searchable versions of periodicals that chronicled British life in the eighteenth and nineteenth centuries.

Britannia. www.britannia.com. Britannia web site has a collection of online documents.

British and Irish Legal Information Institute. www.bailii.org/uk/legis/num_act. Provides a catalog of British legislation online. (See also: www.legislation.gov.uk/)

British Official Publications Collaborative Information Service. www.southampton.ac.uk/library/bopcris. A large digitization project of British texts, political papers, and images.

Google Books. http://books.google.com. Google has been scanning the collections of major academic libraries around the world. Most books printed in Britain have now been put into the system. Full text is available for books out of copyright (the early twentieth century backwards in time). This includes government publications of all kinds.

Guttenberg. www.guttenberg.org. An important source for digitized texts.

Historical Text Archive. http://historicaltextarchive.com Has many links for the United Kingdom and Ireland.

Internet History Sourcebooks Project. www.fordham.edu/halsall. Internet History Sourcebooks Project, edited by Paul Halsall and supported by Fordham University, has a wide range of documents available on British history and society.

Open Library. http://openlibrary.org Open Library is attempting to scan every book ever printed and is making an increasing proportion of their collection available.

Spartacus School Net. www.spartacus.schoolnet.co.uk. This site has many online documents relating to a wide range of topics.

The Victorian Dictionary. www.victorianlondon.org. The Victorian Dictionary web site has many digitized documents.

Victorian Web. www.victorianweb.org. Has a range of digitized documents on the nineteenth century.

Wikisource. www.wikisource.org. A vast and ever growing collection of books and documents many of which relate to British history.

Printed Collections of Documents

The most important collections:

British Documents on the End of Empire, Series A and B, multiple volumes, 1992–2006.

British Documents on Foreign Affairs is a huge series of volumes covering many periods and topics.

Documents in Contemporary History is a large series on the twentieth century.

English Historical Documents is a comprehensive collection of printed documents and an excellent place to begin a search. Volumes 8 through 12 cover 1660 to 1914, published between 1953 and 1977.

The *Camden Series* of the Royal Historical Society contains many documents, diaries, and other primary sources.

Numerous editors have put together collections of documents in print such as the following: Royston E. Pike, *Human Documents of the Victorian Age* (London, 1967) and J.T. Ward, *The Age of Change 1770–1870: Documents in Social History* (London, 1975). However, such collections are rapidly being made obsolete by online collections. http://c19.chadwyck.co.uk provides a catalog of 30,000 nineteenth-century texts available on microfiche.

Index

Sources and Debates in Modern British History: 1714 to the Present, First Edition. Edited by Ellis Wasson.

Published 2012 by Blackwell Publishing Ltd.